PREFACE

This book was conceived for the express purpose of helping pre- and in-service elementary teachers cope with one of the most frustrating problems confronting educators: making the language arts relevant for culturally different children. Although the professional literature in this field has burgeoned in recent years, there is little evidence that the creative, innovative thinking of language arts specialists is being transmitted to the elementary teacher. Few elementary schools possess adequate professional libraries and fewer teachers have enough time to use them. In our colleges and universities a different problem exists: although the professional libraries tend to be relatively comprehensive, they seldom contain sufficient copies of relevant journals, textbooks, and bulletins. Nor are these materials as accessible as they should be. The readings selected for inclusion in this text seek to fill these gaps.

This text advances several basic propositions that we feel are worthy of careful consideration. We hope that the reader will carefully weigh and analyze the opinions advanced by the authors. Hopefully the propositions advanced below will facilitate such an analysis.

First, culturally different children frequently fail to attain academic success in elementary schools because many of their speech patterns and language habits conflict with those valued by society and promulgated by the schools. These language problems are intensified by teachers who, owing to their different cultural orientation, fail to appreciate the varieties of English that the children speak. Many teachers show blatant contempt for the language spoken and written by their black, brown, and poor white students. Apparently they fail to realize that a child's language is a functional and integral component of his culture and self-identity.

Second, most language programs for culturally different children are designed to *replace* their dialects with standard English. While a replacement approach is unsound because these children must communicate with relatives and peers who tend to speak nonstandard dialects, teachers should provide opportunities for their pupils to explore and master alternative speech patterns accepted by the larger society.

Third, teachers need to help their pupils discover that certain achievements in our society — particularly those involving vocational and social mobility — are largely contingent on the mastery of standard English. While the teacher has a responsibility to expose children to language patterns that differ from their own, they should not be forced to abandon their local language patterns in lieu of the alien dialects of standard English. Only when children see the *need* to master standard English will they develop proficiency in the English spoken and valued by their teachers and the larger society.

Fourth, a pupil's present needs and future goals shape his attitudes toward speech and language patterns that differ from his own. If culturally different children perceive standard English as an *alternative* to rather than as a *replacement* of their modes of speech, they will develop more positive attitudes toward it and will become more adept in speaking and writing in conventional ways. It is useless for a teacher to tell a black ghetto child that "ain't" should never be used when he hears the word used daily by parents, neighbors, and even esteemed community leaders and when he successfully uses it himself in interactions with persons in his immediate surroundings. A teacher who tells his pupils that "ain't" cannot be used advantageously in broader social contexts comes closer to the truth.

Finally, different varieties of English are functional in different social contexts; the value of a particular mode of speech cannot be determined in a vacuum. A white middle-class teacher who speaks highly formal English and attempts to survive in the midst of a black ghetto for several weeks will be judged "weird" and probably experience intense frustration in his attempts to meet his daily needs. A black ghetto child would be similarly disadvantaged in a speech class in a white suburban school. Each person's language is functional in his own environs. Only when we are able to view the dialects spoken by America's minority groups as *different* rather than as *inferior* will we be able to structure meaningful language experiences.

This text seeks to sensitize teachers and administrators to the language problems faced by culturally different children, to sharpen and broaden their perspectives regarding the relationship between language and culture, and to help them devise effective strategies for teaching language skills. In choosing the readings the editors sought to identify articles which suggested widely varying approaches to instruction, out of their deep-seated conviction that there are few general teaching strategies that are effective in most teaching situations.

The text is divided into three major sections, each of which examines the language development of culturally different children from a different perspective. Part One is a prelude to the main body of the text in the sense that it explores broad, fundamental problems and issues related to the general field of language arts education. Chapters One and Two explore the educational consequences of racial and ethnic prejudice, particularly as they relate to deprivation and retardation in language development. Chapter Three focuses on the interaction between language and culture. Part Two is prescriptive in the sense that it focuses directly on the domain of methodology — the daily problems and concerns confronting elementary teachers. Chapters Four, Five, Six, and Seven present an array of strategies for teaching the basic modes of communication and for making effective use of children's literature. Chapter Eight closes this section by attempting to bridge the gap between the language arts and the social studies, two areas of the curriculum that in principle are closely interrelated but in practice tend to be taught as if they were mutually exclusive entities. Part Three, the concluding section of the text, invites the reader to re-examine his beliefs regarding the educability of the culturally different child. Chapter Nine focuses on the central, pivotal figure in this process, the teacher.

It is impossible to properly acknowledge the contributions of the many individuals and organizations involved in the creation of this text. Pre-eminent in this regard were Mary Bosser Joyce and Cherry McGee Banks, our wives. Not only did they work tirelessly on the preparation of the manuscript, but they provided constant moral support, a precious commodity essential to scholarly activity. In addition, we are deeply indebted to the authors and publishers who allowed us to reprint their materials, and to those who contributed original articles to the text. Finally, we would be remiss if we failed to express our gratitude to our colleagues at Michigan State University and the University of Washington for the many helpful suggestions they made during the development of the book.

East Lansing, Michigan
Seattle, Washington
November 1970

W. W. J.
J. A. B.

CONTENTS

PART ONE
PROBLEMS AND ISSUES

The readings in this section explore many of the central problems and issues affecting the education of culturally different children. Three areas of concern are emphasized: (1) the effects of white racism on society in general and on pupils and educators in particular, (2) the causes of educational deprivation and retardation in children, and (3) the relationship between language development and the cultural milieu. The editors' purpose in selecting these introductory readings is to provide the reader with a background of information for testing his perceptions concerning the environment in which culturally different children are raised, and the nature and extent of the language problems they encounter.

CHAPTER 1
RACE, ETHNICITY, AND PREJUDICE

Chapter One focuses directly on the effects of racial and ethnic origins on children's social learning. In the first reading Abraham F. Citron analyzes the effects of white racism on black and white children. The second reading, by James A. Banks, carefully dissects various theories of prejudice that have been proposed over the years, and offers worthwhile lines of inquiry that merit exploration by concerned educators.

THE "RIGHTNESS OF WHITENESS": THE WORLD OF THE WHITE CHILD IN A SEGREGATED SOCIETY

Abraham F. Citron

The white majority in America is achieving some understanding of the degradation heaped for generations upon Negroes through the institutions of slavery and of a caste society, with resultant stifling of Negro potential.

However, whites in general have as yet little understanding of what the discrimination and segregation of caste have done and are doing to them.

The essential problem is not bigots who need to hate, but masses of

Abraham F. Citron, *The Rightness of Whiteness: The World of the White Child in a Segregated Society*, Detroit: Michigan-Ohio Regional Laboratory, 1969. Reprinted by permission of the author.

whites whose minds have been formed in a racist society, padded in illusory concepts, and equipped with a set of unreal presuppositions in a make-believe world.

How are minds formed to operate in a white world?

1. THE BUILDING OF THE SELF IN WHITELAND

A. The White Child's World Is White

The white child in a white milieu, with no essential break in patterns or attitudes in the home, builds into his personality a feeling of the rightness of whiteness. All major sources of his impressions reinforce each other and lead him to feel that whiteness, the way he is, is natural and standard.

White children, in our white-dominant society, come early to feel that their skin color is the same kind of mark of the kind of beings they are as are their hands, feet, eyes, and ears, etc. When they grow enough to apprehend that they are children, they accept unthinkingly that their color is just as normal, proper and right as the rest of them. They feel that their color is the way all children should be. They feel it is right, and that other skin colors, if and when they encounter them, are off-standard deviations.

Reared in a culture in which racial ideology is deeply embedded, white children learn that skin color is salient, and the white children learn that light skin colors are accepted and associated with good and honored things while darker skin colors are rejected and associated with bad, inferior, and fearful things.

The signs, language, rewards and punishments, behaviors of referent adults, peer group norms and behavior, all tell the white child that the people who matter are his color. Children note that white persons almost always hold the positions of respect and authority in the society.

In a white section of the city, in suburbia, or in the countryside (other than the South), all people except some domestic workers and lawn service workers are white.

As the white child grows, he gradually assumes an unconscious feeling of white dominance. He orients himself in a white-centric world. The white self is felt as the human norm, the right, against which all persons of other color may be judged. A white boy in a segregated society thinks of himself as representative of the universe of boys. He feels that the way he is is the essence of boyness; when he thinks of the idea of boy he thinks of beings like himself. Girls make the same unconscious and conscious assumptions about themselves.

The effectiveness of this process of self fashioning lies in its simple absorption of what is. No child questions the syllables referring to his or her parents. No child analyzes or questions the air it breathes. In a white-padded cocoon the white child grows into an acceptance of predominance of whiteness just as he grows into identification and acceptance of himself.

The basis is laid in the sense of identity and self for the emergence of feelings of superiority because of color.

B. Feelings of White Superiority

Mary Ellen Goodman painstakingly elicited concepts and feelings on race of 103 four-year-olds. Of the 46 white children she writes:

> ". . . they share a freedom from the shadow cast by color. They belong to the 'right' race, if not to the right religion or national background. They are looking down at the people under the shadow of color."[1]

also:

> "White children ask (about Negroes) 'Why are they colored?' 'Is she sunburned?' 'Can she change?' The questions are uniform in one respect: These white children do not ask about themselves—why their own color, or lack of it. They take it completely for granted in the fashion of the 'primitive' tribesmen, that they are 'the people.' The others, those under the shadow of color, 'they're different,' as Paul put it. Being different, they are, as Diane says, 'strangers.'"

C. Feelings of Rejection of Darker Skin Colors

Kenneth Clark notes that the child adopts the attitudes of his milieu:

> "When white children in urban and rural sections of Georgia and urban areas in Tennessee were compared with children attending an all-white school in New York City, their basic attitudes were found to be the same. Students of the problem now generally accept the view that the children's attitudes toward Negroes are determined chiefly not by contact with Negroes but by contacts with the prevailing attitudes toward Negroes. It is not the Negro child, but the *idea* of the Negro child, that influences children."[2]

Over half of the white children Goodman and her staff examined through doll play, picture identification and other means, over a period of months, clearly indicate they have already achieved (as the racist institutions intend that they achieve) an emotional rejection of Negroes. There are many examples. (These children are four years old):

> "Joan says: 'black people—I hate 'em.' Stefan says he'd rather play with a white man than with a brown boy (in the picture) 'because he's white.' Later he says 'All I like is the white girl' (in the picture). 'Not the black one, the white one.'"

"Norman says of a picture of a Negro boy: 'He's a freshie.' 'Look at his face—I don't like that kind of face.' The face in question is hardly to be seen, and what does show looks like an unremarkable medium brown. Vivien says the white lady 'is better than the colored lady' in the picture. Billy looks at two pictured men (both ordinary and unremarkable) and says 'A good man—and a black one.' Peter assures us proudly: 'There are no black people at my house.'"[3]

Marian Radke and Helen Trager used doll houses, dolls and picture techniques to elicit children's perceptions of the social roles of Negroes and Whites. They worked with 242 kindergarten, first and second graders of the Philadelphia school. Ninety of their children were Negro; 152 were white. They conclude:

1. 38% of the white children gave interpretations in which stereotyped and inferior social roles were ascribed to Negroes.
2. 14% of the white children gave the Negro doll specific low status roles; 24% gave work roles to the Negro doll and leisure roles to the white doll.
3. The great majority of children (both Negro and white) gave the poorer house to the Negro doll and the better house to the white doll. Verbalizations indicated that they "belonged" there.
4. The children were responding in terms of general cultural stereotypes and prejudices.
5. The white doll was preferred by 89% of the white children. Their reasons indicate self-identification with the whiteness of the doll and rejection of Negroes.
6. Inferior roles are ascribed more frequently to Negroes by white children who express hostile attitudes toward Negroes.[4]

As the child grows he encounters, at various social distances, Negroes and others of different skin colors. There are many accounts of the naivete and floundering of segregated children in their efforts to understand the fact of skin color difference. The ghettoized white child sees Negroes in special locations, in limited economic and social roles; he sees them in sports, in show business, in limited ways on TV; and sees them close up in various special roles, usually not on a level of equality with his parents and his group. Many ghettoized white children know Negroes mainly as domestic servants.

2. THE GROWING MIND IN A WHITE WORLD

A. The White World of the Bible and Religion

The child accepts and imbibes what is presented by the culture. In a White-dominant culture, the symbols of religious respect, reverence and love are white. The fact that they are unthinkingly, "naturally" so makes them more effective as influences on the formation of attitudes and unquestioned assumptions of children.

Adam and Eve were white; white children see this in the Bible story pictures and feel that God created mankind as white men. Children are told that man was created in the image of God.

A child's world of Bible stories, often with impressive pictures, is a segregated world. The child sees Adam and Eve in the Garden of Eden; sees the pictures of David and Goliath; of Joseph and his brethren; Moses and Pharoah; Noah and the Ark; the flood and the white dove; Joshua and the Battle of Jericho; Jonah and the whale; Daniel and the lion's den, and many more.

The lesson is unintentionally but effectively taught, that the important people of the Bible are white, and that God is concerned with white people. The effectiveness of the impression lies precisely in its constant unconscious presentation.

For White Christian children the central figure of their faith is pictured as a white man. Jesus is a loving father figure to countless children brought up in the Christian faith. He is seen by white Christians as white; as a man who, in earthly form, served, taught, suffered and died in a white environment. The Holy Family is a white family; the Apostles are white.

To a white child (and many adults) Heaven is white, angels and angels' wings are white; there are cherubs with happy pink faces. The great white throne of God and the chorus of angels rests upon, and is surrounded by, masses of the purest, billowy white clouds.

In a white-dominant culture purity is white; to cleanse away sin, the soul is washed white as snow. Sin and evil are black.

Although Satan is white, he is a fallen angel, and he has a black heart. White in white culture is a powerful symbol of the rightness of things, of purity, cleanliness, goodness, sweetness, of safety and beauty. White is light as well as right. To a child the dark night is likely to be felt as fearful and dangerous. Black is dirt, unclean, impurity, threatening and unpleasant. "The good guys wear white hats."

B. Santa Claus and the Dolls

Santa Claus is a symbol to Christian children of the benevolence of the Christmas seasons; and every child knows that Santa is a jolly, fat, white man, with twinkling blue eyes and a snow-white beard, who lives in a white snowland of the North, and he says "ho, ho, ho" endlessly over the radio and on TV at Christmas time. All his elves are white, too.

The dolls Santa brings to little white girls are white (almost always) and they look alike, reflecting the standard of beauty and attractiveness of the dominant white culture.

C. The World of Fantasy and Adventure

The white child's world of fantasy and fairies is a white world. Alice is white in a white Wonderland. A main symbol is the white rabbit, hurrying in a thoroughly white, middle-class way, to keep a nameless Kafkaesque appointment and feeling dread lest he be late.

The world of nursery rhymes is a white world. From Old Mother Hubbard, Mary and her lamb, Little Miss Muffet through Tom, Tom, the Piper's Son, The Little Old Man All Clad in Leather, all is a white world. Snow White is, of course, white, as are the dwarfs and the rescuing prince. Make no mistake, Little Boy Blue is white. All Fairyland is white, as is, despite its gaudy colors and odd shapes, the Land of Oz. Dorothy and the Wizard,Glinda the Good, the Shaggy Man, etc., are white. Jack of the Beanstalk is white and his giant, too. Cinderella is white as is her wondrous fairy godmother, and again the Prince. White children feel that all princes are white and that they should ride beautiful white horses.

For the white child the world of heroes is white. The greatly admired virtues of intrepidity and physical bravery are felt to be white virtues. The great panoply of heroes, warrior kings, knights, and fighting men is a roster of Caucasians: Prometheus, Leonides, Hercules, Achilles, Ulysses, Samson, Alexander the Great, Horatius, Beowolf, Siegfried, King Arthur, Lancelot, Charlemagne, Roland, William Tell, Robin Hood, and so on in a lengthy list, down to modern times.

Models for the girls follow the same dominant pattern.

The make-believe world of the American wild West has a hold on the imagination of youth as well as adults. In this world of Billy the Kid, Jesse James, covered wagons, cattle empires, straight shooting sheriffs, we deal with the white man's fantasy world in which white men are dominant, white values supreme. Indians, Mexicans, Orientals, and Negroes enter the script in supporting roles.

D. The World of Knowledge

If the white youth is interested in science, medicine, literature, discovery, history, conquest, invention, space, religion, nature, animals, photography, stamps, or any subject whatever, he is quite likely to read or hear about what white men have felt, thought and done. World history and the history of the United States has, up to the present decade, been presented to white children through the writings of white-minded men in and for a white-dominated culture.

E. Conclusion

Only in modern sports and in the entertainment world is the all-white pattern broken with any impact on children and youth in our caste society.

Nancy Larrick, former president of the International Reading Association and authority on children's books, says:

> "... most of the books children see are all white ... There is no need to elaborate on the damage—much of it irreparable—to the Negro child's personality. But the impact of all-white books on white children is even worse. Although his white skin makes him one of the world's minorities, the white child learns from his books that he is kingfish. There seems little chance of developing the humility so urgently needed for world co-operation, instead of a world of conflict, as long as our children are brought up on gentle doses of racism through their books."[5]

3. THE NEGRO AS SYMBOL

White children are exposed to the racist ideas about Negroes carried by the culture.

(Available to some children are familial or other group influences which effectively counter racial ideology through example, contact, reading, visual materials, and other means. But these children are relatively few.)

In many if not most white children an emotional deposit of strangeness, inferiority, rejection, and fear concerning blacks[6] is laid long before there is "rational" content to support it.

If a group of whites are gathered for any purpose and a white walks in, it is perceived that a person has entered. (Sex, age, dress and other items of categorization may be noted.) If, however, the individual entering is of dark pigmentation, then perception will be more complex; first, fundamentally of a Negro, and then of other characteristics (man, woman, child) pertinent to purposes of the individual. Negroes are seen by whites as members of an out-group.

The emotional saliency of Negroidness to the vast majority of whites is well known. It is this emotionality about blacks that children so quickly sense. In addition to common over-generalization, stereotypic thinking, selectivity of perception and memory, there has occurred and continues considerable projection and symbolization in the way whites see and react to Negroes.

A. Emotionalism

In a national survey of attitudes of whites toward Negroes conducted by William Brink and Louis Harris for *Newsweek* in 1963, the authors state:

> "When the white man in America looks at the Negro he is torn by a conflict between his emotions and his intellect. His intellect tells him that the Negro has indeed suffered years of discrimination, directly contradicting the American Creed of equality for all. But his emotions make him feel uneasy at the prospect of such equality for the Negro.

"In the course of the interviews lasting over two hours each, some more than three, Whites were asked how they felt about contact with Negroes and why. The question released a stream of uninhibited feeling about Negroes. The violent emotionalism of many comments is striking:

Comment (South) "They stink. In cafeterias here you go around and collect your food. Then Niggers paw over your food and then you have to give them a tip to carry your tray. Big old dirty black paws pawing your food, then you got to eat it."

Comment (North) "I never forgot that. (His son shaking hands with a Negro.) It's the idea of rubbing up against them. It won't rub off but it don't feel right either."

Comment (North) "I feel as though I can't trust them. I think they'll start a fight. I might pick up some kind of disease . . ."[7]

B. White Stereotypes about Blacks

In the Brink-Harris survey, ten stereotypes about Negroes were set before white people, who were asked which statements they agreed with and which they rejected. The table on page 10 reports the results from the nationwide cross-section, from the South, and from a special group of those who had had social contact with Negroes. The last group, 25 percent of the total, proved throughout the survey to be the most sympathetic to the Negro cause.

C. The Negro as Sexual Symbol

Gordon Allport notes in *The Nature of Prejudice* that "in America we have in the Negro a preferred target for our sexual complexes." He states:

"There is a subtle psychological reason why Negroid characteristics favor an association of ideas with sex. The Negro seems dark, mysterious, distant, yet at the same time warm, human and potentially accessible. Sex is forbidden; colored people are forbidden, the ideas begin to fuse. It is no accident that prejudiced people call tolerant people 'nigger lovers.' The very choice of the word suggests that they are fighting the feeling of attraction themselves.

"The fact that interracial sex attraction exists is proved by the millions of mixed breeds in the country. . . . The attraction is further enhanced by the fact (or legend) that Negroes have an open and unashamed way of looking at life. Many people with supressed sex lives would like the same freedom. They grow jealous and irritated at the openness and directness of sex life among others. They accuse the males of extreme sexual potency and the females of shamelessness. Even the size of the genitalia becomes a subject of jealous exaggeration. Fantasies easily get mixed with fact. . . ."

Allport quotes Helen McLean as follows on this point:

> "In calling the Negro a child of nature, simple, lovable, without ambition, a person who gives way to his every impulse, white men have made a symbol which gives a secret gratification to those who are inhibited and crippled in their instinctual satisfactions. Indeed, white men are very loath to relinquish such a symbol."[8]

White Stereotypes about Negroes*

Statement	*Percent Agreeing*		
	Nationwide	*South*	*Previous Social Contact*
Negroes laugh a lot	68	81	79
Negroes tend to have less ambition	66	81	56
Negroes smell different	60	78	50
Negroes have looser morals	55	80	39
Negroes keep untidy homes	46	57	31
Negroes want to live off the handout	41	61	26
Negroes have less intelligence	39	60	23
Negroes breed crime	35	46	21
Negroes are inferior to whites	31	51	15
Negroes care less for the family	31	49	22

White Feeling about Contact with Negroes

Would object to:	*Percent*		
	Nationwide	*South*	*Previous Social Contact*
Working next to a Negro on a job	17	31	8
Sitting next to a Negro at a lunch counter	20	50	4
Sitting next to a Negro on a bus	20	47	5
Sitting next to a Negro in a movie theater	23	54	6
Own children going to school with Negroes	23	55	9
Using same rest rooms as Negroes	24	56	9
Trying on same suit or dress that Negro had tried on in clothing store	32	57	16
Own child brings Negro friend for supper	41	76	16
Negro family as next door neighbors	51	74	26
Close friend or relative marrying a Negro	84	91	70
Own teen-age daughter dating a Negro	90	97	80

* From Brink and Harris[7]

Allport indicates some of the dynamics of white male and female attitudes toward Negroes based on sexual feelings. He says of the reactions common to white men:

> "Suppose the white male is anxious concerning his own sexual inadequacy and attractiveness. One study of adult prisoners discovered a close relationship between this condition and high prejudice. Men who were antagonistic toward minority groups, on the whole, showed more fierce protest against their own sexual passivity, semi-impotence, or homosexual trends. The protest took the form of exaggerated toughness and hostility. These individuals committed more crimes of sexual nature than did those who were sexually more secure. And the pseudomasculinity of the former group made them more hostile toward minorities.
>
> "Again, a male who is dissatisfied with his own marriage may grow envious when he hears rumors of Negro sexual prowess and license. He may also resent and fear the approach Negroes might make to white women who are potentially his."[9]

There is revulsion, rage, guilt, fear and suspected attraction in the emotion-laden question often raised in race relations discussions: "Would you like your daughter (sister) to marry one?"

A black psychoanalyst, writing on the blockages to transference processes requisite to successful therapy, blockages which occur when patients are white and therapist is a black, says:

> "The meaning of 'Negro' (black), in a magic, symbolic sense, usually associated with 'evil,' 'badness,' 'inferiority,' may constitute an image which can be interjected into the patient's ego only with great difficulty. 'Negro' may equal 'Devil.' On the other hand, it may equal 'Eros'—blind, emotional abandon—and, therefore an image which some patients may accept more easily."[10]

The myths of the American quasi-caste system about Negroes—that they are primitive, emotional, musical, carefree, irresponsible, criminal, etc.—are carried by the folkways to children and youth. What is actually first conveyed is a feeling of rejection and revulsion. Many white children are early conditioned to the culturally standard shudder-reaction toward Negroes. As they mature, adults, peers, and the milieu fill them in on the myth-content.

White children, watching TV, are likely to feel, just as many adults, that Negroes are apt to appear in connection with some type of violence. Mass media, especially the pictorial content of the media, emphasize tensions, conflict and violent aspects of the interaction of Negroes and whites in the contemporary scene. Further, the media are more likely to catch and identify as conflict and violence those actions in which Negroes attempt to oppose or change the system than they are to catch and reflect the repressive actions of the dominant group to maintain the system. This is because white dominance is pervasive, taken for granted, with low visibility, built into the normal flow of institutional and bureaucratic systems, therefore usually accomplished with non-violence, backed, however, with great institutional power and force; while black objection, insistence and militancy is new, identifiable, visible, abnormal, shocking, and fearful, thus newsworthy.

4. CHILDREN SENSE THE DEEP ATTITUDES

In homes of some gentility crude emotions and stereotypes concerning Negroes are out of countenance, but through countless clues the patterns of rejection and avoidance are well taught to children.

Gilbert Gross, son of a Christian minister who was active in civil rights causes, notes that no Negro ever sat at their table and the children knew "without ever one word said about it" that only the most casual relationships on their part with Negroes were acceptable.[11]

There is evidence that unless the home environment is especially effective in countering impressions from the milieu, or unless reality teaching and counter-stereotyping of the home is reinforced by positive experience with Negro children, or with peer groups which have positive attitudes, the child will make his own the attitudes of his general environment.

A graduate student who is a minister reported to me (April, 1967) the essence of his conversation with his 13-year-old son as they drove home from one of a series of dialogue meetings with Negro adults and youth:

> Father: "What did you think of the program?"
> Son: "It sure opened my eyes."
> Father: "How do you mean?"
> Son: "Well, I've felt that Negroes were just no good. But now that I've met these kids, I've changed my mind."
> Father: "Where did you get the idea that Negroes were no good?"
> Son: "Just about everywhere. My friends think so. Most everybody thinks so. It's just the way people feel. I just know that I felt that way."

Counter-elements of the culture (economic, political, religious, moral, scientific, scholastic) are cutting into these myths, and are now aided by the active forces of black self-determination and black Power, but the traditional supports of a racist system are deep-rooted. Since the middle-class white culture also requires gentility, politeness, restraint, and dissimulation, basic emotions about Negroes threatening to the self-image or to acceptance in the eyes of others are often repressed. But they remain dynamic in the personality and indicate their presence in rationalizations, maintenance of social distance, resentment, anger, guilt, anxieties and over-defense.

Gilbert Gross, quoted above, cannot understand why he must go through life carrying an irrational fear of Negroes. He says: "Why am I so condescending? Why so frightened? Why so angry when a Negro touches my life?"

Children sense the deep attitudes, spoken and silent, the real feelings. they see who is honored and who dishonored. They hear tone and intonation, catch nuance and meaning of behavior; sense and adopt attitudes which adults may be unaware they (the adults) carry, or unaware they transfer to children.

Some of the four-year-olds examined by Mary Ellen Goodman (cited above) had learned feelings of rejection such as the following:

> "During these visits (with us) we learned that four-year-olds see and hear and sense much more about race than one would suppose after watching them at school or even at home. . . . Hostility and rejection appear rather seldom in 'real life' and very often in the testing room. Paul reacts to the brown doll with, 'Bad girl—I hit her.' Ronald is more vehement: 'I don't like dat boy (Negro in picture). He stinks. I don't like Juny (Negro schoolmate). She's a smelly girl. She hits me.' When we show the picture of a Negro man and woman, he is through for the day. He grimaces at the picture and turns his face away. 'I don't want any more,' he says, and departs. Carl, referring to the same picture, says, 'I don't like this man and the lady neither.' Joseph is moved to ideas of violence. 'I don't like that man (Negro). I make an axe. I bang his head off.' Roland says, 'I don't like little black boys—nor my mother neither.' Patsy says, 'I hate them that way—I hate black.' David says, 'He's black, he's a stinky little boy, he's a stinker . . .' "

Eleven out of the 46 four-year-old white children with whom Mrs. Goodman was working talked in these terms. About one half of the 46 expressed definite feelings of rejection of Negroes.

The fears many Whites carry are stereotypic, mythological, symbolic, projective, mixed with elements of reality, fanned by publicity of riots, violence, crime and fed by selective perception.

Through the fears of parents, adults, older children and peers, many children learn to be afraid of Negroes long before they ever have an opportunity to have any meaningful contact with them.

It should by no means be overlooked that attitudes toward Negroes are channeled by aspects of contemporary reality even if these aspects are selectively distinguished and especially weighted.

Uprisings in major cities involving incendiarism, looting, and violence, perceived by many whites as riots against property, law and order, have been an important source of rejective attitudes of Whites toward Negroes.

Crimes of Negroes have been increasingly highlighted as realistic cause for negative attitudes toward all Negroes. "Crime in the streets" has become a major political issue.

Dr. Alvin Rose, [a Negro] Professor of Sociology at Wayne State University, addressing a Northeast Detroit Project Commitment audience of the Catholic Archdiocese, recently received the following as one of a number of written questions: "Can't you understand? We don't run from dislike. We are literally frightened to death of you."

5. THE CONCEPTS AND LANGUAGE OF DOMINANCE

Centuries of white imperialism over darker peoples, over three hundred years of the institution of slavery in this country, and a quasi-caste system since the days of Reconstruction, have produced concepts and language forms fitting the needs of the dominant group. These forms play their part in forming the habits of thought of children. There has been generated a mythology of racism, with its stereotypes of primitiveness, amorality and dangerousness.

Among the racist language forms created to sustain white dominance are contrast-terms referring to skin color. Racism assimilates objective color terms and transforms them into terms of contrast, of super-ordination and subordination. In racist language there are no degrees, one is either "black" or "white". Further, racism invests skin color with an enormous and completely irrational salience in our culture.

If one observes with an eye for color the various hues of lighter-skinned peoples, one sees that these cover quite a range and are clearly not white. Instead of white, the lighter-skinned people could much more accurately be called the "olive-pink-yellow-beige-tan-maroon-grey-browns," or some such.

But the child is forced by the language forms to adopt the ultimate contrast: the blacks vs. the whites.

The term "black" referring to darker skinned groups of African background, formerly derogatory in common folkways, now is being given new meaning and currency. If one uses "colored" he is reduced to nonsense, for all human groups are colored. Further, this term dates from an era of genteel manners when parlance required a term not so crude as "nigger" and not so dignified and formal as "Negro". Just as "black" and "white" emphasize color differences, so does "colored" as a reference term. The best our language will now do is Negro or black or Afro-American; and Caucasian or white or clumsy circumlocutions. The term "race" has been so long misused by ideological movements, propagandists, and racists that it should be avoided by those seeking clarity and objective communication.

The colloquialisms of dominance contain many sayings such as "free, white, and twenty-one," "nigger in the woodpile," "work like a nigger," and such terms as "coon," "shine," and "darky" to refer to Negroes. There is also the custom in a caste-ridden society to refer to Negro men as "boys." One presently hears in bigoted white groups the term "animals" referring to blacks. There is also a large stock of jokes, stories, anecdotes depending for their humor on feeding feelings of white dominance.

There is a large vocabulary, ranging from genteel to coarse to vulgar, expressing racial difference and derogation. These language patterns constitute powerful directives of the ways members of the majority group think about and communicate concerning blacks. Language forms used by blacks to express derogation, contempt, and social distance from white are also common.

6. DISTORTED PERCEPTION OF REALITY

White-centeredness is not the reality of the modern world, but the ghettoized white child is under the illusion that it is. It is thus impossible for him to deal naturally or adequately with the universe of human and social relationships. He learns through selective perception to see, in a white world, what promotes or threatens his ego plans and ego investments, and to (a) react selectively to the stimuli offered, and (b) search out needed stimuli. He learns salience, that is, what portions of his environment are important to him and to which he must react. He learns in his white world the importance of reacting in certain ways to skin color.

It was one of the conclusions of the group of social scientists who signed the "Appendix to Appelants' Briefs" in Brown vs. Board of Education, 1954, that for both majority and minority groups "segregation imposes upon individuals a distorted sense of social reality."

Children who develop this pattern learn dependence on a psychological and moral crutch which inhibits and deforms the growth of a healthy and responsible personality.

7. INNER CONFLICT, CONFUSION; IMPAIRMENT OF CHARACTER

The central point of Gunnar Myrdal's analysis of American race relations from which it derives its title, *An American Dilemma* is the deep cultural and psychological conflict among the American people: of American ideals of equality, freedom, God-given dignity of the individual, inalienable rights, on the one hand, against practices of discrimination, humiliation, insult, denial of opportunity to Negroes and others in a racist society, on the other.[12]

As white children mature in our society, some become aware of this conflict and attempt, in one way or another, to deal with it. Many become aware, for example, of the lack of fulfillment of the Pledge of Allegiance to the Flag: ". . . one nation under God, indivisible, with liberty and justice for all."

Many white children are taught two differing standards of behavior: kindness, friendliness, respect, trust, care for the feelings of others, courtesy, fairness, decency, and justice; but in the case of Negroes, and perhaps other minorities, they are taught dissimulation, superiority, avoidance, and the acceptance of caste arrangements.

Gordon and Roche, writing on the harm that segregation does to whites, state that:

"On the one hand a person is taught that equal treatment for all persons and the brotherhood of man under the Fatherhood of God are the values by which to guide conduct. On the other hand, he is exposed to forces which dictate behavior patterns of hostility, superiority, and avoidance toward certain minority groups. This provides a setting for internal conflict, tension, the feelings of guilt. While it cannot, in the present state of our knowledge, be safely asserted that all prejudiced majority persons in the United States experience this inner conflict, it is entirely likely that at various levels of awareness and consciousness, many do."[13]

Pointing to the moral aspects of this situation, Gordon and Roche say:

"The gap between creed and deed in American life with regard to racial and other forms of group discrimination constitutes a weakening of the moral tone of America and doubtless contributes to the flabbiness of moral codes in other important areas . . . The consequences of this 'American Dilemma' are that American life functions in the constant shadow of a patent evasion of a major moral imperative. The child growing up in such a culture is faced with the perpetual reminder that creeds are one thing, deeds another; and that the adult world, to a large degree, countenances this hypocrisy."

Dan Dodson, Director of the Center for Human Relations and Community Studies of New York University, says that we may be teaching our children to hide from both people and problems:

"More and more city neighborhoods and suburbs are becoming so segregated that a child can grow up in either without any real contact with children of different racial, religious or social backgrounds.

"Do we parents want to teach our children how to hide respectably from those who are different from ourselves? . . . But unless we can develop more authentic values 'the home in the country with grass under our feet' may actually deprive our children of as good a chance as we had. It is a foregone conclusion that they will not get a better chance if the major thing they are taught is to flee from encounters with those who are different. It will be extremely difficult for them to move heroically in this space age, if we supply them with a ghetto mentality."[14]

8. DISADVANTAGED CHILDREN, PRODUCTS OF WHITE SEGREGATION

Whites whose minds and feelings have been produced in ghettoized ways of living are quite likely to experience Negroes (outside of traditional roles) with a sense of resentment, a feeling of discord, a sense of dissonance, like a familiar pattern disarranged. These people are seriously handicapped in their ability to react to Negroes as persons, to interact with naturalness and spontaneity, without anxiety, fear or guilt. They feel at best in a strange and unnatural situation, experience considerable discomfort, and desire, consciously or unconsciously, that the pattern revert to the familiar, proper and the "natural."

Children who develop in this way are robbed of opportunities for emotional and intellectual growth, are limited in basic development of the self so that they cannot accept darker pigmented people. Such persons are severely handicapped in a complex, interactive, multi-ethnic world, undergoing intergroup tension and conflict.

Not only is the ghettoized white child handicapped in accepting and interacting with those different from himself, but he is seriously disadvantaged in recognizing and in dealing with some of the most basic issues of his society in a real world.

9. ESCAPE FROM A GHETTOIZED WORLD

If children are to have attitudes and behavior different from the general culture they will have to be reared in a subculture of equality. The home itself, if it is strong and positive enough and with resources, can furnish such a subculture. However, the child's position is much more solid and secure if there are some peer groups, some adult groups and the school which reinforce the home in the behaviors and the folkways of equality. For then the child can enter into relationships with Negro children and adults much more naturally as a matter of course. These groups furnish valuable support against the general culture norms, definitions, and ways.

It is not enough that parents do not indulge in racist ideas or expressions in the home. The external culture and the peer group folkways are vigorous and demanding. In many American homes, although there may be no crude or overt racism, there is a conscious and unconscious acceptance of racist attitudes and institutional forms so that through their life-style the parents teach aloofness from blacks, social distance, and superiority.

Children should see their parents acting toward blacks as they see them acting toward Whites. This is not easy to achieve in our present divided society but it can be done. We are led to believe, by emphasis on tensions and violence, that mutually satisfying and constructive relationships between blacks and whites are much more rare than is really the case.

A basic step for white parents is involvement in one or more organizations dedicated to building equality of opportunity in an important aspect of our society, such as employment, education, housing, health and welfare, law and justice, and equality of treatment in police procedures and behaviors.

Children discover the real values of parents. To be morally authentic in a racist society means to be a dissenter from common ideas and folkways; it means to be engaged in some way in the struggle to move the society away from racism. It is naive, irresponsible, and escapist to feel that if one personally does not exploit Negroes (many whites are so habituated that they do not know when they are engaging in systematic exploitative relationships with Negroes) and if one treats Negroes one meets with courtesy (special guardedness), he is not a part of a racist system. It is whites as a group who enforce the repressions of the racist system and every white, especially those in middle and upper class positions, because they have more political and economic power, should be actively involved in destroying racist arrangements, practices, exclusions, double standards, folkways and institutions, and should be actively involved in building the conditions of equality.

Intergroup relations theory has held, in the past, that it is beneficial to healthy personality growth for children to have acquaintances, companions and friends across group lines. But from the point of view of many black parents the issue is by no means so simple.

Increasing numbers of black parents are determined to raise their children with feelings of full dignity and worth for blackness, black people, black past, and black future. There is considerable difference of opinion and variety of practice in the attempts to achieve this goal. Some black parents place emphasis on throwing off every vestige of dependence on white standards, influence, or domination as the basis for the self respect of their children. These parents will not subject their children to experiences which are likely to implant or strengthen in a child the feeling that in order to accept himself he must be accepted by whites. They are wary of experiences which might make their children feel in any way psychologically dependent on what whites do, or do not do; accept, or do not accept.

Negroes know that the white world is in general permeated by racism, that it generates devaluation and rejection of Negroes. Some areas and pockets of the White culture are relatively free of this influence, but such areas are sharply circumscribed, and are often unreliable, shifting without warning.

A growing number of Negro parents are wary of going out of their way to expose their children to subgroups of the white majority. They are increasingly demanding change, for example, in school curricula through which their children have been exposed to a white version of history, literature, politics, economics, art, and social studies. Negro parents support school integration resulting from open residential patterns and they resist efforts to gerry-mander school districts to segregate Negro children.

They also fully support the necessity to dismantle the system of legally structured school segregation. This is a matter of basic human dignity.

Although it is possible that black children may risk some security of self image through contacts with whites, it is also quite possible that black children can gain a great deal of fundamental security through equal-status contacts with white children and adults. These contacts must be conducted in mutual respect, involve mutual effort, and be a source of mutual satisfaction.

Parents in white areas and in suburbs should see to it that administrative and teaching staffs are integrated. Negro staff members can be engaged if they are convinced they will be judged as professionals and not pre-judged through stereotypes.

White children need books and stories in the home which are not white-centered and which reflect the heterogeneity of America and of the world.

Administrators and teachers should see to it that text books and teaching materials reflect the reality of a multi-group world, that history and social studies texts contain the realities of Indian-white relationships, of Negro-white relationships in the history of the American people, and materials on other minorities, ethnic and racial. Literature, art, and music courses and materials should contain representative contributions of black poets, authors, artists and composers. Courses and materials in science and medicine should note the contribution of Negroes. Committees charged with reviewing materials and recommending new texts and materials should be integrated "racially," religiously, ethnically.

A parent in a suburb recounts that she was shocked when her seven year old pointed to a Negro on TV and said, "That's a bad man, I don't like him." He made rejective remarks about other Negroes he saw on TV no matter what their role or how briefly they appeared. Among the things she decided to do was to supply him with some good books showing Negroes in a variety of roles. When she went to the library in her suburb to ask for such books for children, the librarian was at a loss. Finally, the librarian found a copy of "Little Black Sambo" which she offered. (For those not familiar with this small, vividly illustrated little book, which a few years ago was quite popular with white parents and children, it is a benignly stereotyped Aunt Jemimah type story of Little Black Sambo who goes for a stroll in the jungle proudly outfitted in his beautiful new purple jacket and bright yellow walking shorts, carrying a green umbrella. Tigers chase him around a tree so fast that they turn to butter, which his Mammy immediately uses to fry huge stacks of pancakes which the whole family enjoys.) Despite the repeated disclosure of the damage done by such White-fantasied, stereotyped impressions of good fun for children, many librarians and others haven't gotten the message. Indeed, many can read the above book and still be at a genuine loss as to what is wrong with such an innocent story.

This points to still another aspect of the task of digging out from the White ghetto outlook and indicates what must be done to aid children to break out of the white cocoon and into the world of real people.

Children reared in the folkways of the rightness of whiteness are condemned to move in the cherry orchard of a dying era, playing roles fast passing from the stage of history.

REFERENCES

1. Goodman, Mary Ellen, *Race Awareness in Young Children*, Cambridge, Mass.: Addison-Wesley, 1952, pp. 44–66.
2. Clark, Kenneth B., *Prejudice and Your Child*, Boston: Beacon Press, 1963, p. 25.
3. Goodman, *Race Awareness*, pp. 2, 49.
4. Radke, Marian, and Helen Trager, "Children's Perceptions of the Social Roles of Negroes and Whites," *Journal of Psychology*, **29** (1950), 3–33.
5. S. Nancy Larrick, 'The All-White World of Children's Books," *Saturday Review* (Sept. 11, 1965).
6. Some now prefer the term black for Negro. Both terms are used in this paper. Usage should follow black consensus on this matter.
7. Brink, William, and Louis Harris, *The Negro Revolution in America*, New York: Simon and Schuster, 1963, pp. 138–152.
8. McLean, Helen V., "Psychodynamic Factors in Racial Relations," *Annals of the American Academy of Political and Social Science*, **244** (1946), 159–166.
9. Allport, Gordon, *The Nature of Prejudice*, New York: Doubleday, 1958, pp. 351–353.
10. Curry, Andrew E., "Myth, Transferrence, and the Black Psychotherapist," *Psychoanalytic Review*, **51**, 4 (Winter 1964–1965), 553.
11. "A White Man Looks at the Negro," *Look* (Dec. 17, 1963).
12. Myrdal, Gunnar, *An American Dilemma*, New York: Harper & Co., 1944.
13. Gordon, Milton M., and John P. Roche, "Segregation—Two-Edged Sword," *New York Times*, April 25, 1954.
14. Dodson, Dan, "Are We Segregating Our Children?" *Parents' Magazine* (Sept. 1963).

THE CAUSES OF PREJUDICE

James A. Banks

We cannot reduce racial prejudice unless we acquire an understanding of its causes. First, however, we shall find it useful to define prejudice.

The literature on racial relations is replete with efforts to define prejudice. While the definitions differ to some extent, most suggest that prejudice is a set of rigid and unfavorable attitudes toward a particular group or groups which is formed in disregard of facts. The prejudiced individual responds to perceived members of these groups on the basis of his preconceptions, tending to disregard behavior or personal characteristics that are inconsistent with his biases. George Simpson and J. Milton Yinger have provided a lucid and useful definition of prejudice. ". . . [P]rejudice is an emotional, rigid attitude (a *predisposition* to respond to a certain stimulus in a certain way) toward a group of people. They may be a group only in the mind of the prejudiced person ... he categorizes them together, although they may have little similarity or interaction. Prejudices are thus attitudes, but not all attitudes are prejudices."[1]

Although social scientists have attempted for years to derive a comprehensive and coherent theory of prejudice, their efforts have not been totally successful. A number of theories explain various components of prejudice, but none sufficiently describes its many dimensions. Social scientists have rejected some of the older, more simplistic theories of prejudice; other theories are too limited in scope to be functional. Still others are extremely useful in explaining certain forms of prejudice directed toward specific groups, but fail to account for its other facets. A serious study of the theories of prejudice reveals the complexity of this configuration of attitudes and predispositions; thus simplistic explanations of prejudice only hinder our understanding of it.

Arnold M. Rose has critically reviewed both the older, simpler theories of prejudice, and the more complex modern psychological explanations.[2] A summary of his analysis is presented below in order to illuminate the strengths and weaknesses of the various theories.

The racial and cultural difference theory maintains that man has an instinctive fear and dislike of individuals who are physically and culturally different from him.[3] Rose dismisses this theory as untenable since research indicates

---

James A. Banks, "The Causes of Prejudice." Published simultaneously in this text and in James A. Banks and William W. Joyce, *Social Studies for Culturally Different Children*, Reading, Mass.: Addison-Wesley, 1971, by permission of the author.

that children are tolerant of other races and groups until they acquire the dominant cultural attitudes toward ethnic minorities. Children must be *taught* to dislike different races and ethnic groups. Writes Rose, "[This theory] should be thought of as a rationalization of prejudice rather than as an explanation of it."[4]

The economic competition theory holds that prejudice emanates from antagonism caused by competition between various groups for jobs and other economic rewards.[5] Although this theory sheds light on many historical examples of racial prejudice and discrimination, it has some gross limitations. It fails to explain why a group continues to practice discrimination when it no longer profits economically from doing so. A number of studies document the severe financial losses attributable to the discrimination against the black American.

The social control theory maintains that prejudice exists because the individual is forced to conform to society's traditions and norms;[6] Thus he dislikes certain groups because he is taught to do so by his culture. While this theory helps to explain why prejudice may be perpetuated when it is no longer functional, it does not consider how it originates.

The traumatic experience theory states that racial prejudice emerges in an individual following a traumatic experience involving a member of a minority group during early childhood.[7] This theory is inadequate because a child does not associate an early unpleasant experience with a particular racial group unless he has already been exposed to the concept of racial differences. In noting another limitation of this theory, Harley writes, "This idea can be discounted because persons can hold extreme prejudice with no contact with persons of the discriminated class, and the traumatic experiences reported by persons as reason for their prejudice are very often found to be either imagined by them or elaborated and embellished beyond recognition."[8]

The frustration-aggression theory is a modern psychological explanation of prejudice.[9] It suggests that prejudice results when individuals become frustrated because they are unable to satisfy real or perceived needs. Frustration leads to aggression, which may then be directed toward minority groups because they are highly visible targets and unable to retaliate. Displacing aggression on stigmatized groups is much safer than attacking the real source of the frustration. Rose illuminates two basic weaknesses in this theory: (1) it fails to explain why certain groups are selected as targets rather than others, and (2) it assumes that all frustration must be expressed.[10] However, a number of writers and researchers have relied heavily on this theory to help explain the emergence and perpetuation of prejudice.

The projection theory states that "people attribute to others motives which they sense in themselves but which they would not wish to acknowledge openly."[11] This theory is severely limited because it fails to explain motives for prejudice or why certain characteristics are attributed to specific groups.

Symbolic theories attempt to explain prejudice as deriving from an individual's ambivalent attitude toward an important phenomena.[12] Rose relates writer Lilliam Smith's interpretation of anti-Negro prejudice. "The heart of this theory is that Negroes are the objects of the whites' desires for, and yet fear of, uninhibited sex."[13] Symbolic theories are basically weak because they are formulated on the basis of inferences and have not been rigorously tested.

In attempting to derive a comprehensive theory of prejudice, Rose suggests that the modern psychological theories are the most useful explanations. He writes:

> The central theories today which seriously attempt to explain prejudice are based on the concepts of frustration-aggression, projection, and symbolic substitution. These theories have a good deal in common despite the differing kinds of evidence which lead to their formation. All of them postulate (1) a need to express antagonism (2) toward something which is not the real object of antagonism. Not only is there an essential similarity among the three theories, but they complement each other at their weakest points. The symbolic theory does most to explain which group is selected for prejudice and why. The frustration-aggression theory does most to explain the strength behind prejudice. The projection theory offers a plausible explanation of the psychological function of prejudice as a cleansing agent to dissolve inner guilt or hurt.[14]

Simpson and Yinger have formulated a comprehensive theory of prejudice "around three highly interactive but analytically distinct factors, each the convergence of several lines of theory and evidence."[15] The first factor is the personality requirements of the individual. As a result of both constitutional and learned needs, some people develop personalities that thrive on prejudices and irrational responses. This theory has been offered by a number of other writers and researchers. Later we will review some of the research on which it is based.

An individual may also develop prejudices based not on personality needs but on the way society is structured.[16] The power structure of society is especially important to this concept, which is similar to the economic competition theory discussed by Rose. Simpson and Yinger write, "It is impossible to interpret individual behavior adequately without careful attention to the social dimension."[17]

The third basic cause of prejudice suggested by Simpson and Yinger is society itself. "In almost every society . . . each new generation is taught appropriate beliefs and practices regarding other groups. Prejudices are, in part, simply a portion of the cultural heritage; they are among the folkways."[18] This explanation is identical to the social control theory summarized by Rose.

Simpson and Yinger stress that all three of these factors interact: "Any specific individual, in his pattern of prejudice, almost certainly reflects all of the causes."[19] Both they and Rose emphasize that multiple explanations are needed to account for the complexity of racial prejudice.

In his review of the theories of prejudice, Rose discusses personality explanations. As we have seen, Simpson and Yinger cite the personality needs of the individual as one of the basic causes of prejudice; earlier researchers considered personality *the* most important variable in the formation of bigotry. The latter attributed different types of personalities to differences in child-rearing practices, some of which were thought to produce personalities that were intolerant of different races and groups, while others helped to develop racial tolerance and acceptance in the child. Else Frenkel-Brunswik and her associates conducted the pioneering research on the role of personality in the formation of prejudice.

In one of a series of studies (1948), Frenkel-Brunswik compared the racial attitudes and personality characteristics of 1,500 children.[20] Interviews were conducted with the subjects and their parents; both personality and attitude tests were administered. Frenkel-Brunswik concluded that there were significant differences in the personalities of prejudiced and unprejudiced children. She found that prejudiced children evidenced more rejection of outgroups, a blind acceptance of the in group, a greater degree of aggression, and a strong rejection of persons perceived as weak. The more prejudiced children also displayed a greater resentment of the opposite sex and an admiration for strong figures. They were more willing to submit to authority, more compulsive about cleanliness, and more moralistic. The unprejudiced children were "more oriented toward love and less toward power than the ethnocentric child . . . and more capable of giving affection."[21] Frenkel-Brunswik notes, in summarizing her study, "It was found that some children tend to reveal a stereotyped and rigid glorification of their own group and an aggressive rejection of outgroups and foreign countries."[22]

Frenkel-Brunswik and her associates also studied the relationship between personality and prejudice in adults.[23] They concluded that certain individuals, because of their early childhood experiences, have insecure personalities and a need to dominate and feel superior to other individuals. These individuals possess an *authoritarian personality* which is manifested not only in racial prejudice but also in their sexual behavior and religious and political views. The authors write:

> The most crucial result of the present study, as it seems to the authors, is the demonstration of close correspondence in the type of approach

> and outlook a subject is likely to have in a great variety of areas, ranging from the most intimate features of family and sex adjustment through relationships to other people in general, to religion and to social and political philosophy. Thus a basically hierarchical, authoritarian, exploitative parent-child relationship is apt to carry over into a power-oriented, exploitively dependent attitude toward one's sex partner and one's God and may well culminate in a political philosophy and social outlook which has no room for anything but a desperate clinging to what appears to be strong and a disdainful rejection of whatever is relegated to the bottom.[24]

While the research by Frenkel-Brunswik and her associates contributed greatly to the literature on the origins of prejudice, recent writers have severely criticized it because of its methodological flaws and theoretical base. We will defer a discussion of the theory on which the research is based and review a number of its methodological weaknesses. Simpson and Yinger have written one of the most perceptive critiques.[25] They point out that the inadequate attention given to sampling techniques limits the generability of the findings. The research is also weakened by the heavy reliance on the subjects' memories of childhood, the inadequate control of variables, such as education and group membership, and the low reliability of the measuring instruments. The F Scale used by the researchers measured many variables simultaneously, failing to measure any one variable well. However, Simpson and Yinger conclude that the flaws in the research do not substantially diminish its import. "Despite the seriousness of such methodological problems, they do not refute, in the judgment of most observers, the significance of personality research for the student of prejudice."[26]

Other researchers have also attempted to explain the emergence of racial prejudice as a personality variable. Lindzey (1950) studied the personalities of 22 individuals judged "high in prejudice" and 22 judged "low in prejudice."[27] The subjects were divided into experimental and control groups. After exposing members of the experimental group to a frustration experience, Lindzey concluded that the individuals high in prejudice evidenced more "frustration susceptibility" and "more overt disturbance in response to frustration than those low in minority group prejudice."[28] The subjects high in prejudice also received higher scores on an instrument which measured "conservative nationalistic statements." Writes Lindzey,

> We have pointed to certain evidence in our data suggesting that the high in prejudice are more "frustratable," somewhat more aggressive, and more conforming to authority norms than the low in prejudice. Further, we have proposed that early exposure to strict norms is one means by which we might account for the behavior patterns that appeared to characterize the high in prejudice in this study.[29]

Allport and Kramer (1946) found that the more prejudiced persons in a sample of college students maintained closer ties with their families, whereas the least prejudiced students "reacted against" their parents' attitudes.[30] The former also had more negative memories of childhood, were better able to identify racial and ethnic groups, were more religious, and expressed more hostility and aggression. "From all these results," they write, "we conclude *that prejudice is woven into the very fabric of personality.* A style of life is adopted. It proceeds by rule of thumb."[31] (Emphasis added.) The subjects who reported that they had studied "scientific facts about race" in school were more often classified as "less prejudiced." However, only 8 percent of the subjects could recall studying racial facts in school.

Like Frenkel-Brunswik, Allport and Kramer believe that prejudice can be explained largely as a product of personality. However, both research teams compared extreme bigots with individuals who manifested few negative racial attitudes, whereas most white Americans exhibit only an average amount of racial prejudice and do not have seriously disorganized personalities. Thus there are severe limitations implicit in an exclusive *personality* approach to the study of prejudice.

Herbert Blumer seriously questions attempts to attribute prejudice and discrimination to personality variables. He almost completely dismisses the role of attitudes in influencing behavior. Blumer asserts that the social setting rather than racial attitudes is the "prime determinant of behavior."[32] In trying to understand discrimination against minority groups, he contends, we should analyze social settings and norms instead of the personal attitudes of the individual. Blumer reviews a number of studies which indicate that there is frequently a discrepancy between an individual's verbalized attitudes and his actual behavior. Saenger and Gilbert found that prejudiced individuals will patronize a racially mixed store when their desire to shop exceeds their antipathy toward blacks.[33] Research by Blalock suggests that discrimination is not always a correlate of racial prejudice.[34] That is, in certain situations, prejudiced individuals may not discriminate, since the prevailing norm may affect their behavior more than their personal attitudes do. Blumer summarizes an important study by Lohman and Reitzes:

> . . . in a study of race relations in a large city . . . the same set of whites behaved entirely differently toward Negroes in three situations—working establishment, residential neighborhood and shopping center; no prejudice or discrimination was shown in the working establishment where the whites and Negroes belonged to the same labor union, whereas prejudice and discrimination toward Negroes by the same whites was pronounced in the case of residential neighborhood.[35]

Blumer seriously underestimates the role of attitudes and personality as determinants of racial discrimination and prejudice. An adequate theory of prejudice must take into account both personality variables and the social setting. Explaining prejudice and discrimination as totally a product of a disorganized personality ignores the fact that humans are social beings, and that their reactions in a social setting reflect not only their individual idiosyncrasies and biases but also the prevailing norms and expectations. Thus a bigoted teacher will be less inclined to manifest her true attitudes toward black children when black parents are visiting her room than she is when she and the children are alone.

However, social setting alone cannot completely explain racial discrimination; nor can it, as Blumer implies, totally diminish the importance of racial attitudes. If the same bigoted teacher were transferred to an all-black school in which there was little tolerance for racial discrimination, her behavior would probably become more consistent with the dominant norms of the new setting, but her *attitudes* would be revealed to her students in subtle ways, and perhaps affect them just as profoundly. *The most equalitarian social setting cannot cause an intense bigot to exhibit behavior identical to the behavior of the person free of racial prejudice.*

Much of the research that Blumer relies on to support his hypothesis is subject to serious criticism, particularly the study by Lohman and Reitzes. These authors found that their white subjects behaved "*entirely differently toward Negroes in different social settings*" and showed "no prejudice" toward them at work.[36] (Emphasis added.) However, this writer seriously questions whether the black factory workers would have endorsed these conclusions, believing instead that they could have cited numerous examples of discrimination directed against them by their white co-workers. It is inconceivable that persons who are so bigoted that they would exclude blacks from their neighborhood could treat them with full equality at work or indeed in any other setting.

The *social setting* explanation of prejudice and discrimination presents other difficulties. In trying to explain an individual's reactions in a given situation, we must consider not only the group norms but the importance the individual attaches to the group and setting. Research suggests that a group or situation must be important to an individual before he accepts its norms and values. Pearlin (1954) classified a random sample of 383 college students into "acceptors" and "rejectors" on the basis of their attitudes toward blacks.[37] A majority of the subjects who accepted blacks in different situations had broken their close family ties and developed identifications with campus groups. The more prejudiced individuals indicated that they had maintained close ties with their families and developed few associations with campus groups. Students who become more racially liberal as a result of their college experience considered college group norms more important to them than their parents' attitudes, while the more prejudiced subjects deemed family norms more important. Thus simply placing individuals in new settings with different norms and values does not necessarily change their behavior and attitudes. Pearlin writes:

> These findings indicate that when a person holds membership in groups having conflicting views on an issue, his own attitudes will be influenced by the relative importance of the groups to him. Generally, in such a situation the attitudes of the individual will approximate most nearly the norms of the groups to which he most closely refers himself . . . attitude change cannot be reckoned solely in terms of exposure to new ideas. Whether or not an individual will undergo modification of his attitude depends in large part on the nature of his relationship to groups holding the opposing sentiments and opinions.[38]

The social setting hypothesis also fails to take into account the fact that individuals collectively determine the group norm. Whether a group sanctions racial discrimination or racial tolerance thus depends on the attitudes of its members. Clearly, then, we must consider both individual attitudes and social norms when attempting to explain the genesis and perpetuation of racial discrimination and prejudice. The most important variables that affect the formation of racial prejudice are summarized in Chart 1.

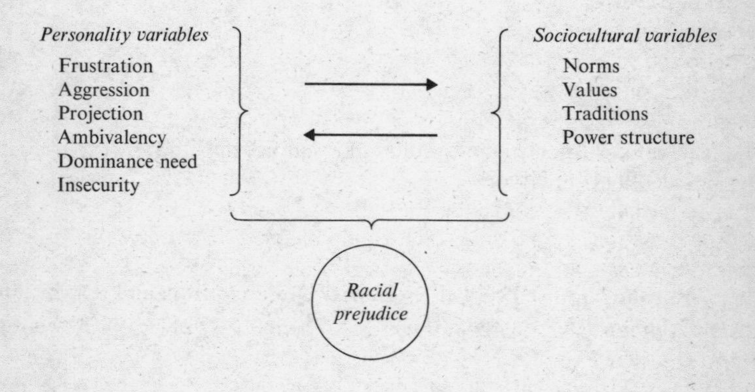

Chart 1. Variables that cause racial prejudice.

REFERENCES

1. George Eaton Simpson and J. Milton Yinger, *Racial and Cultural Minorities*, New York: Harper and Row, 1965, p. 10.
2. Arnold M. Rose, "The Causes of Prejudice," in Milton L. Barron, ed., *American Cultural Minorities: A Textbook of Readings in Intergroup Relations*, New York: Alfred A. Knopf, 1962.
3. *Ibid.*, pp. 77–80.
4. *Ibid.*, p. 78.
5. *Ibid.*, pp. 79–80.
6. *Ibid.*, pp. 80–81.
7. *Ibid.*, pp. 77–78.
8. David Harley, "Prejudice in Whites," unpublished paper, Michigan State University, 1968.
9. Arnold M. Rose, "The Causes of Prejudice," pp. 82–83.
10. *Ibid.*, pp. 82–83.
11. *Ibid.*, p. 83.
12. *Ibid.*, pp. 83–87.
13. *Ibid.*, p. 86.
14. *Ibid.*, pp. 92–93.
15. Simpson and Yinger, p. 49.
16. *Ibid.*, p. 50.
17. *Ibid.*
18. *Ibid.*
19. *Ibid.*
20. Else Frenkel-Brunswik, "A Study of Prejudice in Children," *Human Relations*, **1** (1948), 295–306.
21. *Ibid.*, p. 305.
22. *Ibid.*, p. 296.
23. T. W. Adorno, Else Frenkel-Brunswik, D. J. Levinson, and R. N. Sanford, *The Authoritarian Personality*, New York: Harper and Row, 1950.
24. *Ibid.*, p. 971.
25. Simpson and Yinger, pp. 65–66.
26. *Ibid.*, p. 66.
27. Gardner Lindzey, "Differences Between the High and Low in Prejudice and Their Implications for a Theory of Prejudice," *Personality*, Vol. 19 1950, pp. 16–40.

28. *Ibid.*, p. 39.
29. *Ibid.*, p. 33.
30. Gordon W. Allport and Bernard M. Kramer, "Some Roots of Prejudice," *The Journal of Psychology*, **22** (1946), 9–39.
31. *Ibid.*, p. 35.
32. Herbert Blumer, "United States of America," in *Research On Racial Relations*, New York: UNESCO, 1966, pp. 87–133.
33. Reported in *Ibid.*, p. 112.
34. *Ibid.*
35. *Ibid.*, pp. 112–113.
36. *Ibid.*, p. 112.
37. Leonard I. Pearlin, "Shifting Group Attachments and Attitudes Toward Negroes," *Social Forces*, **33** (1954), 41–47.
38. *Ibid.*, p. 50.

STUDY QUESTIONS

1. According to Citron, what are some of the typical stereotypes whites often ascribe to blacks and members of other minority groups? What stereotypes do blacks and members of other minority groups ascribe to whites? In what ways are such stereotypes changing? for the better, or for the worst?
2. What is the "white ghetto outlook" postulated by Citron? How does he believe that it can be changed? Do you agree or disagree with his recommendations?
3. Studies reported by Goodman and by Radke and Trager are cited as indicative of the extent to which children adopt the attitudes of their cultural millieu. If you were to replicate these studies today, would you expect that your findings would differ from theirs? If so, under what circumstances?
4. Why are black children less likely than white children to make correct self-identifications? What are the implications for the development of self-concept in all children, irrespective of racial or ethnic background?
5. What evidence does Banks offer in support of his contention that social scientists have failed to derive a comprehensive, coherent theory of prejudice? Is there any evidence that such a theory is forthcoming?
6. Of the various theories of prejudice described by Banks, which tend to be most closely associated with ethnic groups? With racial groups? Do these theories suggest any strategies for reducing prejudice in our schools?

7. Why have the schools been so reluctant to make a concerted effort to deal honestly and positively with prejudice in children? Is there any evidence to suggest that the situation is improving? Deteriorating?
8. It is asserted that the pathology of prejudice is far more than merely a school problem. What does this mean? How far do the parameters of this problem extend?

SUGGESTED READINGS

Allport, Gordon, *The Nature of Prejudice*, Cambridge, Mass.: Addison-Wesley, 1954

Ashell, Bernard, "Not Like Other Children," in *The New Impoverished American*, New York: McGraw-Hill, 1963

Bloom, Benjamin S., *Stability and Change in Human Characteristics*, New York: John Wiley & Sons, 1964

Clark, Kenneth, *Prejudice and Your Child*, Boston: Beacon Press, 1963

__________, *Dark Ghetto: The Dilemmas of Social Power*, New York: Free Press, 1962

Gans, Herbert, *The Urban Villagers*, New York: Free Press, 1962

Goodman, Mary Ellen, *Race Awareness in Young Children*, Cambridge, Mass.: Addison-Wesley, 1952

Holt, John, *How Children Fail*, New York: Pitman, 1964

Klineberg, Otto, "Life is Fun in A Smiling, Fair-Skinned World," *Saturday Review* (Feb. 16, 1963), 75–77, 87

Kopp, Sister M. Audrey, *The Myth of Race*, Techny, Ill.: Divine World Publications, 1967

Lewis, Oscar, *La Vida*, New York: Random House, 1966

Lloyd, Jean, "The Self-Image of a Small Black Child," *Elementary School Journal*, **67** (May 1967), 407–411

Miel, Alice, *Children of Suburbia*, New York: Human-Relations Press, 1967

Misiaszek, Lorraine, "The Cultural Dilemma of American Indians," *Social Education*, **33** (April 1969), 438–439

Rose, Arnold M., *The Roots of Prejudice*, Paris: UNESCO, 1958

Rose, Peter I., *They and We: Racial and Ethnic Relations in the United States*, New York: Random House, 1965

Roy, Prodipto, "The Measurement of Assimilation: The Spokane Indians," *American Journal of Sociology*, **67** (March 1962), 541–551

Sexton, P. C., *Spanish Harlem*, New York: Harper and Row, 1965

Simpson, G. E., and J. M., Yinger *Racial and Cultural Minorities*, New York: Harper and Row, 1964

Solomon, Benjamin, "Educators and the Racial Issue in Education," *Illinois Schools Journal*, **48** (Spring 1968), 25–34

Spindler, George D., and Louise S. Spindler, "American Indian Personality Types and their Sociocultural Roots," *Annals of the American Academy of Political and Social Science* (May 1957)

CHAPTER 2
DEPRIVATION, RETARDATION, AND LEARNING

A cartoon published in a New York newspaper several years ago showed an improverished old man describing his predicament in these words:

> I used to think I was poor. Then they told me I wasn't poor, I was NEEDY. Then they told me it was self-defeating to think of myself as needy, I was DEPRIVED. Then they told me deprived was a bad image, I was UNDERPRIVILEGED. Then they told me underprivileged was overused, I was DISADVANTAGED. I still don't have a dime, but I have a GREAT vocabulary![1]

Are educators merely intellectualizing the learning problems of children without attempting to correct them? Or, as Loretan and Umans ask, "Is this what we have been doing—creating a vocabulary, a jargon, a cult, but producing disadvantaged adults to replace disadvantaged children?"[2]

The readings in this chapter seek to answer these questions in terms of their implications for pupils' general educational growth and language development. William H. Boyer and Paul A. Walsh challenge the assumption that children differ innately in their ability to learn, and suggest ways of creating ability, increasing intelligence, and developing interests in learning. The second article, by Nicholas Anastasiow, pursues in greater detail various explosive and confusing issues surrounding the question of racial intelligence differences.

The concluding readings analyze the positive and negative effects of environmental factors upon the language development of children, and offer a series of concrete proposals for action. F. Elizabeth Metz considers language attainment from the standpoint of three definable aspects of language: lexical, phonetic structure, and syntactic structure. Eddie G. Ponder asks, "Should we try to change the language of the disadvantaged child?" and "Can we change the language of the disadvantaged child?" In the final reading James Olsen proposes a series of sweeping changes for instituting a total oral language program for all children, irrespective of family background and home environment.

NOTES

1. Jules Feiffer, "Feiffer," *New York Post*, Feb. 17, 1965, p. 41.
2. Joseph O. Loretan and Shelly Umans, *Teaching the Disadvantaged*, New York: Teachers College Press, Columbia University, 1966, p. 6.

INNATE INTELLIGENCE: AN INSIDIOUS MYTH

William H. Boyer and Paul Walsh

In societies where power and privilege are not equally distributed, it has always been consoling to those with favored positions to assume that nature has caused the disparity. When man himself creates unequal opportunity, he can be obliged or even forced to change his social system. But if nature creates inequality, man need only bow to supreme forces beyond his control, and the less fortunate must resign themselves to their inevitable disadvantage.

The metaphysics of natural inequality has served aristocracies well. The Greeks had wealth and leisure as a result of the labor of slaves. Plato expressed the wisdom of the established order with the claim that nature produces a hierarchy of superiority in which philosophers, such as himself, emerge at the top. Aristotle's belief that all men possess a rational faculty had more heretical potential, but it was not difficult to believe that some men are more rational than others.

In later periods, nations that possessed economic superiority explained their advantages on the basis of innate superiority. Sir Francis Galton was convinced that the English were superior and that the propertied classes were even more superior than the general population. They were the repository of what was the most biologically precious in mankind.

The democracies of the new world shattered many elements of the old order, and brought a new, radical, equalitarian outlook. In principle, if not always in practice, man became equal before the law, and the idea of "the worth of the individual" established a principle of moral equality. Yet legal

---

and moral equalitarianism did not necessarily mean that men were intellectually equal. So the assumption upon which American schools and the American market place developed was that democracy should mean *equal opportunity for competition among people who are genetically unequal.* This creed has satisfied the requirements of modern wisdom even for the more liberal founding fathers such as Thomas Jefferson, and it equally fit into the social Darwinism of an emerging industrial society.

In contemporary American education many of these assumptions remain. People are usually assumed to be not only different in appearance, but also innately unequal in intellectual capacity and therefore unequal in capacity to learn. The contemporary creed urges that schools do all they can to develop *individual* capacities, but it is usually assumed that such capacities vary among individuals. Ability grouping is standard practice and begins in the earliest grades. Intelligence tests and the burgeoning armory of psychometric techniques increasingly facilitate ability tracking, and therefore the potentially prosperous American can usually be identified at an early age. If it is true that people have inherently unequal capacities to learn, the American educational system is built on theoretical bedrock, and it helps construct a social order based on natural superiority. But if people actually have inherently equal capacities, the system is grounded in quicksand and reinforces a system of arbitrary privilege.

Four types of evidence are typically offered to prove that people are innately different in their capacity to learn. The first is self-evidential, the second is observational, the third is logical-theoretical, and the fourth is statistical.

The self-evidential position is based on high levels of certainty which include a strong belief in the obviousness of a conclusion. Many people are very certain that there is an innate difference between people in intellectual capacity. However, such tenacity of feeling is not itself a sufficient basis for evidence, for it offers no method of cross-verification. The mere certainty of a point of view regarding the nature of intelligence must be discounted as an adequate basis for verification.

The observation of individual differences in learning capacity cannot be dismissed as a basis for evidence; useful information for hypotheses requiring further verification can be obtained in this way. For instance, parents may notice different rates of learning among their children. People from different social classes learn and perform at different levels. The city child may learn particular skills more rapidly than the rural child. Observations require some care if they are to produce reliable evidence, but it is possible to observe carefully, and such observation can be cross-verified by other careful observers.

But if people learn particular tasks at different rates, does it follow that people must therefore be *innately* different in their learning capacity? It does *not* necessarily follow. Increasingly, as we know more about the role of environment, we see that there are not only differences between cultures, but also differences within cultures. Even within families, no child has the same environment as the others. Being born first, for instance, makes that child different; he is always the oldest sibling. A whole host of variables operates so that the environment as perceived by an individual child has elements of uniqueness (and similarity) with other children raised in proximity.

Observational evidence can be a useful part of the process of understanding when it raises questions that can be subjected to more conclusive evidence, but it is often used as a way of selectively verifying preconceived notions which are endemic in the culture. Western culture is strongly rooted in the belief in a natural intellectual hierarchy. Few observers have been taught to make observations based on assumptions of natural intellectual equality. Observational evidence must be carefully questioned, for it is often based on a metaphysic of differential capacity which encourages selective perception and a priori categories of explanation. Yet these preconceptions are rarely admitted as an interpretive bias of the observer.

Theories based on carefully obtained data provide a more adequate basis for reaching a defensible position on the nature-nurture controversy than either of the previous procedures. A general theory in the field of genetics of psychology which fits available information would be a relevant instrument for making a deduction about the nature of intelligence. If a logical deduction could be made from a more general theory about heredity and environment to the more specific question of innate intellectual capacity, the conclusion would be as strong as the theory. Such deduction is a commonly used procedure.

Both genetic and psychological theories have often been used to support the belief in inherited intelligence. Genetic connections between physical characteristics such as eye color, hair color, and bodily stature are now clearly established. Certain disease propensity has a genetic basis, yet the best established research is now between single genes and specific physical traits. It is commonplace to assume that if a hereditary basis for differential physical traits has been established, there is a similar connection between genes and intelligence. The conclusion, however, does *not* necessarily follow. Intelligence defined as the capacity to profit by experience or as the ability to solve problems is not a function of a single gene. Whatever the particular polygenetic basis for learning, it does not follow that intellectual capacity is variable because physical traits are variable. Current genetic theory does not provide an adequate basis for deducing a theory of abilities.

Similarly, the Darwinian theory of natural selection is often used to ascribe superiority to those in the upper strata of a hierarchical society. Yet a system of individual economic competition for survival is actually a very recent phenomenon in human history, characteristic of only a few societies, primarily in the eighteenth, nineteenth, and early twentieth centuries. It is very likely that it is irrelevant to genetic natural selection because of its recent origin. American immigration came largely from the lower classes, a fact which could condemn America to national inferiority if the Darwinian theory were used. In the long span of human history, most societies have relied mainly on cooperative systems or autocratic systems for their survival, and individual competition is an untypical example drawn largely from the unique conditions of Western, particularly American experience.

Psychological theories which emphasize individual differences have often assumed that the descriptive differences in physical characteristics, personality, and demonstrated ability are all due largely to heredity. Psychology has had strong historical roots in physiology, but as social psychologists and students of culture have provided new understanding of the role of experience, hereditarian explanation has shifted toward environmentalism. Even the chemical and anatomical characteristics of the brain are now known to be modifiable by experience. Psychologists such as Ann Anastasi point out that, "In view of available genetic knowledge, it appears improbable that social differentiation in physical traits was accompanied by differentiation with regard to genes affecting intellectual or personality development."

Anthropologists, with their awareness of the effects of culture, are the least likely to place credence in the genetic hypothesis. Claude Levi-Strauss, a social anthropologist, claims that all men have equal intellectual potentiality, and have been equal for about a million years. Whether or not this is true, it is clear that the best-supported general genetic or psychological theory does not validate the conclusion that individual intellectual capacity is innately unequal.

Statistical studies under controlled conditions, on the other hand, can provide some of the most reliable information. For instance, when animals are genetically the same, there is the possibility of inferring genetic characteristics through experimental studies. Identical twins develop from the separation of a single egg and have identical genetic inheritance. If human twins could be raised under controlled experimental conditions, much could be learned about the respective role of heredity and environment. Many studies have been made of twins, but none under sufficiently controlled experimental conditions. The results, therefore, permit only speculative conclusions. Most twins are so similar that unless they are separated they are likely to be treated alike. When they are separated, in most cases, one twin is moved to a family of the same social class as the other twin. And people of similar appearance tend to be treated similarly—a large, handsome child is not usually treated the same as a short, unattractive child. The resultant similarity of I.Q. scores of separate twins has not been surprising.

Even if particular identical twins were to show marked differences in ability when they live in substantially different environments, as they occasionally do, the evidence does not prove the *environmentalist* thesis unless a significantly large number of random cases is compared with a similarly random selection of non-identical twins. In a small sample, difference could be due to the experience deprivation of one twin. It is possible to stultify any type of development, and so the variation between identical twins, identified in some studies up to forty points, by no means disproves the hereditarian position. Consequently, current studies do not provide conclusive statistical evidence to support either position over the other.

The second most commonly used statistical evidence to show the hereditary basis of intelligence is the constancy of I.Q. scores at different age periods. Usually, I.Q. scores do not change appreciably, but occasionally the changes are dramatic. It is now understood that a standard I.Q. test is culturally loaded toward middle-class values, and so the general constancy of most I.Q. scores can be explained as the expected result of limited mobility between social class and the resultant constancy of subcultural experiences. So even the statistical "evidence," so often used to support a belief in innate intelligence, is really not conclusive.

Studies of innate intelligence, then, have not produced conclusive evidence to justify the claim for an innate difference in individual intellectual capacity. Equally, there has not been conclusive evidence that the innate potential between people is equal. The research is heavily marked by the self-serving beliefs of the researchers. Psychologists have usually created "intelligence" tests which reflect their own values, predetermining that their own scores will be high. When they have discovered they are high, they have often proclaimed such tests to be indicators of innate superiority.

Many studies are built on simple-minded assumptions about the nature of environment. Physiological environment is related to the subject. A researcher who says that two children live in the "same" environment is quite wrong, for the environment that each child perceives may be quite different from that perceived by the researcher.

Also, it is often assumed that environment is only postnatal, but evidence is now availabe on the role of prenatal environment, both psychologically and nutritionally. Malnutrition of a pregnant mother can, and often does, have permanent debilitating psychological and physiological effects on her child. Certain diseases contracted by the mother (measles, for example) and certain drugs (thalidomide, for instance) can produce destructive "environmental" effects which limit intellectual capacities. Clearly, people do demonstrate varying capacities to learn, but they have had varying prenatal and postnatal opportunities. If they are female, they are generally treated differently than if they are male. Negroes are treated different from whites—one social class is treated different from another. The *kind* of employment people engage in has a profound effect on what they become. They probably become different through different treatment and different experience, yet our institutions, reflecting our culture, usually operate on the assumption that such differences in ability are innate.

There are at least three ability models which can be supported by current evidence. Each is based on different assumptions about human nature and therefore provides a basis for different social philosophies and different conceptions of government and education.

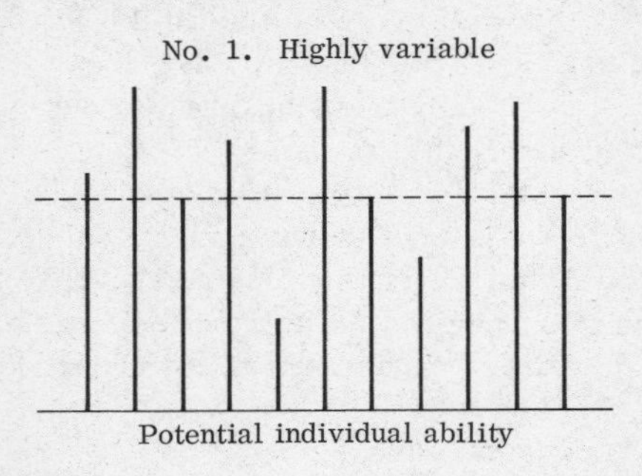

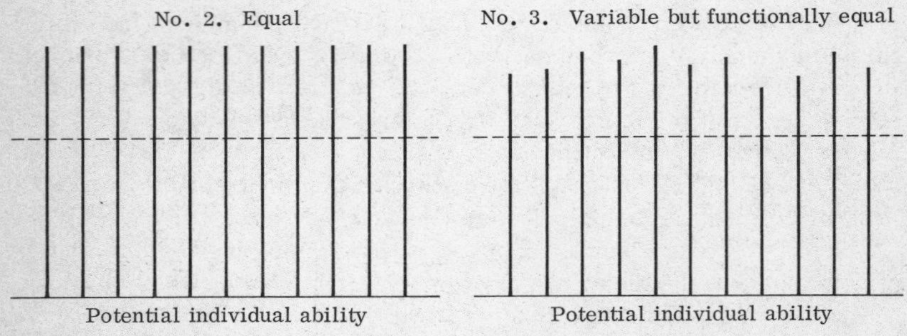

Ability Models. Each model is based on different assumptions about the nature of potential human ability. The dotted line indicates the intellectual level at which individuals must function to meet the requirements of society.

The first model assumes a great variety of innate ability and a high level of intellectual demand on the average person. In this model, there are hereditary geniuses and idiots, while most people have an intellectual capacity about equal to the demands of their society.

The second model assumes that the innate ability potential of everyone (who has not been injured pre- or postnatally) is equal and far exceeds the normal demand level. (The actual opportunities a person has may produce differential *performance* similar to model No. 1.)

The third model assumes the possibility of some variation, but since all of the ability potential is well beyond the normal demand level, the variation makes virtually no operational difference.

In an economic or educational system, model No. 1 would justify the usual culling, sorting, and excluding through screening devices to create a "natural" heirarchy of ability. It would also justify the common belief in "equal opportunity for competition between unequals," where sorting is acheived through competition.

Both models two and three would justify maximum social effort to develop the abilities of all people, and the failure to achieve high levels of ability in all people would constitute social failure rather than individual failure. American society, with its considerable disparity of wealth and power, is largely a success based on the inequality assumed in the first of the three models. It is largely a failure based on the equality assumed in the second and third models.

Schools make little effort to develop the kind of equal ability assumed in models two and three. I.Q. tests are widely used to identify presumed differences in innate ability so that culling and grouping can make the management of the school easier and more efficient. The disastrous effects of the schools on lower-class children are now finally becoming known. The "compensatory" concept has gained some headway, but most educators are so overloaded with work and so traditional in outlook that the schools have become partners with the economic system in reinforcing a system of privilege that usually panders to the children of those in power and finds metaphysical excuses to make only minor gestures toward the less fortunate. The "special programs for the gifted" would be more accurately labeled "special programs for the privileged," for the gifted are primarily the children from socio-economic classes which provide the most opportunities. The less fortunate (usually lower class children) are ordinarily neglected or convinced that they are innately inferior. Once they become convinced, the prophesy is soon realized.

Part of the problem is the way "intelligence" is defined. It can be defined in many different ways, each leading to a somewhat different educational direction. We can view it as environmental adaptation, as ability to solve problems, as ability to use logical convergent thinking, or it can emphasize divergent thinking and the creation of ideas and problems. When intelligence is defined as abstract verbal-conceptual ability drawing on the modal experiences of middle class environment, as it is in most I.Q. tests, a selection has been made which excludes many other plausible and often more useful definitions.

The capacity to become intelligent does, of course, have a genetic basis. A cat is not capable of becoming a psychologist. But this does not mean that demonstrated differences in intelligence among psychologists are innate. What is particularly important is whether intelligence is defined primarily as the input or the output. The input is not subject to control, but the output depends on experience; so it is intelligence as output that should be the central concern of the educator.

Until the particular beliefs, which are endemic in many cultures, including American culture, are seen to be part of the heritage of an ancient, anachronistic, elitist tradition, there is little likelyhood that the official liberal and equalitarian goals of many modern nations are likely to be realized, even though the wealth of modern technology gives every promise that they are capable of being achieved. Government, industry, education, and virtually all other institutions are now part of the problem, hobbled by a metaphysics of innate inequality. Elitist assumptions about the meaning of ability permeate all fields of education. When teachers of music, mathematics, art, or physical education find that a student doesn't demonstrate the requisite ability, they often reject him (low grades can be a form of rejection). Then counselors shuttle the student to courses where he shows "ability." All this assumes that the school should not develop abilities, but only grant them opportunity to be expressed. The Rousseauian belief in the pre-existing self is widespread.

The environmental hypothesis may be wrong, but if it is, it should be shown to be wrong only after a society has done everything possible to develop the abilities of people. We should begin with prenatal care, and should eliminate the experience of economic deprivation, ghettoized living, and elitist schools and businesses. *Lacking definitive scientific evidence about human potentialities, social policy should be based on moral considerations*. We should base our policy on the most generous and promising assumptions about human nature rather than the most niggardly and pessimistic. Men will do their best only when they assume they are capable. Liberal assumptions and conservative assumptions about human nature create their own self-fulfilling prophesies. We now create millions of people who think of themselves as failures—as social rejects. Their sense of frustration and despair is a travesty on the potentialities of an affluent nation.

Poor teaching is protected in the American educational system through the assumption that the child doesn't have the ability. An American environmentalist commitment (toward liberal rather than totalitarian goals) would aim at *creating* ability, at *increasing* intelligence, at *developing* interests. The meaning of "education" would need to be broader than merely institutional schooling. It should also include community responsibility, especially for business and the mass media, which must supplement the work of the school if Americans are to receive more equal educational opportunity. This requires more social planning and more public responsibility than Americans have previously been willing to undertake.

Most American institutions, including the schools, still base their policy largely on the old conservative ideology. This outlook resists change and condemns many to inferiority. Ideological rigidity is not exclusive to the United States; in fact, many other nations are even more rigid. Yet the expanding wealth produced by modern technology is beginning to encourage the have-nots within the United States and throughout the world to demand their share by force and violence if necessary. Violence is likely to be an increasingly common road to social change unless a new public morality based on new assumptions about human potentiality is translated into both foreign and domestic policy. It is not merely racism which bogs down American progress, but also the more pervasive belief in intellectual inequality. The failure to develop the abilities of people was useful to the early American aristocracy and to the power elite of an industrial-scarcity economy. But modern economies of abundance flourish through the maximum development of the abilities of people. There is potentially plenty for all. More widespread development of the capabilities of people would not only add greatly to the wealth of nations, but it can also permit people to participate in a social and cultural renaissance.

Aside from the compelling moral obligation to create equal opportunities within nations and even between nations, the excluded millions in the world are starting to force the changes which should have occurred long ago. Some of them don't believe they are inferior, and they are understandably impatient about changing the old processes of exclusion. All institutions, including the schools, will either need to re-examine their self-consoling elitist beliefs and create real and equal opportunity, or else risk that violence and revolution will increasingly become the dominant instruments of social change.

EDUCATIONAL RELEVANCE AND JENSEN'S CONCLUSIONS

Nicholas Anastasiow

Probably nothing on today's educational scene has created more attention and controversy than Arthur R. Jensen's article in the Winter, 1969 issue of *Harvard Educational Review* and the discussions by Jerome Kagan, J. McV. Hunt, J. F. Crow, Carl Bereiter, David Elkind, Lee Cronbach, and W. F. Brazziel published in the spring issue. National news media gave the original article wide coverage, with focus on specific sections, stimulating a wide variety of continuing reaction. Diverse though the responses may be, remarkably similar issues keep cropping up. I shall review these recurrent themes.

It is generally agreed that Jensen's article exhibits breadth of scholarship, that it makes a contribution to scholarly dialogue, and that there is a genetic factor in intelligence. There has been general disagreement about two of Jensen's conclusions, those two which have been most widely quoted:

Nicholas Anastasiow, "Educational Relevance and Jensen's Conclusions," *Phi Delta Kappan*, **51** (September 1969), 32–35. Reprinted by permission of the author and the publisher.

1. "That genetic factors are strongly implicated in the average Negro-white intelligence difference. The preponderance of evidence is, in my [Jensen's] opinion, less consistent with a strictly environmental hypothesis than with a genetic hypothesis, which, of course, does not exclude the influence of environment or its interrelation with genetic factors."[1]
2. [That] compensatory education has been tried and it apparently has failed.[2]

Several of the *Review* discussants have also raised questions as to conclusions Jensen draws from the data of his research and that of other research he reports, and there has been criticism of his failure to include consideration of the findings of other pertinent studies, particularly in the area of socialization and early child growth and development.

In the main, Jensen discusses intelligence, how it is measured, its correlates, and its hereditability. He reviews a wide range of research studies in genetics, intelligence testing, and psychology, and draws the conclusion that attempts to raise intelligence are fruitless. He concludes not only that there are genetic differences between individuals but that there are genetic differences in intelligence between whites and Negroes. Further, he says that specific aptitudes should be identified and school curriculum and techniques should be designed to teach to these aptitudes.

Jensen argues that the "environmentalists" have misled us in regard to how much environment can modify intelligence. He bases his argument on a series of earlier research studies in which he and his students worked extensively with white, Negro, and Mexican-American students. These studies appear to be well executed and controlled. They suggest that, while there are social class differences in children's performances of complex tasks, there do not seem to be the same kinds of differences among social classes on associative learning tasks.

In general, the discussants in the spring issue of the *Review* agree with the need to recognize special abilities and aptitudes, and consider Jensen's scholarship of high caliber. However, they do not all agree when Jensen attributes the difference in intellectual functions of the lower-class child (particularly the Negro) not to the psychosocio-cultural deprivation hypothesis so ably prepared by Hunt[3] but to basic genetic factors. Jensen suggests that about 80 percent of intelligence can be accounted for by genetics alone. Crow appears to agree. Cronbach[4] raises some question about this figure. And there are newer conceptions of genetics not discussed by Jensen which would set this limit nearer 50–60 percent.

What is troubling about Jensen's hypothesis of racial differences in I.Q. is that he appears to seek truth and make known his findings, yet seems to close off alternative hypotheses to explain the data. At the same time, he asks us to consider the tenability of an older hypothesis of racial differences in I.Q. which his data, to this reviewer, fail to support. Equally ironic is the fact that some of his severest critics in the news media appear to be closed to the hypothesis he suggests. Rather than analyze data and offer alternative interpretations, they condemn Jensen. Neither approach will serve science and education.

To support his hypothesis of racial differences in I.Q., Jensen draws upon data from several areas one of which consists of studies of genetic influence on height and weight. To Jensen, these suggest racial and genetic limitations. As Cronbach indicates in his discussion, Jensen is on weak ground here. Height and weight can be modified and are not under purely genetic control, as an earlier study by Greulich[5] of Japanese-Americans and their Japanese cousins strongly documents.

Gruelich's studies controlled for genetic factors and found marked differences in height, weight, and chest expansion in favor of the California subjects who came from the same gene pool as the comparison group, but whose dietetic, climatic, and other environmental conditions were more conducive to optimum development. Thus supposed racial traits proved modifiable by environmental conditions.

Jensen dismisses the environmental-influence-on-intelligence point of view rather lightly, although he does mention some studies. He questions it by stating that "disadvantaged children are not reared in anything like the degree of sensory and motor deprivation that characterizes, say, the children of the Skeels study."[6] *However*, the breadth of studies by Spitz, Bowlby, Anna Freud, Skodak and Skeels, and Skeels and Heinicke[7] on the effects of deprivation, separation, and adoption have well demonstrated the effects of physical, emotional, perceptual, and environmental conditions on intellectual functioning and adult academic attainments.

Perhaps, in working with 5-year-olds in California, Jensen has not seen the effects of lack of stimulation on the 2–5-month-old infant. There is, however, ample evidence reported by reputable research psychologists to support the fact that there are marked conditions of economic and social and psychological lacks among the poor of this nation.

The issue of environment versus heredity was ably handled by Anastasi and Foley[8] years ago as an interaction phenomenon. As Piaget and Inhelder[9] suggest, mental development is influenced by maturation or organic growth, the role of exercise and acquired experience, social interaction and transmission, and an internal mechanism of equilibration. Knowledge, to Piaget and Inhelder, is derived from action; thus the culture, the socialization processes and techniques used to train the child, greatly influence what we measure on an I.Q. test. If Jensen's otherwise excellent article has a major weakness, it is in its naive conception of growth and development and the critical area of the socialization process on the intellectual functioning of the child. For example, both physical and language development appear globally undifferentiated in the young child and are progressively differentiated through learning and experience. As Elkind[10] states in his review, the Piagetian view is that intelligence develops through experience.

The paradox of Jensen's article is that it contains one of the clearest descriptions of what is required for school success as schools now exist, then states a faulty assumption with respect to the way children acquire skills that lead to school success. Let's look at Jensen's excellent paragraph:

> Our thinking almost always takes as granted such features as beginning formal instruction at the same age for all children (universally between ages five and six), instruction of children in groups, keeping the same groups together in lock-step fashion through the first several years of schooling, and an active-passive, showing-seeing, telling-listening relationship between teacher and pupils. Satisfactory learning occurs under these conditions only when children come to school with certain prerequisite abilities and skills: an attention span long enough to encompass the teacher's utterances and demonstrations, the ability to comprehend verbal utterances and to grasp relationships between things and their symbolic representations, the ability to inhibit large-muscle activity and engage in covert "mental" activity, to repeat instruction to oneself, to persist in a task until a self-determined standard is attained—in short, the ability to engage in what might be called self-instructional activities, without which group instruction alone remains ineffectual.[11]

Children of middle-class homes have been prepared to meet these conditions and are carefully trained to be able to function within the school situation, as shown by Sears, Maccoby and Levin, Loevinger, and Schaeffer.[12] In the majority of cases, children of lower-class homes have not received such training (see Hess and Shipman[13]). When the lower-class child begins school, he is usually required to act as if he has already mastered the necessary prerequisites for verbally oriented group instruction, though in fact he has not because the socialization process—particularly of the Negro—has not so prepared him. Hess and Shipman, Anastasi, Hertzig, Birch, Thomas and Mendez,[14] and others have shown in comparisons of lower-class mothers with middle-class mothers marked differences in what is taught and how it is taught. What is taught by the lower-class mother appears to be nonverbal cognitive systems which may reflect intellectual functionings that our typical intelligence tests do not measure. However, as McNeill[15] states, in our schools verbal facility is usually measured by the most peripheral aspects of language; phonology and morphology are taken as signs of intelligence. Kagan[16] also suggests that the deprived or poverty child has not had the necessary early stimulation which with the middle-class child begins as early as 3–6 months.

The issue of Negro-white intellectual differences is often argued without taking into account those very early child trainings which Piaget[17] and Hunt[18] regard as crucial. Isolated from the main stream of America, many poverty mothers have not been provided with the necessary techniques to maximize their children's intellectual potential.

The Negro is frequently compared disparagingly, as Jensen infers, with European immigrants who have been assimilated into the culture and are functioning successfully within it, acquiring power and prestige positions. The analogy is a gross fallacy, because it fails to take account of two relevant facts: 1) European immigrants were usually motivated toward the same kind of success as white Americans and brought with them a predominantly verbally oriented culture. 2) The immigrant's child, once he mastered the outward manifestations of middle-class acceptability in speech and dress, could not be stigmatized as to ethnic origin and had access to the middle- and upper-class prestige positions. No matter how accurate a Negro's speech, how skillfully he masters the formalities of middle-class attitudinal and value systems, he is still unable to melt into the culture because of his color. Unfortunately, teaching to individual differences will not assure adult success until we cast aside the Neanderthal notion that skin color is related to intelligence. Guskin's[19] recent work is a case in point. Teachers listening to tape recordings of speech by Negro children purportedly reading their own compositions rated them lower than white children who read the same passages.

Jensen does, however, present some very reasonable suggestions for beginning instruction with poverty children. He reviews his own research and that of Lesser, Fifer, and Clark[20] to demonstrate different patterns of ability among ethnic groups which may not be related to social class. If the deprived child uses different modes of thought, we should teach to those modes, Jensen suggests. There is a difference, however, between Jensen's position that there is a limited number of skills that can be taught to poverty children and conclusions that can be drawn from research with lower-class children. Jensen feels that most school skills can be taught and acquired by associative learning, which he calls Level I learning. He appears to imply that racial lower-class groups are so different from others as to preclude their developing abstract reasoning and conceptual thinking (Level II learning). Apparently, he believes that the lower-class minority has failed with these tasks and cannot be expected to master them. Other learning theorists postulate that styles or modes of thought do not preclude problem solving. Rather, they believe that how a child is taught abstract reasoning and problem-solving skills should vary, depending upon the child's strengths or skill profiles. Jensen seems to want to close the door that it has taken a decade of special educators and modern curriculum personnel in the Dewey,[21] Taba[22] tradition to open. That is, the major question is not why a child can't function now but how we can provide him with an educational program so that he can. Therefore, although

Jensen agrees that early education programs have not focused on the relevant tasks, his conclusion that they have failed and will fail does not logically follow from his discussion. Both Hunt[23] and Kagan[24] point out that early education programs have not been developed adequately for assessment to be valid at this time.

Many compensatory education programs have been based upon what has been successful with the "task-oriented" middle-class child. We are only beginning to find out what are appropriate interventions for the deprived child. In addition, the compensatory programs have been built too often upon the weakest of the middle-class pre-school models, which deal largely with drill and practice techniques and total group activities rather than individual child opportunities to explore, manipulate, and deal with the environment. Maturation of functions demands different modes of transaction with the child, and learning requires reward, reinforcement, and tasks near the child's current level of functioning.[25] Our teaching procedures must come to match the competencies and the level of development the child brings with the requirements of the task to be learned. To do this takes time and careful analysis of the learning task and the stage of the child's development. As Tyler[26] long ago pointed out, it often takes teachers three years to be able to perform the teaching procedures that an innovative program intends to implement.

If there are weakness in these programs (and there undoubtedly are), they may well reside in our techniques of training teachers to meet marked individual and subcultural differences and our lack of stronger in-service training programs. Until we are more successful in preparing teachers, we will not identify those components of instruction that enable the child to develop the multiplicity of intellectual competencies available at birth regardless of what the ultimate capacity may be.

Jensen could have assisted us greatly by establishing what the real issue for educators is. It is *not* one of heredity versus environment; it is concerned with discovering what kind of environmental stimulations are necessary to reach the potential of what is inherited. We must adopt a more dynamic approach to intelligence and mental development than that presented by Jensen.

Piaget and Inhelder[27] state it beautifully: "It may even seem that effective dynamic factors provide the key to all mental development and that in the last analysis it is the need to grow, to assert oneself, to look, to be admired that constitutes the motive force of intelligence, as well as behavior in its totality and its increasing complexity."

NOTES

1. Arthur R. Jensen, "How Much Can We Boost I.Q. and Scholastic Achievement?," *Harvard Educational Review* (Winter, 1969), 82.

2. *Ibid.*, p. 2.

3. J. McVicker Hunt, *Intelligence and Experience*, New York: Ronald Press, 1961.

4. Lee Cronbach, "Heredity, Environment, and Educational Policy," *Harvard Educational Review* (Spring 1969), 338–347.

5. William W. Greulich, "A Comparison of the Physical Growth and Development of American-born and Native Japanese Children," *American Journal of Physical Anthropology* (December 1957), 489–516.

6. Jensen, "How Much Can We Boost I.Q.?," p. 61.

7.a Rene Spitz, "Hospitalism: An Inquiry into the Genesis of Psychiatric Conditions in Early Childhood," *Psychoanalytic Studies of the Child*, New York: International Universities Press, 1945, p. 53–74.

b John Bowlby, Marry Arnsworth, Mary Boston, and Dina Rosenbluth, "The Effects of Mother-Child Separation," *British Journal of Medical Psychology*, Part 4, 1956, pp. 211–247.

c Anna Freud, *Infants Without Families*. New York: International University Press, 1944.

d Marie Skodak and Harold M. Skeels, "A Final Follow-up Study of One Hundred Adopted Children," *Journal of Genetic Psychology*, September, 1949, pp. 85–125.

e Harold M. Skeels, *Adult Status of Children with Contrasting Early Life Experiences: A Follow-up Study*, Monograph of the Society for Research in Child Development, Serial No. 105, 1966.

f Christoph M. Heinicke, "Some Effects of Separating Two-Year-Old Children from Their Parents," *Human Relations*, May, 1956, pp. 106–176.

8. Anne Anastasi, and John P. Foley, "Proposed Reorientation in the Heredity-Environment Controversy," *Psychological Review*, May, 1948 pp. 239–249.

9. Jean Piaget and Barbel Inhelder, *The Psychology of the Child*. New York: Basic Books, 1969.

10. David Elkind, "Piagetian and Psychometric Conceptions of Intelligence," *Harvard Educational Review*, Spring, 1969, pp. 319–337.

11. Jensen, *op. cit.*, p. 10.

12.a Robert R. Sears, Eleanor E. Maccoby, and Harry Levin, *Patterns of Child Rearing*. Evanston, Ill.: Row, Peterson, 1957.

b Jane Loevinger, "On the Proportional Contributions of Differences in Nature and Nurture to Differences in Intelligence," *Psychological Bulletin*, December, 1943, pp. 725–756.

c Earl S. Schaeffer, "A Circumplex Model for Maternal Behavior,"

Journal of Abnormal Social Psychology, Volume 59, 1959, pp. 226–236.

13. Robert D. Hess and Virginia C. Shipman, "Early Experiences and the Socialization of Cognitive Modes in Children," *Child Development*, December, 1965, pp. 869–886.

14.a *Ibid.*

b Anne Anastasi, *Differential Psychology*, 3rd ed. New York: Macmillan, 1958.

c Margaret E. Hertzig, Herbert Birch, Alexander Thomas, and Olga Aran Mendez, *Class and Ethnic Differences in the Responsiveness of Preschool Children to Cognitive Demands*, Monograph of the Society for Research in Child Development, Serial No. 117, 1968.

15. David McNeill, "The Development of Language," ERIC, Document No. ED021218, 1968.

16. Jerome Kagan, "Inadequate Evidence and Illogical Conclusions," *Harvard Educational Review*, Spring, 1969, pp. 224–277.

17. Jean Piaget, *The Origins of Intelligence in Children* (trans. by Margaret Cook). New York: International University Press, 1952.

18. Hunt, *op. cit.*

19. Judith Guskin, "Current Approaches to the Study of Language Behavior and Some Recent Research on Mental Retardation," mimeographed, 1968.

20. Gerald Lesser, Gordon Fifer, and Donald Clark, *Mental Abilities of Children from Different Social-class and Cultural Groups*, Monograph of the Society for Research in Child Development, Serial No. 102, 1965.

21. John Dewey, *How We Think*, rev. ed. Boston: Heath, 1933.

22. Hilda Taba, *Teaching Strategies and Cognitive Functioning in Elementary School Children*, Cooperative Research Project No. 2404. San Francisco: San Francisco State College, 1966.

23. J. McVicker Hunt, "Has Compensatory Education Failed? Has it Been Attempted?," *Harvard Educational Review*, Spring, 1969, pp. 278–300.

24. Kagan, "Inadequate Evidence."

25. Robert M. Gagné, "The Acquisition of Knowledge," *Psychological Review*, July, 1962, pp. 355–365.

26. Ralph Tyler, *Appraising and Recording Students' Progress*. New York: Harper & Brothers, 1942.

27. Piaget and Inhelder, *Psychology of the Child*.

POVERTY, EARLY LANGUAGE DEPRIVATION, AND LEARNING ABILITY

F. Elizabeth Metz

For objective consideration of children's linguistic limitations, language should be subdivided into at least three of its definable aspects:

1. Lexical—relating to words or the vocabulary of a language as distinguished from its grammar or construction.
2. Phonetic Structure—relating to spoken language or speech sounds patterned within words.
3. Syntactic Structure—relating to the way in which words are put together or patterned to form phrases, clauses, or sentences in a connected or orderly system or arrangement—i.e., *grammar*.

TYPICAL LIMITATIONS IN THE LEXICAL ASPECTS OF LANGUAGE

The acquisition of vocabularly is dependent upon two mental processes, abstraction and symbolization. A child who calls a *ladder* a *get-up* is demonstrating inability in symbolization, or the knowledge of names or signs to stand for objects, acts, qualities, attitudes, and relationships. When a child calls a *horse* a *doggy*, he is failing in symbolization and also in abstraction, or the ability to generalize from non-identical experiences to form concepts or classes such as *cars, fruit, animals.*

Children who have experienced early language deprivation are often baffled by a standardized measure of vocabularly such as the Peabody Picture Vocabulary Test.

The Detroit Great Cities School Improvement Program in Language Arts[1] used a sound approach to planning vocabularly growth by first assessing the actual spoken language vocabularies of culturally deprived children who had just finished kindergarten.

Shaw[2] in discussing the language problems of culturally disadvantaged children, states, "We have built our aptitude and intelligence tests so that reading and vocabulary count very heavily, and have found them valid as predictors of academic success."

F. Elizabeth Metz, "Poverty, Early Language Deprivation, and Learning Ability," *Elementary English*, **43** (February 1966), 129–133. Reprinted with the permission of the National Council of Teachers of English and F. Elizabeth Metz.

It has long been the writer's opinion that group tests of intelligence measure the young child's language deprivation. Analysis was made of the oral vocabularly required to complete successfully five different group tests of intelligence. In one, the child must understand fourteen geometric terms to comprehend the teacher's oral directions. Language-deprived children often lack the concepts of such terms; for example, *pointed, oval-shaped, opening* (noun), or *partly curved.* This same test includes more than twenty directional words and phrases, among which are *toward the left, opposite from, the next after,* and *exactly under*. How, when we know such tests are valid as predictors of academic success, can we fail to teach the language-deprived child this vocabulary?

Most group tests of intelligence include tasks called *non-verbal* which involve ability in abstraction or classification. The task may involve the selection of an object or design from a series because it is *different* or *not like the others.* It may require the selection of two items from a series because they are related as are no other items in the series. Such tasks involve the ability to relate or isolate items on the basis of mutiple determinants. Choice must sometimes be made on the basis of *use*; for example, isolating an *eraser* from a series of *tools for writing*. In other tasks the choice might be determined by *direction*, up or down or left and right. *Spatial* factors such as symmetric—asymmetric may be involved. Examples of still other determinants are: spatial-numerical; reality testing; series-patterning. Are these tasks really *non-verbal?* Let us compare the responses of children from adequate language environments with those of language-deprived children. On a relatively simple task such as selecting a *tiger* as different from a *pig,* a *horse,* and a *sheep*, both children will probably succeed. When the first child is told, "Tell why," he can easily explain, "Well, the pig and the sheep and the horse are all farm animals, but the tiger is a jungle animal." Many language-deprived children, on the other hand, will be unable to give a verbal explanation of their thought processes. One child responded by pointing to each farm animal saying "Him here," then pointing to the tiger and saying, "Him not here!" Can we doubt that some quality of inner-language is being employed by a child when he performs such so-called *non-verbal* tasks? On more complicated items of a test, the language-deprived child will probably fail the task even without verbalization. Examine the inner-language needed to solve such an item as this:

> Let's see, there are four squares here. Each one is outlined by figures such as triangles, circles, stars, and squares. Two of the large squares use triangles and small squares—the other two use stars and circles . . . no, that won't help find the one that is different. . . . Aha! Three of the large squares have the same small figure in all four corners, with two each of the second kind of small figures filling in each side. The different large

square uses two different small figures and has them arranged first one kind and then the other kind, all around the large square!

It might well be contended that language-deprived children should have motivated learning experiences with classification tasks, with the teacher supplying the necessary oral language to show the child how one thinks through language. Children enjoy these tasks when they are removed from a test situation. Call the activity "Look, Think, and Find Time" and they will participate enthusiastically. Many of Dr. Marianne Frostig's materials[3] for improving visual perception could be used for such activity.

Language-deprived children will need continuing special consideration throughout the elementary grades. For example, if a fourth-grade teacher in a slum school wishes to introduce a creative writing project employing verse to express children's reactions to colors, her work will be quite different from that of a teacher in a school with a middle-income population. She will provide much more preparatory time, possibly sharing some of her own responses and bringing examples from literature into the classroom. Even then, the children may not have in their own mental warehouses the vocabulary needed to express their ideas. It may be necessary for the teacher to cover the chalkboards with words such as *sad, joyous, gloomy, cool, a rainy day, like dying,* etc., to give the children the tools with which to create. Some children may say they respond to no colors. The teacher can then use her knowledge of the individual child to ask such questions as, "Let's see, Sam, you are dreaming of the day when you will own a car. What color would you like it to be? Oh! A red one. Why don't you think about why the car's color matters to you. Think of some words to tell how you would feel at the wheel of a new red car."

Teachers use many ingenious ways of motivating vocabulary growth. Better ways for distributing and sharing such methods are needed.

LIMITATIONS IN THE PHONETIC STRUCTURE OF LANGUAGE

Educators are becoming fully cognizant of the importance of phonic skills in the total language arts instructional program. To be able to spell, for instance, a child must think of written symbols (letters) for the speech sounds he hears. To read, he must think of the sounds of the letters he sees.

It is questionable whether the professional training of elementary school teachers provides sufficient work in the areas of language development, speech improvement, and individual differences in speech and language. Teachers need to be skilled, critical listeners. They should be able to recognize the sound substitutions, omissions, and distortions which children produce. Schools including speech clinicians as part of special staff could provide such information to teachers through an economical amount of in-service training.

Speech errors could be related to the particular phonetic charts employed in the reading program to improve teachers' skills. They could then discriminate between speech errors typical for particular dialects, for non-standard English, and for clinical speech defects.

The goal for speech sound articulation should not be absolute uniformity. Regional expressions and dialect often enrich our total language. Change should be a goal, however, when differences lessen the intelligibility of speech or when they are commonly identified as non-standard English. The Norwegian's *dis* for *this* may be enchanting, but the American Negro high school graduate who says *dis, dem,* and *dose* may not get the job he is seeking! The non-standard English of those from the sub-culture of poverty might almost be considered a *second language*. Golden[4] advises, "Speech improvement must be self-improvement. We cannot change the student's patterns for him, but we can bring about awareness of a need for change, aid him in finding ways to make the change, and encourage his efforts at self-improvement."

LIMITATIONS IN THE SYNTACTIC STRUCTURE OF LANGUAGE

The use of language is the conveyance of meaning. Clarity of meaning depends upon grammatical structure, which involves inflection, word order, intonation, and word variations which indicate number, time action, and other functions. The best way to learn English grammar is the *Mother's Method*, through which the child with an adequate early language environment gains automatic grammatical responses through audition of the language he hears in the home. This *automaticity* of response is essential. Concepts and symbols will not give usable and meaningful speech and language unless the language processes become automatic. Consider, for example, the ability to form plurals, which ranges from simple addition of *s* (*toy—toys*), to the inflectional change demanded by the addition of *es* (*church—churches*), to the formation of irregular plurals, *man—men*, *mouse—mice*, *leaf—leaves*, etc. Ervin's[5] study of structure in children's language indicated that most children had acquired the ability to form plurals before the age of three. Through the writer's experience with language-deprived children, it has become obvious that many children lack this ability at age six or even age eight! The Auditory-Vocal Automatic Test, a sub-test of the Illinois Test of Psycholinguistic Abilities, includes nine items of plural formation. Most slum children form no more than three or four of the plurals correctly. Some creative teacher could easily devise a card game which would make repetition of correct plurals fun for the children.

Another automatic language ability assessed by the Illinois Test of Psycholinguistic Abilities is that of being able to make comparisons by use of the comparative and superlative degrees of adjectives and adverbs. For example, the examiner shows the child a picture of two cakes and says, "This cake looks good. This cake looks even. . . " Few young slum children are able to supply the comparative form *better*. Typical responses are *good, gooderer, gooder*. One eight-year old Mexican-American child pointed to the first cake, saying, "This one little good,"—then, pointing triumphantly to the other cake, "This one *yes* good!"

One group test of intelligence for second-grade children requires the teacher to use in the oral directions ten terms of superlative degree, for example, *largest, nearest,* and *fewest*.

Some language texts introduce this study of degree as late as sixth grade, even though the children need such oral skills for the first years of formal learning.

Is anything more mercurial than the English verb? All children experience some difficulty with the structural shifts and changes required for proper person, tense, and number. The verbs *to be* and *have* are customarily slaughtered by language-deprived children, since *they was* and *we has* sound right to them. One typical distortion by Negro children from language-deprived homes is, "She don't be here today."

The writer made a study comparing written language of three groups of ten-year-old children last year. The groups were: Negroes from low-income public housing; Spanish-speaking from a low-income area; profoundly deaf Caucasian children in a special oral day class. The Negro children made as many verb errors of number and tense as did the deaf children! Spanish-speaking children were unable to employ clauses for better expression. Negro children did not use progressive verb forms. The writer's observations confirm this problem. When shown action pictures and asked, "What is he doing?" the Negro child will usually respond, "He skatin'," omitting the auxiliary, rather than "He is skating."

It seems evident that language-deprived children need repetitive, structured oral experiences with proper language usage early in their school experience. When a six-year-old girl asks, "I doing good a little?" or a seven-year-old boy says, "You know that River Street? Him live Johnnie" it is time for remediation to achieve correct work order and usage.

Some language-deprived children may have vocabularies just good enough to mask their real language problems. *Naming* is not of much use if a child is unable *to tell something about* the object he has named. Such children need oral experiences with guidance in *telling about things*, so they can ask themselves, *What is it? What color is it?*, *What size?*, *What looks like it?*, *How is it used?*, *What is it made of?*

It is important to improve language usage as early as possible in the child's life. A recent study[6] indicates that high school students' awareness of structural relationships in English does not improve significantly after three years of formal study of English grammar! Other evidence supports the hypothesis that early instruction is most effective in changing language usage.

Since language skills and learning ability are so interdependently related, surely our schools have a responsibility to children with limited language. This responsibility involves adequate definition of the problem and commitment to the development of teaching methods that will meet the children's special needs. If the slum child's foundation of language skill can be strengthened through pre-school, kindergarten, and primary programs, he will then be able to compete more successfully during the subsequent years of school. Attention to this one specific symptom of *poverty* is not a total solution. However, as is stated by I. N. Berlin,[7] "Beginning to learn academic material is one way of beginning to deal with the real world. The successes in the mastery of subject matter mean a great deal to a sick child's concept of himself."

No special educational techniques can succeed in the wrong *attitudinal climate*! Progress in teaching slum children will depend upon the feelings of the staff of such schools. If children are viewed as *unteachable* or *hopeless from the start*, both teachers and children will find school a place of frustration and discouragement. Successful education of the children of poverty must be viewed as an exciting professional challenge and as a social and economic necessity.

REFERENCES

1. Wachner, Clarence W., "Detroit Great Cities School Improvement Program in Language Arts," paper presented at Annual Meeting of National Council of Teachers of English, November 1963.
2. Shaw, A. B., "Slums and School People," an editorial, *The School Administrator*, **22** (December 1964).
3. Frostig, Marianne, and David Horne, *The Frostig Program for the Development of Visual Perception*, Chicago: Follett Publishing Company.
4. Golden, Ruth I., *Improving Patterns of Language Usage*, Detroit: Wayne State University Press, p. 5.
5. Ervin, S. M., "Structure in Children's Language," paper presented at International Congress of Psychology, Washington, D.C., 1963.
6. Davis, O. L., Harold C. Smith, and Norman D. Bowers, "High School Students Awareness of Structural Relationships in English," *The Journal of Educational Research,* **58** (October 1964), 69–71.
7. Berlin I. N., "Unrealities in Teacher Education," *Saturday Review* Dec. 19, 1964.

UNDERSTANDING THE LANGUAGE OF THE CULTURALLY DISADVANTAGED CHILD

Eddie G. Ponder

INTRODUCTION

The urban schools of our country are faced with a sizeable number of school-age children who are considered educationally and culturally disadvantaged.[1] This presents a challenge to the public schools which try to provide an effective educational program for the boys and girls of this segment of the population. There is evidence, however, of a wealth of untapped resources among disadvantaged children. Because their self-images, motivations, and cultural horizons are very low, they are prevented from achieving at a level commensurate with their ages and abilities.

PHENOMENA REGARDING THE ORAL LANGUAGE OF DISADVANTAGED CHILDREN

> Lack of verbal symbols for common objects and ideas—Speech patterns which cause frequent misunderstandings in oral communication.

The above statements, extracted from one of the first reports of the Milwaukee Great Cities Study,[2] are indicative of findings and impressions of many school psychologists relative to the oral language productions of the majority of disadvantaged children. One has to take into account, however, that the standardized tests available and used are mostly standardized outside the experiences and language of these children. Most standardized instruments used to measure the language of the disadvantaged child do not tap the kind and quality of language that he possesses. His patterns of speech, usage, and pronunciation do not, for the most part, approximate the standards of language expected by the school (commonly referred to as school language).

The oral language of the disadvantaged child is usually on the "vulgar" level. The "vulgar" level is used here to denote a language category of the people or the crowd (vulgus). In addition, the "vulgar" level is usually designated as the lowest level of language. The common man without ade-

---

Edward G. Ponder, "Understanding the Language of the Culturally Disadvantaged," *Elementary English*, **42**, 769–774. Reprinted with the permission of the National Council of Teachers of English and Edward G. Ponder.

quate educational experiences speaks mostly on the "vulgar" level.

The oral language habits of disadvantaged Negro and white children coming from the same region are similar. In working directly with children and parents from the two racial groups, one can easily discover many similarities in language usage, oral expression, and sentence sense. There are, of course, some differences. The differences, however, are of degree, not kind.

Following are some samples of the oral language (along with comments) of socially disadvantaged children. The first two samples selected for use have been extracted from the final report of the Milwaukee study on Orientation Classes for In-Migrant—Transient Children.[3] The third and final sample was selected from an actual classroom discussion in one of the Milwaukee Orientation Classes for In-Migrant—Transient Children where a tape recorder is familiar equipment and was used to record this session.[4]

Sample 1

An Original Play

Students used the tape recorder in putting this play together.

Boss: Hey you, boy, come here (menacingly). I thought I asked you for two bales. You got a bale and a half here.

Worker: Yes sir, you did and I'm trying to pick the rest of it.

Boss: I hear you been playing and loafing out there in the field.

Worker: No sir, that ain't so, I been working hard.

Boss: You—yeah you, come here. You the one who told me this boy was playing and laughing stead o' doing his work?

Worker (2): Yas sir, and he keeps the rest of us from doing our work.

Boss: I reckon um have to give you a beatin'. Kneel down. (Boss lashes worker on back.) Now get up. You got a woman?

Worker: Naw sir, I ain't married.

Boss: Boy, go get yourself a woman. Maybe you'll work better and get them bales picked.

Worker: (Student goes off stage, selects a girl.) E. says, "I don't want to be in that old play, Mrs. Carter." Other students urge E., "Aw go on, E." E. and worker go to field.

Worker: Bossman, this is my wife.

Boss: You got any children old enough to work in the field?

Wife: No sir, they're in school.

Boss: Send them out here to help this good for nothin' man of yours.

Wife: (Resolutely) They're staying in school.
(as they leave the field) I don't care whether he ever gets his cotton picked. My children are gonna stay in school, even if I have to leave Mississippi and go to Milwaukee and live with my sister. The children wili have a chance up there.

One can readily see how environment helps to shape an individual's attitudes and values. Fortunately, special personnel providing social and developmental histories as well as psychological evaluations were available to the teacher in her efforts to try to understand her students through their use of oral and written expression. In this play, it is interesting to note the male acceptance of the Southern social system from which they came. Too, the teacher observed that the boys laughed as they played these roles and expressed no resentment toward the social system portrayed. (They didn't even react, to the name, *boy*.) On the other hand, the girls did not like the image portrayed. Also, it appears that the female values education. The play seems to suggest that immorality, values, and attitudes often thought of as being *inherently* associated with lower-class status (and sometimes racial minority groups) can be and are influenced or conditioned by authority figures of a supposedly higher social order. In addition, this play seems to support the notion that disadvantaged families are migrating from rural impoverished circumstances to the urban zone to better themselves. The extended family is most often crucial in this regard.

Sample II

> When mama and papa died, my brother sent for us to come live with him. He can't read and write and he's so ashamed. He ain't never had no trouble on his job tho'. He wants to give us a chance to finish high school. My sister-law is nex' to the angels—she's so good to me and my little brothers. There's a baby in the house that loves me so much—I don't know why because I'm only his aunt, but they all say he looks just like me. I do love that little baby.

This sample seems to suggest strong family ties which facilitate the social system of the extended family. Moreover, one can sense the value of education which the family holds even though the male head of the household appears to lack a positive self-image because of his inability to read and write. Nevertheless, there seems to be a sense of pride in the work of the male as well as love of family. Note also the poetic quality of the line, "My sister-law is nex' to the angels."

Sample III

William: Will you have seven years of bad luck if you break a mirror?

Scott: I broke mine and that was bad luck enough cause it was brand new. But, I'm gonna buy me a new one. Bad luck just comes—you don't have to break nothing—But you got to make good luck by working hard and saving—getting an education.

This dialogue between two students indicates adequate language to express interesting ideas, aspirations, and philosophy of life.

The samples contained language of Negro and white students. Was it possible to determine racially one from the other?

The Cratis Williams' studies on Southern Appalachian speech also indicate regional characteristics which are interracial. Further, William asserts that words, more particularly verb forms and even diction, when examined comparatively, reveal little that is confined only to Appalachia.

Following is a selected list of some of the most common verbs used in mountain speech which was developed by Williams:[5]

Present	*Past*	*Past Participle*
(ask) ax	axt	axt
bring	brung	brung
burst	busted	busted
drive	driv	driv
fight	fit	fit
hear	heared	heared
reach	rech	rech
see	seed	seed
sneak	snuck	snuck
take	takened	takened
teach	teached	teached

Although the above list does not indicate acceptable verb forms in our culture, it, nevertheless, displays verb forms with certain systematic characteristics. While the verbs in the past tense and past participle are at the "vulgar" level, they are within the framework of regional speech which is fluent and meaningful. There are many positive aspects of mountain speech. It is colorful, metaphorical, lyrical, rhythmical. Frazier[6] asserts that the great mass of children we consider poorly languaged actually have quite a lot of language. Therefore, Frazier argues, if we let them, they can talk a blue streak about the things they know how to talk about. Thus, it would seem reasonable to suggest that we need to understand and learn the language which the disadvantaged child brings to the school situation if we are to "take him where he is."

Some of the language of the disadvantaged child may be less fluent. For example, these children often answer with a nod or one-word reply for fear of not being able to answer correctly in the school culture. On the other hand, generally speaking, the child is from a home where the parents are educationally and culturally disadvantaged, thereby affording little opportunity for the development of his oral language. Moreover, the child is usually from a large family living in a crowded, noisy apartment. The noise, however, does not represent meaningful stimuli.

The extended family is not uncommon in the family structure of the disadvantaged child. Uncles, aunts, grandparents, cousins, and sometimes very close friends are a part of the family structure. It would appear that the disadvantaged child has only advantages regarding language development with so many people around. The extended family structure, however, may cause serious discontinuity in the language development of the child. He learns language from the many people around him, likely speaking in varied pitches and accents. Lost in the shuffle of so many people, often in a crowded space, the child has limited opportunities for help in learning to label the objects in his environment. His opportunities for enrichment within and outside the encapsulated, socially impoverished environment are also limited.

Allison Davis[7] stated that one night he attended a movie on Chicago's Southside to gain further insights into the language of disadvantaged adults. He sat behind two women who were engaged in a lengthy discussion trying to label two animals (rhinoceros—hippopotamus) which had been flashed on the screen in a zoo scene. Davis discovered (1) that these women were born and reared in the South. (2) that they had never been to a zoo or circus because being Negro in their previous locale of the South prevented them from attending and (3) that the women had not become acquainted with these animals in their sketchy educational or experiential backgrounds. This illustration by Davis would seem to support the notion that the disadvantaged child is the product of a disadvantaged family in which his opportunities for learning to label, including feedback regarding labeling, are limited.

These boys and girls pass innumerable resources and objects going from school each day (also in their travels about the community) without the slightest idea as to how to label them. They label them as a thing, do-hickey, or *somethin' out yonder*. These seemingly crude labels, however, serve an important function in the communication system developed in the disadvantaged populace.

Many idiomatic expressions uttered by the disadvantaged child and his parents seem to baffle the more affluent speaker and often obstruct communication. For example, in some disadvantaged neighborhoods, "I don't care to," can mean "yes, I'm willing," according to the intonation of the speaker. Whether the disadvantaged child utters "twice out of sight" (go around two mountains) in the Kentucky hills or "gwine to tote this poke of 'taters'" (going to carry this bag [sack?] of potatoes) in Mississippi, his oral language is highly clear, understandable, and completely acceptable in his particular social milieu.

SHOULD WE TRY TO CHANGE THE LANGUAGE OF THE DISADVANTAGED CHILD?

It seems of paramount importance that we accept the language of the disadvantage child. To be "accepting," however, does not indicate a reluctance to "build on" or improve the language habits and skills of the disadvantaged child for fear of alienating him from his family and/or peers in the socially impoverished environment.

Disadvantaged parents want their children to improve educationally. In fact, they realize the necessity of a good education. They are perplexed, usually, as to means by which to attain educational ends. Yet, it should be realized that many racial and ethnic groups which presently enjoy high cultural and social positions in the social stratification of our society are descendants of disadvantaged parents and depressed neighborhoods.

There is also concern that it is futile to try to teach the disadvantaged child "correct" language skills because he returns to the impoverished environment only to revert back to his "incorrect" usage of the language. It should be stated that the intent to improve the language skills of the disadvantaged child should not be to train him *only* for a given higher level of language. Rather, he should be made aware of other levels of language, especially as they relate to actual occupational situations in our society. Thus, if the disadvantaged child subsequently becomes verbally mobile, to what degree is his reverting back of importance? Is there a correctness to our language? Tomlinson states that in helping children achieve social standards of language, the teacher should keep in mind that these standards do not deny certain regional characteristics of tone, accent, rhythm, and idiom. Might we think of acceptable ways of expressions for given situations as we work with disadvantaged children (and, indeed, all children)?

CAN WE CHANGE THE LANGUAGE OF THE DISADVANTAGED CHILD?

While it is important to try to assess the amount and quality of the language possessed by disadvantaged children, it is equally important to try to assess their language deficiencies. This will facilitate the establishment of a "communicative" benchmark from which to build more acceptable language usage. Research indicates some interesting findings relative to the language of the disadvantaged child; paucity of language, shorter sentences in speech, poorly structured speech syntactically, and language related to social class.

Cutts[9] states that the utterances, huh—uh . . . huh . . . nuttin . . . naw . . . wuh? . . . cuz . . . unhunh . . . sho! and other *strange noises* [italics mine] that take the place of standard American English reflect the impoverished language background of underprivileged children.

John[10] reports that several studies indicate that children from lower-class backgrounds rely on shorter sentences in their speech than do their middle-class agemates. She further reports from her summary of studies that children from lower-class circumstances have a more limited vocabulary and poorer articulation.

Deutsch,[11] reporting on some of the basic research at the Institute for Developmental Studies, postulates that the lower-class home is not a verbally oriented environment. Moreover, he reports that from observations of lower-class homes, speech sequences appear to be temporally very limited and poorly structured. Thus, Deutsch argues, it is not surprising to find that a major focus of deficit in the children's language development is syntactical organization and subject continuity.

Newton[12] states that the opportunities for language development are stretched on a continuum and the economic "have nots" are often the verbal "have nots" as well.

This brief look into research on language development of disadvantaged children is helpful in providing a frame in which to understand the nature of their language deficiencies. It facilitates the development of an instructional program to more adequately meet their needs. For example, special tapes may be prepared to develop attentional or listening skills. These skills are important first steps with respect to language development. Too, a sequential program may need to be planned which begins with attentional or listening skills and moves to such higher levels as the labeling of objects, and the labeling of similarities and differences in objects and functions of objects. While this example indicates how language may be developed, it also has implications for the development of other skills.

CONCLUSION

In conclusion, it seems of paramount importance that the language spoken and written by the disadvantaged child be understood by the teacher in order to (1) facilitate meaningful communication and (2) provide a starting point from which to build on the language which he does possess.

The teacher will need to develop good rapport with the children and provide a positive classroom climate in order to free them to express themselves orally. Moreover, good classroom climate will help the teacher gain better opportunities to help children develop "other ways" of speaking and using the language. When good classroom climate exists, children can often be heard to say "I know better than that," or "That sounds like me."

Understanding the language of the disadvantaged child is not as difficult a task as is often assumed; the teacher's attitude and the understanding with which he approaches the task will determine to a large extent the degree of difficulty. Moreover, the teacher's awareness of the individual needs of his children will determine the kinds of activities and program to be provided in the classroom. It is quite likely that the approach in helping the disadvantaged child develop language facility is applicable for use with advantaged children. The teacher will in both cases plan his instruction around the language strengths and the language needs which the children bring to the school situation.

NOTES

1. The terms culturally and educationally disadvantaged are used interchangeably with urban disadvantaged, socially disadvantaged, disadvantaged, culturally deprived, experience poor, educationally underprivileged, children with limited backgrounds, and the disaffected.
2. Milwaukee, Wisconsin Board of School Directors, "Orientation Classes for In-Migrant—Transient Children, Report I, Part I," October 1961.
3. Milwaukee, Wisconsin Board of School Directors, "Orientation Classes for In-Migrant—Transient Children, Final Report," March 1964.
4. The comments following the language samples are a result of staff conferences on selected children enrolled in the high school orientation class. The author wishes to acknowledge the professional services of Mrs. Dorothy Carter, teacher of the class, Mrs. Lottie Porter, Project Social Worker, and Mr. Hoyt Harper, Project Psychologist.
5. Cratis D. Williams, "Verbs in Mountain Speech," *Mountain Life and Work*, Berea, Ky.: Council of the Southern Mountains, Inc., Spring 1962, pp. 15–19.
6. Alexander Frazier, "Helping Poorly Languaged Children," *Elementary English* (February 1964), 149–153.
7. In an address at the New York University sponsored conference, *Integrating Diversity Through the Curriculum*, Dec. 1, 1963.
8. Loren R. Tomlinson, "Accepting Regional Language Differences in School," *Elementary English 30*: 420–423, 1953.
9. Warren G. Cutts, "Reading Unreadiness in the Underprivileged," *NEA Journal 52*: 23–24, 1963.
10. Vera P. John, "The Intellectual Development of Slum Children: Some Preliminary Findings," *The American Journal of Orthopsychiatry 33*: 813–822, 1963.
11. Martin P. Deutsch, "The Disadvantaged Child and the Learning Process," in *Education in Depressed Areas*, A. Harry Passow, ed. New York: Bureau of Publications, Teachers College, Columbia University, 1963, pp. 163–179.

12. Eunice Shaed Newton, "Planning for the Language Development of Disadvantaged Children and Youth," *The Journal of Negro Education 39*: 264–274, 1964.

REFERENCES

1. John B. Carroll, "Language Development," in Chester N. Harris, ed., *Encyclopedia of Educational Research*, 3rd ed., New York: Macmillan, 1960, pp. 744–750.
2. Werner Cohn, "On the Language of Lower Class Children," *School Review*, **67** (1959), 435–440.
3. Warren Cutts, "Reading Unreadiness in the Underprivileged," *National Education Association Journal*, **52** (1963), 23–24.
4. Martin P. Deutsch, "The Disadvantaged Child and the Learning Process," in A. Harry Passow, ed., *Education in Depressed Areas*, New York: Bureau of Publications. Teachers College, Columbia University, 1963.
5. Alexander Frazier, "Helping Poorly Languaged Children," *Elementary English*, **41** (1964), 149–153.
6. Vera P. John, "The Intellectual Development of Slum Children: Some Preliminary Findings," *American Journal of Orthopsychiatry*, **33** (1963), 813–822
7. Milwaukee, Wisconsin Board of School Directors, "Orientation Classes for In-Migrant—Transient Children, Report I, Part 1," October 1961.
8. Milwaukee, Wisconsin Board of School Directors, "Orientation Classes for In-Migrant—Transient Children, Final Report," March 1964.
9. Eunice Shaed Newton, "Planning for the Language Development of Disadvantaged Children and Youth," *Journal of Negro Education*, **33** (1964), 264–274.
10. Loren R. Tomlinson, "Accepting Regional Language Differences in School," *Elementary English*, **30** (1953), 420–423.
11. Cratis D. Williams, "Verbs in Moutain Speech," in *Mountain Life and Work*, Berea, Ky.: Council of the Southern Mountains, Inc., Spring, 1962, pp. 15–19.

THE VERBAL ABILITY OF THE CULTURALLY DIFFERENT

James Olsen

"Nothing so needs reforming as other people's habits."—Mark Twain

I.

One of the common stereotypes of the culturally different child is that he is deficient in language skills and abilities. He doesn't talk and discuss topics and events in the classroom. Frank Riesman has even suggested that he has a different learning style. Riesman says that the lower income child is a physical, action-centered learner who tends to work out mental problems best when he can do things physically.[1] (According to this definition, my five-year old son is culturally deprived because the latter description fits him perfectly.) In the past the verbal deficiencies of the culturally different have been ascribed to their low intelligence and emotional immaturity. The child who was not verbally responsive was often labelled "slow," "not too bright," and of "low intelligence." Now that some of the research on our I.Q. tests is in and we admit the "middle-class bias" of these tests, it is no longer fashionable to attribute the so-called verbal poverty of the poor child to his lack of intelligence. Rather his apparent lack of verbal ability is now explained in terms of his "experiential poverty," "the absence of books in the home," "his circumscribed opportunities for talking to his parents," and so on. In other words, the child is not necessarily stupid. He just has not been lucky enough to be born into a middle class family so that he could be read to, taken to museums and concerts, given travel opportunities, and talked to by adults.

But it seems to me that most average middle-class children do not enjoy the latter advantages to any great extent anyway. As a middle-class child, I remember three or four books in my house, no travel opportunities, and a life pretty much restricted to my neighborhood block. I'm not at all sure that even the *majority* of middle-class children have these advantages, and I know of no research that says they do. What we are really talking about here is the *upper-middle-class* child, not the son or daughter of a clerk. But even if *all* middle-class children have *all* of these advantages,

---

James Olsen, "The Verbal Ability of the Culturally Different," *The Educational Forum* (March 1965), 280–284.

how can we be so sure that in the absence of these informal educational opportunities a child becomes verbally destitute? If you can't talk about Bach and how you spent your summer at South Hampton, does that mean you can't talk at all?

Now what I am going to suggest here is that while it is true that many of the children of the poor do not have any apparent verbal ability in formal learning situations like the classroom, most culturally different children are no more verbally destitute than their middle-class peers. And more than that, these children have a great deal of untapped verbal ability of a highly imaginative nature which remains latent primarily because the institutional arrangements of our schools militate against direct and meaningful discussion.

The problem of the lack of verbal ability of the poor, or of anyone else for that matter, is to pinpoint *why* a child is silent and unresponsive and then to treat the causes, not the symptoms. To label any child "underdeveloped in verbal skills" does not define the problem; it obscures it.

We can best begin, I think, by admitting that some children come to school with such a lack of language experience, or experience of any kind, that they are verbally destitute. We know, for example, that the prolonged hospitalization of normal children can result in retarded language development. I remember children in my class who sat in dumb silence for half a year before they put two sentences together. The vocabularies of these children, the length of their sentences, the syntax and grammatical complexity of their speech indicated to me, their teacher, that they needed compensatory work in language development. Increased readiness activities, the passage of time, and the attention of adults can help these linguistically retarded to reach a point where they can enter the regular language program with profit. But the point is that there are very few of these children. In my class of thirty pupils, one would have found two in this category. But what about the others?

Suppose you walk into a classroom. You see the teacher in front of the room giving a lesson on how to use the dictionary. Most of the children are silent and unresponsive. Some are daydreaming; they are looking out the window. Others are doodling or talking to a nearby classmate. The teacher asks a question based on her lesson. Few hands are raised. No one seems to want to talk. Finally, one student answers the question in three or four words. Now to jump from this empiric observation of lack of student responsiveness to the generalization that "these children come to the classroom verbally destitute" is a big and a dangerous jump. If we see this same group of children in the street a few moments later, we may overhear a heated conversation about some baseball player or a party that is being planned. To say that these children were verbally unresponsive in the classroom is true. But to say that these same children are not verbal or that they are, for one reason or another, incapable of verbalization, is false.

This is an extremely important point. If the latter description is true, that is, if in fact, poor children are not verbal children, then the burden of change is with the child. But if we attribute their verbal unresponsiveness to the content of the lesson, that is, the curriculum, the audience situation (teacher to pupil), the strategy of the teacher (question and answer), and the formality of the learning situation, the burden of change is upon the institution rather than upon the child. If you see these children as "verbally underdeveloped," then you will construct a language program in which the child gets "more of the same." Extra periods of work, remedial assistance, special tutoring, and the like are introduced "to bring these children up to par." But a different viewpoint will result in a different kind of program.

2.

Why are children silent? I have already pointed out that some children may be genuinely retarded in their language development. But there are also other possible explanations:

1. Some children may have full language development of a kind that is not accepted by the school. This child may have learned the language of his environment. He may be quite conversant with "hip" talk but not with "standard" language. He can make himself understood to his peers and parents but not to his teachers.

2. Some children may have full language development except in certain areas of activity valued by the school. In this situation the child may not have the concepts which come out of certain kinds of experiences so that he *appears* to be impoverished in his language. If, for example, the teacher is talking about the milkman or "my summer trip," the child will be silent because he literally has nothing to say. These are experiences which are foreign to the child. He appears *word locked* when he is really *concept locked.*

3. Some children may have full language development but hesitate to share what they have experienced because they feel that these experiences will be disvalued. The child from a "deprived" background may be quite widely experienced, but he finds little in the curriculum, textbooks, or school lessons that relates to the world as he knows it. He is silent because his experience is simply irrelevant.

4. Some children may be quite verbal in informal situations but tongue tied in more formal situations like the classroom. In audience situations, both middle-class and lower-class children may be timid and therefore

quiet and reserved. It may be that we have defined our oral language programs *formally* but have missed the informal oral language opportunities that are available to us all day long. We have also stressed talk between teacher and student rather than between student and student. Perhaps we should encourage more conversation among students by arranging our classrooms so that students can converse easily, by putting aside definite times for "student talk" and by encouraging more group work.

When we insist on silence in a classroom, we destroy one of the most powerful instruments we have in education. As Jean Piaget pointed out a long time ago, the very essence of the cognitive development of children is the socialization of thought that occurs within the child's environment. Children learn from one another as well as from adults in the environment. Indeed the research indicates that a child is more likely to accept the communication of a peer than that of an adult. More than anything else language is a social tool which the child uses to extend, analyze, and interpret his personal experience.

5. Children may not talk because we ask questions that do not require much talking. How often do we talk *with* children rather than *to* or *at* them? Indeed, a good deal of our classroom practice is built upon the question and answer. We discourage incorrect answers, and we reward correct answers with a gold star or a smile. Thus a certain amount of anxiety is always built into a classroom learning situation. In spite of the fact that the right answers of today may be the wrong answers of tomorrow, we overemphasize the importance of the right answer. In this way we tend to skew the process of education toward a futile exercise in meaningless memorization. We forget that in the long run it is the child who must idiosyncratically organize the conceptual content of a learning experience. Oral language development results when we think things through out loud, not necessarily from giving right answers.

6. Children may not respond because our teaching technology may be still suffering from the verbal hangover of the Middle Ages. Most of our work with children is almost exclusively verbalized. The questions and answers, the reading assignment, and the textbook still dominate American education. Nonverbal devices like films, tapes, concrete materials like Cuisennaire rods, games, role-playing, are not used extensively and frequently. Many children, whatever their social class position, do not verbalize well in response to words alone. Indeed, for many children action may speak louder than words. Riesman's formulations about the culturally different child may be applicable to *all* children *whatever* their origin. The point here is our schools are not really set up for those children who learn motorically. The formal lesson plan of the American public school teacher makes the route to learning verbal even though not everybody learns in

the same way. It may be that teachers need to develop a whole repertoire of teaching styles in which the same material will he handled or taught in different ways.

3.

If these explanations of retarded language development are correct, then they apply to *all* children and not just to the "culturally different." What we are talking about then is the basis for any good program of oral language development. It is my contention that the schools must provide such a program *because the responsibility for change is primarily with the school, not the child.* What the schools must do is:

1. Broaden their view of what oral language development is so that it includes informal situations and opportunities as well as formal ones. An informal learning situation does not preclude a structured, task-centered content.

2. Change the content of the curriculum so that children are challenged to develop greater precision of meaning in their speech because speech is not simply an isolated skill or group of skills. The unreality of so much of our curriculum materials destroys the child's initiative to express himself. The curriculum itself is the medium through which the child can extend and develop his language skills. There must be real challenging material for the child to want to speak for speech is simply thought made public.

3. Use various kinds of teaching technologies. Different people learn in different ways and the fact is that we make little actual provision for individual differences. Our concept of the act of teaching is still quite primitive because most teachers still see teaching as an act in which the teacher "pours in" information, skills, appreciation, and so on. The children are not called upon to reach out, to inquire, and to explore for what they need to know simply because there is no real practical need except the desire to continue on the next level or grade because of the artificial threat of failure. At its best, language grows out of both concrete and vicarious experience. We have almost completely relied upon the latter. There are many untried roads to verbalization.

There is no reason why we cannot construct a total oral language program for all of our public school children. I suspect that both our middle-class and lower-class children are capable of much more verbalization anyway. Since the research clearly indicates that language growth is unitary in the sense that reading, writing, speaking, and listening are closely related by structure, purpose, and skill, it is unwise to fragment language development into distinct, unrelated areas.[2] The challenge is for us to construct such a total language program and then see to it that it reaches all of our children.

NOTES

1. Frank Riesman, *A Five Point Plan: A Proposed Approach for Teachers of Urban Disadvantaged Children*. Prepared for Syracuse University Conference on Urban Education and Cultural Deprivation, 1964, p. 15.
2. James F. Halcomb, "Reading: The Language Experience Approach" in *Challenge and Experiment in Reading*, International Reading Association Conference Proceedings, **7** (1962), p. 72.

STUDY QUESTIONS

1. Boyer and Walsh allege that traditionally American education has been predicated on the assumption that children differ innately in their ability to learn. What school practices do they cite in support of this allegation? Is there any evidence to refute it?
2. According to Boyer and Walsh, the schools have allowed intellectual inferiority among lower-class children to become a self-fulfilling prophecy. What do they mean? Do conventional grading systems reinforce this prophecy? Under what circumstances might this reinforcement occur?
3. What do Boyer and Walsh mean when they say that "an American environmentalist commitment (toward liberal rather than totalitarian goals) would aim at *creating* ability, at *increasing* intelligence, at *developing* interests"? How could this statement be applied to the teaching of elementary school subjects?
4. What elements of Jensen's hypothesis of racial differences in I.Q. does Anastasiow regard as particularly disturbing? Would Boyer and Walsh agree with Anastasiow's criticisms?
5. What is Anastasiow's rationale for rejecting the heredity versus environment debate? What does he propose as an alternative line of inquiry for education? Is it acceptable to you?
6. On what grounds does Anastasiow challenge Jensen's assertion that "... compensatory education has been tried and it apparently has failed"? What would you regard as minimal criteria for determining the effectiveness of Head Start and various Title I programs? What problems are one likely to encounter in attempting to apply such criteria?
7. What are the distinguishing characteristics of language-deprived children, as described by Metz? On what basis does she defend the use of group intelligence tests as indicators of language deprivation? Why would some educators be inclined to criticize Metz's use of the term "language deprivation"? Can you think of a more precise term?

8. Why does Metz encourage teachers to begin as early as possible to improve language usage? Does the author advocate systematic, formal instruction, or incidental, informal instruction?
9. Is Metz in substantial agreement with Anastasiow and Boyer and Walsh regarding the effect of environment on the learning capacities of elementary pupils? What kind of teacher is best qualified to apply Metz's recommendations? What instruction materials would be most useful to such a teacher?
10. Do Ponder and Metz agree or disagree concerning the language habits of disadvantaged children? The use of standardized tests?
11. According to research studies on Southern Appalachian speech cited by Ponder, some regional speech characteristics are interracial. In what other regions of the U.S. might this phenomenon occur?
12. What does Ponder mean when he refers to a "communicative benchmark" for disadvantaged children? Would Metz's conceptions of lexical, phonetic structive and syntacic structure provide suitable points of departure for establishing this benchmark?
13. Why does Ponder regard the child's language strengths and deficiencies as basic focal points for improving instruction? He seems to express little concern over the eventual tendency of children to revert back to "incorrect" usage of language of their environment. Why does he regard the development of verbal mobility as an advantage and not a disadvantage?
14. Contrary to many authors, Olsen maintains that ". . . most culturally different children are no more verbally destitute than their middle-class peers." What evidence does he cite in support of this assertion? Would Ponder and Metz agree with him on this point?
15. Olsen offers six explanations for the apparent lack of verbal ability in culturally different children, as perceived by teachers and school personnel. Does he regard these problems as insolvable? Do the solutions lie with the school, parents, or both?
16. Olsen proposes a series of curricular changes which he feels must occur before schools can develop viable oral language programs. How drastic are these changes? Under what circumstances might they be acceptable to administrators and teachers? To teacher-training institutions?

SUGGESTED READINGS

Barbe, Walter B., "Identification and Diagnosis of the Needs of the Educationally Retarded and Disadvantaged," *The Educationally Retarded and Disadvantaged*, Sixty-sixth Yearbook of the National Society for the Study of Education, Part I, Chicago: University of Chicago Press, 1967, pp. 97–120.

Black, Millard H., "Characteristics of the Culturally Disadvantaged," *The Reading Teacher*, **18** (March 1965), 465–470.

Brookover, Wilbur B., *et al.*, *Self-Concept of Ability and School Achievement*, Cooperative Research Project No. 1636, East Lansing: Bureau of Educational Research, Michigan State University, October 1965.

Coleman, James S., *et al.*, *Equality of Educational Opportunity*, Washington; D.C.: U.S. Government Printing Office, 1966.

Deutsch, M., "Happenings on the Way Back to the Forum: Social Science, I.Q., and Race Differences Revisited," *Harvard Educational Review*, **39** (Summer 1969), 523–557.

Evans, John W., "The Effect of Pupil Mobility upon Academic Achievement," *National Elementary Principal* (April 1966), 18–22.

Havighurst, Robert J., "Who are the Socially Disadvantaged?" *Journal of Negro Education* (Summer 1964), 210–217.

Havighurst, Robert J., and Thomas E. Moorefield, "The Disadvantaged in Industrial Cities," *The Educationally Retarded and Disadvantaged*, Sixty-sixth Yearbook of the National Society for the Study of Education, Part I Chicago: University of Chicago Press, 1967, pp. 8–20.

Hess, Robert D., and Virginia Shipman, "Early Blocks to Children's Learning," *Children*, **12**, No. 5 (September–October, 1965).

"How Much Can We Boost I.Q. and Scholastic Achievement: A Discussion," *Harvard Educational Review*, **39** (Spring 1969), 273–356. (Series of papers by Jerome S. Kagan, J. McVickers Hunt, James F. Crow, Carl Bereiter, David Elkind, Lee J. Cronbach, and William F. Brazziel.)

Hunt, J. McVicker, "Black Genes—White Environment," *Transaction*, **6** (June 1969), 12–22.

Jensen, Arthur R., "How Much Can We Boost I.Q. and Scholastic Achievement?" *Harvard Educational Review*, **39** (Winter 1969), 1–123.

__________, "Reducing the Heredity-Environment Uncertainty: A Reply," **39**, Summer 1969, pp. 449–483.

__________, "Social Class and Verbal Learning," in M. Deutsch, I. Katz, and A. Jensen, eds., *Social Class, Race, and Psychological Development*, New York: Holt, Rinehart & Winston, 1968, pp. 115–174.

Justman, Joseph, "Academic Aptitude and Reading Test Scores of Disadvantaged Children Showing Varying Degrees of Mobility," *Journal of Educational Measurement* (December 1965), 151–155.

Keller, Suzanne, "The Social World of the Urban Slum Child: Some Early

Findings," *American Journal of Orthopsychiatry*, **33**, 5 (October 1963), 823–831.

Light, Richard J., and Paul V. Smith, "Social Allocation Models of Intelligence: A Methodological Inquiry," *Harvard Educational Review*, **39**, 484–510.

Parson, A. Harry, and Elliott, David L., "The Disadvantaged in Depressed Areas," *The Educationally Retarded and Disadvantaged*, Sixty-Sixth Yearbook of the National Society for the Study of Education, Part I, Chicago: University of Chicago Press, 1967, pp. 20–39.

Pettigrew, Thomas F., "Negro American Intelligence: A new Look At an Old Controversy," *Journal of Negro Education* (Winter 1964), 6–25.

Rowan, Helen, "A Minority Nobody Knows," *Atlantic*, **219** (June 1967), 47–52.

Stinchcomb, Arthur L., "Environment: The Cumulation of Events," *Harvard Educational Review*, **39** (Summer 1969), 511–522.

Tannenbaum, Abraham J., "Social and Psychological Considerations in the Study of the Socially Disadvantaged," *The Educationally Retarded and Disadvantaged*, Sixty-Sixth Yearbook of the National Society for the Study of Education, Part I, Chicago: University of Chicago Press, 1967, pp. 40–63.

Voyat, Gilbert, "I.Q.: God-Given or Man-Made?" *Saturday Review* (May 17, 1969), 73–75, 86–88.

CHAPTER 3
LANGUAGE AND CULTURE

That ours is a highly pluralistic society is an indisputable fact, one that has given purpose and direction to American public education. In principle, our schools have sought to provide free, unrestricted education for all children, irrespective of race, creed, or national origin. Until recently there has been little evidence that this ideal has achieved reality in language arts classes. In their blind, unyielding insistence on teaching one standard, socially-acceptable dialect of white, middle-class society, educators have denied the existence of linguistic pluralism.

What is being done to counteract this philosophy? How can the schools adjust their curricula in accordance with the needs of children whose oral language patterns are anchored in dialects that deviate from standard English? What can be done to re-educate teachers and administrators so that they can cope with this problem?

The readings in this chapter seek to provide answers to these questions. Raven I. McDavid undertakes a penetrating appraisal of prevailing conceptions of American dialects, and then outlines a series of propositions for the reader's consideration. After describing "The Sounds of Society" project in the Chicago public schools, Frederick David Erickson reveals its implications for researchers and teachers. Next, Edward T. Hall reveals promising new insights into a virtually unexplored field—the listening behavior of various minority groups. The chapter closes with an article by Roger W. Shuy, who describes a pioneering program for the study of social dialects in Detroit. The reader may find that this study and the others reported in this chapter do indeed have far-reaching implications for research and curriculum development.

SENSE AND NONSENSE ABOUT AMERICAN DIALECTS

Raven I. McDavid, Jr.

In my boyhood—more years ago than I care to remember—we used to define an expert as "a damned fool a thousand miles from home." Since I am considerably less than a thousand miles from where I grew up, and stand but a few minutes from my residence in Hyde Park, it behooves me to avoid any claim to expertness about the problems faced in practical situations where the dialect of the school child is sharply divergent from what is expected of him in the classroom. For many of these situations, neither I nor any other working dialectologist knows what the local patterns actually are; for some, there has been no attempt, or at best a partial and belated one, to find out the patterns. Nevertheless, the implications of dialectology for the more rational teaching of English in the schools—and not only in the schools attended by those we currently euphemize as the culturally disadvantaged—are so tremendous that I am flattered to have John Fisher ask for my observations. The problems are not limited to Americans of any race or creed or color, nor indeed to Americans; they are being faced in England today, as immigrants from Pakistan and the West Indies compete in the Midlands for the same kinds of jobs that have drawn Negro Americans to Harlem and the South Side, and Appalachian whites to the airplane factories of Dayton. In fact, such problems are faced everywhere in the world as industrialization and urbanization take place, on every occasion when people, mostly but not exclusively the young, leave the farm and the village in search of the better pay and more glamorous life of the cities. In all parts of the world, educators and politicians are suddenly realizing that language differences can create major obstacles to the educational, economic, and social advancement of those whose true integration into the framework of society is necessary if that society is to be healthy; they are realizing that social dialects—that is, social differences in the way language is used in a given community—both reflect and perpetuate differences in the social order. In turn, the practicing linguist is being called on with increasing frequency to devise programs for the needs of specific groups—most often for the Negroes dwelling in the festering slums of our northern and western cities; and generous government and private subsidies have drawn into the act many teachers and administra-

---

Raven I. McDavid, Jr., "Sense and Nonsense about American Dialects," *P.M.L.A.*, 81 (May 1966), pp. 7–17. Reprinted by permission of the author and the Modern Language Association of America.

tors—most of them, I trust, well meaning—who not only have made no studies of dialect differences, but have ignored the studies and archives that are available, even those dealing with their own cities.

Perhaps a data-oriented dialectologist may here be pardoned an excursion into the metaphors of siegecraft, recalled from the time when under the tutelage of Allan Gilbert I learned something of the arts of war and gunnery, if not all their Byronic applications. In confronting our massive ignorance of social dialects, the professional students of the past generation have been a forlorn hope—burrowing into a problem here, clawing their way to a precarious foothold of understanding there, seizing an outwork yonder. Like many forlorn hopes, they have been inadequately supported, sometimes ignored, even decried—not only by their literary colleagues, with the usual patronizing attitude toward anything smacking of affiliation with the social sciences, but also by their fellow linguists who are interested in international programs for teaching English as a second language, in machine translation, in formulaic syntax, or in missionating to convert the National Council of Teachers of English. It is small wonder that some students of dialects have withdrawn from the assault to participate in these better-heeled campaigns; it is a tribute to the simple-minded stubbornness of the survivors that they have not only persisted but advanced. Today their work, their aims, are embarrassingly respectable, as legions spring from the earth in response to the golden trumpet sounding on the banks of the Pedernales. It is inevitable, perhaps even fitting, that the practical work in social dialects should be directed by others than the pioneers in research. But it is alarming that many of those now most vocally concerned with social dialect problems not only know nothing about the systematic work that has been done, about the massive evidence (even if all too little) that is available, but even have a complete misconception about the nature and significance of dialects. At the risk of drawing the fire of the House Un-American Activities Committee, I would agree with my sometime neighbor James H. Sledd that our missionaries should at least know what they are talking about before they set out to missionate.

I have a particular advantage when I talk on this subject: I am one of those who speak English without any perceptible accent. I learned to talk in an upper-middle-class neighborhood of Greenville, South Carolina, among corporation lawyers, bankers, textile magnates, and college presidents, among families with a long tradition of education and general culture. Many of my playmates, like myself, represented the sixth generation of their families in the same county. It never occurred to any of us to tamper with our language; our only intimate acquaintance with non-standard grammatical forms in writing came from stories in literary dialect or from the quaint and curious exercises that infested our textbooks—though we knew that less privileged forms of speech than ours were found in our community, and were not above imitating them for rhetorical effect. Not a single English teacher of an excellent faculty—our superintendent had his doctorate, not from Peabody or from Teachers College, Columbia, but from the University of Berlin in 1910—made a gesture of tampering. Nor have I ever heard anything in the exotic dialects of the Northeast or the Middle West that would make me feel less content with a way of speaking that any educated person might want to emulate. And yet, a few years ago, my younger sister, who has remained in the South Carolina upland, told me over the telephone: "Brucker, you've been North so long that you talk just like a Yankee." Even though I doubt if I would fool many real Yankees, I know that something has rubbed off from my travels and teaching to make me talk a little different from the boys I grew up with. Still, whenever I go back and start talking with them again, I find myself slipping into the old ways; it is natural for us to shift our way of talking, according to the people we are talking with. In fact, it is the people we talk with habitually who give us our way of talking. Here, in essence, is the way dialects originate. And until everybody lives in a sterile, homogenized, dehumanized environment, as just a number on the books of an all-powerful state, we can expect differences in environment to be reflected in those differences in speech that we call dialects.

An appreciation of this fact would avoid a lot of nonsense expressed in categorical statements in educational literature. Two amusing if distressing examples are found in *Language Programs for the Disadvantaged: Report of the NCTE Task Force*, a booklet released at the 1965 convention of the NCTE. These statements, the more distressing because so much of the report is magnificently phrased, probably arose from the inevitable wastefulness of haste (the Task Force was in the field only last summer) and from the imbalance of the Task Force itself: there was only one linguist and not a single sociologist or anthropologist or historian in a group heavily loaded with supervisors and (to coin a term, which is probably already embalmed in educationese) curriculologists:

> Most disadvantaged children come from homes in which a nonstandard English dialect is spoken. It may be pidgin, Cajun, Midland, or any one of a large number of regional or cultural dialects. Many preschool teachers are concerned about the dialect of their children and take measures to encourage standard pronunciation and usage. (p. 70) . . . the general feeling is that some work in standard English is necessary for greater social and job mobility by disadvantaged students with a strong regional or racial dialect. (p. 89)

Among the bits of nonsense to be found in these two statements we may notice:

1. A belief that there is some mystical "standard," devoid of all regional

association. Yet the variety that we can find in cultivated American English, as used by identifiable informants with impeccable educational and social credentials, has been repeatedly shown in works based on the American Linguistic Atlas, most recently and in greatest detail in Kurath's and my *Pronunciation of English in the Atlantic States* (Ann Arbor: University of Michigan Press, 1961).

2. A belief that there are "racial" dialects, independent of social and cultural experiences.

3. A snobbishness toward "strong" dialect differences from one's own way of speaking. Would Bobby Kennedy, politically disadvantaged after the Atlantic City convention, have run a better race in New York had he learned to talk Bronx instead of his strong Bostonian?

4. A glib juggling of terms, without understanding, as in the parallelism of "pidgin, Cajun, Midland." *Pidgin* denotes a minimal contact language used for communication between groups whose native languages are mutually unintelligible and generally have markedly different linguistic structures; typical examples are the Neo-Melanesian of New Guinea and the Taki-taki of Surinam. However scholars may debate the existence of an American Negro pidgin in colonial days, speakers of pidgin constitute a problem in no Continental American classroom, though it would be encountered in Hawaii and the smaller Pacific islands. *Cajun* properly describes the colonial varieties of French spoken in southwestern Louisiana and in the parts of the Maritime Provinces of Canada from which the Louisiana Acadians were transported; even if by extension we use the term to describe the varieties of English developing in the French-speaking areas of Louisiana and the Maritimes, the problems of teaching English in these areas are really those of teaching English as a second language. *Midland* is a geographical designation for those dialects stemming from the settlement of Pennsylvania and embracing a broad spectrum of cultural levels. At one extreme, we may concede, are the impoverished submarginal farmers and displaced coal miners of Applachia; at the other are some of the proudest dynasties of America—the Biddles of Philadelphia, the Mellons of Pittsburgh, the Tafts of Cincinnati, and their counterparts in Louisville and in St. Louis, in Memphis and in Dallas—people it were stupid as well as impractical to stigmatize in language like that of the Task Force Report. So long as such glib generalities are used about social dialects, we must conclude that our educators, however well intentioned, are talking nonsense.

And regrettably, such nonsense is no new phenomenon in American culture; it has long been with us. Much of it, fortunately, runs off us like raindrops off a mallard's back. But enough lingers in the schoolroom to do positive harm. My friend Bob Thomas, the anthropologist—a Cherokee

Indian and proud of it, though with his blond hair and blue eyes he looks far less like the traditional Cherokee than I do—tells of his traumata when he moved to Detroit from Oklahoma at the age of fourteen. Although Cherokee was his first language, he had picked up a native command of Oklahoma English. Since he had always lived in a good neighborhood, and his family had used standard English at home, he had no problems in grammar; through wide reading and a variety of experiences he had acquired a large and rich vocabulary. But his vowels were Oklahoma vowels; and some benevolent despot in Detroit soon pushed him into a class in "corrective speech." The first day the class met, he looked around the classroom and noticed everybody else doing the same. As eyes met eyes, it became apparent that the class in "corrective speech" contained no cleft palates, no stammerers, no lispers, no foreign accents, not even any speakers of substandard English—for again, the school was in a good neighborhood. The only thing wrong with the boys and girls in the class was that they had not learned English in Michigan, but in Oklahoma, Arkansas, Missouri, Kentucky, Tennessee, West Virginia, Mississippi, and Alabama. "We all realized immediately," Bob told me years afterward, "that they were planning to brainwash us out of our natural way of speaking; and it became a point of honor among us to sabotage the program." To this day, Bob flaunts his Oklahoma accent belligerently; if the teachers had let him alone, he might have adapted his pronunciation to that of the Detroit boys he played with, but once he felt that the school considered his home language inferior, nothing could make him change. The first principle of any language program is that, whatever the target, it must respect the language that the students bring with them to the classroom.

Another kind of nonsense was demonstrated by the head of the speech department at the University of Michigan during my first Linguistic Institute. Impelled by the kind of *force majeur* that only a four-star general can exert, I had compromised with my scientific interest in linguistics to the extent of enrolling in a course in "stage and radio diction," only to find myself bewildered, frustrated, and enraged from the outset. Typical of the petty irritations was the panjandrous insistence on the pronunciation/ˈpradjus/, though all my friends who raised fruits and vegetables for market, many of them gentlemen with impeccable academic credentials, said/ˈprodjus/. But far more distressing were the pronunciations advocated in the name of elegance. We were advised to reject the Middle Western and Southern /æ/, not only in *calf* and *dance* and *command*, but even in *hat* and *ham* and *sand*, for an imitation of the Boston /a/ in environments where Bostonians would never use it, so that we would say /hat/ and /ham/ and /sand/, pronunciations legitimate in no American dialect except that of the Gullah Negroes of the South Carolina and Georgia coast. A few departmental underlings even went all out for an equally phony British [ɑ], again in the wrong places, yielding [hɑt] and [hɑm] and [sɑnd], and all of them plumped for replacing the Mid-western [ɑ] of *cot* and *lot* with an exaggerated [ɔ]. Of course, Mid-westerners ordering [hɔt hɑm 'sɑndwɪčɪz] are as suspect as counterfeit Confederate $3 bills. It is possible that some compulsive aspirants to social elegance docilely lapped up this pap; but those of us who were seriously concerned with English structure and usage laughed the program out of court and left the course, never to return. A second principle can be deduced from this experience: to imitate a dialect sharply different from one's own is a tricky and difficult assignment. A partial imitation is worse than none, since the change seems an affectation to one's neighbors, and the imperfect acquisition seems ridiculous to those whose speech is being imitated. Any attempts at teaching a standard dialect to those who speak a nonstandard one should be directed toward an attainable goal, toward one of the varieties of cultivated speech which the student might hear, day after day, in his own community.

At this point, perhaps, some of you may be muttering, "But what do these experiences have to do with dialects? I always thought that a dialect was something strange and old-fashioned." Many will share your opinion, especially in such countries as France and Italy, where an academy accepts one variety of the language as standard and casts the rest into outer darkness. In such countries the word *dialect* implies a variety of the language spoken by the rustic, the uneducated, the culturally isolated. To say that someone "speaks a dialect"—as one Italian professor patronizingly described one of the best soldiers working with me on our Italian military dictionary—is to exclude him forever from the company of educated men. For a dialect, to such intellectuals, is a form of the language they had rather be found dead than speaking.

True, there are other attitudes. Germans and Austrians make a distinction between the standard language—literary High German—and the dialects, local and predominantly rural forms of speech. But educated Germans do not always avoid dialect speech forms; in some areas, such as the Austrian Tyrol, an educated person will take particular pains to use some local forms in his speech, so as to identify himself with his home. The attitude may be a bit sentimental, but it does help to maintain one's individual dignity in a homogenizing world.

A more extreme attitude was prevalent in the Romantic Era. If the Augustans of the seventeenth and eighteenth centuries looked upon dialects as corruptions of an originally perfect language, the Romantics often alleged, in Wordsworth's terms, that people in humble and rustic life used "a purer and more emphatic language" than that to be met with in the cities. In this viewpoint, the dialects represent the pure, natural, unchanging language, unencumbered by the baggage of civilization. This attitude has long prevailed in Britain; even today the English Dialect Survey is heavily slanted toward archaic forms and relics and ignores modern innovations.

Nor are Americans wholly free from this attitude that a dialect is something archaic and strange. Time and again, a fieldworker for our Linguistic Atlas is told, "We don't speak no dialect around hyur; if you want *rale* dialect you gotta go down into Hellhole Swamp"—or up into Table Rock Cove, or at least across the nearest big river. To many of us, as my student Roger Shuy put it, a dialect is something spoken by little old people in queer out-of-the-way places.

When we become a little more sophisticated—as we must become on a cosmopolitan campus—we realize that cities as well as rural areas may differ in the ways in which their inhabitants talk. Thus we next conclude that a dialect is simply the way everybody talks but us and the people we grew up with; then, by force of circumstance, we realize that we speak a dialect ourselves. But at this point we still feel that a dialect is something regional or local. When we notice that people of our own community speak varieties of English markedly different from our own, we dismiss them as ignorant, or simply as making mistakes. After all, we live in a democratic society and are not supposed to have class markers in our speech. It is a very sophisticated stage that lets us recognize social dialects as well as regional ones—dialects just as natural, arising out of normal, everyday contacts.

By this time we have elaborated our definition of a dialect. It is simply a habitual variety of a language, regional or social. It is set off from all other such habitual varieties by a unique combination of language features: words and meanings, grammatical forms, phrase structures, pronunciations, patterns of stress and intonation. No dialect is simply good or bad in itself; its prestige comes from the prestige of those who use it. But every dialect is in itself a legitimate form of the language, a valid instrument of human communication, and something worthy of serious study.

But even as we define what a dialect is, we must say what it is not. It is different from slang, which is determined by vogue and largely distinguished by transient novelties in the vocabulary. Yet it is possible that slang may show regional or social differences, or that some regional and social varieties of a language may be particularly receptive to slang.

A dialect is also different from an argot, a variety of the language used by people who share a common interest, whether in work or in play. Everyone knows many groups of this kind, with their own peculiar ways of speaking and writing: Baptist preachers, biophysicists, stamp collectors, model railroad fans, Chicago critics, narcotic addicts, jazz musicians, safe-crackers. But in the normal course of events a person adopts the language of such subcultures, for whatever part of his life it may function in, because he has adopted a particular way of life; he uses a dialect because he grows up in a situation where it is spoken. Again, some argots may show regional or social variations; the term *mugging*, to choose one example, is largely found on the

Atlantic Seabord; the sport has different designations in the Great Lakes region and on the Pacific Coast.

Nor are dialect differences confined to the older, pre-industrial segments of the vocabulary. Here European and American attitudes differ sharply. The late Eugen Dieth chided the editors of the *Linguistic Atlas of New England* for including such vocabulary items as window shades, the razor strop, and the automobile, such pronunciation items as *library* and *post-office* and *hotel*, on the ground that these are not genuine dialect items. Yet if they have regional and social variants, as all of these have in North American English, they warrant inclusion. In my lifetime I have seen the *traffic circle* of the Middle Atlantic States become the *rotary* of Eastern New England; the *service plaza* of the Pennsylvania *Turnpike* become the *oasis* of the Illinois *Tollway*; the *poor boy* of New Orleans—a generous sandwich once confined to the Creole Gomorrah and its gastronautic satellites—appearing as a *grinder* in upstate New York, a *hoagy* in Philadelphia, a *hero* in New York City, a *submarine* in Boston. Nor will dialect terms be used only by the older and less sophisticated: a Middle Western academician transplanted to MIT quickly learns to order *tonic* for his children, not *soda pop*, and to send his clothes to a *cleanser*. And though some would consider dialect a matter of speech and not of writing, one can find regional and local commercial terms on billboards and television as well as in the advertising sections of local newspapers.

Finally, dialect terms are not restricted to sloppy, irresponsible usage—a matter of personality type rather than of specific vocabulary items. And though regional and local terms and usages are likely to appear most frequently in Joos's casual and intimate styles, the example of William Faulkner is sufficient evidence that they may be transmuted into the idiom of the greatest literature.

All of these comments are the fruit of centuries of observation, at first casual and anecdotal, later more serious and systematic. The grim test of the pronunciation *shibboleth*, applied by Jephthah's men to the Ephraimites seeking to ford the Jordan, the comic representations of Spartan and Theban speech by Aristophanes, the aspiration of the Roman cockney Arrius-Harrius, immortalized by Horace, the Northern English forms in the Reeves Tale—these typify early interest. With the Romantic search for the true language in the dialects came the growth of comparative linguistics, and the search for comparative dialect evidence in translations of the Lord's Prayer and the proverb of the prodigal son. The search for comparable evidence led, in the 1870's, to the monumental collections for Georg Wenker's *Deutscher Sprachatlas*, later edited by Ferdinand Wrede and Walther Mitzka—44,251 responses, by German village schoolmasters, to an official request for local dialect translations of forty-five sentences of Standard German. Designed to elicit fine phonetic data, the collections proved notably refractory for that purpose, but the sheer mass of evidence corrected the unevenness of individual transcriptions. More important, the discovery that questions designed for one purpose may yield a different but interesting kind of evidence —as *Pferd* proved useless for the /p:pf/ consonant alternation in dialects where the horse is *Roß* or *Gaul*—was reflected in greater sophistication in the design and use of later questionnaires. Less happy was the effect on German dialectology, with later investigations, such as Mitzka's *Wortatlas*, sticking to correspondence techniques, a short questionnaire, an immense number of communities, and an expensive cartographic presentation of the data. But the *Sprachatlas* and *Wortatlas*, and the Dutch investigations modeled upon them, provided us with the evidence on which to determine their own defects.

A valuable innovation was made at the turn of the century in the *Atlas linguistique de la France*, directed by Jules Gilliéron. Correspondence questionnaires gave way to field interviews on the spot, in a smaller number of selected communities (some six hundred in this instance) with a longer questionnaire; a trained investigator interviewed a native of the community in a conversational situation and recorded his responses in a finely graded phonetic alphabet. As with the German atlas, however, the communities chosen were villages; larger places were first investigated in the Atlas of Italy and Southern Switzerland, under the direction of the Swiss scholars Karl Jaberg and Jakob Jud, who also introduced the practice of interviewing more than one informant in the larger communities. With certain refinements, then, the basic principles of traditional dialect study were established by World War I. Some subsequent investigations have followed Wenker, others Gilliéron; some, like the current Czech investigations, have combined both methods, relying primarily on field interviews but using correspondence surveys in the early stages, so that the selection of communities can be made most effectively. Only the British Isles have lagged, perhaps because Joseph Wright's *English Dialect Dictionary*, with its claim to have recorded ALL the dialect words of English, has erected a Chinese Wall worthy of Mr. Eliot's scorn. Not till the 1950's did any kind of field work get under way in either England or Scotland; in both countries it was handicapped by a shortage of funds and field-workers, and in England by an antiquarian bias that over-emphasized relics, shunned innovations, and neglected opportunities to provide data comparable to that obtained in the American surveys. Yet both Harold Orton in England and Angus McIntosh in Scotland have enriched our knowledge of English.

Perhaps because American linguists have kept in touch with European developments, the *Linquistic Atlas of New England*, launched in 1930, drew on the lessons of the French and Italian atlases. Although the transition from casual collecting to systematic study was not welcomed by all students, nevertheless—even with the Hoover Depression, World War II, the Korean intervention, and the tensions of the Cold War—a respectable amount of progress has been made toward a first survey of American English. *The Linguistic Atlas of New England* was published in 1939–43; scholars are now probing for the changes that a generation has brought. For four other regional surveys, field work has been completed and editing is under way: (1) the Middle and South Atlantic States, New York to central Georgia, with outposts in Ontario and northeastern Florida; (2) the North-Central States: Wisconsin, Michigan, southwestern Ontario, and the Ohio Valley; (3) the Upper Midwest; Minnesota, Iowa, Nebraska, and the Dakotas; (4) the Pacific Southwest: California and Nevada. Elsewhere, field work has been completed in Colorado, Oklahoma, Washington, and eastern Montana; respectable portions have been done in several other states, Newfoundland, Nova Scotia, and British Columbia; with a slightly different method the late E. Bagby Atwood produced his memorable *Regional Vocabulary of Texas*. In all of these surveys the principles of European dialect investigations have been adapted to the peculiarities of the American scene. Settlement history has been studied more carefully before field work, since English-speaking settlement in North America is recent, and its patterns are still changing. At least three levels of usage are investigated—partly because cultivated American speech has regional varieties, just like uneducated speech, and the cultivated speech of the future may be foreshadowed in the speech of the intermediate group; partly because until very recently general education has been a more important linguistic and cultural force in the United States than in most of the countries of Europe. Urban speech as well as rural has been investigated in each survey, and intensive local investigations have been encouraged. The questionnaires have included both relics and innovations. All of these modifications were suggested by Hans Kurath, first Director of the Atlas project, who is currently drawing on his experience in developing a new theory for the interpretation of dialect differences.

Just as warfare is still decided ultimately by infantrymen who can take and hold territory, so dialect study still depends on competent investigators who can elicit and record natural responses in the field. The tape recorder preserves free conversation for later transcription and analysis, and permits the investigator to listen repeatedly to a response about whose phonetic quality he is in doubt; but the investigator must still ask the right questions to elicit pertinent data. He must remember, for instance, that *chicken coop* is both a vocabulary and a pronunciation item—that the pronunciation in the American North and North Midlands is /kup/, in the South and South Midland /kʌp/, that *coop* in the North designates the permanent shelter for the whole flock, in the South a crate under which a mother hen can scratch without an opportunity to lead the little ones off and lose them in the brush. The full record for such an item may require three or four questions, which only a human interviewer can provide.

But if the fieldworker remains essential, the objects of his investigation may change. Recent studies have turned increasingly to urban areas, urbanizing areas, and minority groups. To a long list of impressive early investigations one can now add such contributions as Lee Pederson's study of Chicago pronunciation and Gerald Udell's analysis of the changes in Akron speech resulting from the growth of the rubber industry and the consequent heavy migration from West Virginia. Among special groups investigated in detail are the Spanish-American bilinguals in San Antonio by Mrs. Janet Sawyer, the American Norwegians by Einar Haugen, the New York City Greeks by James Macris, the New England Portuguese by Leo Pap, the Chicago Slovaks by Mrs. Goldie Meyerstein, the Gullah Negroes by Lorenzo Turner, and the Memphis Negroes by Miss Juanita Williamson. In all of these studies the emphasis has been on the correlation between linguistic and social forces.

Another significant development has been the investigation of the way language attitudes are revealed by the choice among linguistic variants under different conditions. The most impressive work of this kind has been done by William Labov of Columbia University, in his study of the speech of the Lower East Side of New York. Limiting himself to a small number of items—the vowels of *bad* and *law*, the initial consonants of *think* and *then*, the /-r/ in *barn* and *beard*—phonological details that can be counted on to appear frequently and in a large number of contexts during a short interview, Labov gathers specimens of linguistic behavior under a wide range of conditions. At one end of the spectrum is the reading of such putatively minimal pairs as *bed* and *bad*; at the other is the description of children's games or the recounting an incident when the informant thought he was going to be killed. The difference between pronunciations in the relaxed situation and those when the informant is on what he considers his best linguistic behavior is an index of his social insecurity. Almost as revealing is the work of Rufus Baehr with high-school students in the Negro slums of the Chicago West Side. It is no surprise that in formal situations the students with greater drive to break out of their ghetto reveal striking shifts of their speech in the direction of the Chicago middle-class norm. This kind of discovery should give heart to all who believe that a directed program of second-dialect teaching can make at least a small dent in our problem of providing a wider range of economic and educational opportunities for the aspiring young Negro.

Out of all these investigations two patterns emerge: (1) a better understanding of the origin and nature of dialect differences; (2) a set of implications for those who are interested in providing every American child with a command of the standard language adequate for him to go as far as his ability and ambition impel him.

No dialect differences can, as yet, be attributed to physiology or to climate. Perhaps anatomists will discover that some minor speech-differences arise from differences in the vocal organs; but so far there is no evidence for any correlation between anatomy and dialect, and the burden of proof is on those who propose such a correlation. As for climate: it is unlikely that nasality could have arisen (as often asserted) both from the dusty climate of Australia and the dampness of the Tennessee Valley. And though it is a favorite sport among Northerners to attribute the so-called "Southern drawl" to laziness induced by a hot climate, many Southerners speak with a more rapid tempo than most Middle Westerners, and the Bengali, in one of the most enervating tropical climates, speak still more rapidly. For an explanation of dialect differences we are driven back, inevitably, to social and cultural forces.

The most obvious force is the speech of the original settlers. We should expect that a part of the United States settled by Ulster Scots would show differences in vocabulary, pronunciation, even in grammar from those parts settled by East Anglians. We should expect to find Algonkian loans most common in those regions where settlers met Algonkian Indians, French loans most frequent in Louisiana and in the counties adjacent to French Canada, Spanish loans most widespread in the South-west, German loans clustering in cities and in the Great Valley of Pennsylvania, and indubitable Africanisms most striking in the Gullah country.

Speech forms are also spread along routes of migration and communication. The Rhine has carried High German forms northward; the Rhone has taken Parisian forms to the Mediterranean; in the United States, the same kind of dissemination has been found in the valleys of the Mississippi, the Ohio, and the Shenandoah.

If speech forms may spread along an avenue of communication, they may be restricted by a physical barrier. As Kurath has observed, there is no sharper linguistic boundary in the English-speaking world than the Virginia Blue Ridge between the Potomac and the James. The tidal rivers of the Carolinas, the swamps of the Georgia coastal plain, have contributed to making the Old South the most varied region, dialectally, in the English settlements of the New World.

The economic pattern of an area may be reflected in distinctive dialect features. *Fatwood*, for resin-rich kindling, is confined to the turpentine belt of the Southern tidewater; *lightwood*, with a similar referent, to the Southern coastal plain and lower Piedmont. *Case weather*, for a kind of cool dampness in which it is safe to cut tobacco, occurs over a wide area, but only where tobacco is a money crop. *To run afoul of*, a maritime phrase in the metaphorical sense of "to meet," seems to be restricted to the New England coast.

Political boundaries, when long established, may become dialect boundaries; in the Rhine-land, pronunciation differences coincide strikingly with the boundaries of the petty states of pre-Napoleonic Germany. In the New World, on the other hand, political boundaries have seldom delimited culture areas. Yet *county site*, for the more usual *county seat*, is common in Georgia but unknown in South Carolina, and Ontario Canadians speak of the *reeve* as chief officer of a township, the *warden* as chief officer of a county, and a *serviette* instead of a table napkin—terms unfamiliar in the United States.

Each city of consequence may have its distinctive speech forms. The grass strip between the sidewalk and the curb, undesignated in South Carolina, is a *tree belt* locally in Springfield, Massachusetts (and hence unlabeled in *Webster's Third New International Dictionary*), a *tree lawn* in Cleveland, a *devil strip* in Akron, and a *boulevard* in Minneapolis and St. Paul. And only Chicagoans naturally refer to political influence as *clout*, or to a reliable dispenser of such influence as a *Chinaman*.

Nor are differences in the educational system without their effect. Where separate and unequal education is provided to particular social groups, we can be sure that a high-school diploma or even a college degree will be no indication by itself of proficiency in the standard language. That this problem is not confined to any single racial or cultural group has been shown by institutions such as West Virginia State College, which have undergone the process of reverse integration. This particular school, which once drew an elite Negro student body, is now eighty percent white, with the white students mostly from the disadvantaged mountain areas along the Kanawha. Since the teachers in the mountain schools are not only predominantly local in origin, but often have had little education beyond what the local schools offer, and then, since most of them habitually use many non-standard forms, it has been difficult for the college to maintain its academic standards in the face of increasing white enrollment, however desirable integration may be.

Most important, perhaps, is the traditional class structure of a community. In a Midwestern small town, it is still possible for one brother to stay home and run a filling station, and another to go off and become a judge—and nobody mind. But in parts of the South there is a social hierarchy of families and occupations, so that it is more respectable for a woman of good family to teach in an impoverished small college than to do professional work for the government at twice the salary. Here, too, an aristocratic ideal of language survives, and the most cultivated still look upon *ain't* as something less reprehensible than incest—but use it only in intimate conversation with those whom they consider their social equals. Here too we find the cultural self-assurance that leads an intelligent lawyer to ask the linguistically naive question: "Why is it that the educated Northerner talks so much like the uneducated Southerner?"

If social differences among the WASP population are reflected in linguistic differences, we should not be surprised if similar differences among later immigrants are reflected in the extent of linguistic borrowing from particular foreign-language groups, or even from the same foreign-language group at different times. Our longest continuous tradition of borrowing, with probably the largest and most varied kinds of words, is that from various kinds of German. Even the bitterness of two world wars cannot prevent us from seeing that of all foreign-language groups the Germans have been most widely distributed, geographically and socially, throughout the United States—as prosperous farmers, vaudeville comedians, skilled craftsmen, merchants, intellectuals. In contrast, the hundreds of thousands of Italian- and Slavic-speaking immigrants of the last two generations have left few marks on the American vocabulary; most of them were of peasant stock, often illiterate, and settled in centers of heavy industry as basic labor.

Even more striking is the change in the incidence of Texas borrowings from Mexican Spanish. In her study of the bilingual situation in San Antonio, Mrs. Sawyer has shown that although early Spanish loans were numerous, quickly assimilated, and widely spread—*canyon*, *burro*, *ranch*, *lariat*, *broncho*, *silo* are characteristic examples—there have been few such loans in the last seventy years. The explanation is the drastic change in the relationships between Anglos and Latins. When English-speaking settlers first moved into Texas, they found the hacienda culture already established, and eagerly took over culture and vocabulary from the Latins who constituted the local elite. Anglo and Latin, side by side, died in the Alamo 4 March 1836 and conquered at San Jacinto seven weeks later. But since 1890 the Texan has encountered Mexican Spanish most often in the speech of unskilled laborers, including imported braceros and illegally entered wetbacks; derogatory labels for Latins have increased in Texas English, and loans from Spanish have declined. We borrow few words from those we consider our inferiors.

We can now make a few clear statements about the facts of American dialects, and their significance:

1. Even though much work remains to be done, we can describe in some detail most of the principal regional varieties of American English and many of the important subvarieties; we can indicate, further, some of the kinds of social differences that are to be found in various dialect areas, and many of the kinds that are to be found in some of the most important cities.

2. We can be sure that in many situations there are tensions between external norms and the expectations of one's associates. These tensions, most probably, are strongest in the lower middle class—a group anxious to forget humbler backgrounds but not sure of their command of the prestige patterns. Since the teaching profession, on all levels, is heavily drawn from the lower middle class, we can expect—as Marjorie Daunt found years ago—that anxiety is the characteristic attitude of the English teacher toward variations in usage. There is a strong urge to make changes, for the sake of making changes and demonstrating one's authority, without stopping to sort out the significance of differences in usage. This attitude is reflected in the two most widely known programs for teaching better English to the disadvantaged: a socially insignificant problem, such as the distinction between *Wales* and *whales*, is given the same value as the use of the marker for the third singular in the present indicative. Future programs should use the resources of the dialect archives, at least as a start, even though more detailed and more

recent information may be necessary before one can develop teaching materials. The inevitable prescription in a pedagogical situation can be no better than the underlying description.

3. There is evidence that ambitious students in slum areas intuitively shift their speech patterns in the direction of the prestigious local pattern, in situations where they feel such a shift will be to their advantage. Some actually achieve, on their own, a high degree of functional bidialectalism, switching codes as the situation demands. In any teaching program it would seem intelligent to make use of this human facility.

4. The surest social markers in American English are grammatical forms, and any teaching program should aim, first of all, at developing a habitual productive command of the grammar of standard English—with due allowance for the possibility that the use of this grammar may be confined to formal situations in which the speaker comes in contact with the dominant culture.

5. Relatively few pronunciation features are clear social markers, though in many Northern cities there is a tendency to identify all Southern and South Midland pronunciations as those of uneducated rural Negroes. How much one should attempt to substitute local pronunciations for those which are standard in regions from which migrants come would probably depend on the extent to which variations in standard English are recognized and accepted in the community: Washington, for instance, may be more tolerant than New York City. In any event, programs to alter pronunciation patterns should concentrate on those pronunciations that are most widely recognized as substandard.

6. Few people can really identify the race of a speaker by pronunciation and voice quality. In experiments in Chicago, middle-class Middle Westerners consistently identified the voice of an educated urban white Southerner as that of an uneducated rural Negro, and many identified as Negro the voice of an educated white Chicagoan. Similar experiments in New York have yielded similar results. And many white Southerners can testify to personal difficulties arising from this confusion in the minds of Northerners. In Ithaca, New York, I could not get to see any apartment advertised as vacant until I paid a personal visit; over the telephone I was always told that the apartments had just been rented; James Marchand, a Middle Tennessean now on the Cornell faculty, must carefully identify himself as "Professor Marchand," if he wants a garageman to come and pick up his car. And the telephone voice of my Mississippi-born chairman, Gwin Kolb, is racially misidentified with alarming regularity.

7. There can be no single standard in programs for the disadvantaged; the target dialect must vary according to the local situation. In Mississippi, the same program can be used for Negroes and whites, because they share

most of the same grammatical deviations from the local standard, and share phonological patterns with that standard; in Cleveland, grammatical features in writing are sufficient to distinguish Negro college applicants from white better than ninety percent of the time, and deviations from local standard pronunciation are far more striking and numerous among Negroes than among locally-born disadvantaged whites.

8. To the suggestion that Southern Negroes should not be taught local standard pronunciation, but some external standard—the hypothetical variety some call "network English"—there is a simple answer in the form of a question: "Do you want integration in the South?" The Southern patterns of race relations have suffered too long from too many separate standards for Negro and white; it would be ironical if those speaking most loudly in behalf of the aspirations of the Southern Negro should create new obstacles to those aspirations. The language problems of the uneducated Southern Negro are the language problems, even to fine detail, of the uneducated Southern white in the same community: the South may well solve the language problems in its schools before Detroit does. Once the races are brought into the same classroom, a community will need only one intelligent program based on a solid body of dialect evidence.

9. While we are planning language programs for our disadvantaged, we must educate the dominant culture in the causes and significance of dialect differences; it is particularly urgent that we educate teachers on all levels, from kindergarten through graduate school. The disadvantaged will have enough to do in learning new patterns of language behavior; the dominant culture must meet them part way, with greater understanding, with a realization that dialect differences do not reflect intellectual or moral differences, but only differences in experience. Granted that this reeducation of the dominant culture is bound to be difficult, we should not be so cynical as to reject it, on the ground that it cannot take place. In an age when we are turning the head off under the melting pot and accepting the cultural contributions of Americans with ancestral languages other than English, in an age when we are learning the art of peaceful coexistence with a variety of economic and political and cultural systems, it should not be difficult to extend this acceptance to fellow Americans of different cultural backgrounds and linguistic habits, and especially to recognize that cultured American English may be found in many regional and local varieties. It is a poor cultural tolerance that would accept all cultivated speech except that in other parts of our own country.

With my deep-ingrained horror of patent-medicine salesmen, I would not leave you with the impression that we already have all the answers, or even all the evidence we need to arrive at those answers. We need many more kinds of investigation, and we should like to think that John Fisher, with his unlimited license to stalk money-bearing animals, might belp us conduct some of them. We are still to do even the preliminary surveys in such parts of the country as Tennessee and Arkansas; we need many more studies of the actual patterns of social dialects in most American cities. We really have no serious evidence on regional and social differences in such prosodic features as stress and pitch and juncture. The recognition of paralanguage—the non-linguistic modulation of the stream of speech—is so recent that we have no idea as to the kinds of regional and social differences that may be found in tempo and rhythm, in range of pitch and stress, in drawl and clipping, in rasp and nasality and mellifluousness. We have not even begun to study regional and social variations in gesture and other kinds of body movement. But we do have a framework which we can fill in detail, continually building our teaching programs on solid research into the ways in which Americans communicate in various localities, and into the attitudes of specific speakers toward those whose usage differs from their own. In comparison with the immensity of our social problems, our linguistic knowledge is as a little candle in the forest darkness at midnight; let us not hide that candle under a basket, but put it in a lantern and use it to find our way.

BIBLIOGRAPHICAL NOTE

The significance of dialect differences has been often discussed, notably in Leonard Bloomfield, *Language* (New York, 1933), Ch. xix. The most detailed summary of dialect investigations to the mid-century is Sever Pop, *La Dialectologie*, 2 vols. (Louvain, 1950). Kurath's *Areal Linguistics: Problems, Methods, Results* (Bloomington, Ind., 1967), will be shorter but more up to date.

The most widely known summary of American dialects is to be found in Ch. ix of W. Nelson Francis, *The Structure of American English* (New York, 1958); the most accessible bibliographical summary is in the footnotes of Ch. vii of the one-volume 1963 edition of H. L. Mencken, *The American Language*. Annual summaries of research will be found in the reports of the Committee on Regional Speech and Dialectology, in *Publications of the American Dialect Society*; recent research is reported in the quarterly bibliographies in *American Speech*, less extensively in the supplement to *PMLA*. The method of the American atlases is discussed in detail in Kurath's *Handbook of the Linguistic Geography of New England* (Providence, R.I., 1939). For summaries of particular dialect features along the Atlantic seaboard, see Kurath, *A World Geography of the Eastern United States* (Ann Arbor, Mich., 1949); Atwood, *A Survey of Verb Forms in the Eastern United States* (Ann Arbor, Mich., 1952); Kurath and McDavid, *The Pronunciation of English in the Atlantic States* (Ann Arbor, Mich., 1961). Atwood's *The Regional Vocabulary of Texas* was published by the University of Texas Press, Austin, in 1962. For particular regions see articles by A. H.

Marckwardt for the Great Lakes, Harold B. Allen for the Upper Midwest, Marjorie M. Kimmerle and Clyde Hankey for Colorado, David W. Reed and David DeCamp for California. *A Dictionary of American Regional English*, directed by Frederic G. Cassidy, is currently under way at the University of Wisconsin.

The first direct attention to American social dialects is McDavid, "Dialect Geography and Social Science Problems," *Social Forces*, XXV, 168–172; basic for the problems of Negro speech is Raven I. and Virginia McDavid, "The Relationship of the Speech of American Negroes to the Speech of Whites," *American Speech*, XXVI, 3–17. A 1964 conference on social dialects, held at Bloomington, Indiana, is reported in *Social Dialects and Language Learning*, a publication of the NCTE, edited by A. L. Davis and Roger Shuy (Champaign, Ill., 1965); in 1965 the NCTE also published *Language Programs for the Disadvantaged: A Report of the NCTE Task Force*, and reprinted two of McDavid's articles as a monograph, *American Social Dialects*. A teachers' manual on the subject has been requested by the U.S. Office of Education; it is hoped that work can begin in the summer of 1966.

The most familiar American analysis of stress, pitch, and juncture was first sketched in G. L. Trager and H. L. Smith, Jr., *Outline of English Structure, Studies in Linguistics*: Occ. Paper 3 (Norman, Okla., 1951); a more detailed exposition is found in A. A. Hill, *Introduction to Linguistic Structures* (New York, 1958). A different analysis is that of Kenneth L. Pike, *The Intonation of American English* (Ann Arbor, Mich., 1945). The importance of paralanguage, previously discussed by Trager and Smith, is shown in Robert E. Pittenger, Charles F. Hockett, and John J. Danehy, *The First Five Minutes* (Ithaca, N.Y., 1960); the most detailed treatment of gesture is in Ray Birdwhistell, *Introduction to Kinesics* (Washington, 1952), later reprinted by the University of Louisville. A good popular treatment of communication in culture is Edward T. Hall, *The Silent Language* (New York, 1959), now available in paperback. Martin Joos's theories of style are summed up in *The Five Clocks* (Bloomington, Ind., 1962).

"F'GET YOU HONKY!": A NEW LOOK AT BLACK DIALECT AND THE SCHOOL

Frederick David Erickson

F'get you (f'géchoo), *interjec.* Black dialect phrase. Many shades of meaning, from "Get out of here, stupid!" through "You're wrong!" to an affectionate form of banter, "Aw, go on."
HONKY, HONCKY (háwnkee), *n. sing.* A white man, more especially a stupid, racist white man. Black dialect equivalent of wh. dial. *nigger*. Poss. der. from wh. dial. *Hunky* (from wh. dial. *Bohunk*, from stan. Eng. *Bohemian*)

Last summer I was working with a discussion group at a human relations workshop for teachers of ghetto Black children. The group raised the question of what to do about children who spoke non-standard English in the elementary classroom. The response of one teacher was particularly interesting. She said, "I don't believe in making a child feel self-conscious by criticizing his language in front of the other children. So when a child says, 'Teacher, I ain't got no pencil,' I say, 'What did you say?' If he says it again I say, 'What did you say?' and after a few times he realizes he made a mistake." Under such circumstances, one wonders how long it took for the child to get a pencil.

Such "I'm not prejudiced, but . . ." responses are common at workshops I attend. Listening to non-standard English in the classroom seems to make teachers very uncomfortable. They seem to feel a deep responsibility to say, "Don't say ain't." One reason for this may be the tradition of resistence to linguistic pluralism which characterizes the American public school. Until recently a major function of the public school was the Americanization of immigrants. Rigid adherence to standard English in the classroom was one of the school's defensive responses to its inundation by culturally different immigrant children.

"WE HAVE MET THE ENEMY AND HE IS US."

Unfortunately another reason for the resistance of inner city teachers to non-standard dialect may be a new tradition, fostered by workshops for teachers

Frederick David Erickson, "F' get You Honky! A New Look at Black Dialect and the School," *Elementary English*, **46** (April 1969), 495–499. Reprinted with the permission of the National Council of Teachers of English and Frederick David Erickson.

of the "disadvantaged." People like myself—white, professorial, and research-oriented—are responsible for this new tradition. Because of us, terms such as "cultural deprivation," "sensory deprivation," and "linguistic deprivation" have become part of the professional vocabulary of teachers, and part of their folklore as well. Ironically, what began in the university as an analytic term, after being transmitted through the journal and workshop, ends in the public school faculty lounge as a "neo-stereotype." Some teachers used to say that Black ghetto children were dirty, ignorant, came from immoral homes, and couldn't learn. Now those teachers can say "the children are culturally disadvantaged and *that* is why they can't learn."

One of the most persistent neo-stereotypes I have found in working with teachers is the concept of *linguistic deprivation*. In this instance, academic writing seems to have positively reinforced the values already present in the teacher "folk culture" regarding "bad language." Research on Black dialect (with a few exceptions; notably the work of William Stewart and his colleagues at the Center for Applied Linguistics) has been conducted from a perspective of "deprivation." Many of the research designs have been constructed around prior assumptions and hypotheses regarding the "pathology" of the dialect; its inhibiting effects upon cognitive development and its inadequacy in comparison with standard English. Few research propositions have been advanced regarding the adequacy of the dialect.

The setting for much of the research has been the school, or a "school-like" experimental situation. In these settings we can see how the dialect functions (or fails to function) in tasks that *we*, the scholars, define. We do not see the dialect used in tasks defined by the people who use the dialect well. Consequently we have little idea of the effectiveness of Black dialect as it is used on its own terms in congenial settings in which it is appropriate.

THE "BERNSTEIN HYPOTHESIS" AND RECENT RESEARCH

A frame of reference which has influenced many American research designs is the one developed by Basil Bernstein, a British sociolinguist. Briefly summarized, his position is that the social class dialects of the British upper middle and lower classes differ not just in grammar and vocabulary, but in the way the dialects convey meaning. This difference, according to Bernstein, profoundly affects the cognitive development of children.

In the lower class English dialects, the meaning of a word or phrase is not specific. Meaning is determined by the social situation in which the word or phrase is used. Since meaning is dependent upon the social situation, Bernstein terms this type of dialect a *restricted linguistic code*, or *public language*.

In contrast to the restricted code of the lower classes, the British middle and upper class speak an *elaborated linguistic code* in which the meaning of a word or phrase is quite specific. The shadings of meaning conveyed depend on precise construction of language, not on social setting. For this reason an elaborated code can be described as a *private language*.

American Black dialect and standard American English fit quite well into Bernstein's schema. For example, the Black dialect phrase "F'get You," can be classified as a restricted code utterance which "translated" into elaborated code might be, "I disagree with you and wish that you would leave before I hit you."

It is easy to see how such language differences might find expression in child rearing. A mother in the Black ghetto might say, "Boy Ima whup you . . ." while her upper middle class white counterpart in suburbia might say, "Johnny, I'd rather you didn't do that just now." The suburban mother would be teaching by example the ability to use spoken language very precisely and would be fostering the cognitive development of her child.

A critical issue in educational research is whether or not the lack of use of elaborated code in the home *necessarily* limits the cognitive development of lower class children, particularly lower class Black children. The literature on the "language of the disadvantaged" suggests that this is so. This is a reasonable conclusion, if based on the assumption that the vagueness of restricted code utterances *necessarily* limits the communication of abstractions or prevents a precise categorization of experience through language.

THE "CONTEXT PRINCIPLE"— AN ADDITION TO BERNSTEIN'S SCHEMA

Bernstein's schema implies a direct relationship between social class subculture and language style. My own research in a project titled "Sounds of Society" (conducted at Northwestern University with B. J. Chandler under a grant from USOE, Project No. 6–0244) suggests that an intervening factor may exist between social class and language style. Edward T. Hall and I developed a term for this intervening factor, the "shared context principle."

This principle was identified by Edward Sapir, the anthropological linguist, in 1931;

> Generally speaking, the smaller the circle and the more complex the understandings already arrived at within it, the more economical can the acts of communication afford to become. A single word passed between members of an intimate group, in spite of its apparent vagueness and ambiguity, may constitute a far more precise communication than volumes of carefully prepared correspondence interchanged between two governments.

Sapir's statement can be paraphrased in Berstein's terminology as, "When two communicators share considerable experience and point of view, restricted linguistic code can *function as precisely* as elaborated code." The paraphrase places the relationship between subculture, language style, and cognitive style in a new perspective. It provides a framework within which research on Black dialect takes on new meaning. It suggests that while Bernstein's original schema may have descriptive and classifactory value, it may not have analytic value unless altered to include the context principle.

We can think of *shared context* as a continuum, with "high shared context" at one end and "low shared context" at the other. High context communication (restricted code) is appropriate when there is considerable overlap of experience between communicators, and low context communication (elaborated code) is appropriate when little experience is shared. As context increases the volume of necessary communication signals decreases. This is illustrated in Figure 1:

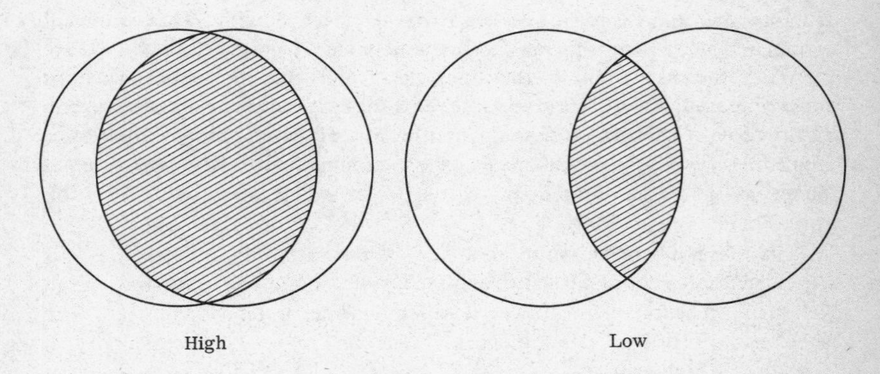

Figure 1. Areas of high and low context communication.

An everyday high context communication situation would be two plumbers loosening a pipe. Plumber *A* could say to Plumber *B*, "Now!" (high context) and *B* would understand that *A* meant, "It is time for you to hand me the medium-sized pipe wrench" (low context). *A* could signal that he wanted a wrench, not a hammer, with a gesture or glance. He could even signal which wrench he wanted. The communication would be very precise, even though a restricted linguistic code was being used. Under conditions of even *higher* context (if *A* or *B* had worked together for some time) *B* would *already know* that a certain size wrench would be needed. *A* would not even need to use non-verbal signals. His "Now!" would be completely unambiguous and would communicate much faster than an elaborated code utterance.

Children in classrooms, of course, are not plumbers. In order to see the relevance of the context principle for the school it is necessary to examine a more "intellectual" setting for communication.

THE CONTEXT PRINCIPLE IN RESEARCH

This setting was provided in the "Sounds of Society" research project mentioned earlier. In the project informal discussion groups of young people were formed in various neighborhoods of the Chicago metropolitan area. Two types of neighborhoods were involved; lower class inner city Black neighborhoods and upper middle class suburban white neighborhoods. Inner city and suburban groups met separately and dicussed the social significance of familiar popular song lyrics. The discussions were recorded and typescripts were prepared. A song was played at the beginning of each discussion to provide a discussion stimulus and a standardized "situational frame" which would permit comparative analysis. Adult leaders provided loose structure, but the discussions were extremely free flowing. They provided a congenial setting for informal language behavior.

When the discussions of the inner city groups and the suburban groups were compared, true to Bernstein's schema the language style of the suburban groups resembled elaborated code significantly ($P > .01$) more than did the language style of the inner city groups (language style was operationally defined as the mean number of words per utterance in a given discussion typescript).

The data, however, showed a very wide variability of means. This suggested that major shifts in language style might be occurring within each group discussion. In a more detailed analysis, independent raters were asked to arbitrarily designate various sections of each discussion typescript as "high context" or "low context". A two-way analysis of variance was conducted in which the data were partitioned by both the context factor (high or low) and by the social class factor (inner city or suburban). A strong relationship between the context factor and language style was demonstrated (context factor $P > .01$, Social class factor $P > .05$, virtually no interaction effect).

The data suggest that both inner city and suburban groups shifted back and forth between relatively restricted and relatively elaborated code, *depending on the context.* If the topic was familiar, high context communication tended to be used. As the discussion trailed off into the unfamiliar, low context communication predominated. Their "restricted code" and "elaborated code" did not seem to be discrete categories directly related to social class. They seemed to be relative categories closely related to shared context and also related to social class (see Figure 2).

Although inner city Black people may generally speak a more restricted linguistic code than suburbanites, neither group seems bound to one language style exclusively. Furthermore, analysis of the typescripts in my sample revealed extremely high context discussions by Black groups in which extremely abstract concepts were communicated (one example was a debate regarding free will and necessity which was conducted entirely in restricted code).

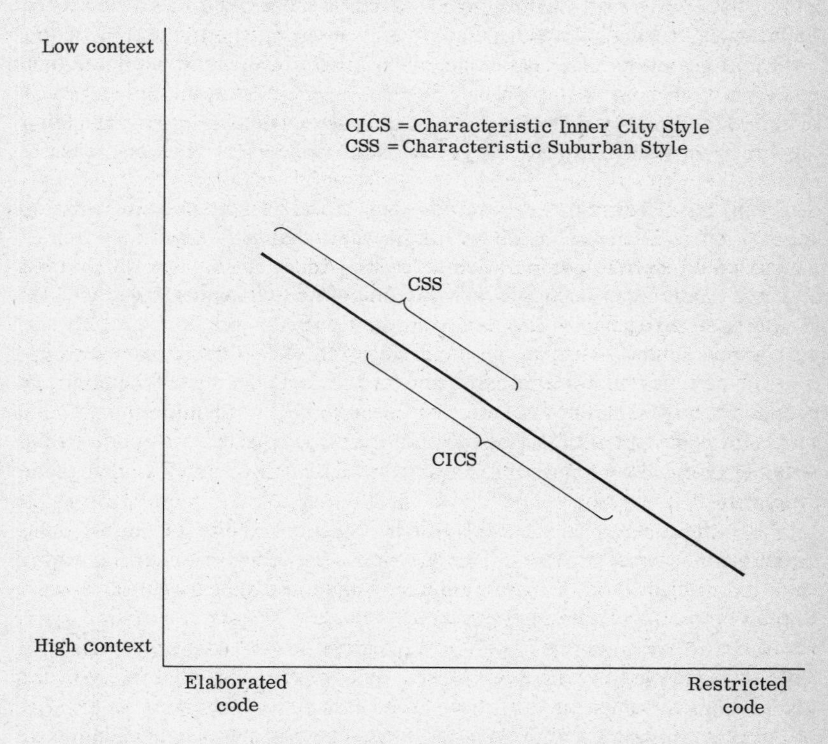

Figure 2. The context principle, language style, and social class

IMPLICATIONS FOR THE SCHOOL

Because "Sounds of Society" was an exploratory rather than experimental study, the findings presented here should be regarded as hypotheses rather than final conclusions. The study suggests a number of implications for research and teaching, however.

First, the concept of "linguistic deprivation" in the Black ghetto needs to be reviewed. It seems that, given a proper context, Black dialect can be used to communicate abstractions with considerable precision. But in order for the researcher to realize this *he must share the context of the speakers he observes.*

Second, teachers need to become sensitive to the context principle. The teaching act itself can be viewed as a continual process of shifting back and forth between high and low context situations. When the direct experience of ghetto children is involved in high context classroom discussions, restricted code may be a very effective mode of discourse. In low context situations, restricted code may be inappropriate. The problem may not lie so much in the nature of the dialect as in the attitude of teachers toward allowing the experience and language of Black ghetto children a place in the classroom.

Third, considering "elaborated code" and "standard English" as synonymous may be misleading. I think that what most teachers teach as "standard English" is a *spoken* form of *written* English—a form that we read but don't often speak. The elaborateness of written language is functional in the most extreme of low context situations: the relationship between author and reader. Spoken language, however, is by definition more "low context" and less elaborate than "standard English." The suburban young people in my sample, who are very successful academically, did not speak "standard English." They did not even speak elaborated code all the time. They did use "standard grammar," which made their spoken language acceptable. (It may be useful to Black children to learn standard English as a second language because it is respectable and because it is occasionally functional in special situations. These, I think, are better reasons for teaching standard English than the assumption that one must learn to speak standard English before he can succeed in school.)

Fourth, high context communication can be very efficient when used in an appropriate setting. As I was discussing the context principle with a class of Black young people recently, one young man observed, "That elaborated code takes too long to get to the point." I know of few suburban mothers who invariably would say "Johnny, I'd rather you didn't do that just now." Many if not most would say, "Stop it!"

This is a time when increasing demands are being made for the inclusion of Black culture in the curriculum of the ghetto school. A hard look at the place of Black dialect in the ghetto classroom seems necessary (and a look at informal language in the suburban classroom as well.) If well-meaning administrators and teachers in the ghetto resist the use of Black dialect on the ground that it is a source of cognitive deprivation the schoolmen may find themselves resisted by the Black community. Perhaps future research will show conclusively that Black dialect is pathological in the educative process. Perhaps not. But Black people will be very skeptical of school-people, white or Black, who tell them that the only way to learn is to "talk white." To this stance Black people today are saying, "F'get you, Honky!"

LISTENING BEHAVIOR: SOME CULTURAL DIFFERENCES

Edward T. Hall

What does it mean to listen? More than you might think! Most of us take listening for granted, yet the way people show they are listening is as varied as the languages they speak. In fact it's part of language; not explicit but implicit; not spoken but silent.

I first became interested in the implications of listening behavior some 15 years ago while developing orientation materials for Americans going overseas for the State Department. Fortunately, I had around me people who represented many of the major languages and cultures of the world. A number of them used to stop in my office and then stay to visit. As is often the case when interacting with people of other cultures, I would find myself impelled (as though pulled by hidden strings) to hold myself, sit, respond, and listen in quite different ways. I noted that when I was with Germans I would (without thinking) hold myself stiffly, while with Latin Americans I would be caught up and involved.

My friends, who were also my subjects, soon began to talk about how hard it was to know whether Americans were "tuned in" or not. When my subjects felt sufficiently at ease to talk freely, they said that we were rude. I slowly learned that how one indicates that one is paying attention is different for each culture. The entire process of being an interlocutor in a conversation is highly stereotyped, culturally patterned, and regulated by rules that are seldom, if ever, spelled out.

These experiences with technically advanced peoples took me back to the early Thirties when I was working with the Navaho Indians. Although I was young at the time, I was fortunate in having friends who were good models for interacting with Navahos. A small point, but one which I learned was

Edward T. Hall, "Listening Behavior: Some Cultural Differences," *Phi Delta Kappa*, **50** (March 1969), 379–380. Reprinted by permission of the author and the publisher.

crucial to the entire tone of a transaction, is the way the Navahos use their eyes. Unlike middle-class whites, the direct open-faced look in the eyes was avoided by Navahos. In fact, Navahos froze up when looked at directly. Even when shaking hands they held one in the peripheral field of the eyes, letting the message of the other person's warmth and pleasure at seeing a friend seep through a long-clasped, but delicately held, hand.

I ultimately learned that to look directly at a Navaho was to display anger. As an illustration of this, a colleague of mine told of seeing an adult Indian in a pickup truck pull up, stick his head out of the window, and chastize two misbehaving boys playing at the roadside with nothing but a look. Another Navaho taboo was the use of the name as a form of direct address. Nor were voices ever raised—except in anger.

By now some of my readers are undoubtedly thinking what it must have been like to be a small Navaho child in schools taught by whites where many teachers were frustrated by behavior they couldn't understand because no one had really analyzed it then. The teacher would raise his voice, while looking directly at the child hanging his head. "What's the matter? Can't you talk? Don't you even know your own name?" Finally some other child would intervene, saying in a barely audible voice, "His name Hosteen Nez Begay." Some teachers were more gentle than others; some were made so anxious by behavior they couldn't fathom they allowed their own frustration and rage to break through. "Stupid Indians can't even tell you their names!"

This experience was 35 years ago and I am sorry to report that things have not changed significantly. The Navahos have changed, though, and they now look at us, which we find reassuring. Yet I've observed they still use the old forms when they're with one another.

Humphry Osmond, the psychiatrist, once wrote to me about his childhood experiences in England:

> When I was a small boy I was always encouraged to look at people "straight between the eyes." It took me some time to learn this art because, particularly where adults are concerned, one's neck got tired looking up, and anyway you couldn't look at anything else. My father, who was usually kindly and sensible, was easily distressed by this for he was of the opinion that not to look at people "straight between the eyes" implied shiftiness or untrustworthiness.

What has all this to do with modern education? It's true the Indians are an important part of our heritage, but the practical educator might ask what percentage of today's school population is Indian? Actually, a very small percentage; but there are others, more numerous than the Indians, who are just as misunderstood and just as inappropriately handled. I refer to the blacks as well as the Puerto Ricans, Mexican-Americans, and Spanish-

Americans of New Mexico. For the moment I will treat only a small segment of black behavior, for there are basic, deep, and important cultural differences which are out of our awareness but result in what Irving Goffman calls "alienation in encounters."

The existence of black culture is implicit in my discussion. The subject is much too complex and emotion-laden to develop here. However, according to my own definition of culture as set forth in *The Silent Language* and *The Hidden Dimension*, the French, the English, the Greeks, and the Navahos—to name only a few groups—use their eyes and set distances in ways which are characteristically French, English, Greek, and Navaho. They behave toward each other in many ways which are distinctive, but particularly in their handling of time, space, and materials. The blacks, too, have a culture that is a reality that must be reckoned with. Just as there are many languages not yet reduced to writing there are informal cultures that have not yet been described technically. However, these cultures are as real as those that have been described.

For several years I did research on listening behavior (showing polite interest and giving correct responses) as a way of discovering how people from different cultures set conversational distances.* I should make it clear at this point that when I started studying black-white encounters in America in detail I wasn't sure that black culture was significantly different from the dominant white culture on the point of listening behavior. My research ultimately revealed that actually there does exist in black culture a series of responses governing use of the eyes, the hands, orientation of the body, position of the body, and tone of voice. Any and all of these are frequently misread by whites and vice versa.

Basically, the informal rule for black culture goes somewhat as follows: If you are in the room with another person or in a context where he has ready access to you there are times when there is no need to go through the motions of showing him you are listening because that is automatically implied. When blacks interact with whites the differences in how one communicates that he is paying attention can cause great difficulty. One of my black assistants, working as a draftsman, got into trouble with his engineer boss who wanted to tell him something. Following his own culture, my assistant continued working at his drafting table without looking up, thus giving the engineer no visible or audible sign that he was listening. The man finally said, "John! Are you paying attention to me?" At which point John looked up and said, "Of course."

How often has a polite black school child cast his eyes downward as a sign of respect and failed to meet a teacher's eye when questioned?

---

* This research has been supported by grants from the National Institute of Mental Health.

How many teachers have thought students were "tuned out" because they gave no visible sign they were listening? How many have said, in angry tones, "Johnny! When I talk, you listen! Is that clear?" What is the child to do? Sometimes blacks feel they are supposed to do something—but just what isn't quite clear (shuffle their feet, perhaps). Sometimes blacks find that if you move around a lot and say "Yawssa Boss" it seems to make some white people less hostile.

When I discussed eye behavior with a black colleague he observed, "When I punish my boy *I look at him*, and when I look at him I'm *mad.* I look at his eyes and they grow big and he *knows* I'm *mad.*" (Note the direct communication back and forth on both sides.)

Imagine, for a moment, what it is like to be a black child or a Navaho child confronted with an adult white person who gives cues with his eyes, his hands, and his tone of voice, all indicating in your own dialectology that there is anger. Those blacks who have begun to understand the rules for the white population are still caught in a double bind, for as we know, the learning process is inhibited by anxiety and situations like these make people very anxious.

Reading cross-cultural behavior is inevitably full of pitfalls for everyone. The fact that blacks often talk in a very loud voice makes it appear to be overly intrusive to whites. There are many forms of over-loudness—loud for emphasis, loud for anger, loud because of distance. I would be very much surprised if white interpretations of the situational significance of black over-loudness is right more often than it is wrong.

Patterns will change, of course, for there are those who have already learned that in certain situations you must show the other person you are listening in his fashion. The main point is that people are beginning to realize that culture encompasses more than beliefs and mores in the conventional sense and that *how* you listen and *how* you talk does make a difference.

DETROIT SPEECH: CARELESS, AWKWARD, AND INCONSISTENT, OR SYSTEMATIC, GRACEFUL, AND REGULAR?

Roger W. Shuy

Teachers of the English language arts frequently view the language of their students from a position shared by many in the teaching profession. From this view, disadvantaged children veer off the accepted path of standard English and are guilty of being slovenly or non-verbal or inexact or lazy. Such observations can be expected, however, when we realize that these same teachers often have been trained in the false assumptions of a single universally accepted norm for English.

This position, as we shall see, is both fallacious and dangerous. It would seem that in an age which witnessed the maturing of liguistics, some of the basic principles of language analysis might have more greatly affected the teaching profession. Yet even contemporary scholars nourish these long held fallacies when they fail to clearly point out that *everyone* speaks a class dialect of some sort. Furthermore, they frequently cite language differences between various groups in terms which are condemnations of one of the groups rather than evidence of a systematic though different language on the part of both. They do not seem to grasp the distinction between language differences and value judgments about these differences. Thus inner city Negroes are said to engage in *unneccessary* repetition, *awkward* arrangements, *inconsistent* use of tense, and *careless* omission of words. Such research does little to get at the nature of the language problems of the disadvantaged child.

If we take the matter out of the realm of value judgment, the question, then, is a bit clearer. How can we identify the features of speech which characterize a person as a member of a social group? One way, as we have seen, is to assume that disadvantaged people deviate from the advantaged. Their deviation is characterized by carelessness, inconsistency, awkwardness, and irrelevance. One danger of this approach is, of course, its lack of objectivity. A second danger is that it assumes a single style on the parts of the advantaged and the disadvantaged. Ever since William Labov's research[1] on stylistic variation within social dialects, simple statements about one

Roger W. Shuy, "Detroit Speech: Careless, Awkward, and Inconsistent, or Systematic, Graceful, and Regular?" *Elementary English*, **45** (May 1968), 565–569. Reprinted with the permission of the National Council of Teachers of English and Roger W. Shuy.

style of speech have become passé, for Labov found that representatives of every social dialect speak in different styles in different situations.

Dialectologists have been working for decades in a heroic attempt to describe American speech as it actually exists. For many years the focus was on the relationship of current speech and settlement history. But, in the past decade, the tremendous pressures of urban life have caused scholars from many disciplines to turn their attention to the city. And dialectologists also find the city fascinating and fruitful, for it is in American cities where the relationship of English and social stratification is most sharply seen.

THE STUDY

It is within this context that the Detroit Dialect Study was started.[2] The basic questions to be answered were these:

1. What are the features of pronunciation, grammar, and vocabulary which set off different soical groups, races, age groups, and sexes from each other in Detroit?
2. What is the most efficient way to gather this kind of data?
3. What is the most efficient way to analyze this kind of data?
4. What will this information say to the teacher of English?

To answer these questions, it was necessary to tape record interviews of a large number of people from all parts of the city. These people, selected randomly, were from four groups:

1. Fourth to sixth graders
2. Secondary level students (older siblings of #1)
3. Parents of #1 and #2
4. Grandparents of #1 and #2

In all, some 700 people were interviewed in this study. For approximately 45 minutes, each informant was encouraged to talk freely about subjects which he found interesting. The fieldworkers followed a general questionnaire but varied freely from it in order to let the informant talk. This part of the interview filled side one of a tape. On the second side, the interview changed somewhat. For about twenty minutes, each informant answered questions intended to elicit single word responses. In the final section of the interview, each person was asked to read aloud a standard prose passage.

These three parts of the interview were designed to elicit at least three styles of oral language—narrative/descriptive style, interview style, and reading style. In addition, certain questions were designed to elicit an emotional style.

The exact speech features which evidence social stratification were first searched for by the staff of the Detroit Dialect Study and currently, since the director and data have moved to the Center for Applied Linguistics, by the Sociolinguistics Program staff. The final report of this study provides the details of the findings.

As for methodology, we feel that many, if not most of our approaches were efficient. A large random sample is a necessity in such a study. Our sample turned up a large number of the most numerous ethnic groups in Detroit—in proportions remarkably similar to the entire population. We did not exclude newcomers, for Detroit is made up of a large number of in-migrants. The sample included lower-, middle-, and upper-income residents, White and Negro, young and old, male and female, Christian and Jew.

As we analyze our data, we are using the most efficient techniques at our disposal. All single answer responses have been transcribed phonetically and coded for key-punching for a computer retrieval program that will display phonological or lexical matters in matrices that describe intra-class distributions.

In addition, several analyses of suspected phonological indices of social stratification are in progress. We are making a special study of final consonant cluster reductions and the loss of final nasal consonants along with their subsequent replacement by nasalized vowels.

Various vowel contrasts are also under investigation but our special interest is directed to the general fronting of all low vowels and, especially among children, the raising of the low front vowel (as in *hat*), so that it is closer to [ɛ] than to [.æ.].

The grammatical index study is more complex for the possibilities of grammatical choice are very great. We are currently typescripting the first (narrative/description) part of selected interviews, then filing each phrase, clause, and sentence by type. This will ultimately yield quantitative data about the use of phrases, clauses, and sentence types. The accompanying chart will illustrate the results of the filling systems being used in this investigation.

The informant whose clause and sentence types have been charted here is a ten-year-old Negro boy whose father is a laborer. With this kind of analysis we will be able to contrast the kinds of syntactic structures used, for example, by all ten-year-old informants with those used by informants of other ages, or we can compare the syntactic structures of informants who are the same age but come from different social backgrounds. One might expect more than 0.3 percent passives in the speech of older or more advantaged children. A great deal of whatever can be discovered about social stratification and age grading can be approached in this way.

Other suspected grammatical indices of social stratification include

Table 1. Clause totals for types of clauses by sentence type in speech of informant 0015

				Independent			
Sentence type	*First clause in resp. to question*	*Not initial not after* and, but	*Not initial after* and, so	*Not initial after* but, or	*Not initial after dep. clause*	*Impera-tive, no subj. expressed*	*Impera-tive, in func-tion, not in form*
S+tV+DO	58	61	84	7	9	22	0
	(8.7%)	(9.2%)	(12.6%)	(1.0%)	(1.3%)	(3.3%)	0
S+iV	32	8	48	3	2	13	1
	(4.8%)	(1.2%)	(7.2%)	(0.45%)	(0.3%)	(1.95%)	(0.15%)
S+cV+S–	14	16	13	2	1	0	0
Comp/adv	(2.1%)	(2.4%)	(1.95%)	(0.3%)	(0.15%)	0	0
S+cV+S–	14	18	7	1	5	0	0
Comp/noun	2.1%	(2.6%)	(1.0%)	(0.15%)	(0.75%)	0	0
Other	10	9	23	3	8	0	0
Totals	128	112	175	16	25	35	1
	(19.2%)	(16.8%)	(26.25%)	(2.4%)	(3.75%)	(5.25%)	(0.15%)

Key: S = subject; tV = transitive verb; DO = direct object; iV = intransitive verb; eV = coula verb;

the use of negation, the copula, the auxiliary, pronominal usage, number concord, and past tense forms. We are also anxious to determine whether or not there are significant quantitative differences in the frequency of relatives and coordination.

IMPLICATIONS FOR ENGLISH TEACHING

Even though this is a mere preview of the methodology and analytical techniques of the Detroit study, let us turn to the potential usefulness of this kind of information for the classroom teacher. As with many research projects, pedagogical application will come in two steps and from two kinds of people. The first step will be the presentation of language data as related to social class, ethnic group, age, sex, race, and geography. The principal tools will be those of description and comparison. The data will reveal, for example, the language features which distinguish twelve-year-old Negro boys from the Inner City from twelve-year-old Negro boys whose parents are professional.

The second step should be taken by people with expertise in pedagogy. The linguist is not always the person to decide how to program the evidence discovered in step number one. He may know too little about child psychology and material sequencing.[3] But the educator will surely benefit from an

Dependent								
Inter-rogative	*Presen-tative*	*Passive*	*With if, when etc.*	*Rel. clause with rel. pair*	*Rel. clause without rel. pair*	*Presen-tative*	*Miscel-laneous*	*Totals*
18	0	2	26	11	8	4	0	311
(2.7%)	0	(0.3%)	(3.9%)	(1.7%)	(1.2%)	(0.6%)	0	(46.5%)
3	1	0	18	8	5	2	1	145
(0.45%)	(0.15%)	0	(2.6%)	(1.2%)	(0.75%)	(0.3%)	(0.15%)	(21.6%)
5	0	0	4	11	1	0	0	62
(0.75%)	0	0	(0.6%)	(1.65%)	(0.15%)	0	0	(9.3%)
7	0	0	1	1	6	0	0	60
(1.0%)	0	0	(0.15%)	(0.15%)	(0.9%)	0	0	(9.0%)
1	1	0	12	10	2	0	0	79
34	2	2	61	41	22	6	1	656
(5.1%)	(0.3%)	(0.3%)	(9.15%)	(6.15%)	(3.3%)	(0.9%)	(0.15%)	

Comp/adv = adverbial complement, Comp/noun = nominal complement.

accurate description of the linguistic situation as it relates to different ages, races, sex, and social status groups.

The major thrust of the Detroit study, then, is in terms of the presentation of linguistic data in a sociological framework. Such data can be gathered and analyzed only by linguists. This information however, should reveal a number of exciting things, including the following:

1. That each social dialect has a structure quite adequate for its users. "Omissions," if they exist, are not merely careless. Variations in tense may be quite patterned. Apparently "unnecessary repetition" may, within that system, be quite necessary.
2. That there are certain features of pronunciation, grammar, and vocabulary which can be considered indices of social stratification. These indices will become the focus of the English teachers attention.
3. That in most cases, it will be best not to destroy a lower class social dialect, for its user may need it to survive in certain social situations. Instead it may be best to add to it a new social dialect which will be useful for getting ahead in the world.
4. That in order to build the second dialect, it is best to know the structure of both the lower class dialect and the target dialect (see point 1).

In a more specific sense, the results of the Detroit Dialect Study will provide at least two kinds of help to the elementary teacher:

> First, it will identify the specific phonological and grammatical features and processes which characterize different groups. We have data on a large number of 9, 10, 11, 12, 13, 14, 15, and 16 year olds. Such a corpus is a natural source for information about increasing sentence complexity, however it is defined. It is possible, for example, to note the increasingly complex syntax in the speech of pre-adolescents as they approach their teens; for example, the embedding of one sentence in another, as "The store where we meet our friends is right over there." With a corpus of this size, it is further possible to check this and other processes across ethnic, racial, sex, and economic boundaries. The usefulness of this information will be obvious to any teacher who has been frustrated by teaching against an unwanted construction which exists in one group but not in another.
>
> Second, we will use the above information to discover the nature of the students' language problems. Frequently such problems stem from interference of the "home" dialect on the "school" dialect. A person learning a foreign language hears the new language through the grids of his own experience. Likewise a person tends to hear a different dialect through his own linguistic framework. The first problem in learning a second language or a second dialect is that of coming in contact with it. The second problem is that of identifying the differences.

Many elementary children are in the first and second stages of learning "school" English. Their home dialect frequently interferes with the second dialect. To the teacher their speech may seem careless, inconsistent, or awkward. But, in the fact, the children are being careful, consistent, and graceful within the only dialect they know.

What many teachers fail to realize is that at least some of the problems of dialect switching are of this sort. The inner-city child actually must unlearn a perfectly good pattern in favor of one which has a characteristic which he must later come to scorn again—in other social circumstances. In this case, the home dialect may interfere with the school dialect to the extent that "she looks" may be read aloud as "she look." If the teacher understands the *system* of the home dialect, he will realize that the "omission" of the *s* in "looks" is not necessarily a matter of carelessness, inconsistency, awkwardness, or irrelevance. Nor is it necessarily a problem of failure to pronounce an [s]. It appears, instead, to be a matter of grammatical interference of home grammar system with school grammar system.

Whether this kind of problem appears in reading or composition, it is good to know the reasons which underlie it. By identifying the major features of the phonological and grammatical systems of various groups in a city such as Detroit, we can more efficiently come to grips with the reasons why students make specific switching errors.

I am reminded here of a former student from West Virginia who spelled *basement* with an i—*basemint*. His problem was *not* one of carelessness, inconsistency, awkwardness, or irrelevance. He simply had a good ear for pronunciations, and he pronounced the word with an [ɪ] sound not an [ɛ] or a [ə]. The point here is that by understanding *his system*, I could better understand his problem and discover a remedy for it. The implications of the illustration are at the heart of the task of the Detroit research. We need to identify the significant differences between groups of all sorts (social, racial, age, *etc.*) in order to understand the failures in the normal and expected switching in which socially mobile people engage.

NOTES

1. William Labov, *Social Stratification of English in New York City*, Washington, D.C.: Center for Applied Linguistics, 1966.
2. Roger W. Shuy, Walter A. Wolfram, and William K. Riley, *Linguistic Correlates of Social Stratification in Detroit Speech*, Final Report, Cooperative Research Project 6-1347, U.S. Office of Education, 1967.
3. But see my "Some Sociolinguistic Implications for the Teaching of English," (a paper presented at the First International Conference on the Teaching of English, Vancouver, 1967) for ways in which the linguist does have something to say about pedagogical sequencing.

STUDY QUESTIONS

1. How does McDavid define dialect? Why does he define this term differently than do other linguists? Do you accept his definition? If not, what is your definition of dialect?
2. What conceptions of social dialects does McDavid regard as nonsense? To what extent do his views on teaching standard English as a second language correspond to those of other scholars?
3. McDavid maintains that "while we are planning language programs for our disadvantaged, we must educate the dominant culture in the causes and significance of dialect differences." For whom would McDavid recommend this training? What would he regard as essential elements in this training?
4. Do you agree with Erickson's explanation of why inner-city teachers resist nonstandard dialects? What related hypotheses that might be deduced from the theories of prejudice described by Banks in Chapter 1?
5. Why does Erickson take issue with researchers who are preoccupied

with studying the inadequacies of nonstandard English? How might you test the validity of Erickson's assertions?

6. What is the "shared context principle" postulated by Erickson and Hall? To what extent does this constitute an elaboration of Bernstein's concept of "public and private language"?
7. If you applied the findings of the Sounds of Society Project to language arts instruction, what changes in teaching methodology might be implemented? Is there any evidence to suggest that these findings might have different applicability for children of different subcultures? Might they be applicable to language problems of individual children, irrespective of their cultural antecedents?
8. How does Hall define listening behavior? How does he define "conversational distances?" How might both phenomena facilitate communication between pupils and teachers?
9. Hall's article underscores the need for awareness training for teachers. Do you agree or disagree with Hall's rationale for this training? Should it be limited to teachers of Indian, black, Puerto Rican, and Mexican-American children?
10. How might the methodology utilized in the Detroit Study be adapted to smaller communities? Would any change in instrumentation be necessitated by the nature of the community?
11. On what grounds does Shuy challenge the assumption that disadvantaged people deviate from advantaged people? How might one describe the essential differences in dialects used by various segments of the population?

SUGGESTED READINGS

Ausubel, David P., "How Reversible are the Cognitive and Motivational Effects of Cultural Deprivation? Implications for Teaching the Culturally Deprived Child," *Urban Education* (January 1964), 16–38.

Bernstein, Basil, "Social Class and Linguistic Development: A Theory of Social Learning," in *Education, Economy, and Society*, New York: Free Press, 1961.

Clark, Kenneth, "Clash of Cultures in the Classroom," *Integrated Education*, **1**, 4 (1963), 7–14.

Davis, A. L., "Dialect Research and the Needs of the Schools," *Elementary English*, **45** (May 1968), 558–560, 608.

Deutsch, Martin, *et. al., The Disadvantaged Child: Studies of the Social Environment and the Learning Process*, New York: Basic Books, 1967.

Deutsch, Martin, "The Role of Social Class in Language Development and Cognition," *American Journal of Orthopsychiatry* (January 1965), 78–88.

Elam, Sophie L., "Acculturation and Learning Problems of Puerto Rican Children," *Teachers College Record*, **61** (February 1960), 258–264.

John, Vera P., and Leo S. Goldstein, "The Social Context of Language Acquisition," *Merrill-Palmer Quarterly*, **10** (July 1964), 265–276.

Lloyd, Donald J., "Sub-Cultural Patterns Which Affect Language and Reading Development," in *Language, Linguistics, and School Programs*, Champaign, Ill.: National Council of Teachers of English, 1963.

Steiner, Stan, *La Raza*, New York: Harper and Row, 1970.

PART TWO/ CURRICULUM AND INSTRUCTION

This section focuses directly on classroom instruction and as such constitutes the major portion of the text. The readings were selected for the express purpose of helping elementary educators evaluate language arts curricula for culturally different children. Admittedly, none of the readings offer surefire solutions for specific instructional problems, but they do describe a wide variety of promising approaches to curriculum building and classroom instruction.

The readings cluster around topics that are of prime concern to elementary teachers and administrators: (1) designing strategies for teaching standard English, (2) building and evaluating oral language programs, (3) developing multisensory teaching approaches, (4) selecting and utilizing elements of children's literature, and (5) bridging the gap between the language arts and the social studies.

CHAPTER 4
TEACHING STANDARD ENGLISH

Why is it essential that all our pupils be taught to use standard English? To what extent do nonstandard dialects facilitate and interfere with the acquisition of standard English? What instructional materials and strategies have proven useful in this regard? The authors of readings in this chapter speak of these and other fundamental questions concerning the teaching of standard English, or the so-called "prestige dialect."

In the first reading, Kenneth R. Johnson delves deeply into the unique language problems of lower-class black children, and demonstrates how second language techniques can be employed with these children. Mildred R. Gladney and Lloyd Leaverton then report the results of their pioneering research on teaching standard English usage in the Chicago public schools.

STANDARD ENGLISH AND DISADVANTAGED BLACK CHILDREN: TEACHING STRATEGIES

Kenneth R. Johnson

Children begin to learn language long before they enter school. By the time they enter school, they have internalized the features of the particular variety of English spoken in their primary cultural environment. Children born into a middle-class culture learn the standard variety of English spoken by their

Written especially for this volume.

parents. Disadvantaged black children learn the variety of English spoken in their sub-culture. This is not the variety of English which facilitates academic, social and vocational success in the larger society.

Disadvantaged black children speak a nonstandard dialect of English. A dialect is a variety of a particular language that differs somewhat in grammar, phonology, and vocabulary from the standard and prestigious form.

Teachers recognize that the language spoken by many disadvantaged black children has numerous phonological and grammatical deviations from standard English. Furthermore, teachers recognize that these deviations occur with great frequency in the speech of disadvantaged black children. The aggregate of these deviations comprise the outstanding features of the non-standard Negro dialect. What teachers frequently do not recognize, however, is that these deviations (phonological and grammatical) operate systematically to interfere in the children's attempts to learn standard English.

Interference refers to the tendency of individuals to make a foreign language conform to the sound and structure of their native language. In other words, when speakers of Spanish learn English, they make English "sound like Spanish." This phenomenon of interference also operates when speakers of one dialect of a particular language learn another dialect of that language. This is the situation when disadvantaged black children attempt to learn standard English: their nonstandard dialect gets in the way—interferes—and their attempts to learn standard English are hampered. The nonstandard Negro dialect has a phonological and grammatical system that is predictably different than the phonological and grammatical system of standard English. When disadvantaged black children learn standard English, they impose the phonological and grammatical system of the nonstandard Negro dialect on standard English.

Individuals who speak foreign languages are taught English as a second language by techniques that account for the problem of interference. That is, techniques to teach English as a second language to speakers of foreign languages focus on the interference points between English and the individuals' foreign languages. For example, the Spanish speaker who lacks the English phoneme represented by the letters *ch* (Spanish does not have this phoneme in the initial position) is given special help in hearing and then reproducing this phoneme.

The essence of second language techniques is identifying the points of interference between the individual's native language and English, and then developing audio-lingual techniques to deal with these interference points.

The problem of teaching standard English to disadvantaged black children who speak a nonstandard Negro dialect is not unlike the problem of teaching standard English to speakers of foreign languages. Specifically, the interference points between standard English and the nonstandard Negro dialect must be contrasted and dealt with in the language program, utilizing the instructional techniques that have been worked out in programs to teach English as a second language.

The phonological and grammatical interference points between standard English and the nonstandard Negro dialect have been identified by linguists and educators. Examples of phonological interference points are: the substitution of /d/ for voiced /th/ in the initial position (*dem* for *them*, *dis* for *this*, *dat* for *that*); the substitution of /f/ for voiceless /th/ in the final position (*wif* for *with*, *mouf* for *mouth*, *paf* for *path*); elimination of /r/ in the final position (*dō* for *door*, *sto* for *store*, *fa* for *far*). Examples of grammatical interference points are: lack of third person singular present tense agreement morpheme (*he go*, for *he goes*; *it run*, for *it runs*; *she walk*, for *she walks*); omission of the copula in present tense (*she running*, for *she is running*; *they talking*, for *they are talking; he busy,* for *he is busy*); reversal of the present and past participle forms of irregular verbs (*I done my work* and *I have did my work*, for *I did my work* and *I have done my work*; *I taken a bath* and *I have took a bath*, for *I took a bath,* and *I have taken a bath*; *I done it* and *I have did it,* for *I did it* and *I have done it*).

Classroom teachers can determine these interference points by noting the phonological and grammatical deviations from standard English disadvantaged black children consistently make. These consistent deviations from standard English can't be considered as simple mistakes, because this would assume that the children know and have internalized the standard English rule and they are carelessly disregarding the rule. Instead, these consistent deviations from standard English must be recognized as the phonological and grammatical features of the nonstandard Negro dialect.

The school must teach standard English to disadvantaged black children who speak a nonstandard Negro dialect. The traditional language program has emphasized the study of grammar and analytic activities in teaching these children standard English. This is not, however, the way language is learned. Language is not learned by parsing, memorizing paradigms, or analyzing sentences. Instead, language is learned by hearing and then imitating sounds of models. Repeated imitation of sounds and structures form linguistic habits. This is how one's native language is learned, and the same is true for learning a second language.

The traditional language program is organized to reinforce and extend standard English. That is, the traditional program emphasizes analyzing standard English, having children do written drills, and having children read descriptions of standard English. The traditional program emphasizes a non-oral approach in language instruction. Language, however, is best learned through an audio-lingual approach. The proof that the traditional language program has been a dismal failure for most disadvantaged black children is that most of these children leave school after twelve years unable to speak standard English. Educators have generally blamed the children for not learning standard English. Perhaps, the blame should be placed on the methods used to teach these children.

Before suggesting a different method for teaching standard English to black children who speak a nonstandard dialect, the reasons the traditional program has failed must be examined further.

The traditional approach has taught standard English to disadvantaged black children as a replacement dialect. In other words, these children were encouraged to discard their functional dialect. As long as most blacks live in segregated communities and confine most of their interpersonal relations to others within the disadvantaged black sub-culture, they will not replace their functional dialect for a nonfunctional dialect. Standard English is nonfunctional in the disadvantaged black sub-culture.

The nonstandard Negro dialect has been described with such labels as "bad language," "lazy lips and lazy tongues language." Language is an identity label that ties one to a particular cultural group. Thus, when the language system of an individual is given a negative or derogatory judgement, this judgement also applies to the individual, and the judgement is generalized to all others who use the language system. Teachers and textbooks that have communicated negative derogatory judgements of the nonstandard Negro dialect to black students have probably alienated these students by rejecting their language, and this is an indirect way of rejecting the students and their culture.

The speech deviations characteristic of the nonstandard Negro dialect have been treated as if these deviations were speech idiosyncracies of each individual student who uttered them. Teachers often recognized that black students utter the same deviations; yet the English program has not treated these deviations as systematic speech occurrences characteristic of a group. The traditional English program for black students who speak a nonstandard dialect has corrected speech deviations "on the spot." There has not been a rationale to deal with these systematic speech deviations. Instead, the traditional program, in capsule, has been to give "on the spot" correction, often accompanied with beratement and extensive written drills to reinforce and extend a dialect (standard English) the students did not speak.

Audio-lingual techniques of teaching language have not been used, and students have been given little opportunity to practice standard English orally. The emphasis of the traditional program has been on written and analytic activities, instead of oral and functional activities.

Disadvantaged black children will not learn standard English until the teaching strategy implied by the reasons for failure of the traditional program is followed, and this teaching strategy is to teach standard English as an alternate dialect through second language techniques. Specifically, this strategy requires that: 1) the children recognize that there is a difference between their dialect and the dialect being taught without the usual accompanying stigma being placed on their dialect; 2) next, the children must hear the standard English sound or pattern being taught; 3) after they are able to hear the standard English sound or pattern, they must be able to discriminate between the standard English sound or patterns and the corresponding interfering sound or pattern in their nonstandard dialect; 4) after the children are able to do these preceding steps, they must be given drills which help them to reproduce the standard English sound or pattern; 5) finally, the children must be given the opportunity to use the standard English sound or pattern in their speech. They must be given the opportunity to practice the sound or pattern so that they can use it whenever necessary. Note that in this sequence of steps the children are not required to reproduce the sound or pattern being taught until they can hear and discriminate the sound or pattern from the corresponding interfering sound or pattern in their nonstandard dialect. The traditional approach of teaching disadvantaged black children standard English fails to do these necessary preceding steps before requiring the children to reproduce the standard sound or pattern. In summary, the traditional approach is a "don't say it like that, say it like this" approach (then, written instead of oral drills are assigned).

These five steps of a second language strategy for teaching disadvantaged black children will be discussed in more detail to clarify a second language strategy.

Before employing a second language strategy, children must recognize that their nonstandard Negro dialect and standard English are different. The traditional strategy recognizes the difference, but the difference is recognized as being the result of careless or sloppy departure from the rules of standard English. Also, the traditional approach places a stigma on the nonstandard Negro dialect. A second language strategy must deal with the difference more accurately. That is, the children must be taught the nature of language and the reasons for language differences between people. This requires that the social factors (language learning in slavery, social isolation caused by segregation, language as an identity label) that produce the nonstandard Negro dialect must be taught. In addition, the children must be taught that the nonstandard Negro dialect is not morally or intellectually inferior to standard English. This teaching strategy also requires a change of attitude in teachers, and this is crucial. It is unlikely that disadvantaged black children will accept the language of the teacher if the teacher will not accept their's. Finally, this teaching strategy accepts, and admits, the social reality and functional value of the nonstandard Negro dialect. At the same time, children must be taught the social situations in which standard English is appropriate.

The tape recorder should be used extensively to get children to hear standard English sounds and patterns. The tape recorder, when used with earphones especially, has the advantage of focusing attention on the feature being taught. In this electronic age, students are more attentive to electronic devices than they are to teachers. Also, the tape recorder has the advantage of being able to present the standard sound or pattern being taught without variation. In other words, once the sound or pattern is put on tape, it can be repeated exactly, again and again. Teachers are likely to introduce variations (particularly in pronunciation) if they attempt to get the children to hear standard features by live oral presentations.

When attempting to get the children to hear the standard sound or pattern, the children must be told what they are expected to hear. This requires that they must be aware of what they substitute in place of the standard feature being taught. Stated another way, the children must be aware of the particular interference. For example, if the standard feature being taught is the voiced /th/ in the initial position, the children must be told that they substitute the sound they hear at the beginning of words like *dog*, *day*, *do* and *dance* (they should not be told that they substitute a "d" sound).

After the children know the nature of the conflict, they should be given a list of words which contain voiced /th/ in the initial position. Next, they should be given auditory exercises which require them to discriminate this sound from other sounds, except the interference sound from their nonstandard Negro dialect. For example, they should be given a list orally such as: *this*, *that*, *them*, *those*, *these*, etc. Then, they should discriminate words beginning with this sound from other words except those beginning like *dog*, *date*, *do* and *dance*.

If the standard feature being taught is a grammatical feature, these same procedures should be followed. The children should be told what they are expected to hear, then the feature is presented. Again, the best way to present it is with the tape recorder. An effective way to present it is to rewrite interesting stories or anecdotes so that they contain many examples of the grammatical feature being taught.

At this point, the teacher can determine if the children are able, at least, to hear that the voiced /th/ in the initial position is heard as a different sound from other sounds, but this is not the crucial factor. Thus, very little time should be spent on this phase. The crucial factor is whether they can discriminate the voiced /th/ from /d/ in the initial position. That is, whether they can discriminate *those* from *doze*, for example.

One activity that can be given to the children to force them to auditorilly discriminate between the standard sound or pattern and the interfering sound or pattern from their nonstandard dialect is to present a series of three words each (standard and nonstandard versions) in which one of the words is said twice (again, this should be presented by the tape recorder). For example, the series to discriminate voiced /th/ from /d/ might be: *doze*, *doze*, *those*; *dat*, *that*, *that*; *dis*, *this*, *dis*; *them*, *dem*, *them*. The children determine which word, standard or nonstandard, was said twice (the same exercise can be adapted for discriminating between standard and nonstandard grammatical features). Another exercise is to give a list of words including both standard and nonstandard versions and have the children write the letters that stand for the sound in the contrasted position. Teachers should collect recorded samples of children's standard and nonstandard pronunciations of particular words in sentences and play these on the tape recorder. The children are required to indicate whether the word was pronounced in a standard or non-standard manner. This exercise has the advantage of presenting the contrasts in meaningful context. This, however, is a more difficult auditory discrimination exercise than presenting word lists.

The old game of bingo can be adapted to teach phonetic discrimination. First, have the children make a bingo card of squares. Then, have them copy in random order words which contrast standard and nonstandard features. For example, *doze*, *those*, *dare*, *there*, *dish*, *this* would contrast voiced initial /th/ and initial /d/; *whiff*, *with*, *laugh*, *math*, *puff*, *path* would contrast voiceless final /th/ and final /f/ (the nonstandard substitution for voiceless final /th/); *flow*, *floor*, *stow*, *store*, *mow*, *more* would contrast r-lessness in the final position (another nonstandard feature of the nonstandard Negro dialect). The phonetic bingo game is played by having the words read, and the children place markers in the squares containing each word as it is read. The winner of this kind of bingo game is determined in the usual way.

Only after the children can discriminate between the standard and non-standard features should they be required to reproduce the standard feature. The simplest way to get children to reproduce standard grammatical features is through pattern practice. The children can repeat sentences which contain the grammatical pattern being taught. For example, if the grammatical pattern being taught is the standard use of past tense forms of the verb *to be*, the children can be required to repeat such sentences as the following after they are presented orally (the tape recorder is the best way to present the sentences . . . A pause between each sentence must be long enough to permit the children to repeat each sentence before the next one is presented): "He was always late;" "They were caught in a storm." A more difficult pattern to teach the same standard feature is to give the children part of a sentence such as ". . . caught in a storm" to be used with the standard past tense form of the verb *to be* (was or were) when a subject is presented. For example, the children are given the subject "she" and they answer, "She was caught in a storm;" or, the children are given the subject "they" and they answer, "They were caught in a storm." Another exercise is to record sentences using the nonstandard form of the grammatical feature being taught, and have the children "translate" the nonstandard sentence into standard English. For example, if the agreement sound of third person singular, present tense verbs is being taught the children would hear the nonstandard sentences "She look serious" and "He dress nice." A pause following each of the nonstandard sentences permits the children to answer, "She looks serious" and "He dresses nice." Other kinds of patterns that can be given are: ask the children questions which force them to use a particular grammatical feature in their answer ("Are you going to school?" "Yes, I am going to school;" "Are they late?" "Yes, they are late"); and, have children repeat sentences which omit the grammatical feature being taught ("I ______ going to the party." "I am going to the party;" "The girls ______ waiting for the bus." "The girls are waiting for the bus.").

The simplest way to get children to reproduce a standard sound is to give them a list of words containing the standard sound and have the children repeat the words after each is presented. A more meaningful way to have them reproduce the standard sound is through pattern practice (standard grammatical features can also be reinforced at the same time). For example, if the voiced initial /th/ is being taught, sentences like the following can be given: "Those apples are cheaper than these." Note that there are three words in this sentence beginning with voiced /th/. In other words, sentences containing many words that include the sound being taught are given to the children. At this point, words containing the interfering sound are not included (in the case of voiced initial /th/ no words beginning with /d/ are presented). After children can reproduce the sound being taught in this kind of pattern, then sentences containing both the standard sound being taught and the interfering sound can be given to the children for them to repeat. For example, the following types of sentences which contain both initial /th/ and /d/ can be given to the children to repeat: "Those dogs that didn't have their licenses were caught;" or, "These double decker sandwiches are more delicious than those." These sentences contain words that begin with the interfering phonological feature and the standard phonological feature being taught.

The final step in a second language technique is to get the children to use standard English in a meaningful situation. This approach requires that children are taught those situations in which standard English is appropriate. However, the school cannot place children in these situations. Therefore, the situations have to be simulated through role playing.

Role playing is a technique that can be used to present children with a situation in which standard English is appropriate. For example, situations like a visit to the dentist's office, an employment interview, a call to the department shore to order merchandise, etc. can be given to children to role play.

During role play, children not actually involved can listen for particular features to determine if the players have used these features in a standard way. The children should listen for only a few standard features. For example, they should listen for one or two standard phonemes, or one or two standard grammatical patterns. In other words, the children not involved in playing the roles in a situation should act as evaluators to determine if a particular standard feature is being used. Role playing activities should be recorded, so that the speech of the players can be played back for evaluation.

When children first begin role playing activities, the duration of the role playing should be short. As they get more instruction in standard English and become more accustomed to role playing, the duration can be increased. The reason for this is that children become so engrossed in the role that they forget about trying to speak standard English. The more they become engrossed in the role, the more they speak their nonstandard dialect.

The final test of second language techniques occurs when children are actually in a situation that requires the use of standard English. If second language techniques have been successful, they should be able to speak standard English. This would be ultimate success. The least that can be expected is that they will be aware of standard English requirements in the situation, and that some nonstandard features will be eliminated from their speech.

This discussion has focused on the particular language problem of disadvantaged black children, and the discussion has suggested a second language rationale to teach these children standard English. This rationale is more consistent with how language is actually learned, especially a second language. Since learning another dialect of a language is similar to learning a second language, the rationale suggested in this discussion should be more effective than the traditional approach for teaching standard English to disadvantaged black children. The traditional approach has demonstrated only remarkable and consistent failure with disadvantaged black children.

A MODEL FOR TEACHING STANDARD ENGLISH TO NON-STANDARD ENGLISH SPEAKERS[1, 2]

Mildred R. Gladney and Lloyd Leaverton

PURPOSE

For some time, we have been interested in the dialect of the Afro-American child of a low socio-economic status and the part it plays in the difficulty of the children in learning the language arts subjects as taught in our public schools.

For instance, the dialect has been used to suggest, at least in some of the literature, that the children are verbally retarded.

Our experience with the children and the comments we have received from their teachers lead us to conclude that this description is not representative of a large number of the children in low income ghetto schools. However, the nonstandard dialect *is* considered a serious problem by their teachers, who work tirelessly, if unsuccessfully, to change it using such methods as constant correction, providing a model of standard English and following the various speech activities suggested in many language arts manuals and supplements.

Part of our difficulty as educators in effectively coping with this problem of teaching the standard dialect has been a failure to recognize that the child's dialect contains a definite structure and organization and is resistant to change. This was clearly demonstrated to us as a result of an investigation we conducted in one of the special summer schools in Chicago in 1965. We tape recorded conversations with entering kindergarten children and with children who had completed the third grade. The third graders were reading at or above grade level and had obviously been exposed to standard speech usage as it appeared in their reading material for at least three years. Their teachers, also, no doubt, had provided a model of standard English usage in their communication with the children throughout each school day. In spite of these exposures to standard English, the children's oral speech

Mildred R. Gladney and Lloyd Leaverton, "A Model for Teaching Standard English to Non-Standard English Speakers," *Elementary English*, **45** (October 1968), 758–763.

contained most of the major differences from standard English that we found in the speech of the kindergarten children.

DEVELOPMENTS OF MATERIALS

While searching for ideas for a language arts program that would be effective for children who used their language fully and well to communicate with the adults and other children in their community and with many of their teachers but who used nonstandard patterns, we formulated three conditions upon which to base our model as an approach to this problem.

First, we must start at a point meaningful to the learner. Translated to the area of oral speech, this suggested to us that the learning sequence in teaching standard speech patterns should start with an actual statement made by the child.

Second, in utilizing the different patterns of the nonstandard dialect, preference should be given to that speech pattern that permits the transition from the child's dialect to the standard dialect by adding to the child's dialect. For example, "My mama pretty," can be restated in standard English by adding *is*—"My mama is pretty." One exception to this is the unique use, "I don't like cake when it be frozen." Here, a complete substitution of verbs is necessary. "I don't like cake when it is frozen."

Third, we felt it essential to focus on one pattern at a time and to proceed systematically in accordance with linguistic principles. This condition we felt was crucial in view of the influence it exerts on the behavior of the classroom teacher. By focusing on one pattern at a time only the verb form relative to the specific pattern is brought to the child's attention as everyday talk and immediately followed by the presentation of the school talk form to the child. The other speech patterns characteristic of the dialect with respect to verb form are permitted in the classroom without comments until the particular verb form is encountered in the sequence of the materials. Needless to say, if the child is "corrected" in an unsystematic fashion each time his speech differs from standard English usage the child will become confused and discouraged. Such systemization is also imperative to avoid the creation of errors which did not originally exist. For example, introduction of the use of *is* in simple statements must be closely followed by the introduction of *am* and *are* so that the child will not begin to use forms such as "I is," "you is," and "they is."

In addition to the tape recorded conversations mentioned previously, we had also taped conversations with kindergarten, first, second and third grade Afro-American students in a school in a different low income ghetto area in June of 1965. All of the conversations were analyzed and four striking differences in verb usage were identified as the focal point of our proposed program of instruction.

They are:

a) The verbs *is* and *are* are omitted:
   1. In simple sentences, e.g.
      He my friend.
   2. In sentences using the present participle form, e.g.
      They playing house.
   3. In sentences expressing the future using the verb go, i.e.
      She gon be a nurse when she grow up.

b) One verb form is used for all subjects in the present tense, i.e.
   Chocolate milk look good.
   The baby look like he do.
   That boy have a piece of bread.

c) One verb form is used for all subjects in the past tense, i.e.
   We was hungry.
   Somebody knock that down.
   Yesterday I write my name.

d) Be is used in place of *is*, *am* and *are* and in sentences describing a recurring event, i.e.
   When my mama be gone, I take care of the babies.
   Sometimes he be riding in the alley.
   I be scared when it be thundering.

The instructional sequence of our program begins with the teaching of Rhymed Pattern Practices developed by Mr. Melvin Hoffman, consulting linguist to the project. These rhymed verses are intended to provide a model of standard English usage (possibly at a preconscious level).

These practices are then followed by activities developed by the authors and Mrs. John Patterson, a project staff teacher, and designed to help the child make the transition at a conscious level from his established dialect form to the corresponding standard dialect form.

The teacher tells a story or asks a question which will elicit from the children their speech patterns in the verb area being studied. The children's statement is nonstandard and standard forms are recorded on chalkboard or paper. For example, some of the sentences given by the children in a conversation about their friends or classmates during a lesson on the use of *is* in simple sentence were:

Terry he bad in school.
Deborah my friend.
Michael is strong.
Gregory brown just like me.

The teacher then describes each sentence as EVERYDAY TALK or SCHOOL TALK pointing out to the children that the sentences that omit *is* are EVERYDAY TALK and the sentences that include *is* may be EVERYDAY TALK and definitely are SCHOOL TALK. The teacher discusses SCHOOL TALK and EVERYDAY TALK as different ways of expressing ideas, neither one "wrong" or "right" but used in different situations, that is, in school, out of school.

After the activities stemming from the children's own statements are concluded, pre-written sentences and stories in EVERYDAY TALK and dialogues in SCHOOL TALK which include the verbs being studied are given to the children for practice in changing the nonstandard dialect to the standard dialect in orally spoken sentences.

The sequence of the verb pattern introduced is as follows:

Unit 1—am, is, are
Unit 2—was, were
Unit 3—"s", "es"
Unit 4—do, does
Unit 5—say, says
Unit 6—have, has
Unit 7—"ed"
Unit 8—be

COLLECTION OF DATA

At the initial stage of the development of the program, considering the ingrained nature of the children's dialect, we did not expect that they would adopt the standard dialect in even the minority of instances in their informal talk after just a year's time. However, we hoped that the children would be able to respond in the standard dialect or SCHOOL TALK if asked to do so at the beginning of an informal conversation.

Therefore, it was determined that the appropriate evaluation at the end of the school year would consist of comparing the SCHOOL TALK conversation of the experimental group with the oral speech of similar children, with respect to age, grade, I.Q., and socio-economic status who had been given the traditional speech lessons.

Two classes were selected from neighboring schools to serve as the control groups. Samples of spontaneous speech were obtained in June, 1966 from both the experimental and control groups in a series of small group sessions consisting of approximately 5 to 6 students. Each session was taped recorded. The sessions were initiated by asking the children how they planned to spend their time during the summer vacation. Two other questions served as stimuli.

1. What would you like to be when you grow up?
2. If you had $100 to spend all by yourself, what would you buy?

The tape recordings were then analyzed with respect to the extent of correspondence to standard English or to nonstandard English when any one of the verb forms comprising the experimental treatment occurred in their speech. For example, the statement, "When it be hot, we go to the beach everyday," was counted as corresponding to the nonstandard dialect; whereas the statement, "When it is hot, we go to the beach everyday," was counted as corresponding to standard English. A count was made for each child as how many times his speech corresponded to the nonstandard dialect or standard dialect with respect to each verb form included in the experimental material.

ANALYSIS OF DATA

These data contained some characteristics that should be discussed before presenting the findings. In the first place, some children used a particular verb far more frequently than did others. For example, the verb form "I be" occurred as many as fifteen times with some children and as few as two times with other children. However, if the latter children used the nonstandard form "I be" only two times and did not use the corresponding standard form at all, one could not conclude that they utilized the dialect form less than the children who used the form "I be" fifteen times. Conversely, if other children used the standard English form "I am" ten times and the form "I be" did not occur in their speech at all, one could not conclude they had mastered standard English usage more than the children who used "I am" two times, but also did not "I be" at all.

In view of these considerations a non-parametric technique seemed most appropriate to test the significance of the differences between the experimental control groups. Each child was therefore rated as a plus or minus with respect to standard English usage for each of six verb forms. The X^2 test was then used to determine the significance of the differences between the groups.

RESULTS

Although each teacher utilized the Language Arts Curriculum Guide prepared by the Department of Curriculum Development and Teaching of the Chicago Board of Education, it is highly probable, we felt, that the language arts activities relative to oral language of the two control groups may have varied because of the teacher variable. Hence, it was anticipated that the two control groups might show some differences in their speech because of this variable. Therefore, the experimental group was compared separately with each control group. The findings of these comparisons are given in Tables 1 and 2.

Table 1. Number of children in experimental group compared with children in control group 1 whose informal speech corresponds to standard English usage with respect to six verb forms

Variable	*Experimental Group*		*Control Group 1*			
	Standard English	*Non-standard Dialect*	*Standard English*	*Non-standard Dialect*	X^2	*P*
Be Present (omission of am, is, are)	33	1	32	7	3.27	$<.10$
Irregular Present (have-has do-does say-says)	5	3	5	12	1.29	$<.30$
Regular Present (work-works)	6	5	3	20	4.62	$<.05$
Irregular Past (write-wrote)	16	0	18	4	1.60	$<.30$
Regular Past (work-worked)	5	0	10	5	.80	—
Conditional With *Be* (if I be)	19	1	6	28	27.27	$<.001$

Table 2. Number of children in experimental group compared with children in control group 2 whose informal speech corresponds to standard English usage with respect to six verb forms

Variable	*Experimental Group*		*Control Group 2*			
	Standard English	*Non-standard Dialect*	*Standard English*	*Non-standard Dialect*	X^2	*P*
Be Present (omission of am, is, are)	33	1	20	3	1.23	$<.30$
Irregular Present (have-has do-does say-says)	5	3	2	7	1.41	$<.30$
Regular Present (work-works)	6	5	2	11	4.56	$<.05$
Irregular Past (write-wrote)	16	0	2	1	—	—
Regular Past (work-worked)	5	0	4	1	—	—
Conditional With *Be* (if I be)	19	1	5	24	25.61	$<.001$

Table 3. Number of children in experimental group compared with children in control groups 1 and 2 whose informal speech corresponds to standard English usage with respect to six verb forms

	Experimental Group		*Combined Control Groups 1 and 2*			
Variable	*Standard English*	*Non-standard Dialect*	*Standard English*	*Non-standard Dialect*	X^2	*P*
Be Present (omission of am, is, are)	33	1	52	10	2.58	$< .20$
Irregular Present (have-has do does say-says)	5	3	7	19	2.01	$< .20$
Regular Present (work-works)	6	5	5	31	5.63	$< .02$
Irregular Past (write-wrote)	16	0	20	5	2.03	$< .20$
Regular Past (work-worked)	5	0	14	6	—	—
Conditional With *Be* (if I be)	19	1	11	52	36.14	$< .001$

It is interesting to note that the significant differences between the experimental group and both control groups were with respect to the same two verb forms i.e., the Conditional with *Be* form and the Regular Present (inclusion of "s" to verb). The findings with respect to the other verb forms showed positive trends favoring the experimental group but were not statistically significant. However, when the two control groups are combined and compared with the experimental groups as shown in Table 3, the trends are more apparent.

Extensive investigations are needed to determine why the experimental treatment appeared more effective with some verb forms than with the others.

The model encourages the teacher to respect and accept the children's established dialect and at the same time provides a framework to help the children recognize, learn, and hopefully begin to use standard English.

NOTES

1. Paper read at the American Educational Research Association, Chicago, Feb. 9, 1968.
2. This research is cooperatively supported by the Office of the Superintendent of Public Instruction, Department of Program Development for Gifted Children and the Chicago Board of Education.

STUDY QUESTIONS

1. In what ways are the audio-lingual techniques suggested by Johnson similar to and different from those proposed by other authors? How might these approaches help disadvantaged children who encounter difficulties in learning standard English?
2. Why does Johnson believe that traditional language programs have been so notoriously unsuccessful when used with black disadvantaged children? Does his "second language strategy" involve modifying existing programs or creating new ones? Which approach would be easier to adopt? Why?
3. Role-playing activities occupy a position of central importance among Johnson's teaching strategies. What are their prime advantages? Potential disadvantages?
4. How might Johnson's strategies be used with non-black disadvantaged children? Would any basic changes in these strategies need to be made?
5. What are the three conditions upon which Gladney and Leaverton based their model for teaching language arts to disadvantaged children? Would Johnson support or challenge these conditions? Why?
6. How do "school talk" and "everyday talk," as defined by Gladney and Leaverton, differ? At what point do these authors believe that teachers should begin correcting the nonstandard dialects of their pupils?
7. Gladney and Leaverton found that the experimental treatment was more effective with some verb forms than with others. Specifically, what verb forms were most visibly affected? Can you explain why this occurred? Why weren't other verb forms similarly affected?
8. If you were redesigning the Gladney and Leaverton study, what would you employ as independent and dependent variables? How might these changes affect your procedures for gathering and analyzing data?

SUGGESTED READINGS

Allen, Virginia F., "Teaching Standard English as a Second Dialect," *Teachers College Record* (February 1967), 355–370.

Arnold, Richard D., "Reliability of Test Scores for the Young Bilingual Disadvantaged," *The Reading Teacher*, **22** (January 1969), 341–345.

Bereiter, Carl, and Siegfried Englemann, *Teaching Disadvantaged Children in the Preschool*, Englewood Cliffs, N.J.: Prentice-Hall, 1966.

Brooks, Charlotte K., "Some Approaches to Teaching English as a Second Language," in William A. Stewart, ed., *Non-Standard Speech and the Teaching of English*, Washington, D.C.: Center for Applied Linguistics, 1964, pp. 24–32.

Ecroyd, Donald H., "Negro Children and Language Arts," *The Reading Teacher*, **21** (April 1968), 624–629.

Finocchiaro, Mary, *Teaching English as a Second Language in Elementary and Secondary Schools*, New York: Harper and Row, 1958.

Hughes, Marie M., and George I. Sanchez, *Learning a New Language*, Washington, D.C.: Association for Childhood Education International, 1958.

Ott, Elizabeth H., *A Study of Levels of Fluency and Proficiency in Oral English of Spanish-Speaking School Beginners*, Austin: University of Texas Press, 1967.

CHAPTER 5
LANGUAGE PROGRAMS

In recent years the professional literature has proliferated with descriptions of language programs for culturally different children. Unfortunately, there is little evidence attesting to the merits of such programs. At issue are such questions as: What should be their purpose? Toward what segment of the school population should they be directed? Should they be build on existing programs, or should entirely new programs be created? How much emphasis should be placed on the skills of listening, speaking, reading, and writing? Granted, these questions have not been answered to the satisfaction of all, but some potentially useful answers have been proposed.

In the first selection, Jean Greenlaw reports the results of her research into the role of minority groups in the selection of basal reading programs. Nicholas P. Criscuolo then assesses the effectiveness of a popular reading program with disadvantaged children. John H. Litcher and David W. Johnson reveal their findings regarding the use of multiethnic readers as a vehicle for changing the attitudes of children.

The balance of the readings covers a wide variety of language programs. Richard D. Arnold describes how teachers succeeded in significantly upgrading the language development of Mexican-American children in Texas by developing a combination science-language arts program. William L. E. Philion and Charles G. Galloway describe how they designed, implemented, and evaluated a language arts program for children residing on an Indian reservation in British Columbia. The final reading, by Mildred B. Smith, presents a thorough, comprehensive description of a model language arts program, and indicates the conditions that must be met to insure the maximum effectiveness of such a program.

A STUDY OF THE INFLUENCE OF MINORITY GROUPS IN THE SELECTION AND DEVELOPMENT OF BASAL READING PROGRAMS

Jean Greenlaw

Millions of dollars are spent every year in the name of education and we are still failing to educate many of our children. One of the greatest areas of failure lies in the realm of reading and the group about which there is so much current public concern is that of disadvantaged minorities. Riessman presents some rather disturbing figures concerning this topic.

> The general estimate of reading inability among school children is fifteen to twenty percent, while among educationally deprived children the disability estimate is as high as fifty percent.[1]

Research dealing with the content of currently-used reading series generally concludes that minority groups are not well represented in basal reading programs and that the stories found in the books are not of particular interest to children.[2] Blom, Waite and Zimet state that writers of textbooks for children need to demonstrate greater sophistication and awareness of real life situations of children and their families and the developmental interests of children.[3] Rogers and Robinson found that children enjoy reading most that which is familiar to them and that good and poor readers share many of the same interests.[4] This leads one to question whether there should not be more written with settings depicting a variety of life styles, which would be of interest to children of various cultures. Ford and Koplyay[5] and Robert Emans[6] have studied the interests of primary children and postulated that realistic materials are preferred to fantasy.

The failure of our schools to teach many children to read and the inappropriateness of some reading materials leads to the consideration of another topic. A discussion of minority groups and reading is pertinent to the general public interest in minority groups. Newspapers, magazines, radio, television and other communications media are focusing upon minority problems in all areas and a central theme of their concern is stated by Ecroyd:

> There are attempts to upgrade the . . . school; to find new ways to train the untrained so they can become employable; to attack the roots of poverty itself. Integral to all of these is the teaching of reading.

Jean Greenlaw, "A Study of the Influence of Minority Groups in the Selection and Development of Basal Reading Programs." Research report published with permission of the author.

> Without the ability to read, economic progress is not an open choice for anyone.[7]

→ Inability to read is considered one of the major problems facing members of disadvantaged minority populations. It is difficult to find an article written by one of the spokesmen for minority groups in which this fact is not cited. If the concern is so great, do these groups influence the selection and development of the reading materials used to teach them to read? If there is an influence, to what extent does it effect school systems and publishers? A search of the literature reveals a dearth of information on this subject.

Despite the availability of research discussing the content of reading materials, there is a need for information concerning the selection and development of these materials. If minorities are an important segment of our society, what influence do they exert in this area?

PROCEDURE

Basal readers were selected as being the most consistently used method of teaching reading. This was confirmed by Mary Austin in her study, *The First R*. She reports,

> Of the multitude of reading material published, the basal readers with their accompanying manuals and workbooks are used more extensively than any other material. Indeed, in a good many classrooms they are utilized as the only tool of instruction.[8]

Five publishers of well-known and commonly used basal readers were chosen to receive a questionnaire. The purpose for questioning publishers was to determine what organized influence, if any, minority groups have on the development of basal reading programs.

For the purpose of this study, minority groups are defined as a part of the population differing in some way from the majority within that selected area. In the instrument designed for the study, Appendix A, specific minority groups were designated as being those most commonly considered minorities in the United States. A designation of "other" was provided to allow any school system to include an unlisted minority influence.

To obtain a broad sampling of minority influence on the selection of basal reading materials the population area of the continental United States was selected. The United States was divided into five geographical areas: Northeast, Southeast, Midwest, Southwest and Northwest. The states included in each of these areas can be found in the questionnaire to publishers, Appendix B. Fifteen selections were made from each geographical area with a lower limit of ten thousand population set as a criteria for selection.

The method used for selection of the communities involved was a stratified systematic unaligned random sampling. Simply stated, this consists of gridding the selected geographic area, assigning numbers to the grid intersections and choosing the intersections with the use of a table of random numbers. This method, in the study of human geography, has the advantage of randomnization and stratification together with the useful aspects of systematic samples. By avoiding alignment of the sample points, it also avoids the possibility of error caused by the natural geography of the area. In studies comparing methods of sampling the above method was consistently superior in producing accurate results.[9]

Two questionnaires were designed and can be found in the Appendix. Appendix A was designed to determine the influence of minority groups on the selection of basal readers by school systems. Appendix B was a questionnaire for publishers to ascertain minority influence on the development of basal readers. Following the selection of the sample the questionnaires were mailed to the seventy-five school systems and the five publishers.

RESULTS

Of the seventy-five questionnaires mailed to selected school systems, forty-seven returns were received. The five geographical areas were all well represented in the replies.

Table 1. Replies Received by Geographical Area

Geographical area	*Possible replies*	*Number of replies*
Northeast	15	9
Southeast	15	8
Midwest	15	7
Southwest	15	12
Northwest	15	11

The information gained from these replies can best be shown in table form. Table 2 shows that reading, as a curriculum area, is a very active subject. All systems replying had adopted a reading program, based on curriculum study, within the past five years, were presently studying reading or intended to study reading within the next two years.

Table 2. Status of Reading Adoptions

Recency of adoption	*Number of replies*
Within the past five years	34
Now being studied	10
To be studied within two years	3

A question was asked to determine whether specific criteria were or must be met in a reading adoption. Of the forty-seven respondents, twenty had developed specific criteria while twenty-seven had not.

The determination of minority influence is shown in the following table. The largest percentage of respondents did not consider minorities in their selection of materials. Negro, Mexican, urban and rural interests received the most consideration of those systems influenced by minority populations.

Table 3. Determination of Minority Influence

Minority group	*Number of considerations*
No group considered	23
Negro	14
Mexican	11
Puerto Rican	3
Oriental	5
Indian	6
Jew	3
Rural interests	10
Urban interests	9
East Indian	1

Fifteen systems considered more than one population in their selection.

Minority influence came from several sources. This writer was most interested in organized influences over curriculum adoptions in reading, but the question permitted more general responses, too. It will be noted in Table 4 that when sources of influence were considered present by respondents they came most frequently from their own personnel. Three systems were influenced by several factors.

Table 4. Sources of Perceived Influence in Textbook Selection

Area of influence	*Total*
Organized group	3
Individuals	6
School personnel	18
National movement	1
Government	1
None	22

It was presumed that where the reading curriculum materials were, or would be, under study, the basis of such study might well stem from recognized weaknesses in basal reading series, as these weaknesses applied to minority groups. Systems were then asked whether they had requested that publishers correct these limitations.

Table 5 compares those systems which discerned weaknesses in the treatment of minorities with the number of requests for material revision.

Table 5. Requests for Change, with Material's Treatment of Minorities Perceived as Inadequate

School systems	*Yes*	*No*
Weaknesses cited	38	9
Request for material change	8	37

Areas of cited weakness fell in three catagories: language, illustrations and content. Table 6 compares these stated weaknesses with the number of requests for change.

Table 6. Type of Material Weakness and Change Requests

Area of weakness	*Number citing weakness*	*Number requesting change*
Language	25	5
Illustrations	30	6
Content	32	6

Again, more than one area was checked by some respondents.

Five publishers of basal reading programs were contacted to determine whether they were influenced by minority populations in developing basal reading programs. Four publishers replied. Of the four respondents, three produced programs which were new since 1965 and one was a recent revision. All made specific references to minority groups in their materials. The method of reference is shown in Table 7.

Table 7. Method of Treatment of Minority Groups in Basal Readers

Method of treatment	*Total*
Language	2
Illustrations	4
Content	4
Authorship	1

Publishers were questioned with respect to the extent of requests for change of reading materials by school systems and organized minority groups. The comparison of these figures is shown in Table 8.

Table 8. Extent of Requests for Change of Basal Reading Materials Made by School Systems and Organized Minority Groups

Extent of requests	*School systems*	*Organized minority groups*
None	2	3
Slight	0	0
Moderate	2	1
Extensive	0	0

A response was requested as to which minority groups most influenced the planning of basal reading series. These are minority groups which received consideration in the published materials.

Table 9. Number of Publishers Influenced by Specific Minority Groups

Minority group	*Number of publishers influenced*
Negro	4
Mexican	3
Puerto Rican	4
Oriental	2
Indian	2
Jew	2
Rural interests	2
Urban interests	4

Areas in which demands for change in materials were specified by school systems or organized minority groups came in this order: illustrations, content and language. Cities demanded the greatest number of changes with state adoptions and towns following in that order.

Demands for change by geographical area are ranked as follows: Northeast, Southwest, Midwest, Northwest and Southeast.

CONCLUSIONS

On the basis of the findings, these conclusions were reached:

1. Minority populations are not specifically considered within the criteria

for selection by a majority of school systems adopting basal reading programs.
2. Organized minority groups are not exerting influence on school systems concerning basal reading adoptions.
3. Where minority groups are considered, the influence for consideration is mainly from school personnel.
4. Many school systems interviewed consider basal reading programs weak in their treatment of minority groups.
5. Few school systems request publishers to change the basal treatment of minority populations.
6. The areas of language, illustrations and content, within basal reading programs, are perceived by school systems as being weak in their treatment of minority populations.
7. Publishers perceive their basal reading materials to be inclusive of minority groups in the areas of illustrations and content.
8. Publishers receive few requests for change of basal reading materials from school systems.
9. Publishers receive almost no requests for change of basal reading materials from organized minority groups.

IMPLICATIONS

The major purpose of this study was to ascertain what, if any, influence was being exerted by minority groups on schools and publishers in regard to the adoption and development of basal reading materials. Though limited by the size of the sample, the study is useful to indicate a rather consistent trend in curriculum and to suggest possibilities for future change.

Though spokesmen for minority groups cite inability to read as one of the major problems facing disadvantaged minority populations they do not seem to be doing much about this problem. As with many situations, it is far easier to criticize what exists than to develop an alternative and actively pursue it. Organized minority groups have exhibited their power in such areas as housing and civil rights; it might be appropriate for them to utilize this same power in requests for basal reading programs more applicable to minority populations.

There is a distinct difference of opinion between the publishers' perception of their treatment of minority groups in basal reading programs and the perception of the school systems which adopt these materials for use. If this discrepancy is so obvious, is it not possible that a concerted effort made by school systems would effect a change in these materials? Whether the failure on the part of school systems to request material changes stems from a sense of impotency or is a product of inertia, the results are the same. Little is requested so little is accomplished. There is power in numbers as well as in size. If many small school systems were to demand specific material changes the publishers might be forced to act.

Publishers must not wait for pressure, however. Progress has been made in recent years in the development of reading programs, but it is evident that treatment of minority populations is not representative enough. Too many times the only minority group changes have been effecting the Negro within an urban setting. From the data collected there seems to be a need for presentation of Indian, Mexican, rural and Oriental populations as well. Publishers must realize that minority group and Negro are not necessarily synonymous terms. There are other minority interests prevelant in the United States. An honest effort should be made to prepare a program which would be more than "color me black".

One further implication will be mentioned. Eighty-five percent of the respondents signifying a lack of minority consideration in their basal reading adoptions cited as their reason the absense of minorities within their school population. This statement, combined with the lack of any response from the Southeast except from the states of Florida and Kentucky, poses another question. What is the purpose of producing a culturally well-balanced basal reading series? Is it to satisfy only those segments of the population who occasionally do or potentially might demand changes? Or, is it to be an attempt to present American culture in all its facets through a medium which is used by a large majority of American school children?

NOTES

1. Frank Riessman, *The Culturally Deprived Child*, New York: Harper and Row, 1962, p. 115.
2. *Ibid.*, p. 30; N. P. Criscuolo, "How Effective are Basal Readers with Culturally Disadvantaged Children?" *Elementary English*, **45** (March 1968), 364–365; A. Gordon, "Throw Out the Textbook," *American Education*, **3** (September 1967), 5–7.
3. Gaston E. Blom, Richard R. Waite, and Sara Zimet, "Content of First Grade Reading Books," *Reading Teacher*, **21** (January 1968), 317–323.
4. Helen Rogers and H. Alan Robinson, "Reading Interests of First Graders," *Elementary English*, **40** (November 1963), 707–711.
5. R. C. Ford and J. Koplyay, "Children's Story Preferences," *Reading Teacher*, **22** (December 1968), 233–237.
6. R. Emans, "What Do Children in the Inner City Like to Read?" *Elementary School Journal*, **49** (December 1968), 118–122.
7. Donald H. Ecroyd, "Negro Children and the Language Arts," *Reading Teacher*, **21** (April 1968), 624.

8. Mary Austin, *The First R*, New York: Macmillan, 1963, p. 69.
9. Peter Haggett, *Locational Analysis in Human Geography*, New York: St. Martin's Press, 1966, p. 198.

APPENDIX A. READING QUESTIONNAIRE FOR SCHOOL SYSTEMS

This questionnaire is being used in an attempt to determine what effect minority groups are having on the development and selection of basal reading programs. Please check the most appropriate response.

1. Reading, as a curriculum area:
   a. was last adopted in (year) __________
   b. is now being studied __________
   c. will be studied within the next two years __________
2. Do you have specific criteria which must be met?
   a. yes __________
   b. no __________
3. If the answer is yes, a copy is:
   a. enclosed __________
   b. unavailable __________
4. Have any of the following minority groups been influential in establishing the criteria? (rank)
   a. Negro __________
   b. Mexican __________
   c. Puerto Rican __________
   d. Oriental __________
   e. Indian __________
   f. Jewish __________
   g. Rural interests __________
   h. Urban interests __________
   i. other (specify) __________
5. Was this influence from:
   a. an organized group __________
   b. individuals __________
   c. other (specify) __________
6. Materials are examined for many qualities and certain aspects of a book might be questioned. Which are the areas of weakness you have questioned, as they pertain to minority groups? (rank)
   a. language __________
   b. illustrations __________
   c. content __________
   d. other (specify) __________
7. Has your system requested any definite material changes by publishers?
   a. yes __________
   b. no __________

8. If so, in which areas? (rank)
   a. language __________
   b. illustrations __________
   c. content __________
   d. other __________

APPENDIX B. READING QUESTIONNAIRE FOR PUBLISHERS

This questionnaire is being used to attempt to determine what effect minority groups are having on the development and selection of basal reading programs. Please check the most appropriate response.

1. Is your basal reading program:
   a. new (1965–1969) __________
   b. a recent revision (1965–1969) __________
   c. in the process of revision __________
   d. in the developmental stage __________
2. Have you made, or are you making specific references to minority groups in your materials?
   a. yes __________
   b. no __________
3. Treatment of minority groups is in the form of: (rank in order of importance)
   a. language __________
   b. illustrations __________
   c. content __________
   d. other (specify) __________
4. Have these changes been requested by school systems?
   a. none __________
   b. slight __________
   c. moderate __________
   d. extensive __________
5. Have these changes been requested by organized minority groups?
   a. none __________
   b. slight __________
   c. moderate __________
   d. extensive __________
6. Which groups have had the *most* influence in your planning? (rank)
   a. Negro __________
   b. Mexican __________
   c. Puerto Rican __________
   d. Oriental __________
   e. Indian __________
   f. Jewish __________
   g. Rural interests __________
   h. Urban interests __________
   i. other (specify) __________

HOW EFFECTIVE ARE BASAL READERS WITH CULTURALLY DISADVANTAGED CHILDREN?

Nicholas P. Criscuolo

INTRODUCTION

Basal readers have been used for reading instruction in our schools for many years. These basal texts are designed to teach reading skills sequentially. The stories read by the children are used to teach the various skills outlined in the teacher's manuals which accompany these readers.

Some critics have attacked the use of basal readers. Their specific criticisms center around the content, rigidity of vocabulary control (particularly in the primary grades), and the inflexible way some teachers use these materials. Recent attention regarding the culturally disadvantaged pupil has renewed the arguments pro and con regarding the use of basal reading materials. They particularly object to the supposedly middle-class orientation of the stories in these books. Critics have felt that culturally disadvantaged children, because of their unique values, attitudes, and backgrounds, find it hard to relate to the content of the typical basal reader.

Since 1962, efforts have been made to design basal readers with the unique needs of the culturally disadvantaged pupil in mind. Since many of these children reside in the cities, the theme of many of the new stories is urban. The story characters are biracial, and in some cases, multiracial. The vocabulary and language used in these texts now supposedly represent the natural speech patterns of these children.

Although changes have been made in style, format, and content of basal readers, some critics continue their sharp attacks on their use and advise the "courageous and effective" teacher of disadvantaged children to shift from the basic reading program to other approaches and materials.[2]

THE STUDY

How effective are basal readers for teaching reading to culturally disadvantaged children? This was one of the questions the author sought to determine in a recent study.[1] The first step was to select two schools: one from a

Nicholas P. Criscuolo, "How Effective are Basal Readers with Culturally Disadvantaged Children?" *Elementary English*, **45** (March 1968), 364–365. Reprinted with permission of the National Council of Teachers of English and Nicholas P. Criscuolo.

lower-middle class area and the other from a lower-lower class area. Warner's Index of Status Characteristics was then applied to gain objective assurance that these two schools represented these socio-economic levels.[3]

The population of the study included eighty-seven third-grade children enrolled in the New Haven public school system. Sixty-four percent of the group was Negro and thirty-six percent was Caucasian. The length of the study was six months—from September, 1965 to February, 1966.

One teacher at each school was randomly assigned to use the enrichment approach and the other the acceleration approach. Enrichment involved doing all the activities suggested in the teachers' manuals accompanying the basal readers of the series used (Houghton Mifflin *Reading for Meaning*, 1963 Edition) which included not only the skill development sections but also the enrichment sections. The two classes randomly assigned to the enrichment group spent the entire six months of the study on one reader for each reading group. Acceleration involved completing the activities suggested in the teachers' guides for skill development, but the children did not do the enrichment program. The time saved allowed each acceleration group to cover two basal readers during the course of the study rather than only one.

Pre- and post-test scores on the Metropolitan Reading Test were statistically analyzed by means of analysis of variance. F ratios proved significant at the five percent level of confidence in favor of the enrichment approach. The enrichment approach for both schools on the two reading sub-tests of the Metropolitan produced an average mean growth of 6.1 months whereas the acceleration approach produced an average of 3.2 months. Thus, the children who had used the basal texts *thoroughly* had grown significantly more than the children who used the basal readers in a more hurried fashion.

Several implications can be drawn from this study:

1) The use of the basal reader will produce highly satisfactory reading achievement if used a sufficient length of time in order to allow for complete mastery of reading skills.
2) Although enrichment is usually advocated only for superior readers, it appears that enrichment is worthwhile for children of lesser reading ability also.
3) Since the content of the basal readers used in this study was not multi-ethnic as such, it is suggested that the criticisms of the basal readers for use with culturally disadvantaged children are not completely justified.

CONCLUSION

Basal readers, if used intensively, are effective tools for skill development with culturally disadvantaged children. Although these materials can be used for effective reading instruction, the author does not suggest that they should be used to the exclusion of other materials and approaches. Rather he wishes to make the point that enrichment, offered in the context of a basal reading program, has demonstrated its usefulness with culturally disadvantaged children. Let us just remember that as we search for new ways to teach children to read competently, we should not overlook or eliminate what we already have just because something is novel or different.

REFERENCES

1. Criscuolo, Nicholas P., "A Comparison of the Enrichment and Acceleration Approaches with Children of Different Socio-Economic Backgrounds and Their Effect on Reading Achievement," unpublished doctoral dissertation. Storrs: The University of Connecticut, 1967. 137 pp.
2. Davis, Allison, "Teaching Language and Reading to Disadvantaged Negro Children," *Elementary English*, **42** (November 1965) 791–797.
3. Warner, W. Lloyd, Marchia Meeker, and Kenneth Eells, *Social Class in America*, New York: Harper and Row, 1960.

CHANGES IN ATTITUDES TOWARD NEGROES OF WHITE ELEMENTARY SCHOOL STUDENTS AFTER USE OF MULTIETHNIC READERS

John H. Litcher and David W. Johnson

This study investigated the effect of curriculum materials which portray Negroes in a way which is contradictory to prevailing prejudices and stereotypes upon the attitudes toward Negroes of white second-grade school children in a Midwestern city. A pretest-posttest design controlling for the teacher, the classroom, the school, and the reading ability of *S*s was used. The 34 children in the experimental groups used a multiethnic reader which included characters from several different racial and ethnic groups for 4 months, while the 34 children in the control groups used

John H. Litcher and David W. Johnson, "Changes in Attitudes toward Negroes of White Elementary School Students after Use of Multiethnic Readers," *Journal of Educational Psychology*, **60**, 2 (1969), 148–152. Reprinted with the permission of the authors and publisher.

the regular reader which included only whites. Use of the multiethnic reader resulted in marked positive change in *S*s' attitudes toward Negroes, supporting the counter-conditioning hypothesis.

Changing racial attitudes on a wide scale basis is one of the most important social-psychological problems of our society. It is evident that from a very early age white children are prejudiced against Negroes (Blake and Dennis, 1943; Goodman, 1948; Gregor and McPherson, 1966; Horowitz, 1936, 1939; Katz and Braly, 1933; Landreth and Johnson, 1953; Radke and Trager, 1950; Radke, Trager, and Hadassah, 1949). There is some empirical evidence which indicates that under certain conditions (which have not been adequately researched) the attitudes of whites toward Negroes may be changed through direct experience. Singer (1967), for example, in a recent study of the effects of integrated classrooms upon the racial attitudes of fifth-grade children, found that white children in integrated schools, compared with white children in segregated schools, are more accepting of Negroes and more familiar with Negro celebrities. The more intelligent the white child in the integrated school, the more favorable are his attitudes toward Negroes.

It is not possible, however, to provide every white child with direct experiences with Negroes. In Minnesota and North Dakota, for example, the Negro population is so small that such direct experiences are impossible. One alternative to direct experience with Negroes is exposure to materials which portray Negroes in a positive way, contradicting prevailing prejudices and stereotypes. Research in social perception (Allport and Postman, 1945; Bartlett, 1932) and in the learning of controversial material (Edwards, 1941; Jones and Aneshansel, 1956; Levine and Murphy, 1943) suggests that materials portraying Negroes positively would be either distorted in various ways to support the prevailing stereotypes and prejudices or ignored and quickly forgotten. Research in counter-conditioning (Bandura and Walters, 1963), however, would predict that such an approach would be effective. If, for example, the stimulus "Negro" (which elicits a negative response) is repeatedly paired with the cluster of stimuli characteristic of "middle class" (which elicits a positive response), the stimulus "Negro" wiil elicit the positive response associated with "middle class"—if the stimulus "Negro" does not elicit a more powerful response than the response elicited by the stimuli characteristic of "middle class".

An exploratory study was conducted contrasting the social perception, social learning, and the counter-conditioning hypotheses by investigating the effect of multiethnic readers upon the racial attitudes of white elementary students. Multiethnic readers are readers which contain characters from several different racial and ethnic groups. In the readers used, Negroes are portrayed as having middle-class characteristics (works hard, dresses nicely, is clean, etc.) in integrated situations.

METHOD

This study employed a pretest-posttest control group design. Experimental groups used a multiethnic reader for 4 months while control groups used the traditional reader. Both groups were interviewed before and after the experimental treatment. The study was conducted from February 1967 through May of the same year. Sixty-eight white, middle-class children were studied, 34 classified by their teachers as upper group readers and 34 classified as middle group readers. Both the multiethnic and the regular second-grade readers were used by each teacher in each classroom. Eight reading groups in four second-grade classrooms in two public elementary schools participated in the study. Through random assignment, two classrooms (one in each school) used the multiethnic reader in their upper reading group and the regular reader in their middle reading group. The other two classrooms (one in each school) used the regular reader in their upper reading group and the multiethnic reader in their middle reading group.

The four teachers who participated in the study were randomly selected from volunteers within the school system. The teachers' interest in this study was prompted by the opportunity it offered them to participate in research. They were generally informed as to the nature of the study and asked to teach the experimental and control groups as similarly as possible. Since the basal approach to reading instruction was followed, the teaching included the development of work recognition skills, comprehension skills, reading skills in other content areas, oral and silent reading, and emphasis on a personal reading program. A record of any discussion relating to race relations was requested. According to their reports, the teachers did not at any time initiate a discussion of the fact that many of the characters in the multiethnic reader were nonwhite. Neither did they encourage student discussion of the racial differences of the characters in the reader while the study was in progress. The students commented very little on the differences in race of the characters about whom they were reading. The multiethnic readers were the only multiethnic materials in the classroom.

The Scott-Foresman multiethnic (Robinson, Monroe, and Artley, 1965) and regular (Robinson, Monroe, and Artley, 1963) second-grade readers were used in the study. These readers are identical except for the pictures (some of the characters in the pictures in the multiethnic reader are nonwhite) and the names used to represent the characters of the racial and ethnic groups found in the readers.

For both the pretest and the posttest each child was interviewed individually. Four tests were presented in random order and all were given in one sitting. On the average it took 9 minutes to administer the tests. All questions were asked of each child, but answers were not made compulsory. During the 4 months of the experimental treatment three children, all in the experimental group, moved out of the school district. They were, therefore, not available for the posttest.

The study was conducted in a Midwestern city of 50,000 inhabitants. The total Negro population in this city is less than 100. Of the 6,181 children attending the city's elementary schools, 10 are Negroes. No Negro children attended the two elementary schools studied.

The instruments used in this study were a variation of the Clark Doll Test (Gregor and McPherson, 1966), the Horowitz and Horowitz (1938) "Show Me" and Categories tests, and a Direct Comparison test (Blake and Dennis, 1943). In the Clark Doll Test the children were presented with two dolls which differed only in skin color (one white, one dark brown). The children were asked to point to one doll as a response to the following questions: Show me the doll that (*a*) you would like to play with, (*b*) you like best, (*c*) is a nice doll, (*d*) has a nice color, (*e*) looks bad, (*f*) looks like a white child, (*g*) looks like a colored child, (*h*) looks like a Negro child, and (*i*) looks like you.

The "Show Me" test developed by Horowitz and Horowitz (1938) consists of 12 portraits (3 white boys, 3 white girls, 3 Negro boys, and 3 Negro girls) placed randomly on a large sheet of paper. The following questions were asked of the children: Please show me the one that (*a*) you'd like to sit next to at school, (*b*) you'd want to play with, (*c*) comes from a poor home, (*d*) you do not want in your school, (*e*) you'd like to have as your cousin, (*f*) doesn't look very smart, (*g*) you would want to come to your house for a long visit, and (*h*) you do not like.

In the Categories test (Horowitz and Horowitz, 1938) five pictures mounted on a page were presented to each child. The children were asked to reject one picture as not belonging to the group. Categories of race versus sex and race versus age were used. For example, one page might contain five pictures, three white boys, one white girl, and one Negro boy. If the Negro boy was selected as not belonging, race is a more salient category than sex for that child. If the white girl was selected, sex could be considered as the more salient category. The test was designed to analyze the strength of race, sex, and age categories for the children.

The Direct Comparison test (Blake and Dennis, 1943) required the children to make direct comparisons between Negroes and whites in regard to 18 traits. The children were asked to indicate whether the trait was more characteristic of whites or Negroes or to respond "no difference" or "don't know." Examples of the traits used are: cheerful, honest, lazy, forgetful, neat, clean, lies.

RESULTS

As part of the pretest each child was asked to respond to several questions dealing with racial identification. From Table 1 it may be seen that with the exception of one child, all the children correctly identified the dolls used in the Clark Doll Test with their appropriate racial group. From these data it may be concluded that with one possible exception, all the children studied were able to respond to questions dealing with racial membership.

Each child studied responded to four tests of racial attitudes. Since the investigators were interested only in general changes in racial attitudes resulting from the use of multiethnic readers and not in responses to the specific questions of each test a general score of favorableness of attitudes toward Negroes was derived for each child for each test. A child was given one point

Table 1. Frequency of responses of white second-grade children to items of race identification on the Clark Doll Test—Pretest

Which doll	*Multiethnic reader group*[a]		*Regular reader group*[b]	
	Negro doll	*White doll*	*Negro doll*	*White doll*
Looks like a white child	1	30	—	34
Looks like a colored child	31	—	34	—
Looks like a Negro child	31	—	34	—
Looks like you	1	30	—	34

[a] $N = 31$.
[b] $N = 34$.

for each response which indicated favorable attitudes toward Negroes. For the Clark Doll Test the range of possible scores was 0–5, for the "Show Me" test the range of possible scores was 0–8, and for the Categories test, 0–6. For the Direct Comparison test the proportion of responses favorable to Negroes was used, the possible range of scores being from 0–100 percent.

In order to see if the tests were independent of each other the responses of the children to the four tests were correlated. From Table 2 it may be seen that the tests were only slightly correlated and, therefore, the data for each were analyzed separately.

On all tests there were no significant differences between the experimental and control group on the pretests. In order to control for slight differences between the groups, however, an analysis of covariance was used in analyzing the results of the posttest. The data in Table 3 indicate that on all four tests

Table 2. Correlations between tests of racial attitudes—pretest and posttest

Racial attitude tests correlated	*Pretest*	*Posttest*
Clark Doll and Show Me Test	.19	.25
Clark Doll and Categories Test	.13	.08
Clark Doll and Direct Comparison Test	.12	.35
Show Me and Categories Test	−.08	.22
Show Me and Direct Comparison Test	.22	.26
Categories and Direct Comparison Test	.17	.18

Note.—$N = 65$.

Table 3. Comparison of attitudes toward negroes of white second-grade children—posttest

Test	*Multiethnic reader group*[a]	*Regular reader group*[b]	*Significance*
Clark Doll Test (Range: 0–5)	1.39	0.44	$F = 15.90$; $p < .0002$
Show Me Test (Range: 0–8)	2.58	1.47	$F = 8.71$; $p < .005$
Categories Test (Range: 0–6)	4.42	3.44	$F = 4.38$; $p < .04$
Direct Comparison Test	51%	24%	$F = 14.94$; $p < .0003$

Note.—The higher the score the more favorable the attitudes toward Negroes. An analysis of covariance was used in analyzing the data.
[a] $N = 31$.
[b] $N = 34$.

the children using the multiethnic readers responded significantly more favorably toward Negroes than the children using the regular readers.

DISCUSSION

The results of this study dramatically indicate that the use of multiethnic readers in an elementary school will result in more favorable attitudes toward Negroes. The data from the Clark Doll Test indicate that the use of the multiethnic reader decreased the preference for one's own racial group over the other. While the control group expressed marked preferences for the white rather than the Negro doll, the experimental group *S*s were far less unanimous about their preferences.

In a recent study on the Clark Doll Test, Greenwald and Oppenheim (1967) report that 19 percent of the white children they interviewed (taking their more conservative figure) identified the Negro doll in response to the question, "Show me the doll that looks like you". In an earlier study Morland (1963) found that 14 percent of the white children interviewed responded similarly. Greenwald and Oppenheim (1967) concluded on the basis of these findings that the amount of Negro misidentification found in the Clark and Clark (1940) and other similar studies is misleading as they did not have a control group of white children. The present study (1.5 percent white misidentification) and the study of Gregor and McPherson (1966; 0 percent white misidentification) give no support to their findings or their conclusion.

On the "Show Me" test, the use of the multiethnic reader resulted in a reduction of the amount of social distance placed between the white and Negro racial groups. On the Categories test, the children in the experimental group were less likely to exclude a child on the basis of race than were the controls. The data for the Direct Comparisons test, furthermore, indicate that the experimental *S*s were less likely to attribute negative traits to Negroes and positive traits to whites than were the control *S*s. Examination of the individual items revealed that the experimental group basically became equalitarian in their response. Johnson (1967) found that Negro children who were taught Negro history in a Freedom School became much more convinced that Negroes and whites are equal. Thus, the use of the multiethnic reader had much the same effect on white children as learning Negro history had upon Negro children.

The evidence is quite clear. Through the use of a multiethnic reader, white children developed markedly more favorable attitudes toward Negroes. Under the conditions of this experiment, this finding supports the counter-conditioning hypothesis and does not support the social-perception and social-learning hypothesis. The implications of this finding hardly need elaboration. While it is not possible, due to lack of material resources and the distribution of the Negro population in the United States, for every white child to have direct experiences with Negroes (although the investigators believe it is desirable), it is possible to increase the visibility of the Negro in the curriculum materials of the schools. Such an action should, through the reduction of prejudice, increase racial harmony.

A limitation on the generalization of the results of this study should be noted. The Negro population in the city in which this study was conducted is quite small (Negroes make up less than .2 percent of the total population of the city). The probability is very high that the children participating in the study had no direct experience with Negroes and that the Negro community does not represent an economic or social threat to the white community. The racial attitudes of the children studied, therefore, are probably not firmly rooted in direct experiences or reference group norms.

REFERENCES

Allport, G. W., and L. J. Postman, "The Basic Psychology of Rumor," *Transactions of the New York Academy of Sciences*, Series II, **8** (1945), 61–81.

Bandura, A., and H. Walters, *Social Learning and Personality Development*, New York: Holt, Rinehart & Winston, 1963.

Bartlett, F. C., *Remembering*. Cambridge: Cambridge University Press, 1932.

Blake, R., and W. Dennis, "The Development of Stereotypes Concerning the Negro", *Journal of Abnormal and Social Psychology*, **38** (1943), 525–531.

Clark, H. B., and M. K. Clark, "Skin Color as a Factor in Racial Identification of Negro Preschool Children," *Journal of Social Psychology*, **11** (1940), 160.

Edwards, A. L., "Political Frames of References as a Factor Influencing Recognition," *Journal of Abnormal and Social Psychology*, **36** (1941), 34–50.

Goodman, M. E., "Evidence Concerning the Genesis of Interracial Attitudes," *American Anthropologist*, **48** (1946), 624–630.

Greenwald, H. J., and D. B. Oppenheim, "Reported Magnitude of Self-misidentification Among Negro Children—Artifact?" *Journal of Personality and Social Psychology*, **8** (1968), 49–52.

Gregor, A. J., and D. A. McPherson, "Racial Attitudes Among White and Negro Children in a Deep-South Standard Metropolitan Area," *Journal of Social Psychology*, **68** (1966), 95–106.

Horowitz, E., "The Development of Attitude Toward the Negro," *Archives of Psychology*, **194** (1936), 5–47.

Horowitz, R. E., "Racial Aspects of Self-identification in Nursery School Children," *Journal of Psychology*, **7** (1939), 91–99.

Horowitz, L., and R. E. Horowitz, "Development of Social Attitudes in Children," *Sociometry*, **1** (1938), 301–339.

Johnson, D. W., "The Effects of a Freedom School on its Students," in R. Dentler, B. Mackler, and M. E. Warshauer, Eds., *The Urban R's: Race Relations as the Problem in Urban Education*, New York: Praeger, 1967.

Jones, E. E., and J. Aneshansel, "The Learning and Utilization of Contravaluant Material," *Journal of Abnormal and Social Psychology*, **53** (1956), 27–33.

Katz, D., and K. W. Braly, "Racial Stereotypes of One Hundred College

Students," *Journal of Abnormal and Social Psychology*, **28** (1939), 280–290.

Landreth, C., and B. C. Johnson, "Young Children's Responses to a Picture and Insert Test Designed to Reveal Reactions to Persons of Different Skin Color," *Child Development*, **24** (1953), 63–80.

Levine, J. M., and G. Murphy, "The Learning and Forgetting of Controversial Material," *Journal of Abnormal and Social Psychology*, **38** (1943), 507–517.

Morland, J. K., "Racial Self-identification: A Study of Nursery School Children," *American Catholic Sociological Review*, **24** (1963), 231–242.

Radke, M. J., and H. G. Trager, "Children's Perception of the Social Roles of Negroes," *Journal of Psychology*, **29** (1950), 3–33.

Radke, M. J., H. G. Trager, and D. Hadassah, "Social Perceptions and Attitudes of Children," *Genetic Psychology Monograph*, **40** (1949), 327–447.

Robinson, H. M., M. Monroe, and A. S. Artley, *New More Friends and Neighbors 2–2* and *New Friends and Neighbors 2–1*, Chicago: Scott, Foresman, 1963.

Robinson, H. M., M. Monroe, and A. S. Artley, *More Friends Old and New 2–2* and *Friends Old and New 2–1*, Chicago: Scott, Foresman, 1965.

Singer, D. "The Influence of Intelligence and an Interracial Classroom on Social Attitudes," in R. Dentler, B. Mackler, and M. E. Warshauer, Eds., *The Urban R's: Race Relations as the Problem in Urban Education*. New York: Praeger, 1967.

ENGLISH AS A SECOND LANGUAGE

Richard D. Arnold

INTRODUCTION

Of major concern to many educators is the large number of Mexican-American children who are disadvantaged. In Texas the problem is statewide. Past records indicate that up to 80 percent of these children repeat the first grade, probably because of their inability to read (Texas Education Agency, 1962). Mass failure and deficient reading appear symptomatic of a more funda-

Richard D. Arnold, "English as a Second Language," *The Reading Teacher*, **21** (April 1968), 634–639. Reprinted with the permission of Richard D. Arnold and the International Reading Association.

mental problem. Many of these children have little knowledge of English, the language of instruction in the schools.

In an effort to accelerate growth in English language skills through direct instruction, the San Antonio Language Research Project under the direction of Thomas D. Horn was inaugurated in 1964 as one of twenty-seven first grade reading projects sponsored by the U.S. Office of Education Co-operative Research Project number 2648 (Horn, 1966a). What appears to be a highly successful method of teaching English to children using science as the content vehicle has resulted. Up to this time the highly structured Developmental Oral Language (DOL) program has been taught in first, second, and third grade classrooms.

Though they may have learned to speak English more effectively, data from standardized reading tests indicate that the children receiving the Developmental Oral Language program have not made significant gains in reading. Indeed, the transfer effects from the DOL program in science to the reading content may have been less for the experimental groups than the transfer effects from incidental language development to the reading content for the control groups. What appears to have happened is that the language patterns, vocabulary, and content of the basal reading materials have not been particularly related to the oral language patterns, vocabulary, and content of the DOC program.

It became apparent that it was necessary to establish a closer relationship between oral language and reading. It seemed imprudent to discard the language program specifically designed to teach English to these children and replace it with a language program centered around basal readers designed for an essentially different pupil population. This action appears even more imprudent when one considers the inappropriateness of the middle-class orientation of basal readers for an atypical, disadvantaged population. Another and seemingly more reasonable alternative was selected. A decision was made to develop reading materials centered around the DOL program with its structured experiences in the "culture fair" science content.

The Southwest Educational Development Laboratory, Austin, Texas, sponsored a summer writing seminar in 1967 to develop reading methods and materials that would be complementary to the existing oral language and science programs.

UNDERLYING ASSUMPTIONS

Several assumptions were made in considering the most appropriate way to teach reading to disadvantaged children who are learning English as a second language or dialect. The assumptions are based in part on observation of and experience with the population under study and in part on inferences drawn from reported research on similar children. To date, insufficient empirical data have been gathered to validate these assumptions on the particular population being studied. However, the assumptions seem reasonable and applicable.

First, the disadvantaged Mexican-American children begin school with a highly different experiential background from the more typical Anglo children. Many have never been out of the city limits or have "seen" the country mainly from the rear of a migrant truck, the rate of broken homes is extremely high, and have other environmental deficits associated with disadvantagedness.

Second, these children in general are underdeveloped in visual-perceptual abilities associated with success in learning to read. Relative to other factors, however, this subset of skills is more highly developed than those discussed below. Visual-perceptual factors then are considered a strength in this population.

Third, the children's knowledge of English is highly inadequate, and their expressive abilities are even more depressed than their level of understanding.

Fourth, the auditory perception-discrimination abilities associated with success in beginning reading are grossly underdeveloped in the children. Not only can they not understand what is being said, they cannot discriminate between the differences in many of the sounds being uttered by their teachers. Indeed, some sounds used regularly in English are not even present in Spanish.

EMPHASES IN THE EXPERIMENTAL PROGRAM

With the above assumptions in mind, the writing team devised a method of teaching reading that emphasizes the following:

1. The content of the reading material follows the content of the existent DOL program, science.
2. The experimental reading program utilizes the experiences which are universal to all children in the DOL program.
3. The experimental reading program primarily utilizes the English language patterns which have been learned by all children.
4. The experimental reading program capitalizes on the relative strengths of visual-perceptual skills of these children while strengthening the relative weaknesses of the language associated skills outside of the reading lesson.
5. The experimental reading program emphasizes reading for meaning and understanding.
6. The experimental reading program assures systematic evaluation of reading progress.

The reading content emerges in expository form rather than literary form. The children learn to read about what they have seen and described in their science lessons. With the heavy emphasis on physical rather than life sciences in the AAAS Science program, the resultant reading materials remain primarily at the descriptive level.

Since it is assumed that these children come to school with meager experiences, it was decided to use experiences obtained directly in the classroom through the science curricula. Science lessons commence early in the school year, and reading is delayed until some oral facility is established. Thus, the children have learned the concepts they are to read about before they face the reading task. In this manner, control is exerted over the background of meaning the children bring to the reading task.

The Developmental Oral Language (DOL) program provides for the direct teaching of English language patterns associated with the science materials developed by the American Association for the Advancement of Science (AAAS). That is, the AAAS content is the vehicle around which natural English language patterns are taught. These patterns or sentences which are largely of a descriptive nature are taught using techniques developed in the field of teaching English as a second language. Thus, the children learn the language of science through teacher modeling and child response procedures. The children receive extensive and intensive practice in English language patterns which ultimately are habituated. It should be noted that the science-based language appears to be unique in the sense that these first grade children who are noticeably deficient in their general English language development are quite proficient in describing science materials. It is not unusual to observe a first grade child walk up to a table containing science materials, and accurately describe an object by saying, "This is a rectangular prism. It is a three dimensional shape. It has length and width and thickness."

A major thesis of the experimental reading program is that the teaching method emphasizes the relative strengths of the population being taught. Their weaknesses should be "remediated" outside of the reading program. This means that the visual modality is used extensively and that word recognition is initially taught primarily through visual analysis skills. Children learn to look carefully at words and word parts, as well as morpheme-grapheme correspondences. Phonetic analysis skills are developed as the child's speech improves, thereby eliminating problems which would be confusing to these children if usual phonics instruction is utilized.

The de-emphasis on training in phonics in the beginning reading program should not be construed as a lack of concern for the development of the more phonological oral-aural skills. The point here is that it is deemed very important that special curricular provision should be made to develop these skills. The DOL program and the broader language arts program *do* contain highly structured lessons to remediate these deficits. With this provision, the teacher during reading lesson is relieved of trying to teach children how to hear and say unfamiliar sounds while she also tries to teach them unfamiliar graphic symbols—that is, words.

Many authorities in the field of reading emphasize the need to make reading a meaningful experience. Yet, the research on children's vocabularies upon entering school suggests that the typical first grade child comes to the reading materials with listening and speaking vocabularies sufficient to cope adequately with the meanings. The disadvantaged Mexican-American population of concern here clearly does not. Therefore, meaningful referents and understanding become a critical focus for the reading program.

Several factors are involved. *First*, the science content, preceding the reading program as it does, insures the presence of experiences and concepts needed to understand the printed page. *Second*, all reading occurs within previously learned and habituated oral language patterns. Thus, the reading content becomes a visual representation of the children's language. *Third*, the children learn to read a full sentence at a time. The sentence represents the habituated language pattern and is a full meaning bearing unit. *Fourth*, the teaching method always proceeds from the known to the unknown, from larger units to smaller units. That is, first the children learn several sentences of a similar linguistic structure which is then followed by learning to recognize the language pattern itself, learning individual words which substitute into the slot of that language pattern, and finally learning the individual elements which make the words graphically unique. *Fifth*, word recognition skills are taught from meaningful referents; i.e., known words.

The last emphasis for the experimental reading program is that careful evaluation of the children's reading progress is made. It is considered essential to determine whether or not each child has successfully learned the vocabulary and language patterns taught. Specially constructed evaluation activity sheets based on behavioral objectives for each lesson have been diagnostically designed to determine success or failure. These evaluation sheets accompany every reading lesson. The tests have been designed so that the teacher can see which children have learned the lesson and which have not. For those who have not, it can be further determined exactly which word or language pattern has not been learned. With proper use of these evaluations, the teacher will be able to structure carefully lessons for reteaching to eliminate specific weaknesses of the children.

THE READING METHOD

The experimental reading program utilizes some of the teaching procedures developed in the field of teaching English as a second language. At the beginning of every reading lesson, the teacher reviews orally with the class the language patterns and concepts previously developed in the DOL program. In this procedure a teacher-children dialogue occurs. At this point the teacher typically does not have to model the language patterns except when they emerge incorrectly from the children. Hand gestures indicating "listen" and "talk" accompany the structured dialogue.

Once the language pattern is elicited, the teacher then writes the pattern on the chalkboard. A key procedure for the teacher in the reading method is to say, "Watch me while I write." She then writes the language pattern. When completed, the teacher using one hand signal to tell the children to listen, models the language pattern orally as she simultaneously uses a sweeping left to right gesture under the written language pattern with the other hand. The teacher repeats this procedure an appropriate number of times. She then gives the response hand signal and uses the sweeping gesture as the children respond orally as a group.

The preplanning phase of the lessons is critically important. The teacher must plan carefully the specific questions to ask the children in order to elicit the proper language patterns as responses. Another critical element is the teacher's awareness of the composition of certain language patterns. Different types of language patterns require different types of class participation.

The experimental reading method is similar in many respects to the sentence method of past years. This method, of course, has as its strength the development of the sense of meaning in a sentence. It brings to the child's attention that thoughts are expressed in sentences. The sentence method, however, is only one aspect of the experimental program. Word recognition skills are also stressed. Focus on individual words occurs in the same lesson but within the context of the language patterns. Activities such as matching words with word cards and framing individual words are stressed.

The experimental reading method is somewhat related to the language experience approach to teaching reading. The difference, however, is that the experimental program is highly structured and utilizes preplanned concepts, language patterns, and experience charts.

A final important characteristic of the experimental reading method is the evaluation activities. For every lesson involving new material to be learned, child behavioral objectives are established. Specific terminal behaviors, usually the reading of certain words or language patterns, are written down in the lesson plan objectives for the teacher. Upon completion of the lesson, evaluation activities are presented to them. Each behavior specified in the objectives is then "tested" with a cluster of items on the activity sheet.

This method, based on a set of assumptions different from what is typically used for the general population in developing reading methods and materials, will be field tested on a limited scale this year. It is hoped that some progress will be made toward developing a method to improve the reading of disadvantaged children learning English as a second language.

REFERENCES

Horn, T. D., *A Study of the Effects of Intensive Oral-aural Spanish Language Instruction, Oral-aural English Language Instruction, and Non-oral-aural Instruction on Reading Readiness in Grade One*, Austin: University of Texas, 1966.

Horn, T. D., "Three Methods of Developing Reading Readiness in Spanish Speaking Children in First Grade," *The Reading Teacher*, **20** (1966), 38–42.

Ott, Elizabeth H., *A Study of Levels of Fluency and Proficiency in Oral English of Spanish-speaking School Beginners*, Austin: University of Texas, 1966.

Texas Education Agency, *The Preschool Instructional Program for Non-English Speaking Children*, Austin: Texas Education Agency, 1962.

INDIAN CHILDREN AND THE READING PROGRAM

William L. E. Philion and
Charles G. Galloway

"In an area where facts are few and speculation runs high, it is perhaps inevitable and to the good that people should look far afield for bodies of fact and theory that might be relevant. The price paid for this intellectual speed-trawling, however, is that some far-fetched ideas occasionally capture the imaginations of people who do not understand them well enough to appreciate their fundamental irrelevance."[1] Such has been the case with reference to many of the problems of Indian education. Solutions to questions which range from what the language arts program should include, to whether Indian schools should be integrated, are commonly sought far afield from the area in which the problem exists. If the problems are to be solved, however, much more data than are available at present must be gathered and analyzed in terms of immediate relevance to the problems at hand. This becomes especially true when considering a basic question such as the reading achievement

William L. E. Philion and Charles G. Galloway, "Indian Children and the Reading Program," *Journal of Reading*, **12** (April 1969), 553–560, 598–602. Reprinted with the permission of William L. E. Philion, Charles G. Galloway, and the International Reading Association.

of a certain group of children, for example, the Indian children of a certain specified population.

Going far afield for bodies of fact and theory that might be relevant to the problem of reading difficulty among certain Indian children leads to a consideration of many possible explanations for the difficulty. Among the possibilities available for consideration is Bereiter and Engelmann's suggestion that cultural deprivation be looked at as language deprivation.[1] Lest we err, however, in our zeal to do missionary work among the disadvantaged, we must be cautious in bringing this promising but far-fetched idea, born of the Negro ghetto, to the Indian reservation.

Language deprivation among disadvantaged Negro children, referred to by Bereiter and Engelmann, seems to center around two special weaknesses of language usage that are of primary importance for success in school. "One is the tendency to treat sentences as *giant words* that cannot be taken apart and recombined. This leads to an inflexible kind of language that does not make use of the full potentialities of the grammar and syntax, and it makes the learning of new vocabulary and structures more difficult. The second weakness . . . is a failure to master the use of structural words and inflections which are necessary for the expression and manipulation of logical relationships. The problem for culturally deprived children is not so much learning to speak in sentences as learning to speak in sentences that are composed of discrete words."[1]

Before setting about the construction of a language arts program for Indian children in order to take advantage of these interesting findings with regard to language disadvantage of Negro children, it is necessary first to question whether language disadvantage of Negro children is in fact isomorphic with or even similar to that of certain Indian children. We must ask about the nature and extent of language disadvantage of the population of Indian children in question and then on the basis of the answers we are able to arrive at, try to formulate a language arts program for that specific group of children. Do Indian children show the special weaknesses of language development which seem to be characteristic of lower-class non-Indian children? That is, do they tend to treat sentences as *giant words* and also fail to master the use of structural words and inflections which are necessary for the expression and manipulation of logical relationships? If so, are these the only weaknesses of the language development of certain Indian children?

There are several related ways of going about seeking this kind of information. Two approaches which are reported here have to do with direct observation of children and item analysis of children's responses made to diagnostic test items. Both approaches have the property of being complementary to each other and in addition immediately available to the classroom teacher who, in the final analysis, carries the responsibility for the implementation of all learning programs.

BACKGROUND

The approach being followed in the present attempt to identify specific difficulties in the language development of a specific group of Indian children in the elementary grades and then to plan a language arts program for them involves going far afield for the idea that it might be useful to consider cultural deprivation as language deprivation and then to question how this general idea might be relevant to the particular language and reading difficulties of a certain group of children. The general methods of procedure become that of teacher observations of language patterns of Indian children and item analysis of responses made to diagnostic test items. Information so gathered then serves as clues, giving guidance for the construction of meaningful language arts experiences. Item analysis of responses to tests, such as those in reading, is an absolute must if tests of this sort are to be useful in terms of planning new learning experiences for disadvantaged children. It isn't very helpful simply to know that certain children are reading at a particular level. Knowledge of a grade placement score really provides no information with regard to what the learning experiences should be. This information is available only through careful observation of children's daily behavior and item analysis of the responses children make to specific test items.

The children involved in the present study are residents of a community on Vancouver Island in British Columbia. The area is composed predominantly of loggers and farmers numbering approximately 15,000. The data presented represent reading test scores and observations made by teachers of a group of Indian and non-Indian children from this area. All the children are in the intermediate grades (grades four-seven) of the integrated elementary school. The total school population is approximately 225, of which one third are Indian children.

In September these children were grouped for reading on the basis of their grade placement scores on the Gates Reading Survey, Form One. There were three groups:

Group I . . . . grade placement 2.5–4.5
Group II . . . . grade placement 4.5–6.0
Group III . . . . grade placement 6.0–above

Throughout the school year, September–June, the children were instructed in more or less a conventional reading program as outlined by West, Bowers and Parliament.[5] In June, Form Two of the Gates Reading Survey was administered. The score reflecting achievement levels and increases for various sections of the test were recorded for all Indian and non-Indian children.

Test results from this reading program indicated a difference both for level of achievement and gains made by Indian and non-Indian pupils. These

Table 1. Comparison between Indian and non-Indian children of scores made from September to June on speed, comprehension and vocabulary sub-tests of the Gates reading survey

Reading Speed

Date	*Group*	*Number*	*Mean*	*S*	*t*
Sept.	Indian	28	13.46	4.50	4.13*
	Non-Indian	36	18.47	5.09	
June	Indian	28	17.00	4.29	3.66*
	Non-Indian	36	20.93	5.49	

*(p < .05)

Reading Comprehension

Date	*Group*	*Number*	*Mean*	*S*	*t*
Sept.	Indian	28	17.89	4.84	2.25*
	Non-Indian	36	20.50	4.27	
June	Indian	28	18.94	4.41	4.84*
	Non-Indian	36	25.07	5.52	

*(p < .05)

Reading Vocabulary

Date	*Group*	*Number*	*Mean*	*S*	*t*
Sept.	Indian	28	23.18	4.43	2.23*
	Non-Indian	36	26.00	5.53	
June	Indian	28	26.29	5.18	5.64*
	Non-Indian	36	33.12	5.55	

*(p < .05)

results, reported in terms of achievement level and gains made for vocabulary, comprehension and speed, are presented in Table 1.

It is immediately apparent that the Indian children do not achieve as well as the non-Indian children in any of the areas of reading. It is also apparent that increases made in vocabulary and comprehension by Indian children are significantly less than those made by non-Indian children (Table 2) during the ten-month school year.

These observations suggest that as time progresses Indian children fall further and further behind non-Indian children in reading achievement. In fact, it is noted that by the end of a ten-month period, achievement for this

Table 2. Comparisons between Indian and non-Indian children of increases from September to June, on speed, comprehension and vocabulary sub-tests of the Gates reading survey

Groups	*Number*	*Mean Scores* *September*	*June*	*Increases*	*Standard Deviation*	*t*
Speed						
Indian	28	13.46	17.00	3.54	4.93	.86
Non-Indian	36	18.47	20.93	2.46	4.55	
Comprehension						
Indian	28	17.89	18.94	1.05	4.33	2.75*
Non-Indian	36	20.50	25.07	4.57	5.60	
Vocabulary						
Indian	28	23.18	26.29	3.11	5.29	2.70*
Non-Indian	36	26.00	33.12	7.12	6.21	

*($p < .05$)

group of Indian children has not reached the non-Indian's initial (September) level of achievement.

Although increases made in reading speed are not significantly different for the two groups, the Indian children read much slower than the non-Indian children. However, when one examines the relatively poor gains made by the Indian children in vocabulary and comprehension, their normal gain made in reading speed leads one to suspect that perhaps these children are really gaining only in word-naming skill rather than in understanding of word concepts. Whereas the non-Indian children appear to achieve satisfactorily, the Indian children do not. This suggests that the conventional reading program designed essentially for non-Indian children is not adequate for Indian children.

ITEM ANALYSIS AND OBSERVATION: A MODEL

In the past it has been common practice among teachers to gather from tests grade placement information about children and then to use this information as an aid for grouping. For the most part, such a practice has proved to be fairly successful when considering progress of average white children for whom reading programs are essentially designed. However, when one is concerned with progress of less advantaged groups, for example, certain groups of Indian children, it becomes apparent that the design and methodology of the reading program must be modified. It is questionable to generalize a reading program designed for *all* children to a group of *similar* children in any specific classroom; it is even more questionable to generalize such a program to a specific group which shows the wide range of differences displayed in culturally integrated classrooms.

When grade placement scores are used as a major variable in grouping children for reading, the assumption is often made that the important differences among children are those of reading rate (amount of material covered to date, number of books completed, . . .) rather than the kinds of language experiences to which children have been exposed. Test scores used for this purpose have the limitation of not providing information with regard to exactly what the reading program should include for each group, let alone for each individual. It is not sufficient to apply the same program to all children even if at different rates. This view is in agreement with current thinking; for example, Stones[4] believes that extending the range of experience to children who are backward will not automatically remedy existing difficulties. He suggests that a systematic attack on the specific deficiencies underlying failure to learn is needed. That is to say, even a continuous progress approach is inadequate. Individualization must occur. However, before a teacher can individualize a reading program, he must be able to determine the specific strengths and difficulties of each child.

PROCEDURE

Those teachers involved in this study were dissatisfied with the progress in reading being made by most of the Indian children. The teachers felt the reading program was not very meaningful in terms of helping certain Indian children progress at a satisfactory level. Over a period of time these children tended to fall further and further behind the non-Indian children in all areas of reading, especially in vocabulary and comprehension as measured by the Gates Reading Test. Even though the teachers were well aware of the fact most Indian children were not progressing satisfactorily, they found the grade placement scores of little value in offering suggestions for modification of the reading program. What the teachers desired for planning language experiences was a method of making effective use of information at hand, especially of their observations of language patterns and children's responses to test items.

The teachers were instructed in a technique of conducting an item analysis of the children's responses to reading test items. They were also given instruction in making and recording careful observations of language patterns of children.

In conducting an item analysis the teachers recorded all incorrect responses made to all test items. This was done by listing the number of each test item in rows on squared grid paper. Identification numbers assigned to children were listed in columns. The number of the incorrect response, as well as an *X* for omissions was recorded for each child in a separate square to the right of the item number in the column assigned that child.

With this procedure an examination of the incorrect responses by rows results in a graphic representation of the frequency with which particular items are missed by the group as a whole as well as an indication of the specific kinds of errors the group is making. An examination of the incorrect responses by columns provides information about each child with regard to his specific strengths and weaknesses on that reading sub-test; furthermore, this examination provides specific information which may serve as a basis for grouping according to similar strengths or deficiencies rather than simply grouping on the basis of grade placement scores.

As a result of following the procedure outlined above, the teachers were able to detect specific strengths and deficiencies of each child. At the same time they gained specific information about the total group's performance on each item tested. The simple act of recording the students' responses in such a manner made it immediately apparent that there was no alternative for flexible grouping, and that grouping must be based on the need for specific kinds of experiences.

Their results indicated that for some kinds of reading experiences the class could be treated as one group. For other kinds of specific reading experiences, however, their results suggested the formation of groups of one or more on a temporary basis.

Examination of their data revealed that certain children were having difficulty in the areas of vocabulary and comprehension because of very limited and narrow concept development; for example, the concept *combat*, for most of the Indian children and to a lesser degree non-Indian children, meant *army* . . . the specific army involved in the television program "Combat." Another example of certain children's limited and narrow concept development was evidenced through observation of their language responses to the meaning they attached to the word *core*. For many Indian children this word held no meaning; an applecore was simply the *bones* of an apple. The word *leaf* for many of these children meant only the leaf of a maple tree. The word leaf did not refer to the leaves of other trees in the area, for example, evergreen leaves, not to mention the leaves in a book or magazine. Imagine the meaning for these children of a teacher's direction: "Leaf through your book, please." (The teachers observed that when given this direction the children did turn their pages at the command, suggesting they understood the meaning of leaf in this context. Upon closer observation, however, it was also noticed that many children turned pages only after others started to do so, indicating they were imitating the behavior of others.)

Other sources of difficulty in concept formation for certain children within the specific areas of vocabulary and comprehension were found to involve the following examples:

1. Word configuration: *inspiration* chosen as a synonym for *vibration* from a choice of *offense, inspiration, spirit, flying, shaking; adventurous* chosen as a synonym for *tumultuous* from a choice of *fluffy, grand, cloudy, adventurous, disorderly.*
2. Word sounds: *growl*, chosen as a synonym for *haul* from a choice of *push, hold, drag, tear, growl.*
3. Confusion of synonyms with antonyms: *little* chosen as synonym for *big* from a choice of *little*, *large*, *easy*, *new*, *fix*.
4. Confusion in the identification of word roots: *embrace* chosen as a synonym for *bracelet* from a choice of *jewelry, pair, tool, embrace, splint; tale* chosen as a synonym for *talent* from a choice of *trade, time, prize, skill, tale*.
5. Environmental influences: *arrive* chosen as a synonym for *overcome* from a choice of *play, fear, cut, arrive, defeat; hymn* chosen as a synonym for *miracle* from a choice of *hymn, wonder, peak, atom, shackle; group* chosen as a synonym for *massacre* from a choice of *group, enlarge, manage, slaughter, section.*

The teachers were at a loss to explain conceptual errors such as those listed in section 5 above in terms of the usual deficiencies in word attack skills. It was only through careful observation that a logical explanation could be made for such choices. The explanations seemed to lie in environmental experiences; for example, it was learned through talking with the children that *arrive* meant *come over*, hence *overcome*; that *hymn* and *miracle* were terms heard frequently in church; and, a *group* of people attended *mass*, hence, *massacre*. There were many additional examples of how item analysis helped these teachers focus their observations in an attempt to discover explanations for incorrect responses. It was learned that for many children the words *cool* and *cold* could be associated only with winter and hence could not be understood when used as adjectives to modify nouns such as *clothes* and *lemonade*. Limited environmental experiences were again evidenced in many Indian children's belief that plant life depends upon soil to the exclusion of other necessities, light, water and air. Sailing vessels of all kinds are *boats* and only boats for most of these children. *Ship* refers to an airplane. In similar fashion, the word *fashion* exists for only a small number of these children and then only in the context of something being *old-fashioned*. Fashion in the sense of style, or a conventional manner simply has no meaning.

Observations which derived from the process of item analysis led to observations in other areas of language development. It was observed that for purposes of getting along socially and of self-expression, language was more a convienience than a necessity for the young Indian child. It was quite possible to make one's wants known, to enter actively into play and other social relationships, and to give vent to one's feelings with little or no use of language. As Bereiter and Engelmann[1] point out, young deaf children do this and it appears that Indian children also rely to a considerable extent on nonverbal means for these purposes. Language is apparently dispensable enough in the life of the young Indian child for an occasional child to get along without it altogether. Frequently was the report given by these teachers of instances in which a child failed to speak even a single word in class for periods of time extending to months. Such children, however, were often indistinguishable from their peers in other areas of behavior, for example participation in games on the playground.

Furthermore, it was observed that certain Indian children tended to be weak in their ability to make effective use of connecting words such as prepositions and conjunctions. Rather than following through with appropriate responses cued by certain verbal directions, many Indian children seemed to rely on nonverbal cues provided by the teacher for information on what response to make. The important cues for appropriate responding to directions such as "please go around the desk," or "line up in front of the door," seemed to be pointing, looking and other gestures made by the teacher while giving the direction, or the behavior of some child who understood the verbal direction. Upon close observation, it was discovered that nearly all verbal directions were accompanied by a variety of nonverbal cues. With experimenting it soon became apparent that without nonverbal cues many Indian children were not able to follow through with responses appropriate to the requests.

Typically speech of the Indian children seemed to consist not of distinct words, but rather of whole phrases or sounds that function like huge words. Expressions such as "What are you doing?" sounded like "Wa-ch-dn?"; "Where are you going?" like "Whr-ya-gn?" These *large words* which come to stand for the complete expression are not really uncommon in non-Indian language patterns. They occur frequently in the everyday conversation of most English-speaking groups. In fact, as Bereiter and Englemann[1] find with certain Negro children, once the listener, and for that matter even the teacher has become accustomed to this type of speech, the teacher may actually begin to hear it as if all the sounds were there, and may get the impression that articles, conjunctions, prepositions, and so forth are being heard when in reality there may only be a pause where the ommitted word should be. The teacher may believe the child is using these words when in fact he may be using one sound for all of them or leaving them out entirely.

This pattern of early speech development could be expected to create more of a problem for Indian and other groups with language handicaps than for middle-class white children. Whereas white children have in their repertoire of responses the necessary information to fill in the hurried-phrases, Indian children do not seem to recognize that their *large words* are a kind of substitute for a more explicit and precise phrase. For many of these young Indian children, the *large words* are all there is to an expression. And such inflexibility of words to combine and re-combine, to be transformed from statements to questions, and so on, presents serious difficulties for young Indian children in learning to read.

DISCUSSION

Language becomes a virtual necessity when one moves from the social uses of language to the transmission of knowledge from one person to another and to the performance of certain operations with concepts[1]. From what was observed by teachers about verbal communication in many Indian homes, it would appear that the cognitive uses of language are severely restricted, especially in communication between adults and children. Language appears to be used primarily to control behavior, to express feelings and to a degree emotions, and to keep the social machinery of the home running smoothly. These, of course, are important uses of language. Many Indian people seem more skillful in them than better-educated non-Indian people. Especially skillful are Indian people and even very young Indian children in completely nonverbal communication. Indian children learn early to pay particular attention to nonverbal directional cues from parents as well as brothers and sisters in order to gain information about how they should behave. These children display remarkable ability in visual discrimination and in imitating the behavior of others. With no verbal directions at all, even very young Indian children, ages four or five, follow complicated sets of directions.

What appears to be lacking, however, is the Indian child's use of language to explain, to describe, to instruct, to inquire, to compare, to analyze and so forth. And as pointed out by Bereiter and Englemann,[1] who found very similar language difficulties in culturally deficient Negro children, these are the very uses that are not developed in Indian homes to the degree normally observed in middle-class white homes because deliberate verbal teaching does not seem to be a normal or necessary part of the adult Indian role. Hence, neither the skills nor the language peculiar to teaching are developed and maintained. Bernstein[2] discusses similar language difficulties among other disadvantaged children. He refers to this distinction as public and formal language development.

Language deprivation, then, has a double edge. The Indian child is not without language, but he is deprived of that part of language that can only be acquired through verbal teaching—the knowledge, the meanings, the explanations, the ability to question in search of information. Beyond that, the child seems to spend his early childhood in an environment where verbal teaching does not frequently take place and where language with which verbal teaching is carried out is not used; therefore, he may never learn *how* to be taught, and when he is exposed to the typical verbal teaching of the classroom, he may behave much as if he were mentally retarded or devoid of language altogether.

IMPLICATIONS

Essential to the formation of an effective language arts program for these Indian children seems to be a continuing emphasis on concept development; that is, a continuing effort must be directed towards the expansion of *meaning* for limited and narrow concepts.

Caution and precision must be exercised by the teacher in the verbal models she presents which make use of connecting words and prepositions. Care must be taken to emphasize the small words in sentences which are often not heard clearly by the Indian ear.

Teachers must be aware of the fact that Indian children learn effectively through a process of imitation. This has its advantages as well as its drawbacks. Non-verbal cues which might be imitated may be effective in helping bring about certain desired responses, however, while so doing many opportunities for language development are missed. Indian children come to rely on the nonverbal cues to the exclusion of the verbal exchange necessary for language growth. An advantage of this highly developed ability to imitate may be capitalized upon through providing clear, verbal models of the desired responses to be made by the child; for example, the teacher encouraging the child to speak in clear, complete sentences by providing him a model of the sentence in clear diction and intonation. A further drawback of a highly developed ability to imitate is the danger of Indian children learning to parrot the names of words without understanding their meanings. Consequently, words should appear always in a context meaningful for these children. This drawback, coupled with limited and narrow concepts suggests that perhaps an important part of the language program should involve an emphasis on word games, oral reading and the development of listening skills. As Luria[3] suggests, the aim should be to unlock words from single and restricting situations. Perhaps teachers with these children should read and discuss more stories than they might do with other children with fewer language handicaps.

Although many of the components of the language arts program as designed by these teachers for these children are common to other programs of language development, the specific emphases based upon their observations and test item analysis are applicable only to this group of children. To assume that their results will generalize totally to other groups of children is as dangerous as to group children simply on the basis of grade placement scores.

REFERENCES

1. Bereiter, Carl, and Siegfried Engelmann, *Teaching Disadvantaged Children in the Preschool*, Englewood Cliffs, N. J.: Prentice-Hall, 1966.
2. Bernstein, B., "Aspects of Language and Learning in the Genesis of the Social Process," *Journal of Child Psychology and Psychiatry*, **1** (1961), 313–324.
3. Luria, A. R., *The Role of Speech in the Regulation of Normal and Abnormal Behaviour*, New York: Pergamon, 1959.
4. Stones, E., *An Introduction to Educational Psychology*, London: Methuen and Co., 1967.
5. West, W. A., J. L. Bowers, and H. E. Parliament, Eds., "New Challenges in Reading," *The Canadian Teacher's Guide*, **15**, 1 (Autumn 1964).

CURRICULUM INNOVATIONS FOR DISADVANTAGED ELEMENTARY CHILDREN—WHAT SHOULD THEY BE?

Mildred B. Smith

INTRODUCTION AND GUIDELINES

The typical elementary school program does not meet the needs of disadvantaged children because it is founded on the assumption that each child is predisposed to learning what is offered. Children from impoverished backgrounds are not, however, predisposed to learning this curriculum for several reasons:

1. Inadequate language skills—listening and speaking.
2. Poor work habits.
3. Poor physical health.

Mildred B. Smith, "Curriculum Innovations for Disadvantaged Elementary Children—What Should They Be?" *The Teachers College Journal*, **37**, 1 (October 1965), 7, 32–39. Reprinted with the permission of the author and Indiana State University.

4. Frequent tardiness and/or absenteeism.
5. Inadequate model figures in the home and community.
6. Unfamiliar content in textbooks.
7. Inadequate motivation.
8. Initial school failure, caused by the above factors, which damage self-esteem and self-confidence.

Planning a program for the disadvantaged is challenging, and it raises many questions for school people. "If the traditional school program is inadequate, what modifications should be made for these children?" "What about charges made by Civil Rights leaders that curriculum changes in schools in ghetto-type communities, when modified, are 'watered down'?" How do we meet the needs of these children without lowering standards?" is a question which baffles many educators.

It appears to this writer that a school program for disadvantaged children would be similar in many ways to a good typical elementary school program, and yet there would be differences. We would agree that *any* good elementary school has qualified, competent teachers, capable administrative leadership, adequate library facilities, and sufficient quantities of books and other instructional materials for the number of children enrolled in the school. The program in the school for disadvantaged children would be different since these children have deficiencies which will not be adequately met in the typical program. The program for disadvantaged elementary children is therefore compensatory—to compensate for deficiencies of environmental origin. It not only includes additional personnel, resources, facilities, and administrative innovations; but it requires innovations in the day school program as well.

CLASS SIZE NEEDS TO BE REDUCED

The class size should reflect these children's need for special attention. They require more attention from teachers because they lack self-confidence, have difficulty following directions, have little motivation, use materials poorly, and are underachievers. Little can be accomplished if teachers must work with these children in large groups. Class size in schools with a concentration of disadvantaged children should be considerably smaller than for other schools within the same school system. Classes should be smaller for primary children than for later elementary children within the same building. Although it is difficult to designate a numerical figure, many educators agree that all classes should be under twenty-five, and primary classes should be considerably less than twenty-five.

TEACHING STAFF SHOULD BE STABILIZED

Inexperienced staff members and a high staff turnover, characteristic of many schools for disadvantaged children, undermine attempts at program improvement. Experienced teachers and principals in the same school system should be reassigned so as to give equal strength and stability to each elementary school.

SPECIAL SERVICES AND RESOURCES ARE NEEDED

Disadvantaged children have many problems which require special attention. A large portion of the teacher's time is therefore consumed with non-teaching activities brought about by health and behavioral problems, tardiness and absenteeism, and lack of motivation which undermine the instructional program. Teachers must be freed from many such activities in order to give more time to the teaching-learning situation.

These special resources and services are needed by disadvantaged children and their teachers:

1. A school library containing many easy-to-read books with exciting stories, stories about experiences familiar to these children, highly illustrative stories, and stories about these children's heroes.
2. An instructional materials center in each building staffed by professionals and non-professionals who research, catalog, and dispense curricular materials needed by disadvantaged children.
3. Dental, medical, and visual care.
4. Cultural speech specialists to provide help with speech problems which interfere with phonics training.
5. Resource teachers and curriculum consultants who assist teachers with new materials, techniques, and curriculum planning.
6. Facilities for educational trips and tours which compensate for environmental deficiencies.
7. Home-school communication, coordinated by an individual with sufficient training and maturity to work with teachers and parents.
8. Sufficient services from a diagnostician to help teachers assess needs and progress as well as to assist with placement of transient children who frequently enroll with inadequate records.
9. A school photographer to take pictures of children in academic situations for display, thereby enhancing their academic self-concepts and providing an academic aura in the building, which is frequently lacking.
10. Psychological and psychiatric services such as those provided at a Child Guidance Clinic.

11. A hot breakfast (and lunch) for children who need it.
12. A petty cash fund which allows staff members to purchase needed materials and services, thereby improving instruction and staff morale.
13. A comprehensive continuous inservice program to improve teacher competence and morale.
14. An extended school program—extension of the school day, week, and year, allowing these children *more time* to compensate for deficiencies.

PARENT EDUCATION IS NEEDED

A continuous parent education program, jointly planned by staff members and parents, should be developed. Parents in these communities do not respond readily to parent-school activities although they are interested in their children's education and wish the best for them. Their apparent reluctance may stem from a lack of social skills or a feeling of inadequacy about helping their children achieve academically.

Several techniques which may help to involve parents in the school program are home visits made by teachers to invite each parent to a special program, telephone calls, and follow-up home calls by community leaders. At such programs, parents can be helped to understand how important they are in helping motivate their children to achieve in school. They can assist their children by the following:

1. Providing a quiet period at home each day for reading and other constructive activities.
2. Reading daily to children, including pre-school age children.
3. Taking children to the library.
4. Listening to their children read.
5. Buying books for their children.
6. Talking with their children and listening to them.
7. Showing interest in school by asking questions, giving praise and encouragement.
8. Buying games and puzzles and playing with them when possible.
9. Getting children to bed at a reasonable hour.
10. Getting children up with ample time for breakfast, and preparing them for school—checking to see that teeth are cleaned, that hair is combed and brushed, and that face, hands, and clothes are clean.
11. Sending children to school with the attitude that they are going to learn and the teacher is there to help them.

CONTINUOUS EVALUATION IS NEEDED

Evaluation improves the quality of the ongoing program because it discloses which procedures and techniques are most effective, and it points up new directions and new areas for emphasis. Evaluation should be continuous and should be instructionally oriented. It has the added benefit of giving encouragement to parents and rewarding staff members.

No single device is adequate for evaluating programs for disadvantaged children. Many techniques should therefore be utilized. Evaluation techniques should include standardized tests and teacher judgment. Intelligence tests should be eliminated unless administered on an individual basis by a diagnostician for special placement of a child. Such tests assume to measure innate ability or potential; but deprived children will earn low scores because of reading, vocabulary, and concept deficiencies, as well as a lack of test-taking sophistication. This situation penalizes these children since many teachers interpret such test results as a predictor of what a child can learn. Such teachers will therefore expect less of children and not challenge them to reach their fullest potential.

Attendance and tardiness records should be analyzed. Health records should be kept and evaluated to determine progress in health protection—immunizations, visual and dental corrections, and medical examination and treatment. Teachers should observe children and keep individual growth charts on work habits, care of materials, personal grooming, teacher-student relationships, and student-student relationships.

The evaluation should reflect the extent to which parents and community residents are involved in the school program. Parents and community residents should also be involved in the evaluation process. This might include informal discussion as well as the questionnaire technique. The evaluation process should be continuous.

THE ROLE OF REMEDIAL SERVICES

Good programs for disadvantaged children should begin when the child enters school. This, combined with good preschool programs, should reduce the need for remedial programs in later years. A smaller class size will allow each child more personal attention so that remediation is given on a continuous basis. Mobility and other causal factors will create a need for *some* special remediation work, however. Early identification of remedial cases should be made, and remediation should begin before children become severely retarded and discouraged.

Special remedial reading and arithmetic teachers should work very closely with regular classroom teachers so that both are simultaneously focusing on the same problem; otherwise, additional problems are created for these children.

Remedial services, though needed, are not the answer. When children are retarded enough to qualify for these programs, their academic self-concepts are already temporarily or permanently damaged. Efforts must therefore be made to prevent retardation. This requires innovation in the day school program—in content, materials, and teaching procedures in all subject areas, from the time these children enter school.

A description of model language arts programs for primary and later elementary children follows.

A MODEL PRIMARY LANGUAGE ARTS PROGRAM

Disadvantaged children who enter school with inadequate language skills which severely retard readiness for reading and subsequent progress need a prolonged and enriched *reading readiness program* to compensate for these deficiencies.

In order to implement this program, interested and colorful "talking" pictures, clipped and filed by instructional center aides, were used to stimulate children's conversation, build a speaking vocabulary, and clarify concepts. Children were taken on trips to see things, places, and events which are common experiences for children in other communities. Field trips were made to the grocery store, drug store, hardware store, library, fire station, farms (fruit, vegetable, animal), and horticultural gardens. In addition, vicarious experiences were provided through materials available in the Instructional Materials Center, such as filmstrips, recordings, mounted pictures, and imitation realia (toy fruits, vegetables, flowers, animals). After each trip, children talked about their experiences to clarify concepts and to enlarge their speaking and listening vocabularies. Since so much of the teacher's spoken language was "foreign" to these children, the teacher utilized techniques commonly employed in teaching children to speak a foreign language. For example, the teacher showed a toy to a child and named the toy, and the child repeated; or the teacher used a new word in a sentence, and the child repeated the sentence. Materials such as the Peabody Language Development Kit were helpful.

In addition to the typical reading readiness experiences, auditory and visual discrimination training, left-to-right training, "story telling," and reading aloud to develop interest in books, various techniques were utilized to improve skills in which disadvantaged children are especially deficient. This included the skill of listening and the ability to follow direction. Sets of earphones were provided each child and were used with specially prepared tape recordings, records, and radio programs that enhance listening skills. "Listen and do" materials helped with the skill of following one, two, and three step directions.

The children had many experiences with books. They were taken to the school library frequently for "story telling," and they listened to stories from an illustrated book at least twice each day. Older children came to their classrooms and read to them when possible, providing a good model for the children. Parents participated in the reading program through a "read-to-me" program at home. Totally illiterate parents encouraged their children to read by holding the book with the child and discussing the pictures with him. These children learned from some "significant others" (parents) that reading was important and therefore developed an interest in learning to read.

The initial reading program utilized children's experiences through pupil-dictated experience stories, in lieu of a basal reader approach. Storybooks depicting life experiences familiar to the children were also used, such as Follett's City Schools Series, Scott Foresman's Multi-Ethnic Readers, Macmillan's Urban-oriented Readers, and the Chandler Language-experience Readers. In addition to lack of motivation, many reading problems are caused by limited vocabulary and inability to use phonics clues to pronounce words. Metal file boxes (recipe boxes) and file cards were provided each primary child to give special help with vocabulary development. This technique enabled each child to keep his own record of words that cause difficulty and to study them at school and at home, thus improving word recognition and word meaning. Teachers instructed parents to help by flashing the word cards and helping the child follow the study steps outlined:

1. Look at the word.
2. Say it.
3. Tell what it means.
4. Use it in a sentence.
5. Check his card to see if he has used the word correctly.

Teachers reported that this was one of the most helpful of the reading innovations for these children, whose particular speech patterns caused difficulties with the regular phonics approach to word recognition and whose meaning vocabularies were limited by environment. Children printed their own word cards when able to; otherwise, aides in the Instructional Materials Center typed or printed them. Stories in typical basal readers lack appeal to disadvantaged children because the illustrations and story content depict life experiences unfamiliar to them. The basal reader approach was therefore eliminated in lieu of multi-level, self-help reading materials which are individualized for students. Science Research Associates reading and listening laboratories were especially desirable. This program was enriched with supplementary materials: library books, literary collections, word games, listening skill building materials, "bookworm" club materials, individual stories constructed by aides from outdated reading booklets (providing students with the satisfaction of reading several "books"), and real-life stories dictated by pupils, typed and duplicated in the Instructional Materials

Center and distributed for classroom reading. Another incentive which motivated children to read independently was the monthly award—toy or game—given to the child in each classroom showing the greatest improvement in the library program. These supplementary reading materials met the criteria established for disadvantaged children for several reasons.

1. Illustrations showed pictures of people like themselves.
2. Fictional stories were short and packed with action.
3. Real-life stories depicted experiences familiar to children.
4. Materials were highly illustrative and colorful.

The *spelling, writing, and listening program* included the utilization of self-help materials. Follett's *Spelling and Writing Patterns* and Science Research Associates' Listening Skill Building materials are examples of types used. In addition, children learned to write about their own experiences and to use and to spell vocabulary from all subject areas.

A MODEL LATER ELEMENTARY LANGUAGE ARTS PROGRAM

The *reading program* based on a basal reader approach was eliminated for several reasons:

1. The content of such books lacks interest because it depicts experiences unfamiliar to these children: books are middle-class oriented.
2. The illustrations show pictures of people unlike themselves.
3. These children, having previously experienced failure, abhor thick hard-covered books which require a semester or a year to complete.

An individualized program consisting of short, exciting stories and self-help oriented materials replaced the basal reader program. Included were such materials as Science Research Associates' Reading Laboratories and Libraries; Macmillan's Reading Spectrum; Scott Foresman's Personal Development materials; and Follett's Beginning-To-Read series; Steck's Animal Stories; The Owl Books by Holt, Rinehart and Winston; the Button and Cowboy Series by Benefic Press; and the Skyline Series by McGraw-Hill.

Basal textbooks in other areas of the language arts program were also eliminated in lieu of multi-level, self-help type materials such as Science Research Associates' Spelling Laboratories, Follett's Spelling and Writing Patterns, and Science Research Associates' Writing and Listening Skill Building materials.

The reading and language arts program which incorporated the individualized self-help approach aided these children experiencing difficulty in these areas:

1. They accommodate individual differences.
2. They allow each child to begin at a functional level.

3. They provide immediate feedback.
4. They are highly structured and sequential, thereby giving security to children.
5. They keep each child aware of his progress, thus providing immediate reinforcement and gratification.
6. The self-help feature of the materials gives these children self-reliance, self-confidence, and a degree of independence which they otherwise lack.

An extensive library program enriched the reading program. Children visited the library twice weekly to check out books and for "story telling." Parents were encouraged to participate. Fathers provided encouragement by taking turns with library duties as well as by reading to the class during the library period, thus demonstrating to their children, particularly boys, that men value reading. Culturally disadvantaged boys need especially this kind of masculine support since most prodding to read is normally associated with mothers and female teachers, resulting in the idea that boys who take their school work seriously are "sissies."

Library aides and volunteer mothers made single-story reading booklets by cutting up out-dated reading books into individual stories and adding covers. Later elementary children, like primary children, found thick hard-covered books difficult to "read for fun." and these children therefore were delighted to discover they could finish a thin booklet and get the added satisfaction of reading several books. *Bookworm clubs* in each classroom encouraged children to read independently, a characteristic of any good reader. Each child was given a bookworm card, containing a sixteen-segment worm. Each placed a bright color sticker on one segment upon reading one book. When all of the 16 segments were covered, the child was given a "Certificate of Achievement," and a lapel button entitled "I'm a Bookworm." Children also kept a record of books read in their copy of "My Reading Record Booklet." A monthly reward (game, puzzle, toy) was given to the child who had shown the most progress, thus enabling less-able readers in the class to compete successfully. The reward was encouragement and the record keeping gave reinforcement because each child could see immediate progress. Both techniques are especially suited to reluctant readers.

Book fairs for children and adults were held periodically. Books were sold at cost and below cost to enable individuals to *own* books and to encourage families to build home libraries. One reason disadvantaged children do not value property is that they themselves do not own property. When such a child purchased a book, even at a minimal cost of 5¢, 10¢, or 15¢, and wrote *his name* on the cover page, he gained a feeling of pride, self-worth, and self-esteem far greater than most teachers imagined. Since these children's parents do not take them to the downtown book store to purchase books, the school's program compensated for this deficiency. Mothers' clubs underwrote the cost of this program through bake sales and carnivals.

Disadvantaged children require special help with vocabulary development. This includes both word recognition and word meaning, which is a deficiency of environmental origin. A metal recipe box similar to those used by primary children and index cards were given to each child, thus enabling him to keep his own record of words that caused difficulty in reading and other subject areas, and to study them independently at school and at home. The difficult word was written on one side of the card and the definition(s) and its use(s) in a sentence were written on the opposite side. Children and parents were taught the study steps:

1. Look at only one word at a time; think about how it begins and ends.
2. Say it softly; think about how it sounds.
3. Give the meaning(s) in your own words.
4. Use the word in a sentence that makes good sense.
5. Check your card to see that you have given the correct meaning and used it in a sentence.

Parents were taught the study procedure at parent meetings and then helped the children at home by flashing the cards. Teachers reported that this device was one of the most helpful innovations for the children because: (1) Children's vocabularies are limited by environmental conditions, (2) Emphasis on the sight approach to word recognition is helpful because phonics skills are handicapped by cultural speech differences, (3) Children enriched their vocabularies by learning words not only from all subject areas, but also from newspapers, magazines, television and street signs, (4) Children developed the "dictionary habit" which was lacking.

"The Word for the Day" activity consisted of placing a new word each day, printed on cardboard, in a pocket chart set aside for this purpose. Children learned the new word and were encouraged to use it in conversation during that day, thus enriching their speaking vocabularies. Disadvantaged children do not use specific vocabulary to communicate. These children generally use implicit rather than explicit vocabulary; therefore, "hardly any at all" would represent "limited," or "get up the papers" might be said for, "collect the papers." This problem handicaps these children on intelligence tests because the ability to give specific definitions for words enhances one's score on such tests. Disadvantaged children therefore earn a lower score because of their vocabulary deficiency. Easy-to-read dictionaries were provided for each child, on a long-term loan basis, for home use through the school library. The Thorndike-Barnhart Dictionary was especially desirable because of its simplified vocabulary.

Typewriters utilized for after school enrichment classes were used daily by children in the regular school program. Children typed spelling lists, outlines, vocabulary lists, and helpers lists. Teachers reported this to be one of the most valuable techniques for motivating children to learn to spell and improve vocabularies. These children learned to type in the after-school typing classes.

The model programs cited above give some suggestions for curriculum innovations to raise the achievement of children who are educationally disadvantaged. Experienced teachers will no doubt have many additional ideas for innovations. The important point to be made is that the curriculum should be implemented in the regular school program rather than to rely heavily on remedial programs for these schools.

STUDY QUESTIONS

1. The Greenlaw study indicates that publishers of basal reading programs and school systems differ significantly in their perceptions of the need for developing reading programs for culturally different children. Does this finding surprise you, in view of the seeming proliferation of new reading materials? Does Greenlaw offer any evidence of a perceptible trend toward consensus among publishers and schools?
2. What revisions in reading texts are minority groups demanding? Can you cite any instances in other areas of the language arts in which publishers are responding to the demands of organized minority groups? What minorities are in the best strategic position to make their demands felt? Is the advent of the black studies movement influencing the development of basal reading programs?
3. Does Greenlaw's study point to the need for developing basal reading series for *particular* minority groups, or for minority groups in general? Based on your own experience, which approach seems more feasible? Why?
4. Why has the publishing industry been slow to meet the perceived needs of disadvantaged children? Is this a common phenomenon in other curricular areas?
5. Why does Criscuolo refrain from hypothesizing that he might have obtained similar results with another basal reading program? Does he present evidence to indicate that it might not have been the program he used, but the amount of exposure the students received to it, that accounted for the difference in achievement between the two groups of pupils?
6. According to Criscuolo, what are the major criticisms leveled against basal reading programs? Do you regard these criticisms as legitimate? Is there any evidence to indicate that publishers are sensitive to them? Does Greenlaw's study indicate that publishers are taking concerted action to

produce texts that meet the perceived needs of disadvantaged children?

7. What are the major variables operative in Criscuolo's study? Which ones were controlled? What uncontrolled variables could have affected the outcome of the study?
8. Litcher and Johnson found that after using multiethnic readers white children developed more favorable attitudes toward Negroes than did those who had used a regular reading series published by the same company. Do the authors cite any limitations that would limit the generalizability of their findings? Would you expect the findings to have been different in communities with a large Negro population?
9. Litcher and Johnson studied pupils' attitude changes rather than their actual reading achievement. To what extent might the first factor affect the second? How might one assess the permanence of the attitude changes reported in this study?
10. How could the classroom behavior of the teachers who participated in the Litcher and Johnson study have affected its outcome? Are there any other variables beyond the control of the researchers that might have made a difference? If so, what might these be?
11. What are the essential differences between the multiethnic and regular readers used by the subjects in Litcher and Johnson's study? Do these differences appear in other reading programs? In speaking, listening, and writing programs? Should they?
12. The Developmental Oral Language (DOL) program, as described by Arnold, utilizes content drawn from the AAAS program. What appear to be the major advantages and disadvantages of this approach for Mexican-American children? For children of other minority groups? Are there other instances in which language arts programs have been combined with other science programs or with programs in other content areas?
13. Why did the original DOL program fail to measure up to expectations? In what ways is the experimental reading program different from its predecessor? Is there any evidence to indicate that the experimental program can promote greater language facility in Mexican-American children?
14. A major focus of the experimental reading program described by Arnold is its emphasis on making reading a meaningful experience. To what extent did the program achieve this objective? Are the findings reported by Arnold acceptable to you?
15. What type of in-service training for teachers does Arnold envision? Would these need to be adjusted to the experimental backgrounds of teachers? How might this be done?
16. On what basis do Philion and Galloway conclude that ". . . the conven-

tional reading program designed essentially for non-Indian children is not adequate for Indian children"? Is this conclusion warranted? Are there alternative conclusions that might be drawn?

17. To what extent did data obtained from direct observation and test-item analysis support Bereiter and Englemann's attempts to equate cultural deprivation with language deprivation? Do these data suggest other hypotheses regarding reading retardation among Indian children? If so, what might these be?
18. How generalizable are Philion and Galloway's findings? Do they have implications for Indian children residing in the United States? For children of other minority groups?
19. What in your opinion are the major advantages of Philion and Galloway's item-analysis techniques? Could they be used with other reading tests? What modifications might be warranted?
20. In what ways does Smith's language program differ from those recommended by other authors? Would you regard Smith's program as broadly or narrowly construed? What criteria would be of value in establishing the parameters of any language program for culturally-different children?
21. Could Smith's program be implemented in the absence of an in-service training project? If not, how comprehensive would the project need to be? If so, under what circumstances might an in-service project be unnecessary?
22. What personal qualities and abilities would a teacher need to possess if he were to succeed with Smith's program? What would this mean for pre-service selection and training of teachers?

SUGGESTED READINGS

American Institute for Research, *A Study of Selected Exemplary Programs for the Education of Disadvantaged Children*, Final Report, Parts I and II, Palo Alto, Calif.: American Institute for Research, September 1968.

Bereiter, Carl, "Academic Instruction and Preschool Children," *Language Programs for the Disadvantaged: Report of the NCTE Task Force on Teaching English to the Disadvantaged*, Champaign, Ill.: NCTE, 1965, pp. 195–205.

Campbell, Clyde M., ed., *Toward Perfection in Learning*, Midland, Mich.: Pendell, 1969.

The Center Forum, **4**, 1 (September 1969). Entire issue is devoted to bilingualism and bilingual programs.

Loban, Walter, "A Sustained Program of Language Learning," *Language Programs for the Disadvantaged: Report of the NCTE Task Force on Teaching*

English to the Disadvantaged, Champaign, Ill.: NCTE, 1965, pp. 221–229.

Miller, Wilma H., "A Reading Program for Disadvantaged Children," *Illinois Schools Journal*, **49** (Summer 1969), 111–116.

Newman, Ellen, "An Experiment in Oral Language," in Staten W. Webster, ed., *The Disadvantaged Learner: Knowing, Understanding, Educating*, San Francisco: Chandler Publishing Co., 1966, pp. 510–514.

Whipple, Gertrude, ed., "Curriculum for the Disadvantaged," in Harvey Goldman, ed., *Education and the Disadvantaged*, Milwaukee: School of Education, University of Wisconsin—Milwaukee, 1967, pp. 91–105.

Wrightstone, J. Wayne, *et al.*, "Evaluating Educational Programs," *The Urban Review*, **3**, 4 (February 1969), 5–22.

CHAPTER 6
MULTISENSORY APPROACHES

American elementary education is in the throes of a series of revolutions unparalleled in the history of our nation. Their major thrust is toward improvement of instruction in all areas of the elementary curriculum. Instructional aims, subject matter, and methodology—all are undergoing agonizing reappraisal by educators in their attempts to make the elementary school program a source of rich and meaningful experiences for all elementary pupils.

Closely paralleling the creation of new curricular programs has been a movement toward using an ever-increasing variety of instructional strategies. No longer are language arts teachers compelled to follow slavishly the proverbial read-recite-test pattern of instruction. Increasingly they are becoming aware of the virtually unlimited possibilities of dramatic play, role-playing, sociodrama, instructional games, puppetry, creative writing, and countless expressive experiences afforded by the fine arts. Not only do these strategies help teachers meet the unique needs of children, but they also are capable of making language learning an enjoyable experience for both pupils and teachers.

Space limitations do not permit the inclusion of readings reflecting the many promising strategies currently used in elementary language arts classes. However, the editors have included readings that describe various approaches that might have escaped the reader's attention. In the first reading, David A. Sohn describes how he used films as a vehicle for implementing his "Look, See, and Write" method. Betty Halpern then demonstrates the many exciting possibilities for using creative writing, dramatics, and role-playing with Mexican-American children. The potential of incidental, out-of-school learning experiences for reading development is dramatically illustrated in a case study reported by Jane A. Torrey. In the final reading Lessie Carlton and Robert H. Moore demonstrate that self-directive dramatization has some intriguing possibilities for reading instruction.

READING, WRITING, AND SEEING: THE VISUAL APPROACH TO STIMULATING READING AND COMPOSITION

David A. Sohn

> At their best, films communicate valid and significant human experiences which illuminate our common humanity and which we should want to share with our students. At their worst (and they share this fault with all media), they present a dehumanizing view of man against which the best defense is trained intelligence and aesthetic judgment. The power of the moving image to manipulate, to editorialize, and to form values and attitudes makes it imperative in this age of film and television that the audience be equipped with the competence needed to understand the rhetoric of the projected image.
>
> Rev. John M. Culkin, S.J.,
> "Film Study in the High School"

The basic word in my course was *See*. When Hart Leavitt and I wrote the book *Stop, Look and Write*, we described our purpose: "What this book proposes to do is provide a method whereby both students and adults can learn something about the art and power of observation. You might call the method, 'A Beginner's Course in How to See.'" To "notice," to "perceive," to "see" in the best possible way, one needs to practice looking for such things as similarities, differences, emotions, gestures, colors, details, and conflicts. They are all part of the technique of the art of observation. Archibald MacLeish, the poet, has cited the goal: it is to learn to see feelingly.

Using *Stop, Look and Write* and *The Family of Man* throughout the course as springboards for discussion and observation provided texts of photographs that the student could observe again and again. A wide variety of films, however, was the major medium for stimulating reading, writing, and discussion.

The film "Rainshower" (Churchill Films) was one of the first films screened. It is a specific film about the progress of a rainshower and its effects on animals and people. The only dialogue in the film is at the beginning,

David A. Sohn, "Reading, Writing, and Seeing: The Visual Approach to Stimulating Reading and Composition," in Peter G. Kontos and James J. Murphy, eds., *Teaching Urban Youth: A Source Book for Urban Education*, New York: John Wiley & Sons, 1967, pp. 45–56. Reprinted with permission of the publisher.

where it is explained that a photographer started out one day to see what he could see. It was about to rain, and these were the things he saw. The color photography was particularly striking as the students followed the progress of the storm from the country to the city. Shots of animals doused by the rain, a spider drenched by water, a boy chasing the animals to the barn for cover, work stopping in the city, and many others prompted discussion and gave the students a vivid example of how the camera can tell a story without words.

Following this introduction, which was concerned with beauty and specific imagery, we pursued the theme of *Horror*, both real and imagined. Through an error, we received a feature film based on "The Tell-Tale Heart" (but certainly a radical departure from Poe's original) instead of the color short subject with the same title. This film, nevertheless, motivated the students to read the story "The Tell-Tale Heart" in *Great Tales of Horror*, by Edgar Allan Poe. "The Cask of Amontillado" was also shown to stimulate reading. Students were encouraged to read other stories by Poe in the same volume, but they were not required to do so. Several read "The Masque of the Red Death" and "Hop-Frog." Poe's imagined horror was then related to the horror of the real world.

A large reproduction of Picasso's "Guernica" was pasted on the board in front of the class. We discussed what it might mean—how it depicted the horror of war. We then saw the short film "Guernica," in which sections of Picasso's picture are juxtaposed with scenes of the bombed village of Guernica and the horrors of the Spanish Civil War. Next we saw "Night and Fog," the Resnais documentary on the Nazi concentration camps. Contrasts between the empty camps after the war and the film clips and still photographs taken by the Nazi during the war revealed the extreme horror of persecution, starvation, and death in these murder factories clearly and vividly to the students. These films "out-Poed" Poe, certainly, and offered the chance for a discussion that differentiated "real horror" from "imagined horror." Before showing "Night and Fog," we examined the picture of the Warsaw Ghetto prisoners being herded out of hiding by the Nazis. "Night and Fog" is a powerful, realistic film that involved the students. Several asked, "How could something like this happen?"

Moving from the theme of *Horror* to the theme of *Fantasy*, we showed "The Red Balloon" and "Moonbird." "The Red Balloon" was another film that told a story without dialogue. It was possible to bring out such elements in this story as conflict, symbolism, and narrative line. The fantasy, of course, lies in the fact that the balloon takes on human characteristics as it becomes attached to the boy and is finally destroyed by a gang of boys at the end of the film. "Moonbird" was a short film about two boys who dig a hole to catch the moonbird. It is an excellent fantasy. I followed these with a reading of the first few paragraphs of Theodore Thomas' "Test" (from *Ten Top Stories*), which is about an automobile accident, to encourage the students to read it over the week-end.

In regard to the first units, the participating teachers commented in various ways. "I felt 'The Red Balloon' was a good opener for the summer school session. I think it surprised the students to see something new in English, and it nicely tested their powers of observation. The showing of Poe's films was indeed a success. They encouraged a reading of Poe, and the discussions that followed were filled with details that showed an alertness and interest on the part of the students."

Another wrote, "I found this to be an interesting week for several reasons: first, the holding power of the film was vividly demonstrated when *the entire class* gave up its break to see a film through to the end ('The Tell-Tale Heart'). Second, the use of the film to stimulate reading was amply displayed. From a completely 'cold' start on Tuesday, most of the class read several Poe tales by Friday, and I believe all of them will read Monday's assignment ('Test,' by Theodore Thomas.)"

Still another wrote, "When Mr. Sohn asked, ten or so said they'd read 'The Tell-Tale Heart.' Several mentioned they'd read other stories. In a class this size that I taught last year, not more than five read the stories—even though they had the threat of a daily quiz as 'motivation.'"

A fourth commented, "It may be a minor point, but I was impressed by the fact that everyone brought his book on the second day. No mention was made of bringing books—and this was a constant battle in my school. Who can blame the students for not wanting to weight himself down with several huge tomes? Small paperbacks, such as the ones we gave out, are much less imposing and troublesome."

The second week, we showed the following films: "The Pearl"; "New York, New York"; "Corral"; "Morning on the Lievre"; "Diary of Anne Frank"; "White Mane"; and "Dream of Wild Horses." The aim of this week's lessons were to:

1. Interest students in reading by developing interest through seeing films—"The Pearl" and "The Diary of Anne Frank."
2. Develop a sense of seeing details—*Stop, Look and Write*.
3. Develop a sense of interpretation of values—"The Pearl."
4. Understand the term *conflict* and determine the conflict(s) in a story—"White Mane."
5. Recognize film as an art form—"New York, New York" (abstract art) and "Morning on the Lievre" (a series of beautiful scenes and poetry combined).
6. Draw conclusions and develop judgments—"The Pearl."
7. Understand how mood is developed—"The Diary of Anne Frank."

8. See relationships (similarities and contrasts)—"The Diary of Anne Frank" and "Night and Fog."

Before I showed "The Pearl," I passed out the paperback novel and suggested that the students might like to read it. One teacher observed, "Jasper doesn't do homework, but he became involved with *The Pearl* and it was a wonderful thing to watch. Oblivious to the before-class hustle and bustle, Jasper sat reading the book. All during the movies, he read it. Mr. Sohn passed out *The Family of Man*, and Jasper kept reading. Finally he became interested in the pictures, so he kept his place with his finger in *The Pearl*, and glanced at *The Family of Man*. Soon he was back to reading *The Pearl*. He glanced up occasionally to see the movie 'The Diary of Anne Frank,' but most of his attention remained with *The Pearl*. The next morning I asked him, 'How do you like that book *The Pearl*?' He answered, 'Oh, it's all right.'"

While teaching *The Pearl*, the word "parable" was introduced in connection with the film. Pages 10 and 17 of *Stop, Look and Write* were used to emphasize seeing details, and the "seeing" theme was related to the film "New York, New York," which is a film of distorted images shot through trick lenses—everyday scenes during a day in New York City. "Morning on the Lievre" is a more literal treatment visually of a trip down the Lievre river in Quebec—a visual translation of a poem by a Canadian poet.

"Corral" and "White Mane" told simple stories and contained the elements of a good tale. "Corral" is a short film about the roping and saddling of a wild horse in Canada. It contains no dialogue. "White Mane" is a beautiful story about a French boy's love of a horse. It compared nicely with "The Red Balloon," for both concerned a young boy's love for something beautiful that in the end is destroyed by the evil in men's hearts.

"Dream of Wild Horses" is a surrealistic no-dialogue film in slow motion of wild horses playing, then running through fire. One teacher called it "a strangely haunting study of odd colors and motion." It is, in effect, a visual poem.

One conclusion made by the students was that "The Red balloon" could not have been as effective in black and white, whereas "The Diary of Anne Frank" was better in black and white because most of the film takes place in one room. The effect of this variable on the impact of a film is an important one to discuss.

After seeing "The Diary of Anne Frank," students were given the opportunity to borrow and read the book if they wished to do so. At least seven students read the book. This film put the "horror" so vividly shown in "Night and Fog" into specific terms as the students saw the effect of the Nazi terror on one family. As one teacher commented, "For all its horror, 'Night and Fog' stays somewhat abstract, 'The Diary of Anne Frank' makes it real."

"Animal farm" was shown to combined classes. The book was then given to students who felt they might like to read it. Many of them did so. "I was surprised at how well 'Animal Farm' came over," wrote one teacher. "I had seen it before on TV and was not particularly impressed." The animated film was done in color, whereas the TV version had been seen in black and white. This film related nicely to the theme of tyranny and oppression that we had discussed.

"The Big Fair" was used to teach the concepts of "comparisons," "contrasts," and "theme." This is a short film that develops the theme, "The playthings of youth can become the weapons of maturity." Teacher reactions were interesting:

"Ah, the word *theme* finally emerges!" commented a teacher, "Although it was presented in a very broad sense at first, as the whole series of comparisons was presented in 'The Big Fair,' it later emerged quite clearly."

"After watching 'The Big Fair,' the students were able to list comparisons," said another.

"Pat, for instance, would barely manage to mumble something when called on at the beginning of the course. Now she is an eager volunteer, waving her hand on almost every question," one reported.

"The Great Adventure" was one of several films made by the Swedish director Arne Sucksdorf. "'The Great Adventure' gave rise to a whole host of ideas including conflicts of various sorts, some values, pursuit, a cycle of life in the forest, of the animals, of man, and of boyhood, to list a few," commented a teacher. A link of similarities was developed with this film and "The Red Balloon," "White Mane," and "The Diary of Anne Frank." The other films of Sucksdorf, "Shadows on the Snow," "A Summer Tale," and "A Divided World" were brief ones that developed the contrasts between the world of nature and the world of civilization. Such films can be related to reading Jack London, Mary O'Hara, John Steinbeck, and others.

"The Golden Age of Comedy" illustrated the nature of humor and the art of communicating through purely visual language. The elements of surprise and cruelty in much visual comedy were discussed.

"Hand in Hand" is a film about the nature of prejudice. It is about two English children, one a Catholic, the other a Jew. As they investigate their respective religions, they come to realize that they do not differ fundamentally in purpose, but that the adult world imposes prejudice on the young.

Four of the films which most involved the students were shown toward the end of the course. "A Raisin in the Sun," "On the Waterfront," "Nobody Waved Goodbye," and "The Wild Ones" proved to be outstanding in their power to stimulate thought and discussion. Unfortunately we did not have the books for "A Raisin in the Sun" or "On the Waterfront," although several students asked for them day after day. As one teacher put it, "Anyone in the audience must know by now just how powerful a device films can be. Any doubters should have seen the reaction to 'A Raisin in the Sun,' 'On the Waterfront,' etc." The gripping power of these films was a joy to watch.

Through the courtesy of Brandon Films, we were able to show "Nobody Waved Goodbye," a Canadian film about a teenager who is unable to communicate with his family and so rebels, causing his eventual embroilment in a great deal of trouble. It was a remarkable film because of the reality of the problems and the honesty with which it was made. The students identified readily with the main character, Peter. One teacher commented, "By far the best thing we saw this week was the Canadian film 'Nobody Waved Goodbye,' a study of a 'misunderstood' teenager who has no contact with and cannot communicate with the adult world. He has no values, no goals, no ambitions, and no understanding. This film could easily lead to a study of *Catcher in the Rye*, *A Separate Peace*, and perhaps *David Copperfield* and 'Henry IV, Part One.' "

We also saw "Bartleby," the remarkable film made by George Bluestone at the University of Washington. This version of the Melville story was excellent for discussing "character." It also related well to the theme of rebellion. One teacher wrote a comparison of the two films, "Bartleby and Peter (of 'Nobody Waved Goodbye') are two individuals who, motivated into rebellion, react completely differently. Bartleby, a would-be free spirit who lacks spirit, withdraws from society. In a sense he is another Ghandi, for he makes use of passive resistance to gain his end which, in this case, it really does. Peter, on the other hand, stands up and fights against the forces which would restrain him from the freedom he seeks. These two films can, I believe, be used in developing a lesson on civil rights. A parallel can be drawn between Bartleby, a believer in nonviolence, and Peter, who strikes out to gain his ends. Also, they can be used in discussing the recent tower killings (in Texas) by Charles Whitman, for it can be argued that his actions are indicative of his discontent with society."

"The Wild Ones" could also be used in this unit, for it shows the rebellion of motorcycle gangs and the problems of law and justice versus mob violence and chaos in society. The students were given copies of *Mid-Century*, the paperback anthology that contains "Cyclists' Raid" by Frank Rooney, the short story on which "The Wild Ones" was based. Coincidentally *The Hunterdon County Democrat*, published in Flemington, New Jersey, ran a story only a few days before the screening of "The Wild Ones" which reported that a group of 50 to 60 cyclists had invaded a nearby tavern and terrorized the customers. The news story, which sported the headline "Chain Gang Motorcyclists Invade County and Keep Police Jumping," virtually paralleled "The Wild Ones" except that the result was not as violent, for the Flemington police did come to the rescue. The story did show, however, that it could happen here, even in New Jersey.

The film "Runner," a short Canadian film, showed the experiences of a track star. It is an excellent study of motion and rhythm. It was used to lead the students to read *See How They Run*, a story about a long distance runner in *Ten Top Stories*. One teacher suggested that the film could also be related to the film "The Loneliness of the Long Distance Runner."

Perhaps the films done by Norman McLaren for the National Film Board of Canada should be treated as a group. During the course, we viewed "Serenal," "Horizontal Lines," "Rhythmetic," "Short and Suite," and "A Little Phantasy on a Nineteenth Century Painting." The films were among the most imaginative shown to the students, and perhaps among the most imaginative ever made. "Serenal" is a conglomeration of moving colors that seem to tell a story. An extremely op projective film students see many different things in it. It runs only four minutes, but is a powerful stimulus for writing. "Horizontal Lines" is a film that shows lines multiplying to the accompaniment of Pete Seeger's banjo. One line eventually spawns a great number of others, then there is a scrambling, and finally a recession to only one line again. The film seemingly is simple and foolish to some when they first see it, but when it is viewed again, one realizes that it contains the elements of a story that has conflict and builds to a climax, then to the denouement. The other films are just as imaginative, and just as usable for teaching the elements of fiction and for stimulating writing.

"A Short Vision" is a brief animated film about a thing that flies over a town, drops a bomb, and destroys the world. It is tremendously effective in its unexpected shock effect as the mood develops and the bomb drops. This film was used to motivate the students to read *Hiroshima*, by John Hersey, which was passed out to them after they saw the film. Before the film, students examined pictures of destruction and war in *Stop, Look and Write* and *The Family of Man*. One picture in *The Family of Man* was a photo of a girl who had survived the bombing of Hiroshima and had suffered severe burns.

The film "1800 Days" was made for Westinghouse by Hugh and Suzanne Johnston. In four minutes this remarkable film compressed the salient events of a five-year period. It is excellent for teaching time concepts and precise observation.

STUDENT REACTIONS

The students were positive about the course. The visual approach was a new experience to all of them. The following comments are representative of their reactions:

"I've seen many movies these weeks, and they have made me want to read more. The selection of books and movies was very good. I think I have improved in writing and thinking. I will always remember these six weeks."

"I have really enjoyed myself most of all in English. It is sometimes interesting and sometimes dull, but I have never had an English class like this. I wish that the regular English classes in school were like this."

"During this summer course I became more interested in English. I wish we could have movies in our own English class in school. I feel that it encouraged me to read books and stories. If we were lucky enough to have it this way in school, we could have a movie one day a week and discuss it the rest of the week. It was so nice to have all the books. They were interesting and I enjoyed them. I had a wonderful summer and I really enjoyed English."

"I have seen movies that have urged me to read the book. So I did and then compared the two. I also wrote compositions on the movies and books. We all wrote them and got different ideas. To me this English is the most interesting course I have ever had or heard of."

". . . It's a great way to get some of these children (Including Me!!!) to open up books and read them. You really didn't come right out and tell us that you were trying to increase our will to read, but I found out that's exactly what you were doing, and I'll never forget your methods or the enjoyment I got out of this class."

TEACHER REACTIONS

The following excerpts from the final papers of the participating teachers will give some idea of their feeling about what we did during the course:

"I would have to conclude that what we saw in regard to using the film to stimulate writing was new and fresh, that the students find it interesting and enjoyable, that it's fun to teach this way, and best of all, that it works. It can promote a great deal of writing. No one could ask any more of a method."

"I should say one other thing about the use of films, and that is that I learned that properly selected and used films have a universal appeal and a tremendous capacity to grip and move an audience. I was a dying fox, but I was also a mad killer clutching a bloody, throbbing heart, a horse plunging in a fiery surf, a red balloon deflating pomposity, a man anguished to learn that riches can bring terrible grief rather than anticipated joy, an imprisoned girl with a soaring spirit and a free mind, a cowboy, an autumn leaf floating toward winter on the Lievre, a brutal boxer, a boy in love with an otter, a pie-in-the-face comedian, and a dot frantically looking for a place to rest. I'm saying that I didn't just watch a lot of pictures. I was involved. I am not exceptional. What happened to me happened to everyone there. We were all involved. Therein may lie salvation for English teachers, who constantly fret about the same dilemma: 'How can we get our students involved?'"

"This is my first experience with a new medium for teaching, and I found it to be extremely effective. I am most impressed. The use of films has the advantage of conveying ideas to the student more quickly and effectively than a textbook. It has the further advantage of being able to convey a whole range of ideas and themes in a shorter time period than I imagined. It bypasses the problem of having a teacher force a student to read a book, and it alleviates the added problems for a teacher of: (1) wondering whether the student has read the books, and (2) wondering if he understood what he has read. The observation of a film gets a point directly to a student in the surest and quickest way possible."

"Showing a novel or short story in film form to a group of disadvantaged youth is a great equalizer. It gives this type of student something to talk about both to the students in his own group and even students in a so-called higher class. In a way, it can be said that a book to be read is unfair to certain youth, whereas a film to be seen is fair to all youth . . ."

"Maybe some traditional teachers will conclude that Mr. Sohn is opposed to reading. On the contrary, Mr. Sohn has done a great deal to bring about a desire on the part of the student to do more reading. In Mr. Sohn's room there is an abundance of paperback books of the best type. Students are given these books and they are encouraged to read them. No student is ever forced to read. He reads because he wants to read or because he knows the choice is his. There is no fear of failure or punishment of any kind."

"Are the students in Mr. Sohn's class reading? A goodly number of them are. Whenever Mr. Sohn asks a question about a comparison between the book and the film, the response has been surprising to at least one person. As a participating teacher, I was somewhat amazed at the amount of reading that took place on a voluntary basis. One student in particular said that he had read three books. Even if this student told a half-truth, he still has accomplished a great deal."

"If I could utilize any of the techniques I have encountered here, I would employ the Look, See and Write method. I would show lots of movies with the intention of stimulating reading and writing. I would employ the saturation technique with books. Fader's library borrowing technique was an excellent mechanical device: give the child two books; every time he wants a different book, he trades one in."

"Mr. Sohn's technique has made me aware that children, even those who are classified as 'slow,' can handle profound ideas. Movies are an excellent way to present these profundities. 'The Great Adventure,' for example, dealt with many of these weighty issues: the short life of grief and joy in the forest (and in society, perhaps?); no one can catch and hold a dream alive for long; the inevitable pain in growing up; the conflict between man and nature, man and boy, etc. Fader said in his book, semiliterate children do not need semiliterate books. Many aspects of this Institute have combined to tell me not to underestimate the capabilities of these children, not to treat them with condescension. They can cope with the great moral issues. They will, in fact, become deeply involved with great issues such as civil rights, Naziism, prejudice, etc. Since an English class should relate with life in the outside world, I plan to stop avoiding these issues. I plan to bring my classes out of that foreign, Victorian world of Silas Marner and into the world of the midtwentieth century."

CONCLUSION

The students reacted enthusiastically to the course. Many were moved to read the books we provided. Many became more aware of such relationships as comparisons and contrasts. The uses of positive reinforcement and the consequent lack of pressure had beneficial results. In such a short time writing fluency could not be developed. Writing must be taught and developed in class with these students. Assigned homework in writing simply does not work. Time limitations prohibited doing a great deal of "in-class" writing, but those compositions that were written frequently showed a great deal of imagination and potential.

The films were shared with the afternoon program on film-making, and many participating teachers were exposed to the films in evening screenings.

The participating teachers in my course read four books: *How Children Fail* by John Holt, *Summerhill* by A. S. Neill, *Revolution in Teaching* by DeGrazia and Sohn, and *Teacher* by Sylvia Ashton-Warner. The general reaction to the readings was favorable. They felt that many of the ideas in these books were provocative.

I had the feeling at the end of the course that a great deal of enthusiasm was generated for the visual approach to learning from both the students and the participating teachers, and such interest, of course, was my objective. It should be interesting to see *if* and *how* these visual techniques will be applied in the actual school situations.

The following is the prospectus handed out to participating teachers before beginning the courses.

THE VISUAL APPROACH TO STIMULATING READING AND WRITING

Various types of visual stimuli will be used to motivate the student to read and write. The course will be based on the paperback text *STOP, LOOK AND WRITE*, with other types of media related to it. For example, a number of films will be shown to the student for a variety of purposes—such as "The Pearl," which will be shown to the student to motivate him to read the novel; "White Mane," which will be used to stimulate writing and motion; and "On the Waterfront," which will be used both as a springboard for writing and an illustration of the motion picture as a work of art.

In regard to writing, there are three objectives: to teach the student to observe carefully and to interpret his observations imaginatively; to teach the student to think in terms of metaphor and imagery; and to help the student to develop fluency in his writing.

To stimulate reading, books and collections of short stories related to motion pictures and filmstrips will be available. Most of the time, the student will be encouraged to read the printed work, but not required to do so. It is hoped that he will want to read further and will develop a desire to read more. Paperbacks will be used exclusively. Students will do one individual project related to the visual approach.

More positive attitudes toward reading and writing are outcomes that we wish to achieve. Reinforcement theory will be emphasized as part of commenting on student work (no negative comments but accentuation of the positive). We also hope that teachers may find new ideas and methods to use with their classes.

USING CREATIVE WRITING, DRAMATICS AND ROLE-PLAYING WITH THE MEXICAN-AMERICAN CHILD

Betty Halpern

The Mexican-American child comes to school aware that his language is not the language of the larger society. However, with the growing trend of bilingualism in the school environment[1] we may be moving toward a less stigmatized learning situation for the Mexican-American child.

I would like to look at the child's language developmentally, designating three separate stages only to facilitate analysis. These stages are the given language of the child, the language of the "here and now," and the language of beauty and imagination.

Betty Halpern, "Using Creative Writing, Dramatics, and Role Playing with the Mexican-American Child." Published with the author's permission. Written for this volume.

THE GIVEN LANGUAGE

The task of the teacher of Mexican-American children is to be a facilitating and enhancing adult. To achieve this task, two things seem most vital. One, the teacher must accept the child and, two, really listen to his given language.

How do we go about accepting the child where *he* is and utilizing his experience in the teaching process?

First and foremost, while listening, observing and participating in the learning process, the teacher must treasure the uniqueness of each child. He must be aware of the positive qualities in the child's language, especially its simplicity and directness. To simply substitute a "formal" language cuts him off from traditional relationships and alienates him from his culture.

Here are some suggestions for helping the child see and know and deeply feel that the teacher accepts both him and his language:

1. First, find out what the child's experiences have been and capitalize on them—language learning is intrinsically bound up with experiencing.[2]
2. Have children dictate their experiences at home and at school for a newsletter to link the community to the school. (What a wonderful use for an aide or volunteer as recorder, or second-best, a tape recorder.)
3. Respect the child's name—this is the most intimate part of him—label his things, know his name, his whole name.
4. Foster teaching that is non-bookish and intutive, sensitive, flexible, imaginative and responsive to the child.
5. Let each child have time to tell something about himself, his interests and his aspirations.[3]
6. Try to bridge the linguistic double life of the child—the language of the home and language of the school—by encouraging much talking. (Be careful about saying too often: "Speak louder," "Pronounce your words more clearly," "Don't talk funny.")
7. Use non-verbal language (touching, kneeling, smiling, gesturing) to really communicate with the whole of your self.

The following suggestions will reinforce acceptance through involving family relationships:

1. Encourage parents to feel comfortable in the school.
2. Have a parents' corner in the classroom where coffee, reading materials, samples of each child's work and plans for the year are available.
3. Call parents in as resource people to help reflect their culture.
4. Cooking projects, music, dances, holiday celebrations.

5. Invite older school-age siblings for exchange of ideas and school experiences.

Of course, all the techniques in the world—the use of mirrors, self-portraits, photographs, etc. will not do what we must do for a child's feeling about himself if the adults around him do not respect his uniqueness.[4]

THE LANGUAGE OF THE "HERE AND NOW"[5]

The language of the "here and now" is very closely related to the experiences of the child. However, it is an expansion of those experiences through bringing greater meaning and structure to the given language.

We can start out with "Who Am I?" Children can make books about themselves, relating their name, their age, their weight, height, their family, their home life.[6]

Then they can go on to "Where Am I?" Children can make books or dictate stories about the classroom, school, school grounds.

"What Is Around Me?" can be developed by taking walks in the neighborhood, seeing differences in housing and observing stores, the library, the park, other schools, etc.

In the classroom we can simulate many experiences through dramatic play: running a grocery store, enacting home experiences in the doll corner, "building a city" in the block corner.

The teacher must provide the props and the experiences for learning. At appropriate times he should introduce new materials and equipment. By providing time after play for a) questioning, answering and discussing what has happened; b) telling and listening and acting out stories expanding play experiences;[7] c) going on trips to nearby places to gain more concrete experiences; and d) viewing pictures and films symbolizing these concrete experiences the teacher will provide for the child's growing cognitive powers.

For the older child (3rd through 6th grade) the teacher can introduce pantomime and improvisation to expand some of the freer dramatic play the child has engaged in.[8] Children can pantomime the sports they enjoy and the simple tasks they do around the home and school. Improvisation (spontaneous and free) may deal with life at home, at school, on the street. Children should be free to choose their own topics for enactment and play them out in a non-judgmental atmosphere. After the enactment discussion can take place about accuracy of characterization, clarity of the problem, and authenticity of the resolution.

When children have had experience with creative dramatics (pantomime, improvisations, story enactments) they may want to do role-playing.[9] Role-playing allows children to act out new alternatives and solutions to life-size situations which in real life may have punishing consequences. For minority group children the power to even imaginatively control their environment is crucial.

The methodology of role-playing depends upon the group and its setting. The following guidelines should be of use to the classroom teacher in creating an environment for effective role-playing:

1. A majority of the group chooses a common problem to be acted out. For example: how it feels to be the newest (and maybe oldest) child in the class due to "living on wheels", how it feels to experience cultural and family values and standards different from those of the group, how it feels to have personal ambitions or interests which have little opportunity for fulfillment.
2. Group members voluntarily choose to participate in the role-playing.
3. The teacher should provide adequate warm-up to elicit group creativity. For example: how the room looked, how the people in the room felt, how they were dressed, what the weather was, etc. This will help the group understand the setting of the role-playing.
4. Each member should have sufficient support to speak and act freely.
5. After the completion of the role-playing, the players and the audience should analyze the enactment.
6. Alternative solutions suggested in the group criticism should be re-enacted for further analysis.

So, here are some ideas. But the reader can supply many more when he has listened to the child, when he has helped the child to feel a stronger self-concept, when he has allowed language to flow as the child dictated stories, acted, read, role-played—and therefore encouraged the third component of developing the child's language—that of beauty and imagination.

NOTES

1. For example, Head Start, which uses Mexican-American teachers and aids and provides for a Spanish-speaking teacher along with the regular classroom teacher in some elementary schools.
2. In Marie Hughes and George I. Sanchez, *Learning a New Language*, Washington D.C.: Association for Childhood Education International, 1958. Hughes translated mental tests into Spanish. She found that children cannot have a vocabulary for things, objects, and relationships that they do not experience. On the test, the children did not put cup and saucer together because they had (in their homes) only assorted cups without saucers. They had no word for a thimble. They responded to a picture of a kitchen sink with "to wash the hair," "to get water and wash and wash."

3. Mexican-American children are language shy. Although a generalization, Mexican-American children in a classroom are very quiet—could this be attributed to lack of openness and lack of opportunity in the classroom?
4. In a significant new book—Robert Rosenthal and Lenore Jacobson, *Pygmalion in the Classroom*, New York: Holt, Rinehart & Winston, 1968—the authors point out that teacher's attitudes and behavior might be contributing factors to pupil failure.
5. The author is deeply indebted to the late Lucy Sprague Mitchell, and the work of the Bank Street College of Education, for her insights on this topic.
6. Three books that might be helpful in this project are: Ruth Krauss, *Is This You?* New York: Scott, 1955; Ruth Krauss, *The Growing Story*, New York: Harper and Row, 1947; and Mary McBarney Green, *Is It Hard, Is It Easy?* New York: Young Scott Books, 1960.
7. See list of books dealing with the life and experiences of Mexican-American children at the end of the article.
8. Association for Childhood International, *Creative Dramatics*, Washington, D.C.: 1961; Albert Collum, *Push Back the Desks*, New York: Citation Press, 1967 [paper]; Burdette S. Fitzgerald, *Let's Act the Story*, San Francisco: Fearon Publishers, 1957; Geraldine Brain Siks, *Children's Theatre and Creative Dramatics*, Seattle: University of Washington Press, 1961; Viola Spolin, *Improvisation for the Theater*, Evanston, Ill.: Northwestern University Press, 1963; Winifred Ward, *Playmaking With Children*, 2nd ed., New York: Appleton-Century Crofts, 1957.
9. Mark Chesler and Robert Fox, *Role-Playing Methods in the Classroom*, Chicago: Chicago Science Associates, 1966; Fannie R. Shaftel and George Shaftel, *Role Playing for Social Values*, Englewood Cliffs, N.J.: Prentice-Hall, 1967; Betty Halpern, "Role Playing: Its Therapeutic and Educative Application to the Black Ghetto Child," Ed.D. dissertation, University of California, 1968.

BIBLIOGRAPHY OF CHILDREN'S BOOKS IN SPANISH

Berlitz School of Languages, *Spanish for Children: Cinderella, Sleeping Beauty*, New York: Grosset, 1961.

De Brunhoff, Jean, *La Infancia de Babar*, New York Package Library, 1957.

Franconi, Antonio, *See and Say*, New York: Harcourt, Brace & World, 1955.

__________ *The Snow and the Sun*, New York: Harcourt, Brace & World, 1961.

Galdone, Paul, *La Vieja y Su Cerdo* (*The Old Woman and Her Pig*), New York: McGraw-Hill, 1961.

Guilfoile, Elizabeth, *Nadie le Hace Caso a Andres* (*Nobody Listens to Andrew*), Chicago: Follett, 1961.

Keats, Ezra Jack, *My Dog is Lost*, New York: Crowell, 1960.

Latham, J., and B. Lewi, *Cuando Domingo Grazno!* New York: Macmillan, 1961.

Leaf, Munro, *El Cuento de Ferdinando* (*Ferdinand the Bull*), New York: Viking, 1955.

Lenski, Lois, *Cowboy Small* (*Vaquero Pequeno*), New York: Henry Z. Walck, 1960.

———, *Papa Small* (*Papa Pequeno*), New York: Henry Z. Walck, 1960.

Lionni, Leo, *Suimi*, New York: Pantheon, 1963.

Meeks, Esther, *La Vaca Curiosa*, Chicago: Follett, 1961.

———, *Mother Goose* (in Five Languages with Pronunciation Guides and Two Records), New York: Allied Publications, 1964.

Politi, Leo, *Pedro, El Angel de la Calle Olvera*, New York: Scribner's, 1961.

Potter, Beatrix, *Pedrin, El Conejo Travieso*, New York: Warne.

Strumpen-Darrie, R., *Berlitz Spanish Zoo Animals for Children*, New York: Grosset, 1963.

BOOKS ABOUT MEXICAN-AMERICAN CHILDREN

Agnew, Edith J., *Treasure for Tomas*, New York: Friendship, 1964 [paper].

Buffler, Esther, *Rodrigo and Rosalita*, Austin: Steck, 1949.

Bulla, Clyde Robert, *Benito*, New York: Crowell, 1961.

Clark, Ann Nolan, *Paco's Miracle*, New York: Farrar Straus and Co., 1962.

De Grazia, Nich, and James Fraser, *Las Posadas*, Flagstaff, Ariz.: Northland Press, 1963.

Ets, Marie Hall, *Gilberto and the Wind*, New York: Viking, 1963.

Ets, Marie Hall, and Aurora Labastida, *Nine Days to Christmas*, New York: Viking, 1959.

Gordon, Alvin, *Inherit the Earth*, Tucson: University of Arizona Press, 1963.

Krumgold, Joseph, *And Now Miguel*, New York: Crowell, 1953.

Politi, Leo, *Juanita*, New York: Scribner's, 1948.

———, *Song of the Swallows*, New York: Scribner's, 1949.

Schweitzer, Byrd Baylor, *Amigo*, New York: Macmillan, 1963.

Also available: A multiracial list of books and instructional aids (free) from

Educational Reading Service
East 64 Midland Ave.
Paramus, N.J.

Film: "Starting English Early," from
c/o Miss Evelyn Lane
Academic Communication Facility
U.C.L.A. 405 Hilgard Ave.
Los Angeles, Calif. 90024

LEARNING TO READ WITHOUT A TEACHER: A CASE STUDY

Jane W. Torrey

INTRODUCTION

Most children are taught to read after they are in school, but a certain number have some reading skill already when they enter first grade. Dolores Durkin (1966) reports that about one percent of approximately 5000 children who entered the Oakland, California public school system in 1958 were able to read as many as 18 out of 37 words in her simple test. Since reading is a language skill, it is reasonable to suppose that children who read earlier than usual do so because of especially high language ability or especially appropriate exposure to language. When children fail to learn reading, it seems reasonable to look for lower verbal ability or lack of appropriate exposure to language. Thus, the reading problems of slum children are commonly attributed to a lack of knowledge of language, and it is suggested that if they were given special training that would make their articulation, vocabulary, or grammatical patterns more like those of middle class children; they would be able to compete also in reading.

In view of the explanations that suggest themselves both for early reading and for reading problems in disadvantaged children, it is worthwhile to examine a case of one child of average general and verbal ability according to tests, whose language deviates from standard English both in articulation

Jane W. Torrey, "Learning to Read Without a Teacher: A Case Study," *Elementary English*, **46** (May 1968), 550–556. Reprinted with the permission of the National Council of Teachers of English and Jane W. Torrey.

and in grammar, but who has nevertheless mastered very early and without much help the difficult art of reading.

BACKGROUND

I had the opportunity to spend three hours a week for four months with a five-year-old child whom I will call John. John had entered kindergarten in a Negro school in a large southern city at the age of four years ten months. His teacher discovered that he could both read and write and that he was not interested in doing much else. The school asked me to "tutor" him, that is, to observe his reading in detail and help him put his skills to good use. These sessions took place in the living room of his home, so I was able to observe his background and environment in some detail.

John's father had approximately eight years and his mother about ten years in the Negro schools of southern cities. The father drives a truck while the mother works as a maid in a hospital. With five children, their combined income is low enough for them to qualify for subsidized housing. They suffer from those "disadvantages" that go with limited education in poor school systems plus all those others that go with having a dark skin. Although these are real deprivations, the family has the same kinds of desires and ambitions as most middle class Americans for a home of their own and good education for their children. They seem to be making the best use of their resources toward these ends. Theirs is not a case of hard core poverty with the hopelessness and disorganization that sometimes go with it.

John is the third of five children. At the time I was seeing him, they ranged from less than a year to eleven years. The older sister and brother had begun their education in a school that had recently gone from all white to all Negro and in the process had become badly over-crowded and full of severely deprived children. Their reading was average for the school, which meant a year or more behind national norms. By the time John entered kindergarten, the family had moved into the area of a much newer and less crowded but still virtually all Negro school. (Later John entered first grade in an integrated school.) John seemed to be on good terms with his siblings, and they all seemed happy and well cared for, either by their mother or grandmother. The home, a new three bedroom garden apartment, was well kept and had the normal equipment such as washing machine, TV, Hi-Fi and so forth. The children had toys and books.

HISTORY

John's mother reported that he had not begun talking especially early, but that he had been able to read almost from the time he could talk. She said no one had read to him or taught him to read. At five he read better than his older brother and sister and was occasionally able to tell his father a word. His mother once said that he must have received the gift directly from God, (perhaps along with the gift of tongues). The only plausible earthly source of instruction she was able to mention was television commercials. She reported that when he was younger, he had known all the commercials by heart and recited them as they appeared on the screen. She said she could never get his attention until the commercial was over. My own check on television showed that an average of about 40 words per hour are simultaneously shown and pronounced. On children's programs a high proportion of these words are labels on cans and boxes. John's grandmother reported that her earliest evidence of his reading knowledge came when he read labels of cans in the kitchen.

Durkin's survey studies of early reading provide a background for comparing John with other early readers. In many respects he is quite typical of this unusual group. Of her sample of 49 early readers only seven came from professional or upper middle-class homes, the rest being like John, from lower middle-class or lower. John also resembled many early readers in that he took the initiative in learning rather than having the skill taught to him at someone else's behest. Like most early readers he took a great interest in identifying words and numbers he saw. Like them, he enjoyed writing and spent much time printing words and numbers. John's earliest reading material, TV commercials and can labels, is quite typical. His social life is also similar to many others in that he was something of a loner, a Mama's boy. He had good relations with adults but lacked enough aggressiveness to be happy and hold his own with other children. He got along well with his own brothers and sisters, being particularly fond of his brother who is two years older. However, he probably did not have the benefit of his older siblings' help in reading, since he read better than either one. His mother reported that he read stories to his brother at night, stories his brother could not read for himself. He took great pride in reading and in showing off that he knew better than his brother. Durkin reports that high competitiveness is typical of early readers.

The principal difference between John's case and the others is the absence of any report of his receiving help. His mother insisted, even under cross-examination, that he had learned by himself. All reports of his reading from her or from his grandmother were simple accounts of their surprised discovery of something he already could do. His grandmother had been unprepared for his spelling and reading can labels and written TV notices. His mother had been worried about damage he might do to the library books his sister brought home. She said she often took them away from him and did not know he could read them until one day he read aloud to visitors all of what she described as a "third grade library book."

Although John's mother's reports of his reading were all cases simply of his showing off what he knew, it is quite possible that she gave him help without realizing that she was doing it. For example, in getting him to demonstrate how he could do arithmetic, she told him the answer when he guessed wrong. She and others may have done this kind of thing with words, too. She did report his playing bingo and concentration with some teen-age relatives. He could have been told numbers and words by them.

The one known source of instruction remains television commercials. It has already been mentioned that John watched and memorized them. Commercials are frequently repeated, so that whatever a child fails to learn in one showing can be drilled ad nauseam in subsequent days and weeks. Commercials are designed to get attention, so they are usually loud, lively and simple. Memorizing of short sentences is facilitated by catchy tunes. Many common words are shown and the unfamiliar brand names (e.g. "Ban," "Sominex") are usually short or easy to pronounce. It seems possible that from commercials a child could get a start on a basic vocabulary and make a few inferences about phonics, extend his reading knowledge through phonics, use the redundancy of language in simple books, ask occasional questions and be corrected by an adult.

DESCRIPTION OF READING

The tutoring situation made possible a number of direct observations of John's verbal skills. His spontaneous speech gave the basic data on his use of language. All the sessions were taped. He resisted any lengthy reading for me on the reasonable grounds that I was able to read things for myself. However, if he had to read something in the context of a game or other task, he never hesitated. Most samples of his reading were obtained in this way. Another kind of evidence came from his dictating, which occurred when he asked me to type things that were too hard for him to type himself. He took great pleasure in seeing his words emerge in print. His style of speaking changed considerably in this context from his spontaneous speech. His grammar and articulation were at their very best in dictating and it was rarely necessary to ask him to repeat or spell. It was as though he were conforming to the special style of language as it normally occurs in print.

John's oral reading was fast and confident. He showed no sign of word calling, but always read with normal sentence intonation. He could sound out words, but preferred to ask about those he did not know. Although the material might contain unfamiliar words and very unusual grammatical constructions, he was frequently able to grasp the sentence structure. For example, two rather unusual verses he read with correct sentence intonation were

The bunny now gets twenty hops,
While in the woods the lolly pops.

and

Two more hops for the bunny and then
Look out for the Pipsissewah in his den.

Although he asked for help with the word "hops" and "Pipsissewah" he read the sentences without hesitation, including the noun-verb intonation of the phrase "the lolly pops." I interpret this kind of performance as indicating that John treated written language as a natural alternate version of spoken language. He seemed to expect that print represented sentences and words with meaning. Two other kinds of behavior seemed to support this view. One was his silent reading, evidenced by the fact that he could quickly fill in blanks in written sentences without pronouncing either what he read or what he wrote. Given pictures as guides, he filled in the underlined words below without reading aloud or mouthing.

Here are some *flags*.
These are *shoes*. They belong to a *lady*.

The other evidence of his "natural" use of the written medium was his writing. Nearly all of his written production was in sentences and conveyed direct messages to me, although some were more or less on a fantasy level in that he did not expect compliance. Examples include

Put candy in the machine.
Touch the candy. Touch the jar of candy, John.
Look under the table.
Pour candy out the jar. (sic)
Jump rope.

Once, when I had been pestering him to read aloud, he printed "Get out." In print he seemed not to be afraid of offending me or provoking his mother. Although he used upper case letters wherever possible, he was capable of printing as well as reading lower case. He rarely misspelled a word, but did ask how to spell some words, for example, "laugh," apparently knowing it was a peculiar one. His grasp of the English writing system obviously went far beyond any simple sound-symbol association.

John's oral spelling was also fast and confident. Although his articulation was frequently so different from mine that I could not understand his words even when he tried very hard, he could readily spell anything he could say. For example, on one occasion, there was the following conversation, transcribed as well as possible.

John: They were tired of shopping over there. Buying toys for Christmas for the ch???s.
Me: Toys for the what?
John: Ch???s.
Me: Oh, churches.

John: Uh-uh, ch???s.
Me: Turkey?
John: Uh-uh, chrns. (Louder and very carefully articulated.)
Me: Can you spell it?
John: C. H. I. L. D. R. E. N.

Although he pronounced a final /s/ clearly, his spelling was the correct plural without "s." On another occasion he asked for help in finding one of a set of chips bearing single words. The word he wanted was /uh/, a single schwa vowel pronounced very clearly. He rejected the word "a," as in "a boy." Asked to spell what he wanted, he said:

Uh, A. R. E., uh.

It is obvious that John found little difficulty in the fact that standard English spelling was not perfectly consistent with his pronunciation. Although his own dialect of English lacked many of the sounds, especially terminal consonants, of more standard English, sounds that correspond to letters in traditional orthography, he was apparently able to take these inconsistencies in stride, along with the many others that exist for even the most articulate speaker of standard English. John's lack of difficulty raises a question about the need for some kinds of language training as preparation for reading. Although a single case can not prove that careful articulation of standard English is irrelevant to reading, it does demonstrate that it is not a necessary precondition. John's accurate reading of sentences whose grammar deviated radically from anything he would say himself is an example on the syntactic level of this same adaptation to the peculiarities of the language found in print.

John's spelling does not convert all aspects of his language into standard English, however. At one time he dictated an unusually long sentence to be transcribed on the typewriter. Asked to make clear what one of the words was, he responded by spelling the entire sentence, pausing briefly between words. It came out as follows:

Gregory put a candy in Johnny and the baby face.

Standard English would have inserted "'s" after "baby" and possibly also after "Johnny." John's dialect typically omits this possessive inflection. This particular dialect feature was carried over into his writing.

John's language development seemed not to be advanced for his age. The mean length of his utterances in morphemes at 62 months was equal to that of Brown's male subject, Adam, at 43 months. (Brown, 1967.) In grammatical development, he was also somewhat behind Adam. Brown found that when Adam was about 44 months old, he did not normally transpose the subject and verb in forming a wh question. For example

Adam's Question	*Standard English*
What John will read?	What will John read?
Where it goes?	Where does it go?

When the original sentence contains an auxiliary, the auxiliary is transposed with the subject in forming a question in standard adult English. Without an auxiliary, an inflected form of "do" is placed before the subject in forming a question. By John's age (63 months) Adam was transposing nearly all such questions, but John produced the following:

What CBS stands for?
What they say?

John rarely transposed in casual speech but in dictation he did transpose.

Where do you live at?

In reading questions with "do," he commonly omitted the word, thus producing a question in the form he would have used. Here are some sentences with his reading.

John's Reading	*Text*
When you eat breakfast?	When do you each breakfast? (sic)
When you go to school?	When do you go to school?

In other cases where "do" appeared, he misread in other ways.

John's Reading	*Text*
What does he after school?	What does he do after school?
Do he goes to school?	Does he go to school?
Does he can read books?	Does he read books?
Can he write?	Can he write?

John's handling of "may" was parallel to his use of "do." He rarely or never used either in casual speech, but did dictate correct sentences with both. He dictated the following sentences, clearly enunciating "may."

May I go outside?
May I play with the blocks?

However, in reading he avoided or stumbled over the word.

John's Reading	*Text*
Help Uncle Wiggly a hop along	You may help Uncle Wiggly a hop along.
You have to go . . .	You might have to go . . .

Several of the misreadings shown above seem to deviate from the text in the direction of conforming to John's own language. These errors suggest that John expected to find in print the things that he would normally say, that is, that writing to him was firmly understood as a natural alternate form of language. It was as though he read, not the words, but the meanings, and then expressed that same meaning his own way. John's ability to see the meaning of forms he did not use casually would be harder to account for if it were not for the evidence from his dictation showing that he did have some speaking knowledge of these forms.

TEST DATA

The Metropolitan Readiness Test was given to John when he entered kindergarten, four months before I first saw him, and again when he entered first grade a year later. Table 1 shows his scores.

Some observations of John in the tutoring situation seem consistent with

Table 1. Metropolitan Readiness Test

	Kindergarten	*First Grade*
Total	59	51
Percentile	59	42
Word meanings	7	6
Listening	9	8
Matching	10	8
Alphabet	16	16
Numbers	9	9
Copying	8	4

his pattern of scores. He was preoccupied with letters, words, and numbers and not at all interested in nonsense shapes. Although he took great pleasure in digits, his concept of the quantities they represented was very limited. For example, although he could count as high as needed or identify any number, he was not able to determine the number of objects put before him by counting them. Only after several weeks of training with counting solid objects, was he able to play a parchesi type game in which a counter moves a certain number of spaces. He could write the sequence "6 + 6 = 12," but showed no sign of understanding that if you saw three elephants and then two more elephants, you could say there were five elephants. Similarly with words, he cheerfully read words from a French picture dictionary, pronouncing them as if they were English and showing no concern about their meaning. It is consistent, therefore, that John's high performance should be on the alphabet with scores of average or below on other aspects of readiness. Table 2 shows John's performance on the Wechsler Pre-Primary

Table 2. Wechsler Pre-Primary Scale of Intelligence

Verbal		*Performance*	
Information	7	Animal House (color-form matching)	7
Vocabulary	11	Picture Completion	11
Arithmetic	9	Mazes	12
Similarities	14	Block Design	16
Comprehension	6	Geometric Design	13
Verbal I.Q.	96	Performance I.Q.	111
Full Scale I.Q.	104		

Scale of Intelligence, given to him at exactly six years after he had entered first grade. There is no evidence here that his extraordinary reading ability is a matter of unusually high intelligence, or of extraordinary verbal ability. Block design is his high point, with performance scores generally above verbal scores. On the Bender-Gestalt Visual Motor Test he showed superior visual motor ability. He drew the required figures quickly and surely, retaining the form in all but the last two figures. He drew the diamond correctly as only about 50 per cent of seven year olds can do. On the Benton Visual Retention Test, whose norms begin at eight years, his ability to reproduce figures from memory was high average to superior.

Three other tests were administered. On the Peabody Picture Vocabulary Test his I.Q. score was 111. On the Wide Range Achievement Test his reading at age six after two months in the first grade was 4.8 and spelling 5.0. However, in arithmetic achievement was 1.0. His Draw-A-Man was average for his age, done quickly and labeled "A man."

CONCLUSIONS

The following "conclusions" are presented, not as research "findings" from a single case, but rather as hypotheses suggested by its unusual aspects. Reading for John seems to have been learned but not to have been taught by anyone who was consciously aware of teaching him. He appears to have asked just the right questions in his own mind about the relation between language and print and thus to have been able to bridge the gap between his own language and the printed form. His case may have some implications for the more general task of teaching and learning reading.

1. Reading is learned, not taught.

Even in school the teacher can only provide guidance, motivating circumstances, and answers to questions. No teacher has time to tell each child everything he has to learn, much less to drill him enough times on each element. The key for learning to read may be the child's asking the right questions of his environment. If the child does that, he will be able to get the answers from a variety of sources, not necessarily including a consciously teaching older person.

2. The key question is "How does something I can say look in print?" or, vice versa, "What does that print say?"

Effective reading ultimately requires that these questions refer to whole utterances, not to phonemes and graphemes or even words. John's phonic knowledge and his word attack skills were strictly subordinate to the task of reading what it said. I interpreted his intonation patterns in reading to signify that he understood that strings of printed symbols represented language as it is spoken, not a series of sounds or words. When he did not understand what he was reading, he slurred over it, skipped words, converted it into something that was normal for him to say or just rejected the task of reading it. He never did anything remotely like sounding letter by letter a sequence that wasn't a word he knew or calling word by word a sentence whose meaning escaped him. He read as though he always expected it to say something understandable.

3. However useful high verbal ability and high cultural privilege may be in stimulating reading, neither is necessary.

John has no more than average tested verbal ability and perhaps even less than average cultural stimulation in the direction of reading. The key factor in reading therefore must be something else. Large vocabulary, sophisticated thinking, accurate articulation of standard English, active encouragement and instruction in reading skills, may very well help a child learn to read. However, even a single case like John's shows that they are not indispensable, that is, that neither success nor failure in reading can be predicted in individual cases from these factors alone.

The above comments are based on the assumption that the test scores represent a fairly accurate measure of John's intellectual ability. It may be, however, that the tests, which are based on a different cultural milieu from John's, actually underestimate his ability. For example, the Otis Quick Scoring Mental Ability Test, Form A, contains a sample item consisting of pictures of a hammer, saw, chair, and pliers. The subject is supposed to pick out the object that is "different" and name the concept represented by the three that are alike. John pointed to the pliers and asked what they were. When I pointed to the saw and asked him if he knew what it was, he said yes, it was a knife. Obviously the point of the item is lost on a child who can identify only one of the "alike" objects. Since many standardized test items assume vocabulary and knowledge that John does not have, it is quite possible that his true abilities are higher than his test scores indicate, but we have no direct evidence that this is so.

REFERENCES

Brown, R., "The Development of Why Questions in Child Speech," *Journal of Verbal Learning and Verbal Behavior*, **7**, 2 (1968), 279–290.

Durkin, D., *Children Who Read Early*, New York: Teachers College Press, 1966.

THE EFFECTS OF SELF-DIRECTIVE DRAMATIZATION ON READING ACHIEVEMENT AND SELF-CONCEPT OF CULTURALLY DISADVANTAGED CHILDREN

Lessie Carlton and Robert H. Moore

In recent times the failure of culturally disadvantaged children to make satisfactory progress in reading has come to be associated with the concept they have of themselves. For the purpose of bringing about changes in the self-concept of such children and of helping them to make more satisfactory progress in reading, self-directive dramatization was employed in this study.

The study was conducted to obtain answers to the following questions: (1) Can significantly greater gains in reading be achieved with groups of culturally disadvantaged elementary school children through the use of classroom self-directive dramatization of stories than through methods involving the traditional use of basal readers in small groups or in the whole class? (2) Can favorable changes in the self-concept of culturally disadvantaged elementary school children be brought about through classroom self-directive dramatization of stories?

RELATED LITERATURE

Self-directive dramatization was used in this study for the purpose of bringing about a change in the pupil's self-concept from a negative to a positive one,

Lessie Carlton and Robert H. Moore, "The Effects of Self-Directive Dramatization on Reading Achievement and Self-Concept of Culturally Disadvantaged Children," *The Reading Teacher*, **20** (November 1966), 125–130. Reprinted with the permission of Lessie Carlton, Robert H. Moore, and the International Reading Association. Based on research supported by the Co-operative Research Program of the U.S. Office of Education.

and for the improvement of reading. Wylie has defined the term *self-concept* as the self as a subject or agent, or the self as the individual is known to himself[13]. The latter meaning, that of how the individual sees himself, is the one given direction in this report. Wylie referred to the self-concept as good or bad, or positive or negative, while Prescott used the terms healthy and unhealthy[9].

Snygg and Combs said that how a person behaves is determined by the concept he has of himself and his abilities. They added: "What a child thinks about himself is seen in his continuous talking, beating up the younger children . . . ; and always trying to be the center of attention".[11]

Symonds advanced the theory that the goals selected by a person are related to the concept he has of himself. He said he who values himself highly will strive for high goals, while he who has a low opinion of himself will be content with mediocre attainments.[12] Kelly expressed the belief that the individual's frame of reference is highly related to accomplishing a task.[8]

Rogers,[10] Snygg and Combs,[11] and Cantor[5] have expressed the belief that changes in the self-concept occur through non-directive (or self-directive) therapy. Snygg and Combs described non-directive therapy as "a method which relies almost entirely upon the client himself to make changes in his phenomenal field when and how he chooses and in which the therapist's role is solely to provide a situation which will facilitate that process."

Axline, one of Rogers' associates, is often credited with being the first to use non-directive play therapy successfully with children.[2] With children, play therapy provides an approach not possible by other means because young children usually do not possess the necessary verbal concepts to express problems directly, even if they feel free to do so. Too, play therapy materials give a child a considerable measure of protection, for he feels that he can always deny any hint of self-involvement in the situation, "for any reasonable creature can see that this is only play".[11] Symonds said: "Every child needs an opportunity to try out, in fantasy-like play, methods of meeting emotional needs".[12]

Axline,[1] Bills,[3] and others have noted that when non-directive play therapy was used along with help in reading, the pupils made gains in reading. From Bills' conclusions comes this challenging statement: "If personal changes do result from non-directive therapy and if these techniques are adaptable to the classroom, then an approach to teaching is indicated which would include a corrective mental hygiene aspect."

Bottrell[4] and Havighurst[7] suggested ways in which a classroom teacher may help the individual child establish a self-concept that is satisfying to him. Finding work situations for the child in which he feels at ease and helping each child to feel that he is accepted by the children and teacher are some of the ideas suggested.

Carlton, in an attempt to adapt the principles of non-directive play therapy to the classroom as the medium of non-directive therapy, created and employed self-directive dramatization of stories within the frame of reference of the regular classroom. The work was done by the classroom teacher with all the children in a regular classroom as a part of the reading program for the purpose of improving achievement in reading and bringing about changes in self-concept from a negative to a positive tone.

After testing the technique at different times during a three-year period in laboratory and public schools with mostly middle-class white children, she secured the cooperation of three other classroom teachers in conducting similar experiments in as many additional classrooms of laboratory and public schools. Favorable changes in self-concept occurred in all classes, and in all classes but one a positive correlation between self-concept changes and gains in reading achievement was found. The mean gains in all classes during the experimental periods of three and one-half months ranged from 0.75 to 1.36.

The investigators have not discovered any situation in which self-directive dramatization has been employed as a basic reading instruction technique with classes made up wholly or in large part of culturally disadvantaged children.

DEFINITION OF TERMS

Self-directive dramatization of stories as it is used in this study refers to the pupil's original, imaginative, spontaneous interpretation of a character of his own choosing in a story which he selects and reads cooperatively with other pupils in a group which is formed only for the time being and for a particular story. It places emphasis upon what the child does instead of upon what the teacher does not do. It is not a new term used for an old activity such as "creative dramatics," although there may be a degree of similarity. Self-directive dramatization involves self-selection of stories, and for this purpose many books of many levels and varieties are available at all times in the classroom.

Self-concept involves "what a child thinks he is, what he thinks he can do, and what he thinks he cannot do".[6] It is assumed that a positive self-concept is conducive to progress in reading and that a negative self-concept is not conducive to progress in reading.

A *regular classroom* denotes a room which contains pupils who have been placed there only because they are in a particular grade. Pupils have not been place in such a classroom because of any intelligence or achievement test results nor because they do or do not need help in reading or other areas.

A *self-directive dramatization period* consisted of three and one-half months.

SOURCES OF DATA

The experimental groups in the study consisted of one first, one second, one third, and one fourth grade class in a public elementary school of a large city. The average number of pupils in each class at the beginning of the year was thirty. The pupils came from a low socio-economic area. Eighty-five per cent of the school population was Negro.

The teachers consisted of one man and three women. The amount of their experience in teaching ranged from student teaching to five years. Only one had worked with culturally disadvantaged children. However, all had been taught the techniques of using self-selection and self-directive dramatization in a regular classroom, the technique used with the experimental group.

Matches for each pupil were selected from other classes in the same school and from classes in another elementary school in the same system. The pupils in the control groups received reading instruction chiefly through the traditional use of the basal reader in small groups or whole-class situations.

The second school, from which many of the pupils in the control groups were drawn, had an enrollment similar in racial make-up and socio-economic level to the school in which the children of the experimental groups were enrolled. However, children in this school appeared to be more stable emotionally than those in the school in which the experimental groups were enrolled.

The teachers of the children of the control groups had spent more total years in teaching, more total years in teaching culturally disadvantaged children, and more total years in the school than had the teachers of the experimental groups.

PROCEDURES

Preceding the first dramatization period, the intelligence quotient of each child was determined by administering the California Short Form Test of Mental Maturity, S-Form (1957), Pre-Primary Grades in grade one, the California Short Form Test of Mental Maturity, S-Form (1957), Primary Grades in grades two and three, and the California Short Form Test of Mental Maturity, S-Form (1957), Intermediate Grades in grade four.

In order to obtain some measure of progress in reading, the reading section of the Gray-Votaw-Rogers Achievement Test on vocabulary and paragraph meaning, Primary Grades, Form B, was administered as a pretest preceding the first dramatization period in grades two and three, and the reading section of the Gray-Votaw-Rogers Achievement Test on vocabulary and paragraph meaning, Intermediate Grades, Form B, was administered as a pretest preceding the first dramatization period in grade four. Grade one was not tested in reading until the second dramatization period. Following the first dramatization period, comparable forms of achievement tests in reading were administered. These posttest scores were used as the pretest scores for the second dramatization period. As posttests for the second dramatization period, comparable forms of the achievement tests in reading were administered.

Self-concept questions,[6] which identified such negative behaviors of children as: "Does he refuse to do something because he says he cannot do it well?" were checked for each pupil in the experimental group preceding and immediately after each dramatization period. Since the questions were stated negatively, a decrease in the number of questions checked meant a gain for the pupil.

To determine the significance of the difference between the gains achieved through the traditional use of self-directive dramatization of stories and those achieved through the traditional use of basal texts in reading, t for matched pairs was used.

Each pupil in the four experimental classes was matched on the basis of grade, sex, intelligence score, and reading grade score with a pupil from another class in the same school or from two classes in each grade from another school in the same system. (The investigators recognize that, because of the emotional instability of these children, the intelligence scores did not give a true indication of their mental ability. However, the tests were useful in selecting matches for pupils in one culturally disadvantaged class from other culturally disadvantaged classes.)

RESULTS

In Table 1 the mean reading grade score for each of the four experimental and control groups, as determined by the first pretest administered in each grade, is given.

In grades two, three, and four only the combined data for both dramatization periods of three and one-half months are given in this report. Because first grade children were not tested in reading during the first semester, data were obtained in grade one during the second experimental period only.

Table 1. Mean reading grade scores on first pretests of experimental and control groups

Grade	*Experimental Group*	*Control Group*
1	0.58	0.85
2	1.26	1.34
3	2.17	2.05
4	3.39	3.47

Table 2 shows the gains made in reading in grades one, two, three, and four during the experimental periods.

The data show that the mean gain in reading for the first grade experimental group during the three and one-half months dramatization period was more than one year. This gain exceeded the mean gain of the control group by 0.89. The difference in mean gains was significant at the .01 level of confidence ($t = 7.42$) in favor of the experimental group.

Table 2. Gains in reading by experimental and control groups during the self-directive dramatization periods

Grade	*Experimental Group Gain*	*Control Group Gain*	*Difference**
1	1.13	0.24	0.89
2	1.87	1.25	0.62
3	1.18	0.79	0.39
4	0.85	0.43	0.42

*Difference in favor of experimental group in all four grades.

The second grade experimental group made a mean gain of 1.87 during the two experimental periods. This gain was 0.62 greater than the mean gain of the control group. The difference in mean gains was significant at the .01 level of confidence ($t = 4.43$) in favor of the experimental group.

The mean gain for the third grade experimental group during the two experimental periods was 1.18. The difference in mean gains of the experimental and control group was 0.39 in favor of the experimental group. This difference was significant at the .02 level of confidence ($t = 2.79$) in favor of the experimental group.

The main gain of the fourth grade experimental group during the experimental periods was 0.85 and the control group gain was 0.43. The difference in mean gains was significant at the .02 level of confidence ($t = 2.63$) in favor of the experimental group.

Table 3. Numbers of self-concept checks in all grades before and after self-directive dramatization periods.

Grade	*Before*	*After*	*Decrease*
1	519	204	315
2	480	82	398
3	318	104	214
4	558	105	453

Changes in self-concepts of the children, in addition to progress in reading, was of concern in this study. A decrease in the number of checks on the self-concept questions immediately after the dramatization periods led to the inference that changes did occur in the self-concept of the pupils. Table 3 shows that the pupils were checked on fewer self-concept questions following the self-directive dramatization period than preceding the dramatization periods. This was an indication of a gain in self-concept for the pupils.

CONCLUSIONS AND IMPLICATIONS

Significantly greater gains in reading were achieved in the study by groups of culturally disadvantaged elementary school children through the use of classroom self-directive dramatization of stories which pupils selected and read than through the use of methods involving the traditional techniques of the basal readers in small groups or in the whole class. There is also evidence to indicate that through the use of self-directive dramatization favorable changes occurred in the self-concept of the children.

The results obtained may well be a breakthrough in the effort to help disadvantaged children make more rapid progress in reading.

REFERENCES

1. Axline, Virginia, "Nondirective Play Therapy for Poor Readers," *Journal of Consulting Psychology*, **11** (March–April 1947), 61–69.
2. Axline, Virginia, *Play Therapy*, Boston: Houghton Mifflin, 1947.
3. Bills, R. E., "Nondirective Play Therapy with Retarded Readers." *Journal of Consulting Psychology*, **14** (April 1950), 140–149.
4. Bottrell, Helen K., "Child Society," in Harold R. Bottrell, ed., *Applied Principles of Educational Sociology*, Harrisburg: The Stackpole Company, 1954, pp. 135–157.
5. Cantor, Nathaniel, *Dynamics of Learning*, Buffalo: Foster and Stewart, 1946.
6. Carlton, Lessie, "A Report on Self-Directive Dramatization in the Regular Elementary School Classroom and Relationships Discovered with Progress in Reading Achievement and Self-Concept Changes." Unpublished doctoral dissertation, University of Houston, 1963. [Esp. pp. 4, 95–97.]
7. Havighurst, Robert J., *Human Development and Education*, New York: Longmans, Green, 1953, pp. 74–76.
8. Kelley, Earl C., "The Fully Functioning Self," *Perceiving, Behaving, Becoming*, Washington, D.C.: Association for Supervision and Curriculum Development, 1962. [Esp. p. 10.]

9. Prescott, Daniel A., *The Child in the Educative Process*, New York: McGraw-Hill, 1957. [Esp. p. 42.]
10. Rogers, C. R., *Counseling and Psychotherapy*, Boston: Houghton Mifflin, 1942.
11. Snygg, Donald, and Arthur W. Combs, *Individual Behavior*, New York: Harper, 1949. [Esp. pp. 59–78, 268–269, 309.]
12. Symonds, Percival M., *The Ego and the Self*, New York: Appleton-Century-Crofts, 1951. [Esp. pp. 10, 97.]
13. Wylie, Ruth C., *The Self-Concept*, Lincoln: University of Nebraska Press, 1961, pp. vii, 82.

STUDY QUESTIONS

1. What did the teachers in Sohn's workshop regard as the major advantages of using films in teaching the language arts? What criteria for selection and use of films are revealed in the teacher comments? Are these criteria acceptable to you?
2. How does Sohn define the "Look, See, and Write" method? How does this method train one's powers of perception? One's ability to meaningfully apply the skills of reading and writing? Could this method be adapted to the needs of younger children? How might this be done?
3. What area of learning theory was stressed in Sohn's course? To what extent does Sohn's approach build on the relationship between cognitive and affective learning?
4. What are the three developmental stages of language cited by Halpern? How do they differ? To what extent does agreement exist regarding these developmental stages and those postulated by other authors?
5. Are the teaching strategies suggested by Halpern more appropriate for Mexican-American children than for children of other minorities? Which of the four fundamental modes of communication (listening, speaking, reading, and writing) is most closely related to Halpern's strategies?
6. Why does Halpern regard pantomime and improvisation as important activities for minority-group children? How might these activities affect achievement in the language arts? What other elements of creative dramatics might be useful?
7. Would you agree that John's test scores represent an accurate measure of his intellectual ability? What elements of mental ability are not measured by the tests used by Torrey? How might these tests be changed to mitigate their cultural biases?

8. Does Torrey's case study document the importance of commercial television as an informal device for teaching reading skills? Is there any evidence to suggest that other features of John's environment played a role in his reading development? If so, what were they?
9. Why does Torrey conclude that "John's phonic knowledge and his word attack skills were subordinate to the task of reading what is said?" What does this tell you about John's attitude toward reading for meaning?
10. If you were John's teacher, what type of reading program would you recommend for him? Would you recommend a similar program for other early readers?
11. What are the implications of Carlton and Moore's findings for planning reading programs? What pre- and in-service training would be most useful to teachers desiring to implement the results of this study? What other areas of the language arts could be taught, using the authors' self directive approaches?
12. Do you have greater confidence in Carlton and Moore's findings regarding differences in reading achievement or in self-confidence? Are there other instruments that might be used today in measuring growth in the two areas? How might these compare with the instruments used by these researchers?
13. How do Carlton and Moore define "self-directive dramatization"? In what ways is it different from and similar to creative dramatics, role-playing, and dramatic play?

SUGGESTED READINGS

Ausubel, David P., "A Teaching Strategy for Culturally Deprived Pupils: Cognitive and Motivational Considerations," *School Review*, **71** (Winter 1963), 454–463.

Barrows, Marjorie Wescott, *Good English Through Practice*, New York: Henry Holt, 1956.

Blank, Marion, and Frances Solomon, "How Shall the Disadvantaged Child be Taught?" *Child Development* (March 1969), 47–61.

Dale, Edgar, *Audio Visual Methods in Teaching*, 3rd ed., New York: Dryden, 1969.

Davis, Allison, "Teaching Language and Reading to Disadvantaged Negro Children," *Elementary English*, **42** (November 1965), 791–797.

Edwards, Thomas J., "The Language-Experience Attack on Cultural Deprivation," *The Reading Teacher*, **18** (April 1965).

Fantini, Mario D., and Gerald Weinstein, "Toward Contact Classroom Methods," in *The Disadvantaged: Challenge to Education*, New York: Harper and Row, 1968, pp. 376–415.

Golden, Ruth I., *Improving Patterns of Language Usage*, Detroit: Wayne University Press, 1960.

Johnson, David W., "Freedom School Effectiveness: Changes in Attitudes of Negro Children," *Journal of Applied Behavioral Science*, **2** (1966), 325–330.

Kirchenbaum, Howard, "Teaching the Black Experience," *Media and Methods* (October 1968), 28–31.

Kohl, Herbert, *36 Children*, New York: The New American Library, 1967.

Lamb, Pose, *Guiding Children's Language Learning*, Dubuque, lowa: William C. Brown, 1967.

Ornstein, Allan C., "Techniques and Fundamentals for Teaching the Disadvantaged," *Journal of Negro Education* (Spring 1967), 136–145.

Smith, E. Brooks, Kenneth Goodman, and Robert Meredith, *Language and Thinking in the Elementary School*, New York: Holt, Rinehart & Winston, 1970.

Strickland, Ruth G., *The Language Arts in the Elementary School*, 3rd ed., Lexington, Mass.: D.C. Heath, 1969.

Taba, Hilda and Deborah Elkins, "Creating Conditions for Learning," in *Teaching Strategies for the Culturally Disadvantaged*, Chicago: Rand McNally, 1966, pp. 264–281.

Tiedt, Iris M. and Tiedt, Sidney W., *Contemporary English in the Elementary School*, Englewood Cliffs, N.J.: Prentice-Hall, 1967.

Tiedt, Iris M., "Developing Language Abilities," in *Teaching the Disadvantaged Child*, New York: Oxford University Press, 1968, pp. 44–76.

CHAPTER 7
CONTRIBUTIONS OF CHILDREN'S LITERATURE

Educators are expressing growing concern over the use of children's literature with culturally different children. Initially much of this concern centered on the treatment various minority groups received at the hands of authors and publishers of tradebooks. An array of studies conducted in the '50's and '60's documented the tendency of many books to present distorted characterizations, concepts, and stereotypes of Negroes, American Indians, Spanish-Americans, and Orientals. With few exceptions these studies alleged that because tradebooks failed to present children with accurate portrayals of the life styles of American minorities, they promoted, reinforced, and perpetuated racial and ethnic prejudice.

Gradually this criticism is subsiding. Increasingly the intellectually honest, unbiased tradebooks that critics have demanded are now becoming a reality. Recent publications of the American Library Association, the Combined Book Exhibit, the Children's Book Council, and the Center for Children's Books are beginning to identify new books that meet these criteria. But this is only the beginning; there is every reason to believe that children's tradebooks dealing with minority groups will continue to improve qualitatively and quantitatively.

As tradebooks pour from publishing houses, the problem of selection and use increases. What criteria ought to govern the selection of literature for culturally different children? How can materials be used most advantageously? What is the relationship between literature and other elements of the language arts program?

The readings selected for this chapter speak of these questions. Dorothy Seaberg opens this chapter by asking, "Is there a literature for the disadvantaged child?" How literature can promote racial understanding is described in readings by James A. Banks and Nancy Arnez. In the final reading, Robin C. Ford and Janos Koplyay reveal their research findings regarding story preferences of urban children.

IS THERE A LITERATURE FOR THE DISADVANTAGED CHILD?

Dorothy I. Seaberg

With the stress today on education of the urban poor, many writers have focused on the need for selecting literature for the young child's "here and now" world that provides identification with a story character from his own racial or ethnic group.

The Negro in Schoolroom Literature, an annotated bibliography of resource materials compiled for the Center for Urban Education, is a typical example of reading material recommended to teachers for meeting the needs of the ghetto child.[1] Although it is not the intent of compilers to shut the ghetto young off from the complete spectrum of children's literature, nevertheless most books on this and similar lists portray "integrated" and "interethnic" situations. The teacher may think that if he provides enough opportunities for this kind of personal identification, the child will suddenly emerge as one who has discovered the "joy of reading" and will henceforth be a "lifelong reader." Although culled with utmost care, these recommended lists may be misleading. It is entirely possible that book selection helps for the disadvantaged may have a subtle brainwashing effect upon teachers who unconsciously misconstrue the intent of these guides and assume the child's literary diet should be selected exclusively from "integrated" or "interethnic" realistic fiction and biography.

A number of teachers with this orientation were recently enrolled in an NDEA Institute in children's literature. The writer served as consultant when this group became engaged as resource teachers of literature in local public elementary schools in disadvantaged neighborhoods of Brooklyn.

IDENTIFICATION, PERSONAL INVOLVEMENT

Very early in the experience, one resource teacher confessed to me his disappointment over the reaction of primary children to Joan Lepau's book, *Benjie* (Dial Press). He had counted too heavily on the sociologist's precept that, if the child is put in contact with stories and pictures of children of his own skin color and environment, identification and personal involvement

---

Dorothy I. Seaberg, "Is There a Literature for the Disadvantaged Child?" *Childhood Education*, **45**, 9 (May 1969), 508–512. Reprinted by permission of Dorothy I. Seaberg and the Association for Childhood Education International, 3615 Wisconsin Ave. N.W., Washington, D.C.

are likely to occur and therefore he will enjoy the story. What the teacher expected to be easy victory had terminated in dismal defeat. He wondered whether *Benjie* was a poor book selection or whether sociologists might be wrong in their hypothesis.

The setting of this incident was a school in the Crown Heights section of Brooklyn, a community in transition. All but two of the children in this third-grade classroom were Negro or Puerto Rican; and without exception all the children were reading below grade level. It was after one of the initial meetings with his group that the resource teacher decided to share *Benjie*, a story of a small Negro boy living in an urban setting familiar to the pupils. The teacher assumed the book would meet with the sociologist's criterion of "identification"; but, to his dismay, the story left the children with no sense of wonder or excitement—only bleak apathy. The teacher had planned to let the children express their feelings through drawing a scene which had appealed to them in the story, but they countered with complete indifference.

By contrast, Claire Hutchet Bishop's *The Five Chinese Brothers* (Coward-McCann) was received enthusiastically. In this modern folk tale each of the five identical brothers is saved from fearful punishment through his adroit use of a unique ability: one can swallow the sea, one has an iron neck, one can stretch his legs to any height, one cannot be burned, and the last can hold his breath indefinitely.

"Not only was the story very appealing to the pupils," the resource teacher reflected in his daily log, "but the illustrations also filled them with

> fascination and delight! One child exclaimed, 'That brother is going to bust if he doesn't let out the sea!' Another child mused pensively, 'I wish I could stretch my legs like him.' 'I wish I could be a Chinese brother!' added a third child, caught up in the wonder and magic of the story. During the reading, the pupils listened intently, laughed at some of the illustrations, and gave every appearance of enjoying the ingenious tale."

A spontaneous outbreak of pantomime and creative dramatics followed and later the children shared a choral speaking version of the story in the auditorium. After thinking it over, the resource teacher decided *The Five Chinese Brothers* had appealed to the children because of its simple, imaginative text and intriguing illustrations. "The chief criterion for interesting children in reading," he concluded, "is the same as it has always been—a well-told story that stirs a child's imagination and fancy. Young children," he deduced, "prefer this to harsh realism." In making his observation, the resource teacher was saying that children have universal needs, one of which is the need for fantasy. Disadvantaged children are no exception. When one considers the culture of poverty from which these children come and when one also realizes the needs these people have for immediate gratifications, we realize that escape valves are necessary for coping with the hard realities of life. We might hypothesize that disadvantaged children, of all children, stand most in need of the magic of the fairy tale in their literary fare. This suggests that if teachers want to "hook disadvantaged children on books" they should tip the scale in favor of fiction fantasy when selecting books to read to children or in locating material for the child to use in the process of learning to read.

Since the Institute, I have thought a good deal about the literature resource teacher's experience and two generalizations that occurred again and again in one form or other in the participants' final papers. On the basis of their summer's experience with these inner city children (but also drawing upon their experience in working with many other children in similar and dissimilar situations), these teachers observed that:

1. Folk literature and fantastical fiction seem to have the greatest appeal of all types of literary genre for the urban child.
2. If realistic fiction is employed with the urban young, it must possess realism related to the real life experiences of the child. It is only then that identification can take place.

I have been pondering the ideas presented by Kornei Chukovsky, noted Soviet Children's author, in his book *From Two to Five*[2] and those set forth by Susanne Langer in her chapter on "Life Symbols: The Roots of Myth," from *Philosophy in a New Key.*[3] These two writers have delineated the substance of the two above generalizations in a remarkable way and support the notion that fiction fantasy is the literary genre most needed by all young children. Included in the fiction fantasy is the traditional folk and fairy tale as well as the fantastical tale in which fantastic happenings are introduced into an otherwise realistic setting, such as the well-known stories of *Peter Pan* and *Mary Poppins*.

In describing the fairy tale, long known to be a perennial favorite of children, Susanne Langer writes:[4] "It is irresponsible; it is frankly imaginary,

> and its purpose is to gratify wishes. Its heroes and heroines, though of delightfully high station, wealth, and beauty are simply individuals; 'a certain prince,' 'a lovely princess.' The theme is generally the triumph of an unfortunate one—an enchanted maiden, a youngest son, a poor Cinderella, an alleged fool—over his or her superiors, whether these be kings, bad fairies, strong animals, stepmothers, or elder brothers. In short, the fairytale is a form of 'wishful thinking.' It is a personal gratification, the expression of desires and of their imagery fulfillment, a compensation for the shortcomings of real life, an escape from actual frustration and conflict. The fairytale technique transports a natural individual to a fairyland outside reality."

Susanne Langer points out that "the real use of the fairy tale is for supplying vicarious experience—a self-centered fancy from which all realistic thinking springs."[5]

When one considers the power of the fairy story, as a wish-fulfilling device or a way of escape from the hard realities of life, it is no wonder the fairy tale lives forever and appeals to *all* children. Certainly, if children are "disadvantaged" the wish-fulfillment appeal should be all the more convincing and they, of all children, stand most in need of this form of vicarious escape. Yet in pursuing this circuitous path of escape, if Susanne Langer is right, the child will come full circle back to the realm of realistic thought, enabling him better to cope with the world as it really is.

Is it mentally healthful to use fiction fantasy as an escape from reality, even temporarily? Furthermore, if it is legitimate escape, do children of the poor have time for such frivolity? Should they not be reading factual material? Expressing a concern regarding an after-school program for the disadvantaged, a community leader said, "The extra time spent in school should be spent on drill in the reading skills and not in entertaining the children with stories, creative dramatics or art activities." Little did he realize that this precisely may be the place in which the real deprivation lies.

NONSENSE VERSE AND FAIRY TALES

Kornei Chukovsky speaks out to Soviet educators and parents about similar adult concerns: Should young children be exposed to nonsense verse? Is there danger that unrealistic stories will displace the realistic, factual and informational books about radios and diesel engines? If a child reads fairy tales will he turn away from technology and henceforth dream about firebirds to the end of his days?

Chukovsky defends nonsense verse and the fairy tale as not only legitimate literary material for young children but as necessary for their emotional and mental health and development. He reasons that because fantasy is in itself a valuable attribute to the human mind, it should be nurtured and cultivated from earliest childhood. Fanciful literature achieves this purpose, for it enhances the child's imagination and thereby contributes to creative thought. At the same time, reality is strengthened for the child through his recognition of the distortions that appear in nonsense verse and the fairy tale. According to Chukovsky, *"topsy-turvy" verse has an educational value because it helps the child orient himself to the world around him*. In the lines

The piglet meowed—
Meow! Meow!
The kitten oinked—
Oink! Oink!

it is obvious that piglets do not "meow" and kittens do not "oin[illegible] therefore this bit of nonsense verse strengthens a sense of the real[illegible] child's mind. The incongruity of the situation is self-evident and the child enjoys the opportunity this topsy-turvy rhyme affords him for verification and self-examination. *The child's self-appreciation is enhanced because he realizes his power in being able to detect the unreal as he juxtaposes it against the real.*

"The function of similar rhymes and fanciful stories is obvious," Chukovsky writes. "For every wrong the child realizes what is right, and

> every departure from the normal strengthens his conception of the normal. Thus he values even more highly his firm, realistic orientation. He tests his mental prowess and invariably he passes this test, which appreciably increases his self-esteem as well as his confidence in his intellectual abilities; this confidence is most essential to him in order that he may not become discouraged in his chaotic world. I'm not the kind that burns himself with cold 'kaska'; I'm not one to get scared of a snail. I will certainly not look for strawberries on the bottom of the sea."[6]

Even when fairy tales are withheld, children often become their own Andersen, Grimm or Ershov, creating fanciful escapades and imaginary playmates or animal friends with supra-magical powers. Later on, the child arrives at a stage in his development when the fairy tale loses its charm and he exposes the fantasy as relentlessly as he previously espoused it. When his need of the fairy tale has ended, the child himself does away with it. "But up to the age of seven or eight," Chukovsky maintains, "the fairy tale is as important to the psychological development of the child as is a wholesome balanced diet to his physical welfare." "Now it is regarded," he says, "as a generally recognized truth that the fairy tale develops, enriches, and humanizes the child's psyche,

> since the child who listens to fairy tales feels like an active participant and always identifies himself with those characters who crusade for justice, goodness, and freedom. It is in this active sympathy of little children with the high-minded and brave heroes of literary invention that lies the educational value of the literature of fantasy."[7]

How do Langer's and Chukovsky's writings enlighten the discoveries made by the resource teachers in the NDEA Institute? *These two writers have built a strong case for the inherent need of all children to feed upon fantasy; both agree that fantasy assists the child in sorting out the realities that lie within his world.* Langer seems to feel that fantasy as expressed in the fairy tale provides for vicarious wish-fulfillment as well, but from this self-centered fancy realistic thinking eventually springs.

Chukovsky does not stress the "escape from reality value" of nonsense poetry and the fairy tale as does Langer but he argues strongly for the developmental need of the child to slip into fantasy, juxtaposing it against real life situations to give reality to the norms that exist. Furthermore, *fantasy develops the imagination and the fairy tale helps the child to identify with the side of justice, goodness and freedom.* If Chukovsky is right, all children—and especially the disadvantaged—need an ample dose of fanciful fiction from at least Head Start through the primary grades.

REALISTIC STORIES THAT FIT

It should not be assumed from these arguments, however, that children of this age have no need for the "here and now" story or for stories about children similar to themselves in skin color and background. These stories they should have, too, but the problem seems to be in finding the story that has an actual real life "fit." Though primary-age children did not especially seem to care about *Benjie*, Ezra Jack Keats' *Whistle for Willie* (Viking) was a favorite. *Whistle for Willie* (only the illustrations show he is Negro) does not emphasize skin color but rather the problem of a small boy achieving the skill of whistling for his dog after the manner of the "big" boys. "Happiness," in this story, "is learning to whistle"—the kind of realistic wish-fulfillment any boy could long for.

In searching for the right "here and now" book, it is difficult to find one with the appeal of *Whistle for Willie*, as many books are too generalized in the experiences they portray or else they are written for children in a specific urban setting without a generalized appeal (impossible to achieve, in fact) for all urban settings. Therefore, these books are not congruent with the child's actual life experience. This is probably the reason so many of the recommended books fail to speak to urban children and explains why the NDEA literature resource teachers made this observation:

> If realistic fiction is employed with the urban young, it must possess realism related to the real life experiences of the child. It is only then that identification can take place.

Whether making a selection from fantasy or from a true-to-life story, the symbols entailed need to be within the experience of the child. One resource teacher found that the poem, "The Ups and Downs of the Elevator Car," did not appeal to the children because they didn't know what an elevator was. An appreciation for the poem was immediately obvious once this perplexing problem was cleared up. Chukovsky is making the same point when he says the child will miss the humor in the verse

> The children skated on the ice
> on a hot summer's day

if they do not know there is ice only in cold weather. However, stories and poems with unfamiliar concepts, whether they be fanciful or realistic, need not necessarily be omitted from the child's reading or listening diet provided the teacher can find a skillful way of making the unknown known to the child.

Is there, then, a special literature for the disadvantaged young? In selecting literature for disadvantaged children, we need to remember first that they are children possessing a kinship or common bond with all childhood. Therefore we need to guard against setting up artificial barriers in the selection of literature but rather let the child share in the heritage of timeless and ageless classics highly prized by all children. This should perhaps be the first priority as we search also for the meaningful realistic books with which a given child can identify.

If fiction fantasy has the advantage of making the child's life more buoyant and fulfilling and of enhancing his self-concept and appreciation for his own mental powers as Chukovsky has suggested, then all the evidence points clearly in the direction of more fiction fantasy for all young children—and most especially for the disadvantaged child. If he is carried away on the wings of the fantastical more frequently, perhaps he will be helped to find his own identity, realize more self-assurance, and have his imagination kindled and come alive to reading and to books. And what more can we ask of literature for the disadvantaged child—or any child for that matter?

NOTES

1. Minnie W. Koblitz, *The Negro in Schoolroom Literature*, New York: Center for Urban Education, 1966.
2. Kornei Chukovsky, *From Two to Five*, translated and edited by Miriam Morton, Berkeley: University of California Press, 1963.
3. Susanne K. Langer, *Philosophy in a New Key*, Cambridge, Mass.: Harvard University Press, 1951.
4. *Ibid.*, p. 151.
5. *Ibid.*, p. 154.
6. Chukovsky, *From Two to Five*, p. 102.
7. Chukovsky, *Ibid.*, p. 130. Reprinted by permission of the Regents of the Univ. of Calif.

DEVELOPING RACIAL TOLERANCE WITH LITERATURE ON THE BLACK INNER-CITY CHILD

James A. Banks

When white suburban children read that 47 blacks lost their lives in the explosive Detroit riot of 1967, and that an unarmed black teenager was gunned down by a white policeman in the Algiers Hotel amidst that disturbance, their emotions are not likely to be deeply aroused because such cold statistics and incredible incidents seem remote from their lives and experiences. It is only when we are well acquainted with an individual or people that we suffer intensely when they are hurt or harmed. In literature, children can read about individuals from different cultures and subcultures, come to know them as human beings, develop intense feelings for them, and experience agony when they are exploited or mistreated.

Young readers are saddened when Lonnie is murdered by a white racist and David Williams is attacked by a white mob in *Whose Town?*. They react strongly to these incidents because author Lorenzo Graham builds his characters so successfully that children feel that Lonnie and David are their pals. When Lonnie is killed, children lose a cherished and delightful friend. They are enraged when David is beaten, because no sensitive child wants to see his pal beaten mercilessly, especially when he has done nothing to warrant attack. Some children conclude that limp and starving Zeke, a black ghetto child vividly and sympathetically portrayed in *The Jazz Man*, dies at the end of the story and weep because Zeke captures young children's hearts. Henry in *Durango Street*, Jethro and Fess in *The Soul Brothers and Sister Lou*, and Jimmy in *Dead End School* are other memorable characters of the black ghetto who evoke deep feelings and concern in young readers.

Given the immense racial crisis which pervades the nation, it is imperative that we help "culturally sheltered" children to develop positive attitudes toward persons who are different from themselves racially and culturally. An acquaintance with different cultures and groups *can* contribute to the development of the kind of tolerance so desperately needed in our highly polarized society. Since most American children live in tightly segregated communities, they have little opportunity to interact and to become acquainted with people of different races and groups.

Literature can help bridge the gap by acquainting children with people who belong to other racial and ethnic groups. However, like actual social contact, familiarity with other groups through literature *can* help develop racial understanding and tolerance, but *may* also reinforce stereotypes and misconceptions. A child who reads *The Jazz Man* may feel intensely negative toward Zeke's parents because they desert him, and conclude that all black parents in the inner-city are irresponsible and heartless. If inappropriate teaching strategies are utilized, literature will enhance rather than mitigate the development of racial bias.

To use such a book as *The Jazz Man* effectively in social studies, the teacher *must* help children see how characters such as Zeke's parents are the victims of harsh and painful discrimination. Zeke's father is unable to find a meaningful and challenging job; his mother deserts the family when she becomes disillusioned with her husband's working situation. Father turns to drinking when his wife leaves because he feels that he has failed as a man. He physically escapes from Zeke's life. With carefully structured questions, and by leading the children to factual informational sources on the black inner-city, the teacher can help children develop empathy and concern for both Zeke and his parents. The teacher could ask the children questions based on why Zeke's father can't find a good job, and why his mother buys groceries daily, and why the family lives in a dilapidated apartment. After carefully researching these kinds of questions, the students will discover that the real villain in the story is neither of Zeke's parents, but a society which discriminates against poor and black people. The teacher could ask the children to think of actions which could be taken by the larger society to eliminate the kinds of problems encountered by Zeke's family. They should also be encouraged to predict possible consequences of the actions they propose.

Other aspects of black ghetto life portrayed in children's literature might reinforce stereotypes without careful and effective teacher guidance. Most of the families depicted in children's novels lack a father, the home is crowded, mother works as a domestic and is the dominant family member, formal education is not often encouraged, and the family attends a store-front church. It is extremely important that the teacher help the child understand *why* these conditions frequently *do* exist in the black ghetto. However, it is imperative that children become aware of the extent of these conditions in the inner-city. For example, while nearly one-fourth of the black families in America are headed by females, a highly significant three-fourths are headed by men.[1] Recent educational literature suggests that most black parents *do* want their children to attain a formal education, but that they are often unaware of ways to actualize their aspirations.[2] If maximum benefits are to accrue from the utilization of realistic fiction in the social studies, the teacher must encourage students to ascertain the extent to which "realities" portrayed in literature can be generalized to the actual world in which they live. When children read about riots in *Northtown*, they should make a survey of the cities in which riots have actually occurred, and determine the degree to which Mr. Graham's description of racial violence and conflict reflects factual information.

Children will be unable to fully understand and appreciate the American black experience unless they are acutely aware of the devastating effects of slavery on both the black man and his master. The legacy of slavery is still manifested in the black inner-city. Literature can help children gain insights into American slavery. In her beautiful yet poignant biography, *Amos Fortune: Free Man*, Elizabeth Yates vividly describes how Amos Fortune, an African prince enslaved in America, emerges from an overwhelmingly dehumanizing experience "humanized" and perhaps more human because of it. At times children may find this book excruciating beyond tolerance, but perhaps it is this kind of grim realism which helps us attain deeper insights and empathy. The stark realism which permeates this book would be difficult to portray in a social studies textbook.

Julius Lester's *To Be a Slave* is a highly selected and edited collection of documents dictated by former slaves which includes helpful editorial comments. The former slaves' vivid descriptions of suicides, merciless beatings, and the huts in which they lived will evoke intense emotions and reactions. This description of the scars inflicted upon an escaped slave will give children some feeling of what it was like to be a slave:

> My friend desired me to look at his back, which was seamed and ridged with scars of the whip and hickory, from the pole of his neck to the lower extremity of his spine. The natural color of his skin had disappeared and was succeeded by a streaked and speckled appearance of dusky white and pale flesh color, scarcely any of the original black remaining.[3]

At the turn of the century, most black Americans lived in the Southern states which had made up the Confederacy. Later they began an exodus to Northern cities to escape the poverty, violence, and discrimination which they experienced in the South. The jobs which opened up in Northern cities during World War I and the prevalence of lynchings and other violent acts in the South were cogent factors which pushed the black man northward. Blacks poured into Northern cities again during World War II when jobs were prevalent in defense industries.[4] *South Town*, *North Town*, and *Whose Town?* by Lorenz Graham will acquaint children with the problems faced by a typical black Southern family, and how the Williams attempted to solve them by migrating North. *South Town* is a poignant, gripping, yet realistic story about the family's painful experiences with racism in a Southern community. The book is replete with examples of harsh, overt, and unrelenting incidents of bigotry. The book is extremely powerful because the characters are completely believable.

In *North Town*, the Williams discover, like many other Southern black migrants, that the North is no promised land. Their small house is in a slum, David no longer has a room of his own, and he gets into trouble with the police because he lives in a "bad" neighborhood. The family gradually discovers that prejudice "Northern style" is more covert and subtle but no less insidious than Southern racism. The adjustments which David and his family must make in North Town and the disillusionments which they experience epitomize the problems encountered by the black Southern migrant in the Northern city. The reader will sympathize with David's awkward attempts to adjust to a racially-mixed school which is covertly racist, and admire his courage as he leads the family through a major catastrophe. While most children's books on the black inner-city portray a fatherless home, this one depicts a closely-knit family whose greatest strength and power lie in a strong, loving, and understanding father. For this reason, it should be given special emphasis.

In the third and most outstanding book in his trilogy, *Whose Town?*, Graham effectively and poignantly describes the black revolt of the 1960's as manifested in fictional Northtown—which could be Newark, Detroit, Chicago or any other American city in which riots have occurred. In candid detail, he relates how the racial tension in Northtown results in brutal and unprovoked attacks against blacks, killings, and finally a riot when a small black boy is drowned by a white mob at a public pool. The author makes it clear that the pool incident merely triggered the riot, but that it had deeper causes. Gross unemployment, constant indignities and insults, stark poverty and slum housing, and white racism, which permeated the city, were the root causes. The teacher could ask the children to compare this description of the riot in Northtown to newspaper accounts of outbreaks in cities such as Los Angeles, New York, Detroit, and Chicago in the 1960's:

> Gradually the crowd fell back. The people began moving toward the east side. They left behind a block of stores and business places about half of which had been smashed open and several of which had been burned. Merchandise was strewn in the street. Some of it was carried away by looters. David could not tell how many had been arrested. Some who had been hurt were carried off in ambulances and police cars. Others whose heads were bruised and whose faces were bloody were helped away by friends.[5]

Other harsh social realities are revealed in this seminal and gripping novel. The white man who kills Lonnie in cold blood is freed because of what the jury dubs "justifiable homicide." Children could compare this slaying with the Detroit Algiers Hotel incident. When David is attacked by a white mob, he, rather than the attackers, is jailed and humiliated.

Mr. Williams' perpetual unemployment disrupts the family, forces Mrs. Williams to work as a domestic, emasculates him, and turns him into a bitter and disillusioned man. The strength and power which he evidences in the earlier novels are dissipated. Children can study factual informational sources on the inner-city to validate the reality of Mr. Williams' experiences. This novel vividly illuminates the powerlessness and alienation of the black community, and indicates how the black migrant's dream of finding a heaven on earth in Northern cities was almost completely shattered in the 1960's. *Whose Town?* is destined to become a classic in children's literature. In it, Mr. Graham attains the acme of his literary career.

One of the characteristic groups in the inner-city is the gang. Novels whose setting is the black ghetto can help children understand why boys sometimes join gangs, the needs they satisfy, and how a gang can be transformed into a constructive group when gang members are encouraged and helped to satisfy their group needs in more legitimate ways. Frank Bonham studied a number of gangs in Los Angeles and embodied what he learned in *Durango Street*, an interesting story about Rufus Henry and the Moors. When he is released from a camp for delinquent boys, Rufus and his sister are attacked by the Gassers, a local gang. After his attack, Rufus realizes that he must violate his parole and join a rival gang if he is to survive in his neighborhood. Young readers will sympathize with Rufus as he longs for a father, and will share his triumphs as he leads the Moors to street victories and finally into more constructive pursuits. In using this book, the teacher could ask the children to think of ways Rufus might have solved his problems without joining the Moors. They may conclude that he had few other alternatives.

Kristin Hunter's powerful novel, *The Soul Brothers and Sister Lou*, is a story about 14-year-old Louretta Hawkins, and her friends the Hawks, a Southside gang. A strong person, Lou persuades the Hawks to use their group efforts constructively. However, their attempts to pursue legitimate activities are continually frustrated by the local police, who perpetually harass them and brutally kill Jethro. The author skillfully and effectively handles police brutality and other violent acts which take place on the "rough" Southside. When reading this book, the class could study the causes of police brutality in the black ghetto and use factual sources to study actual cases. This book will also help the reader attain many insights into black family life in the inner-city. *The Soul Brothers and Sister Lou* has many strong characters and memorable incidents which will help the child develop empathy for ghetto residents. Fierce but brilliant Fess, talented and lonesome Blind Tom, shy and sensitive Calvin, and Lou, who searches relentlessly for her black identity, will deeply impress the reader.

Poetry by black American writers can be used in the social studies to help children develop empathy and understanding of the black experience and life in the inner-city. Most black poets express their feelings, emotions, and aspirations in their poetry. They have been preoccupied with themes dealing with oppression, freedom, and the meaning of blackness in America. In "Montage of a Dream Deferred," Langston Hughes asks what happens to a deferred dream and implies that it explodes. When studying race riots, this poem would be especially appropriate. The teacher could ask the children what dreams of black people have been deferred, and in what ways have they exploded. Claude McKay's anguished and evocative poem, "If We Must Die," can also stimulate a discussion on race riots. McKay penned this poem when riots broke out in our cities in 1919.

An infinite number of beautiful, poignant, and revealing poems are available for use to teach children the facts of ghetto life. *Bronzeville Boys and Girls* by Pulitzer Prize winning poet Gwendolyn Brooks is a collection of poems about children in the inner-city. This book includes happy, sad, as well as thoughtful reflections by urban children which reveal their feelings and emotions. *On City Streets*, edited by Nancy Larrick, is a collection of poems about the inner-city which urban children helped to select. The book includes captivating photographs which enhance the appeal of the poems. Stephen M. Joseph's *The Me Nobody Knows: Children's Voices from the Ghetto* includes poetry and prose written by children who live in the inner-city. In their accounts they reveal their fears, aspirations, and a limited, but eventful, world.

American Negro Poetry by Arna Bontemps, *I Am the Darker Brother: An Anthology of Modern Poems by Negro Americans* by Arnold Adoff, and *The Poetry of the Negro* by Langston Hughes and Arna Bontemps are excellent and comprehensive anthologies of black poetry. Poetry can evoke interest and help children gain deep insights into the moods and feelings of black inner-city residents.

Our very existence may ultimately depend upon our creative abilities to solve our urgent racial problems. The flames that burned in Watts, the blood that ran in Detroit, and the willingness of black leaders to chance assassination by taking strong stands on social issues indicate that the black American is willing to pay almost any price to secure those rights which he believes are his by birthright. The reactions by the white community to the black man's new militancy have been strong and intense. A "law and order" cult has emerged to stem the tide of the black revolt.[6] Since our major social problems grow from the negative attitudes which whites have toward blacks,[7] we must modify the racial attitudes of whites if we are to create the democratic society that we verbally extol. When used effectively, literature can help white children in our sheltered suburban areas to develop racial tolerance and a commitment to the eradication of social injustice.

NOTES

1. James A. Banks, "A Profile of the Black American: Implications For Teaching," *College Composition and Communication*, vol. 19 (December, 1968), pp. 288–296. See also Andrew Billingsley, *Black Families in White America* (Englewood Cliffs, N.J.: Prentice-Hall, Inc., 1968).
2. Robert L. Green (editor), *Racial Crisis in American Education* (Chicago: Follett Educational Corporation, 1969).
3. Julius Lester, *To Be a Slave* (New York: The Dial Press, Inc., 1969), p. 124.
4. James A. Banks, *March Toward Freedom: A History of Black Americans* (Palo Alto: Fearon Publishers, 1970).
5. Lorenz Graham, *Whose Town?* (New York: Thomas Y. Crowell Company, 1969), p. 194.
6. James A. Banks, "Racial Prejudice and the Black Self-Concept," in James A. Banks and Jean D. Grambs, *Black Self-Concept* (New York: McGraw-Hill Book Company, in press).
7. *Report of the National Advisory Commission on Civil Disorders* (New York: Bantam Books, 1968).

CHILDREN'S BOOKS CITED

Arnold Adoff, *I Am the Darker Brother: An Anthology of Modern Poems by Negro Americans* (New York: The Macmillan Company, 1968). Illustrated by Benny Andrews.

Frank Bonham, *Durango Street* (New York: E. P. Dutton and Company, Inc., 1965).

Arna Bontemps (editor), *American Negro Poetry* (New York: Hill and Wang, 1963).

Gwendolyn Brooks, *Bronzeville Boys and Girls* (New York: Harper and Row Publishers, 1965). Illustrated by John Kaufmann.

Natalie Savage Carlson, *The Empty Schoolhouse* (New York: Harper and Row Publishers, 1965). Illustrated by John Kaufmann.

Robert Coles, *Dead End School* (Boston: Little, Brown and Company, 1968). Illustrated by Norman Rockwell.

Lorenz Graham, *North Town* (New York: Thomas Y. Crowell Company, 1965).

Lorenz Graham, *South Town* (Chicago: Follett Publishing Company, 1958).

Lorenz Graham, *Whose Town?* (New York: Thomas Y. Crowell Company, 1969).

Langston Hughes and Arna Bontemps (editors), *The Poetry of the Negro 1746–1949* (Garden City: Doubleday and Company, 1949).

Kristin Hunter, *The Soul Brothers and Sister Lou* (New York: Charles Scribner's Sons, 1969).

Stephen M. Joseph (editor), *The Me Nobody Knows: Children's Voices from the Ghetto* (New York: Avon Books, 1969).

Nancy Larrick (editor), *On City Streets* (New York: Bantam Books, 1964). Illustrated with photographs.

Julius Lester, *To Be a Slave* (New York: The Dial Press, Inc., 1968). Illustrated by Tom Feelings.

Mary Hays Weik, *The Jazz Man* (New York: Atheneum, 1967). Illustrated by Ann Grifalconi with woodcuts.

Elizabeth Yates, *Amos Fortune: Free Man* (New York: Dutton and Company, Inc., 1950). Illustrated by Nora Unwin.

RACIAL UNDERSTANDING THROUGH LITERATURE

Nancy L. Arnez

The best way of knowing what it means to be a Negro is to be a Negro. To put it more poignantly, as Baldwin says, "Search in his shoes, for a job, for a place to live, ride, in his skin, on segregated buses, see with his eyes, the signs saying 'White' and 'Colored' and especially the signs saying 'White Ladies' and 'Colored Women'."[1] Griffin, author of *Black Like Me* (New American Library of World Literature), tried this approach by medically darkening his skin to discover what it is like to be black in America. Obviously, there are obstacles inherent in this direct kind of education. Seemingly, the next best approach to obtaining a close inside feeling for what is going on in another man's life is through day-to-day interaction with him and his. Complexities prevent our use of this approach too. So we settle for a third best way. We seek to approximate the Negro's experiences as closely as we can by use of literature (novels, short stories, biographies, autobiographies, diaries, poetry, and drama), in which the author has

---

Nancy L. Arnez, "Racial Understanding Through Literature," *English Journal*, **58** (January 1969), 55–61. Reprinted with the permission of the National Council of Teachers of English and Nancy L. Arnez.

expressed himself in such a way that we can identify with him and live the experiences, albeit vicariously. Thus literature can give us a closer inside feeling for what is going on in our Negro culture.

Harrington in *The Other American: Poverty in the United States* (Penguin), also alludes to our difficulty of truly knowing both intellectually and emotionally what it means to be what we are not in the following passage:

> The poor can be described statistically; they can be analyzed as a group. But they need a novelist as well as a sociologist if we are to see them. They need an American Dickens to record the smell and texture and quality of their lives. The cycles and trends, the massive forces, must be seen as affecting persons who talk and think differently (p. 24).

The purpose of this approach is not to make literary judgments. Rather, the approach here is to view each piece of literature in relation to understanding the ethos of the Negro and in so doing minimize his complexities by bringing his similarities and differences to the general consciousness.

By pointing out the similarities and differences in the life style of the Negro, we hope to show that his behavior and cultural response arise from the situation in which he finds himself. What we are suggesting is that literature through its dramatic impact can inculcate in the reader certain social and anthropological insights which the reader may not glean from reading sociology or anthropology texts.

From these insights, the reader should be able to move from the literary selections into meaningful discussions which can lead to an appreciation for the ethos of the Negro who, though different from others superficially, does share a common humanity of anguish, pain, desires, and ambition.

Thus, the Negro is no longer invisible but stands visibly etched upon each reader's pupils. His half-blindness is dispelled, his dark glasses removed, and he is no longer a lyncher of souls. He will discover in this approach that life is people, and people are individuals one by one. He will also discover that he is connected to Negroes singly by taste and sensibility. Each one separately whom the reader selects as his friend will reaffirm the general contours of his life. In this way the reader can learn from another's experiences by investing bits and pieces of his own experience into the sighs and laughter of others as he projects himself into a synthetic situation.

The point then is to destroy group prejudices by getting acquainted with characters who are giving and receiving and interacting. In this way the reader can take the idea of humanity from the story books and make it his.

Therefore, reading literature written by Negroes is in an important sense one of the best bridges of communication between the Negro and the non-Negro. In this way other people will learn how some Negroes have fared in the job market, in housing, in social relationships, in education.

It is necessary to remember though that there is no one Negro experience in America. There are twenty-two million separate experiences, for it is absurd to think of one Negro writer as the spokesman for the group, even though some of the experiences are shared ones in the sense of having been experienced by other Negroes. But to make generalizations for the Negro race on the basis of novels and poems and plays by Negroes is dehumanizing and stereotyping. Each story is what the author experienced, felt, said.

Nevertheless, one can learn something about the quality of tenement living, the crowdedness, the lack of privacy, the lack of economic security, the rats and roaches and the rancid, penetrating, distinctive smell of garbage. One can learn, too, about the jobs Negroes are allowed to have—as maids, porters, elevator operators, laborers, dishwashers—which siphon off all energy except that required to fight, to love, to pray. One is exposed to the hangups about color and hair, the high society crowd of boot-leggers, the professionals, the self-hatred, the denigration, the laughter, the crime, the dope, the alcohol.

Therefore, we do not stop at a description of conditions as portrayed, but we use this mass of descriptive material about how things are and why to fashion and mold a saner approach to how life must become for universal survival.

One may then ask the question "How did Claude Brown survive in spite of the debilitating forces of Harlem?" Performing his many roles in the auditorium of his peers, on the stage of his family, in the arena of Harlem's public, Claude Brown was an efficient actor. He survived by playing his roles well. Or one may ask how the men of the master poet Langston Hughes' era survived cleaning spittoons? Or, again, how did Baldwin shove the sea of hate aside and survive? Or, how did Malcolm X snatch sanity from the air and survive? In spite of it all, they did survive. But many do not, many lose the fight and the war. The operation fails so the patient dies.

Reading reveals a vivid picture of the lives of Negroes in such areas as housing, education, family relations, child rearing practices, delinquency and crime, the life space of the inhabitants of the ghetto, religion, and employment. Readers of this literature can come to feel as the Negro feels as he wends his way through his wretched existence in America.

The Negro has obviously been discriminated against in the area of job opportunities and social expansion. Some examples from literature can vividly illustrate this point. Claude Brown in *Manchild in the Promised Land* (Signet) has this to say about job opportunities:

It was all right for a while, until I realized what was happening. After

> I became accustomed to the job, I found out I just couldn't stay there. I was doing more work than anyone else and getting less money. It seemed that they always kept one Negro around to do the heavy work, the jobs nobody else wanted to do. So I decided to get fired and collect unemployment compensation for awhile (p. 360).

And again he writes in the same book:

> A guy who worked in the garment center wouldn't say he had a job; he'd say, "man, like, I got a slave. . . . They looked like they were sixty years old, but they were still pushing trucks through the snow" (p. 33).

For another view, listen to the truth as propounded in this excerpt of a poem by Langston Hughes:

> Detroit
> Chicago
> Atlantic City,
> Palm Beach.
> Clean the spittoons.
>
> The steam in hotel kitchens,
> And the smoke in Hotel lobbies
> And the slime in hotel spittoons;
> Part of life.
> Hey, boy!
>
> A nickel,
> A dime,
> A dollar,
> Two dollars a day,
> Hey, boy!
>
> A nickel,
> A dime,
> A dollar
> Two dollars
>
> Buy shoes for the baby.
> House rent to pay,
> Gin on Saturday,
> Church on Sunday.
>   My God!
> . . . .[2]

Perhaps one of the most frustrating problems that still face the American Negro today is the continual joblessness due to unfair employment practices.

Although there appears to be great pressure exerted by the federal government upon firms that hold government contracts, too many firms have hired Negroes only as a token gesture.

Langston Hughes gives a vivid description of ghetto housing, which is not too different from a description of the South and West side of Chicago today.

> South State Street was in its glory then, a teeming Negro street with crowded theaters, restaurants, and cabarets. And excitement from noon to noon. Midnight was like day. The street was full of workers and gamblers, prostitutes and pimps, church folks and sinners. The tenements on either side were very congested. For neither love nor money could you find a place to live. Profiteers, thugs, and gangsters were coming into their own.[3]

A poignant passage from Richard Wright's *Black Boy* (Harper, 1945) illustrates the deep feeling which Negroes have for education, and their determination to keep the bright flame of the spirit burning despite *de facto* segregation and its concomitant conditions. Thus, he says:

> I was building up in me a dream which the entire educational system of the South had been rigged to stifle. I was feeling the things that the State of Mississippi had spent millions of dollars to make sure that I would never feel; I was beginning to dream the dreams that the State had said were wrong, that the schools had said were taboo (p. 48).

But, in spite of the taboo on Negro learning, Wright coped. He survived.

When the lower class Negro child reaches school age, it is said he comes to the school so "deprived" and "disadvantaged" that he lacks in verbal skills and is cognitively deficient, that he is doomed to failure before he begins. Perhaps we cannot deny that the lower class child does come poorly prepared to meet the demands of the middle-class school and that failure is almost inevitable, but this question comes to mind: Is it this difference that causes the failure or is it the attitude on the part of the teachers and the system toward those whose way of life differs from that of the mainstream?

Dick Gregory, in *Nigger* (Pocket Books), tells of his educational experience as a very young child in the public schools. He says he never learned hate or shame at home. He had to go to school for that. The teacher thought he was stupid, couldn't spell, couldn't read, couldn't do arithmetic. Just stupid. Teachers were never interested in finding out that you couldn't concentrate because you were so hungry.

Claude Brown constantly played a cat and mouse game with the truant officer. For a long while school had no meaning for him. Yet when Brown reached the point in life when he realized the value of an education and that it was a "way out," he met discouragement from his parents. His father said, "Boy, you don't need all that education. You better keep that job, because that's a good job." The job was that of a busboy in a hamburger shop.

Although Malcolm X kept close to the top in scholastic standing in his class, his white English teacher discouraged him from becoming a lawyer.

> "Malcolm, one of life's first needs is for us to be realistic. Don't misunderstand me now. We all here like you, you know that. But you've got to be realistic about being a nigger. A lawyer—that's no realistic goal for a nigger. You need to think about something you can be. You're good with your hands—making things. Everybody admires your carpentry shop work. Why don't you plan on carpentry? People like you as a person—you'd get all kinds of work."
>
> What made it really begin to disturb me was Mr. Ostrowski's advice to others in my class—all of them white. Most of them had told him they were planning to become farmers, like their parents. . . . But those who wanted to strike out on their own, to try something new, he had encouraged. . . . They all reported that Mr. Ostrowski had encouraged whatever they had wanted. Yet nearly none of them had earned marks equal to mine.[4]

At this point, Malcolm X began to change inside and to realize that he still was not considered intelligent enough in the eyes of the whites to be whatever he wanted to be.

This experience can be multiplied thousands of times in the lives of young lower-class Negro children.

> It is not to be wondered at that a boy, one day, decides that if all this studying is going to prepare him only to be a porter or an elevator boy, well, then, the hell with it. And there they go, with an overwhelming bitterness which will dissemble all their lives and complete their ruin.[5]

Few apparently escape as did Gregory and Brown.

The lower class Negro's restriction to the ghetto is more than just a physical confinement. Its residents are restricted mentally, emotionally, and spiritually as well. Claude Brown points out so well how the constriction and narrowness of the life of his parents on a plantation in the south had stifled any ambition they had, and coming to the ghetto of New York only served to limit them even further, so that for them all life had meant was liquor, religion, sex, and violence.

Claude Brown, in *Manchild in the Promised Land*, writes of his brother, "Man, this place is . . . it just ruins me, Sonny I feel like I'm being smothered to death. . . ." "My whole life has revolved around Harlem. . ." (p. 403).

The Negro woman finds that she must cope with every facet of life—poor housing, menial employment, threats of hunger, exploitation from anyone and everyone, child rearing, and guidance just to mention a few. This coping capacity of the Negro woman is surely an indication of her strength, devotion, and dedication to the continuation of a family unit.

Dick Gregory, in *Nigger*, speaks of the coping capacity of his mother, which reflects the beauty of her attitude:

> Like a lot of Negro kids, we never would have made it without our Momma. When there was no fatback to go with the beans, no socks to go with the shoes, no hope to go with tomorrow, she'd smile and say: "We ain't poor, we're just broke" (p. 25).

Mrs. Gregory's philosophy of life was surely an influencing inspiration to her children as is indicated in the following passage from her son's autobiography:

> "Poor is a state of mind you never grow out of, but being broke is just a temporary condition." She always had a big smile, even when her legs and feet swelled from high blood pressure and she collapsed across the table with sugar diabetes. "You have to smile twenty-four hours a day," Momma would say. "If you walk through life showing the aggravation you've gone through, people will feel sorry for you, and they'll never respect you." She taught us that man has two ways out in life—laughing or crying. There's more hope in laughing (p. 25).

Malcolm X, in his autobiography, describes his mother's struggle against hunger:

> Our mother knew, I guess, dozens of ways to cook things with bread and out of bread. Stewed tomatoes with bread, maybe that would be a meal. Something like French toast, if we had any eggs. Bread-pudding, sometimes with raisins in it. If we got hold of some hamburger, it came to the table more bread than meat. . . .
>
> But there were times when there wasn't even a nickel, and we would be so hungry we were dizzy. My mother would boil a big pot of dandelion greens, and we would eat them (p. 13).

Dick Gregory also had cause to reflect on the working conditions endured by his mother and other women. He wonders what it is about these women that causes them to endure:

> But I wonder about my Momma sometimes, and all the other Negro mothers who got up at 6 A.M., to go to the white man's house with sacks over their shoes because it was so wet and cold. I wonder how they made it. They worked very hard for the man, they made his

> breakfast and they scrubbed his floors and they diapered his babies. They didn't have much time for us (p. 26).

As the reader wends his way through the literature of the Negro, he cannot help but be struck by the degradation the Negro has suffered on all sides. In biographies, novels, and poetry, the story of his hardships has been eloquently told. To be a Negro in white America is to be branded as a lesser mortal. Yet even against these tremendous obstacles, the Negro has forged a culture which Americans of every race are only now coming to understand and to appreciate.

NOTES

1. James Baldwin, *The Fire Next Time*, New York: Dell, 1963, p. 77.
2. From *The Big Sea* by Langston Hughes. Copyright 1940 by Langston Hughes. Used with permission of Hill and Wang, Inc.
3. *Ibid.*, p. 33.
4. Malcolm X, *The Autobiography of Malcolm X*, New York: Grove Press, 1965, p. 37.
5. James Baldwin, *Nobody Knows My Name*, New York: Dial Press, 1961, pp. 106–107.

CHILDREN'S STORY PREFERENCES

Robin C. Ford and Janos Koplyay

Zimet's summary (1966) of recent research in the area of children's story preferences recommends that instruments to be employed in investigating children's interests should be refined. The summary also notes the absence of work done with very young children and reports discrepancy between first graders' free choice library selections (Smith 1962) and the content of most basal reading series. Drawing on Zimet's recommendations, the present report summarizes an attempt to construct a reliable instrument for assessing the reading interests of very young children.

Robin C. Ford and Janos Koplyay, "Children's Story Preferences," *The Reading Teacher*, **22** (May 1968), 233–238. Reprinted with permission of Robin C. Ford, Janos Koplyay, and the International Reading Association.

Any investigation of young children's reading interests must control those factors that interfere when verbal reports are given by these children, either to their teacher or to an outside investigator. This kind of data is clearly open to the influence of the response set of providing a teacher with information the child believes she wishes to hear. In addition, open responding in a group situation, especially with young children, enables one child to repeat the responses of another. Furthermore, if the subjects are primary grade pupils from a lower socioeconomic group, any kind of verbal reporting is likely to require a more sophisticated level of language than disadvantaged children can cope with.

The limitation of verbal data could be overcome by a non-verbal instrument designed to measure young children's story preferences. If a reliable and valid instrument could be used across socioeconomic levels, educators might be able to arrive at more precise estimates of the effect of motivation, and the impact of cultural disadvantagement on story preferences.

This kind of information would be particularly useful in light of publishers' current desire to produce relevant and interesting material for the inner-city child. Revised and new editions of basal reading series aimed at disadvantaged children include a heavy emphasis on presenting themes and locales that would be familiar to their prospective readers. The rationale behind this choice is usually stated in this form: the better a student can identify with a story, the more motivated he will be to read it.

The research reported here describes the construction of a non-verbal test of children's story preferences and explores in a tentative way the use of the instrument to disclose story preferences among kindergarten, first, second, and third grade children, one group from an upper-middle class suburban school system and another group from a predominantly Negro, urban school district.

STORY PREFERENCE TEST

Ten pictures in each of six categories were chosen from currently available children's literature in light of definite criteria. The six categories were children in general, children in inner-city and ghetto areas, Negro heritage, history and science, animals, and fantasy. These pictures were reproduced in black and white in a test booklet, four to a page. No two pictures in the same category appeared on the same page; otherwise, the grouping occurred on a random basis. In addition, sixty sentences were constructed to match the action portrayed in each picture. These were also randomly mixed and presented in groups of four sentences, five groups to a page.

The subjects of this study were 373 children, of which 169 were suburban upper-middle class and 204, urban Negro lower-class. Approximately half of each group were girls, half boys; and approximately one fourth of the total number of children represented each grade, kindergarten through grade three. The tests were administered by the classroom teachers according to directions accompanying the booklet. On each page the child was asked to circle the one picture that indicated a story he would most like to read and to cross out the picture that indicated a story he would *not* want to read. Second and third grade pupils were asked to complete the sentence groups in similar fashion.

Due to limitations of space only the major findings of this study are presented in the paragraphs that follow.

LIKED AND DISLIKED PICTURES

Table 1 reports the number of times that pictures in each category were picked as "most liked" or "most disliked." The categories are listed in descending order of the percentage of the total number of choices designated as "most liked." The chi-square value of 36.70 with 6 degrees of freedom is statistically significant beyond the .01 level. The percentage in the last columns of the table suggest the popularity of Negro-heritage stories and the unpopularity of animal stories. Two more categories stand out, i.e., children in the inner city and ghetto, "most liked" and fantasy, "most disliked." These facts indicate that the children who participated were more attracted by stories in the areas of Negro heritage and children in inner-city environments than by stories built around animal or fantasy themes.

Table 2 shows that five of the ten best liked pictures belonged in the history-science category. Of the ten most disliked pictures, four related to fantasy and four to animals. This finding confirms the data in Table 1 regarding these themes.

Table 1. Number and Percentage of Choices Accorded Pictures in Each Category

Category	*Most Liked*	*Most Disliked*	*Total*	*Percentage of Times Most Liked*
Negro heritage	23	6	29	79
Children in ghetto	24	13	37	65
History and science	33	23	56	59
Children in general	19	22	41	46
Fantasy	17	31	48	35
Animals	12	42	54	22

Table 2. Categories Represented by the Ten Pictures Most Liked and the Ten Least Liked

Category—Most liked	*Content of Picture*
History/science	Columbus landing at San Salvador
History/science	An astronaut seated in capsule
History/science	Odysseus, at mast, listening to sirens
History/science	Twenty dinosaurs in battle
History/science	Knights jousting—tournament
Inner-city/ghetto	Four children (integrated) laughing while reading
Inner-city/ghetto	Boy looking at crowded row houses
Negro heritage	African village scene
Children—general	Boy talking while mother irons
Fantasy	Jack atop beanstalk
Category—Least liked	*Content of Picture*
Animal	Bunny muzzling doe
Animal	Wild horses running
Animal	Lion family at rest
Animal	Elephants playing in pool
Fantasy	Children holding tilting sea back from themselves
Fantasy	Sharks attacking children and their troll friend
Fantasy	Witch and ghost in graveyard
Fantasy	Two clothed mice talking, one has knapsack on his back
History/science	Twenty dinosaurs in battle
Children—general	Boy watching stevedores unload

From further analysis of the data for kindergarten through grade three, it appears that age and sex are primarily responsible for variance in preferences. The percentage of "like" scores within most categories shows that girls tended to score slightly lower in interest than boys. For example, the category, Negro heritage, changes little for girls from grade to grade, but for boys it shows strikingly higher "like" scores in the second and third grades. No clear explanation for this surge of interest could be found. The pattern of sex preferences within the category, history and science, was the most surprising. Here the data showed an increasing interest throughout the grades for the girls rather than the boys.

LIKED AND DISLIKED SENTENCES

The groups of sentences were read to all second and third grade children by their classroom teacher. The children were told that each sentence stood for a story and they were asked to indicate which of the four stories they would most like to read and which they would least like to read. A tabulation of the responses revealed that the category, Negro heritage was the most frequently chosen as "liked" and the category, fantasy, was the most frequently chosen as "disliked." Analysis of the context of the sentences suggests that children liked to hear about "water" and things described as "cool," and "refreshing," as well as aggressive themes or those suggesting a high level of activity. The children seemed to dislike stories describing passive happiness or those mentioning helpful cooperation with adults. Boys' and girls' responses were similar.

Only cautious interpretation of the foregoing results can be given because of the small number of sample pictures and sentences used and the large number of uncontrolled variables. For example, there is no way of knowing whether or not the manner in which teachers read the sentences cued their pupils as to the sentences the teachers preferred. There is no evidence from this project that in any way deals with the underlying bases for the selection of either the pictures or the sentences as "liked" or "disliked."

DISCUSSION

Interpretation of the children's choices is made even more difficult because it was necessary to impose artificially created categories in choosing the pictures and assigning the responses to subject matter. In spite of this, it seems clear that children's interests are related to age and sex to a much greater extent than to socioeconomic background. It is difficult to propose a rationale for the great popularity of the Negro heritage category. If suburban middle-class children chose these pictures out of novelty, then what was the basis for the similar choices made by their inner-city Negro counterparts? Perhaps these pictures represented to both groups of children an extention of one of the most favored categories, history and science. It would seem that the impact of the technological changes of the last two decades, and especially the relative sophistication of information conveyed through television to very young children have altered their tastes. Earlier studies (Witty, *et al.*, 1946; Norwell, 1958), consistently mention animal stories, humor, and fantasy as favorite areas of children in the middle grades. If real change has occurred since these findings, it appears to be in the direction of history and science topics and away from the animal and fantasy content that comprise the bulk of young children's television shows.

When the results of this investigation are compared with a recent analysis of reading content in primers and preprimers (Blom, Waite, and Zimet, 1968), there are striking discrepancies between what children indicate they want, and what, in fact, they get. In two areas, character and environmental setting, published first-grade readers are providing content children in this sample "dislike." For example, only 1 per cent of the stories analyzed occur in urban settings, while interest in stories dealing with children in an inner-city environment appears high among children in the early grades.

In light of these findings, the investigators are planning further refinement and validation of the test. First, the test should be expanded to include new and more finely delineated categories (i.e., humor) and used to replicate this project with a larger and more representative sample of youngsters. Second, a corresponding test of short stories should be constructed as a substitute for the sentences used in the current investigation. Third, an expanded instrument should be prepared in the preferred areas of Negro heritage and history/science to ascertain, if possible, the bases for their popularity.

REFERENCES

Blom, G. E., R. R. Waite, and Sara Zimet, "Content of First Grade Reading Books," *The Reading Teacher*, **21**, (1968) 317–323.

Norvell, G. W., *What Boys and Girls Like to Read*, New York: Silver Burdett Co., 1958.

Smith, Ruth C., "Children's Reading Choices and Basic Reader Content," *Elementary English*, **39** (1962), 202–209.

Witty, P., Ann Coomer, and Dilla McBean, "Children's Choices of Favorite Books," *Journal of Educational Psychology*, **37** (1946), 266–278.

Zimet, Sara, "Children's Interests and Story Preferences," *The Elementary School Journal*, **67** (1966), 122–130.

STUDY QUESTIONS

1. Does Seaberg believe that there is a literature for the disadvantaged child? What is her opinion of "integrated or interethnic" realistic fiction and biography? What does this author regard as the function of literature, when used with children?
2. Why does Seaberg contend that stories of fiction and fantasy fulfill a universal need of children? Do you agree with her reasons? On what basis does Chukovsky defend the use of nonsense verse and fairy tales with children? Would his rationale be applicable to disadvantaged children?
3. What are Seaberg's criteria for selecting literature for disadvantaged children? Do you agree with them? What additions or deletions would you suggest? How does literature fit in with the total language arts program?

4. What were the major variables controlled by Ford and Koplyay in their study? What two uncontrolled variables do they cite? Could there have been additional ones of any consequence? What might these be?
5. Do Ford's and Koplyay's findings agree with Seaberg's observations? How do these findings compare with content emphases of current primary-grade readers?
6. Why do Ford and Koplyay conclude that children's interests are more a function of age and sex than of socioeconomic status? What factors may account for this discrepancy? Would you expect this to be true in the case of fourth, fifth, or sixth graders? Would a longitudinal study shed light on these questions?
7. Why do Ford and Koplyay indicate that they intend to further refine and validate their instrument? Is there any value in using the instrument again in its original form? What type of research design would accommodate original and revised versions of the instrument?
8. What are Banks' objectives for exposing white children to the realities of black ghetto life? Do you agree with his rationale? Under what circumstances would parents and teachers be willing to support Banks' approach?
9. What does Banks regard as the basic advantages of exposing children to literature on black inner-city people? What are some pitfalls to be avoided by teachers?
10. To what extent are Banks and Arnez in agreement regarding the role of literature in promoting racial understanding? Why does Arnez express a preference for literature written by Negroes? Do you agree with her rationale? Why or why not?
11. At what point in a child's life is he psychologically ready to learn about life in the black ghetto? How can a teacher determine whether her pupils have reached this point? Do the selections quoted by Arnez and Banks offer any cues regarding their suitability for pupils of a certain age? of a given subculture?

SUGGESTED READINGS

Arbuthnot, May Hill, *Children and Books*, 3rd ed., Chicago: Scott, Foresman, 1964.

Blatt, Gloria T., "The Mexican-American in Children's Literature," *Elementary English*, **45** (April 1968), 446–451.

Cianciolo, Patricia J., and Jean M. LePere, *The Literary Time Line in American History: Rx for Social Studies*, Garden City, N.Y.: Doubleday, 1969.

Crosby, Muriel, *Reading Ladders for Human Relations*, 4th ed., Washington, D.C.: American Council on Education, 1963.

Gast, David, "Minority Americans in Children's Literature," *Elementary English*, **44** (January 1967), 12–23.

Haines, Helen E., *Living With Books*, 2nd ed., New York: Columbia University Press, 1963.

Huck, Charlotte S., and Doris A. Young, *Children's Literature in Elementary School*, New York: Holt, Rinehart & Winston, 1967.

Kircher, Clara J., *Behavior Patterns in Children's Books*, Washington, D.C.: Catholic University Press, 1966.

Korey, Ruth Ann, "Children's Literature of Integrated Classes," *Elementary English*, **43** (1966), 39–42.

Millender, Dharathula, "Selecting Our Children's Books: Time for Some Changes," *Changing Education*, **1** (Fall 1966), 8–13.

Robinson, Evelyn R., *Readings About Children's Literature*, New York: David McKay, 1966.

Siks, Geraldine, *Children's Literature for Dramatization*, New York: Harper and Row, 1966.

Tiedt, Iris M., "Literature Learnings," in Sidney W. Tiedt, ed., *Teaching the Disadvantaged Child*, New York: Oxford University Press, 1968, pp. 109–138.

CHAPTER 8
LANGUAGE ARTS AND THE SOCIAL STUDIES

Two areas of the elementary curriculum that bear a particularly strong affinity for each other are the language arts and the social studies. The extent of this relationship becomes readily apparent when one realizes that more than in any other subject, achievement in the social studies is predicated on mastery of the fundamental modes of communication. The major categories listed in Johns and Fraser's chart document this dependency:

Social studies skills: a guide to analysis and grade placement[1]

Part One: Skills which are a definite but shared responsibility of the social studies.

I. Locating information
II. Organizing information
III. Evaluating information
IV. Acquiring information through reading
V. Acquiring information through listening and observing
VI. Communicating orally and in writing
VII. Interpreting pictures, charts, graphs, and tables
VIII. Working with others

Part Two: Skills which are a major responsibility of the social studies.

I. Reading social studies materials
II. Applying problem-solving and critical-thinking skills to social issues
III. Interpreting maps and globes
IV. Understanding time and chronology

Although the categories listed in Part One consist almost entirely of language arts skills, they also play an indirect but nevertheless vital role in Part Two.

To what extent do the social studies contribute to the language arts? One of the more obvious examples involves the content of basal reading and writing programs. Most of the stories in these materials deal with human relationships—between individuals, between groups of individuals, between individuals and various social, political, and economic institutions, between individuals and groups and their physical environment. Similar examples might be drawn from other areas of the language arts, including listening, speaking, and writing. These instances reinforce the proposition that as the social studies rely on the language arts for the skills of communication, so do the language arts rely on the social studies for subject matter content.

Clearly this reciprocal relationship between language arts and social studies establishes the relevance for this chapter. In the first reading, which explores one facet of this relationship, William W. Joyce asserts that although textbooks and tradebooks have traditionally presented a distorted image of the role of minority groups in American society, this image is beginning to improve. The balance of the readings describes various teaching strategies wherein the language arts and social studies serve as vehicles for promoting social learning in pupils. In this process the two fields become virtually indistinguishable. First, James A. Banks demonstrates how an elementary teacher used various communication skills in the study of historiography with black pupils. Donald Hugh Smith then shows how resource persons can significantly affect the self-concept of pupils. In "Not Unteachable—Just Unteached" Lawana Trout describes how she taught a unit on prejudice and propaganda to urban pupils. In the final reading Grace Graham gives a clear, concise account of how teachers can use sociodrama, irrespective of grade level.

NOTE

1. Eunice Johns and Dorothy McClure Fraser, "Social Studies Skills: A Guide to Analysis and Grade Placement," in Helen McCracken Carpenter, ed., *Skill Development in Social Studies*, Thirty-Third Yearbook for the National Council for the Social Studies, Washington, D.C.: NCSS, 1963, pp. 313–327.

MINORITY GROUPS IN AMERICAN SOCIETY: IMPERATIVES FOR EDUCATORS

William W. Joyce

> Little Indian, Sioux or Crow,
> Little frosty Eskimo,
> Little Turk or Japanee,
> Oh don't you wish that you were me.

Admittedly the world has shrunk dramatically since Robert Louis Stevenson penned this stanza. But the spirit if not the intent of this blatantly chauvinistic attitude toward other cultures has endured, deriving its sustenance from an "accepted" view of the social studies that in theory advocated such values as the dignity and worth of the individual, the inviolability of the human personality, and the belief in justice and equality of opportunity, but in practice negated even the best-intentioned efforts of teachers to inculate these values in their pupils. An examination of instructional materials and curricular documents used extensively in elementary schools throughout our nation strongly suggests that over the years teachers have given their children a distorted view of American minority groups, one that has extolled the virtues and accomplishments of the white, Anglo-Saxon, Protestant sector of society, while denigrating the role of the Negro, the American Indian, the Spanish-American, and the Oriental—four groups that in varying degrees have been barred from assimilation into American society.

Indeed, our nation's experiences in minority group relations demonstrate that the proverbial American melting pot has been a colossal fraud perpetrated by a dominant white Anglo-American majority for the purpose of convincing society at large that all cultural groups, irrespective of race or ethnic origin, were in fact eligible for full and unrestricted participation in the social, economic, political, and religious life of this nation. To be sure the American melting pot did achieve reality in some instances—initially for the white Western European immigrant and later for his Eastern European counterpart, but for the non-European, non-white immigrant, the melting pot had little meaning.

William W. Joyce, "Minority Groups in American Society: Imperatives for Educators," *Social Education*, **33** (April 1969), 429–433. Reprinted by permission of the author and the National Council for the Social Studies.

It is no mere accident that the process of amalgamation had little effect on other minorities—particularly American citizens of American Indian, Chinese, Japanese, African and Spanish descent. These people differed significantly from the dominant American image—in racial, religious, and other ethnic characteristics. Various theories have been offered as explanations of why the dominant white majority has denied minority groups access to the mainstream of American society. Couched in anthropological, economic, sociological, and psychological terms, these theories range from simplistic rationalizations to highly sophisticated hypotheses. The essential elements of these theories as recounted by Arnold Rose, the eminent sociologist, are summarized below:

1. *The race-difference theory* postulated that man has an instinctive aversion to people who are different from himself, and that these feelings of repulsion are confirmed and strengthened through incidental social contacts with the offending group.
2. *The theory of economic competition* maintains that prejudice is absent when minority and dominant majority groups earn their livelihoods in separate sectors of the economy, but when thrown together in direct competition for limited jobs and resources, the majority group will oppress the minority.
3. *The traumatic experiences* explanation states that racial prejudice is a consequence of painful or unpleasant emotional experiences suffered at the hands of the minority group.
4. *The frustration-aggression theory* states that a person thwarted in his attempt to attain a given goal often experiences an internal tension that can be relieved by lashing out against the source of his frustration or toward an innocent third party. Typically this theory of prejudice is known as "scapegoating."
5. *Trait-factor theories of personality* attempt to describe the interrelationships between authoritarian personality types, familial and other socialization experiences, and prejudiced attitudes.
6. *The social control or caste structure theory* hypothesizes that the dominant and often ascendant sub-culture or caste within a society will strive to maintain its hegemony over other sub-cultures rigorously imposing various physical, social, psychological punishments and rewards.[1]

In recent decades a growing body of sociological, psychological, and anthropological research has documented the devastating effects of white racism on minority-group children. The vast majority of these studies focus on the Negro and variously underscore his negative racial attitudes, his poor self-image, and his low educational and occupational aspirations and achievement. Granted, the dearth of authoritative research prevents us from ascertaining the extent to which these generalizations apply to American children of American Indian, Spanish, and Oriental ancestry, but there is sufficient evidence to indicate that all of these children have suffered at the hands of a society that has knowingly perpetrated social injustices against them.

RACIAL ATTITUDES HELD BY WHITE CHILDREN

But what about the white child? What are his attitudes toward American minorities? There are many serious gaps in the literature, but several studies reveal an emerging, if not fragmented, picture of racial attitudes held by white children. Moreland's study of social perception in Southern children reveals that racial self-recognition was significantly higher in white than in Negro children, and more significantly, white children accepted the socially communicated distinctions of racial inclusion and exclusion at an earlier age than Negro children.[2] Trager and Yarrow found that over two-thirds of their white subjects in the primary grades verbalized hostility toward Negroes.[3] That negative racial attitudes intensify as children grow older was revealed in a study reported by Radke, Trager, and Davis.[4]

How have these attitudes affected the mental health of children? Here too the evidence is scanty, but increasingly psychologists express growing concern over the long-range effects of racial and ethnic prejudice on white children. As early as 1955 the psychologist Kenneth B. Clark hypothesized:

> In observing normal forms and expressions of prejudice among average Americans, one observes certain types of reactions, which if demonstrated in relations with other members of an individual's own race, would be considered symptoms of emotional disturbance.[5]

Since that time other psychologists have confirmed Clark's suspicions.

Why have our children acquired negative attitudes toward minorities? If we accept the proposition that American schools reflect the society they serve, then our total educational enterprise must share the guilt for propagating a white, Protestant, Anglo-Saxon view of society that is totally inconsistent with the past and present realities of American life. In some educational circles it has become fashionable to label the publishing industry as the prime offender. If we acknowledge that universally the textbook has been and still is the most widely used teaching device, it becomes axiomatic that the text largely determines the social studies content that is taught in American schools.

THE "SLANTED TEXT"

In recent years a growing number of critics have documented the failure of social studies textbooks to present our children with an intellectually honest view of American society. Witness the following statement by Vincent R. Rogers and Raymon H. Muessig:

Too many texts are filled with slanted "facts," stereotypes, provincial and ethnocentric attitudes, and superficial, utopian discussions which skim over conditions as they actually exist in life today. Texts which have sections devoted to "life in our United States," for example, too often portray "Americans" as white, Anglo-Saxon, Protestant, white collar, and middle class. Perusing a number of books, one gets the impression that all Americans live on wide, shady streets in clean suburban areas, occupy white Cape Cod style houses, drive new automobiles, have two children (a boy and a girl, of course), and own a dog. Characters in texts have first names like Bill, Tom, and John, rather than Sid, Tony, Juan and last names like Adams, Hill, and Cook rather than Schmidt, Podosky, and Chen. . . .[6]

A recent study on the treatment of minorities in American history textbooks used in elementary and secondary schools in Michigan reinforces these allegations. Although the primary focus of the study was on the Negro, the conclusions and recommendations apply to other minority groups as well:

> Through errors of both omission and commission, through their avoidance of nearly everything of a controversial nature, through their reliance on outdated and even antediluvian historical research, and through their inadequate treatment of the current Civil Rights scene and the backgrounds to it, these books . . . are historically inaccurate, misleading, and distorted . . . These reviews do indeed constitute a severe indictment of the American history textbooks that are in widespread use in the state of Michigan, and undoubtedly in other states as well.[7]

The publishing industry maintains that because of their heavy investment in textbooks (often a publishing house will have invested $250,000 or more in a single social studies text before realizing one dollar of income), they need to insure that their products will sell on a nationwide market. And as Hillel Black points out, "This means he will censor his own books if he thinks the offending passages may hurt sales, [or] submit to censorship from outside sources if the potential market is big enough. . . ."[8]

The effects of such censorship are legion throughout the publishing industry. One executive, addressing a seminar sponsored by the American Educational Publishers Institute and the National Council for the Advancement of Educational Writing, remarked,

> . . . educational materials will be as good as the marketplace wants them to be . . . those of us in the publishing business [know] that when we have tried to do innovative things we very often have taken a blood bath.[9]

One firm that found this to be an expensive lesson was the Follett Publishing Company of Chicago, one of the first houses to produce an integrated social studies series. When Follett released these books in 1959, there were few purchasers, presumably because school systems found them too advanced for the times. Robert Follett, the firm's president, ruefully recalls:

> Even New York was not asking for the integrated text then. . . . Nor was there an overwhelming demand in the suburban areas except for those communities heavily populated with liberal Jewish people. You know, I have the feeling we'll be selling our integrated books in Atlanta and Dade County before we sell them in some of our lily-white suburbs.[10]

This is but one of many instances over the years where publishers have taken the initiative in advocating social change—and paid dearly in the process. Viewed from this perspective, their reluctance to become innovative becomes a bit more understandable.

TRADEBOOKS PROJECT DISTORTED IMAGES

Social studies textbooks have not been the only proponents of white racism. Children's tradebooks have been equally guilty of projecting distorted images of minority groups. After surveying more than 5,000 tradebooks published during the period 1962–1964, Nancy Larrick concluded that only 6.7 percent included one or more Negroes. Indeed, among the four major publishers of children's books, the percentage of books including a Negro in text or illustration is one-third lower than this figure. But even these figures may be misleading, since more than half of the books dealing with Negroes placed them outside the continental United States or prior to World War II, an event that Larrick contends is ". . . as remote to a child as the Boston Tea Party."[11] Further, the author noted that only four-fifths of one percent of the entire list of books surveyed dealt with the American Negro in today's world.

A study conducted by David K. Gast focused on the treatment of contemporary American minority groups in children's literature. Gast's findings not only underscore the biased, distorted portrayals of American Negroes but also reveal the tendency of tradebooks to ascribe distorted characterizations, concepts, and stereotypes to American Indians, Chinese, Japanese, and Spanish-Americans.[12] A few basic conclusions reported by Gast are summarized below:

> —American Indians, Chinese, Japanese, and Spanish-Americans are portrayed as having adopted such dominant middle-class American values as cleanliness, kindness, intelligence, ambition, and hard work. The stereotypes associated with these groups are complementary, but with one exception: "Negroes are musical."
>
> —Children's tradebooks depict American Indians, Chinese, and Spanish-

Americans as possessing lower-class status. Negroes are shown to be of lower- and middle-class and Japanese are treated as middle-class.

—Occupational stereotypes are associated with all minority groups except the Negro, who appears in many occupations, including white-collar and professional positions. The Indian craftsman, the Chinese cook, the Mexican shopkeeper, the Japanese gardener, and the Spanish shepherd persists in these books.

—Tradebooks foster the impression that Japanese and Negro minorities have been assimilated into the dominant culture and have more social contact with Anglo-Americans than American Indians, Chinese, and Spanish-Americans. In contrast, they relegate Indians to reservations, Chinese to Chinatown, and Spanish-Americans to rural areas.

—American Indians and Spanish-Americans are depicted as living simple, serene, and virile lives, close to nature. The male-superiority tradition permeates books dealing with these minorities, while males and females appear to enjoy equal status in books dealing with Negroes, Japanese, and Chinese.

—Few instances are cited when American Indians, Chinese, and Spanish-Americans have lost or abandoned their ethnic cultures; rather, the reader is led to believe that these minorities are fiercely proud of their traditional life styles and have accepted few economic motivations from the dominant culture.

—Primary-grade books in particular stereotype American Indians and Mexican-Americans as wearing their ethnic garb, presumably as evidence of their resistance to assimilation and their desire to be treated as friendly foreigners of the American Southwest.

—Stereotypes associated with physical characteristics are changing. Today's tradebooks portray Negroes as brown-skinned people with straight hair and Caucasoid facial features—a marked departure from traditional portrayals which caricatured Negroes by exaggerating facial features, kinky hair, and coal black skin.

—Social acceptance is a persuasive theme in books about the Negroes but receives incidental treatment in books about American Indians, Chinese, and Spanish-Americans. These books create the impression that the Japanese-American has encountered no prejudice and has gained total acceptance by the Anglo-American majority.

HOW REALISTIC SHOULD BOOKS BE?

Pervading these criticisms is the constant, recurring theme that the contents of social studies textbooks and tradebooks are not only inconsistent with social reality but that they consciously or unconsciously promote, reinforce, or perpetuate racial and ethnic prejudice. But how realistic should these books be? Should they expose children to the social injustices endured by American minorities? Should they explain why and how these injustices were perpetrated? Should they tell the story of America "like it is"? Bruce R. Joyce maintains that "A textbook *can* be constructed to teach children about human interaction, and a sophisticated social studies textbook *can* be used to teach them how to use the strategies of social science to analyze human relations." Nonetheless, he questions whether society is actually ready for realistic textbooks at the primary level.[13]

Admittedly the situation is beginning to improve, as evidenced by recent efforts of publishers to produce materials that present accurate portrayals of American minority groups. *William, Andy, and Ramon*; *Five Friends at School*; and *Living as Neighbors* are noteworthy efforts on the part of Holt, Rinehart, and Winston to publish primary-grade textbooks that tell about the lives of minority-group children. McGraw-Hill's *Skyline Series* utilizes printed materials, films, and filmstrips in depicting problematic situations confronting children in the inner-city. One of the stories in this series, "A Place of My Own," is a poignant account of how a little Puerto Rican girl copes with a perennial problem confronting many people of the inner-city—overcrowded living conditions and the resultant loss of privacy.

Increasingly publishers are developing non-verbal materials, some of which deal with minorities. The John Day Company's *Urban Education Series* is a brilliantly executed collection of photographs on American cities, while Fannie and George Shaftel's *Words and Action Series* is a role-playing kit employing photographs depicting everyday problems of Negro and white children. Both series should be especially useful with pupils encumbered by reading problems and by those encountering difficulty in analyzing social situations.

These are but a few of the new teaching resources on minority groups that have appeared on the market. On display at annual meetings of the National Council for the Social Studies in Washington, are other promising materials, particularly an amazing array of tradebooks for children. Despite recent cutbacks in Federal aid to education, school systems will purchase many of these materials to partially alleviate the shortage of intellectually honest, accurate resources for teaching about American minorities.

THE ROLE OF THE TEACHER

But what about the teachers? Over the years we have subscribed to the time-honored principle that teaching materials are only as good as the teachers using them. This principle, coupled with the inescapable fact that educators, like most other Americans, are likely to harbor negative attitudes toward racial and ethnic minorities, suggests that before the classroom teacher can present his pupils with the accurate, realistic image of minority group relations that is so desperately needed, he will need to re-examine, clarify, and modify his own attitudes and predispositions toward minorities. In these times he can ill afford to do less.

NOTES

1. Arnold M. Rose, "The Causes of Prejudice," in Milton Barron, ed., *A Textbook of Readings in Intergroup Relations*, New York: Alfred A. Knopf, 1957, pp. 82–92.
2. J. Kenneth Moreland, "Racial Recognition by Nursery School Children in Lynchburg, Virginia," *Social Forces*, **37** (1958), 132–137.
3. Helen C. Trager and Marian R. Yarrow, *They Learn What They Live*, New York: Harper and Brothers, 1952, pp. 140–155.
4. Marian Radke, Helen C. Trager, and Hadassah Davis, "Social Perceptions and Attitudes of Children," *Genetic Psychology Monographs*, **40** (November 1949), 440.
5. Kenneth B. Clark, *Prejudice and Your Child*, Boston: American Book Company, 1963, p. 77.
6. Vincent R. Rogers and Raymond H. Muessig, "Needed: A Revolution in the Textbook Industry," *The Social Studies*, **54** (October 1963), 169.
7. *A Report on the Treatment of Minorities in American History Textbooks*, Lansing: Michigan Department of Education, July 1968, p. 15.
8. "Textbook Publishers Discuss Their Product," *Phi Delta Kappan*, **50** (November 1968), 190–191.
9. *Ibid.*, p. 191.
10. Hillel Black, *The American Schoolbook*, New York: William Morrow, 1961, p. 117.
11. *Ibid.*, p. 64.
12. David K. Gast, "Minority Americans in Children's Literature," *Elementary English*, **44** (January 1967), 12–23.
13. Bruce R. Joyce, "The Primary Grades: A Review of Textbook Materials," in *Social Studies in the United States: A Critical Appraisal*, C. Benjamin Cox and Byron G. Massialas, eds., New York: Harcourt, Brace & World, 1967, p. 22.

RELEVANT SOCIAL STUDIES FOR BLACK PUPILS

James A. Banks

> . . . the negro race is inferior to the white race, and living in their midst, they would be far outstripped or outwitted in the chase of free competition. Gradual but certain extermination would be their fate.[1]

A class of seventh grade black pupils was confronted with this argument as they analyzed a series of historical documents that their teacher had duplicated for their study. The document from which this statement was taken, like the other documents the pupils studied, was slightly edited and simplified so that they could read it more easily. Another document that the pupils read stated:

> . . . (Negroes) were born slaves of barbarian masters, untaught in all of the useful arts and occupations, reared in heathen darkness, and sold by heathen masters. . . . They were transferred to shores enlightened by rays of Christianity.[2]

The pupils also read a letter written by a Virginia slave owner to his sister about a slave named Polly. It said in part:

> . . . On last Monday week, I had to whip Polly for her impudence to me. . . . I regret it very much but there must be one master in a family or there can be no peace. I told her that she should never be sold. . . provided she would behave herself . . . she still tells me that she is perfectly willing to be sold.[3]

Another account told about an overseer who was called Mr. Severe:

> Mr. Severe was rightly named; he was a cruel man. I have seen him whip a woman, causing the blood to run half an hour at the time; and this, too, in the midst of her crying children, pleading for their mother's release. . . .[4]

In addition to reading primary sources, the pupils studies excerpts and sections from elementary American history textbooks and from Negro history books. One of the selections read:

James A. Banks, "Relevant Social Studies for Black Pupils," *Social Education*, **33**, 1 (January 1969), 66–69. Reprinted by permission of the author and the National Council for the Social Studies.

> Being indentured servants, some of the first Negroes were later freed and given land. But Negro workers proved very valuable on plantations, and more of them were needed. Gradually, settlers came to think of Negroes not as indentured servants, but as slaves who would never be set free.[5]

Another selection noted:

> One famous social scientist, Nathan Glazer, has called American slavery "the most awful the world has ever known." . . . The slave in this country had no protection from society.[6]

The class read a selection from another book that included this statement:

> . . . in the sale of slaves there was the persistent practice of dividing families. Husbands were separated from wives, and mothers were separated from their children. There was never any respect shown for the slave family.[7]

The pupils read *I Juan de Pareja* by Elizabeth B. De Trevino, *Up From Slavery* by Booker T. Washington, *The Book of American Negro Spirituals* by James Weldon and Rosamond Johnson, and *Amos Fortune Free Man* by Elizabeth Yates. In her poignant yet inspiring biography, Miss Yates tells the story of an African prince who was captured at the age of fifteen and enslaved in America. The author relates how Amos Fortune withstood his torture, turned hostility into humility, and dedicated his life to bringing freedom to others after forty-five years of servitude. The book vividly depicts the horrors of slavery and the dehumanization of the slaves by the early American slave traders.

The pupils pondered a poem by Phillis Wheatley who tells about her own slavery in the United States. It begins:

> No more America in mournful strain
> Of wrongs, and grievance unredress'd complain,
> No longer shall thou dread the iron chain,
> Which wanton Tyranny with lawless hand
> Has made, and which it meant t' enslave the land.[8]

The pupils read the primary sources, the sections from history books, and the biographical and fictional works to help them solve the problem that they had identified, "What was black slavery like in the United States?" Their teacher had helped them define their problem in clear, specific terms. The class, with the teacher's guidance, formulated specific questions related to their central problem. These are some of the questions:

How were the slaves treated?
How did people who were not slaves feel about slavery?

How did slavery in the United States compare with slavery in other parts of the world?
How hard did the slaves have to work?
How did master and slave feel toward each other?
Did slaves ever try to escape?

After the pupils had identified their problem and formulated specific questions related to it, the teacher asked them to tell what black slavery was like in the United States. They had picked up ideas about black slavery from textbooks used in previous grades, from biographical and fictional works they had read, from the mass media, and from discussions they had heard about slavery from their parents and grandparents. The pupils had many erroneous notions about slavery, as revealed below:

Many slaves were happy and contented.
While a few slaves were treated badly, most were well treated.
Most slaves worked on large plantations rather than on small farms.
Everyone except slave owners was against slavery.
Slavery in the United States was just like slavery in other parts of the world.

After they had told the teacher about their notions of black slavery, the pupils read the series of documents and selections their teacher had duplicated and searched for other sources in the school and room libraries. They viewed several films and filmstrips on black slavery, told about accounts of slavery that had been handed down in their families, and role-played a slave auction and the Vesey slave rebellion.

As the class evaluated the selections, they encountered highly divergent and conflicting accounts of slavery. In one source they read that slaves were "enlightened by rays of Christianity"; in another they read that compared with other slavery systems, "American slavery was the worst." It is difficult to accept both of these statements as historical facts. The pupils felt that if black slavery in North America was "the most awful in the world," slaves were not "enlightened by rays of Christianity." Ascertaining the validity and reliability of the sources proved most challenging for the pupils. With the teacher's guidance, the class formulated a list of questions that they used as a guide in ascertaining the value of the various sources in helping them to discover what black slavery was really like in America. They asked such questions as:

In what region of the country did the author live?
For what purpose was the author writing?
What audience did the author have in mind?
What were the author's probable biases?
What were the author's training and qualifications?

When was the document or selection written (approximate year)?
Does the author often use emotionally laden words?
How does his account compare with others that we have read?
Does the author cite sufficient evidence to support his conclusions?
Does the author base his arguments on fact or opinion?
What was the author's social class?
What was the author's race?
What are the author's basic assumptions about slavery?
What are the author's basic assumptions about black people?
Are the author's assumptions grounded in facts?

After answering these kinds of questions about the sources they had read, the pupils were able to generalize about the nature of history and the extent to which history has been written to support racist views. They concluded that because the historian can never discover all of the information about any single event or present all of the data that he uncovers, he must use some criterion for selection. They discovered that his selection is influenced by his personal bias, his purposes for writing, and by the society and times in which he lives and works. The discrepancies found in the accounts of black slavery that the pupils read were classical illustrations of the impact of cultural, racial, and regional influences on written history.[9]

The teacher in our example used the topic of slavery to help his black pupils develop inquiry and problem-solving skills. These skills enable black children to learn the truth about themselves, the contributions that their people have made to American life, and how history was written for years to justify, rationalize, and perpetuate racial myths that portrayed the Negro as a cruel, ruthless savage who was content in his misery. The writing of U. B. Phillips and Jefferson Davis epitomized racism in history. When black pupils gain critical insights into the nature of history as a discipline, they are able to understand why the achievements of their people are often omitted in books, and why Negroes are frequently treated in a patronizing, stereotypic fashion in textbooks. Equipped with this understanding and awareness, black pupils are better able to mitigate their feelings of worthlessness and to develop more positive self-images. Research has documented the fact that black youngsters typically have ambivalent racial attitudes, low self-images, and low occupational aspirations. Social studies teachers should implement strategies to help black pupils perceive themselves and their racial group more positively and realistically.

In addition to developing critical insights into the nature of historiography, black pupils need to make a realistic appraisal of the nature of the social conditions confronting them.[10] They should be guided to inquire into the problems of racial discrimination, the meaning and social functions of the concept of "race," and the struggle that ensues when one race dominates others in a society. Black pupils need to learn the real reasons why they are poor, full of self-hate, and possess hostility that sometimes explodes in the ghetto streets. They should understand that they are not poor because they possess certain deficient traits but because they are victims of a racist society. Without this understanding, black youth will feel that the social conditions they endure are morally justified. Clark writes:

> Children who are consistently rejected understandably begin to question and doubt whether they, their family, and their group really deserve no more respect from the larger society than they receive.[11]

James Baldwin illuminated the need for this kind of instruction when he wrote:

> . . . I would try to teach them—I would try to make them know—that those streets, those houses, those dangers, those agonies by which they are surrounded, are criminal. I would try to make each child know that these things are the results of a criminal conspiracy to destroy him. I would teach him that if he intends to get to be a man, he must at once decide that he is stronger than this conspiracy and that he must never make his peace with it.[12]

Inquiries into black power, poverty, racism, the black revolt, and historical reactions to oppression should characterize social studies for black pupils. Social studies teachers must help the black child become a social critic so that he can ". . . develop critical awareness of the immorality of his condition."[13]

Black children should not only inquire into the problems of racism in history books and into the problems of institutional racism in our society, they should be introduced to the achievements of individual black heroes who have made outstanding contributions to American life. When the Spanish explorers are studied, pupils can be introduced to the black men who accompanied the first Spanish explorers to the New World. Children will be surprised to learn about the thirty black men who were with Balboa when he discovered the Pacific Ocean. They will also be intrigued by black men such as Estavancio who was a guide for Naveza and Cabeza de Vaca. Estavancio, in search of the Seven Cities of Cibola, never reached his destination but was the first man, except for the natives, to behold what is now the state of New Mexico. When studying about Columbus's voyages, children can be introduced to Pedro Alonzo Niño, a black man who navigated one of Columbus's ships when he sailed to the New World. During a study of the Revolutionary Period famous Negroes such as Benjamin Bannaker, the mathematician and inventor, could be studied.[14]

One teacher used a creative approach with disadvantaged fourth grade black pupils. Using the book *Great Negroes Past and Present,*[15] he rewrote and duplicated the biography of one famous Negro each day along with discussion questions and study exercises. As each great Negro was studied, his picture was placed on the bulletin board. At the end of the unit the portraits of all of the Negroes under study were displayed.[16] Then each child chose one Negro who he wanted to portray in a pageant that they wrote and presented to the school assembly. For his part each child dramatized a significant event in the life of a famous Negro whom he had studied in depth. For example, the boy who portrayed Crispus Attucks shouted, "Don't be afraid!" and fell on the stage dramatizing the killing of Attucks at the Boston Massacre, the first man to die for independence. The child who portrayed Harriet Tubman said, "You'll be free to die," dramatizing the way Harriet Tubman forced slaves to escape and join the Underground Railroad. The children also made a mural chronicling the roles that great black Americans have played in the building of this country since they landed on American shores in 1619. They called their mural "They Showed The Way."

The unit was correlated with the other learning areas so that when a famous Negro such as Gwendolyn Brooks was studied, her book of poetry *Bronzeville Boys And Girls* was read along with her biography. When Duke Ellington, Aretha Franklin, and Marian Anderson were studied, the class listened to their records. During the unit many children also read longer biographies of famous Negroes that were borrowed from the school or public libraries.

The teacher's attitudes toward the black child, his perceptions of black history and culture, and his expectations for the child are more important than the materials and methods that he uses. As Cuban insightfully notes:

> Less attention should be paid to additional books and courses . . . and more to the craftsman who will use the tools. Preachers of Black History know that the person is far more important than the materials he uses.[17]

Much research indicates that teachers typically have negative attitudes toward poor and black youth. Gottlieb found that white teachers described Negro pupils as talkative, lazy, fun-loving, high-strung, and rebellious.[18] Becker interviewed teachers in an urban school system who felt that slum children were difficult to teach, uncontrollable, and morally unacceptable on all scores from physical cleanliness to the spheres of sex and ambition to get ahead.[19] It is imperative that teachers develop more *positive attitudes* toward black pupils and their culture if they are to play effective roles in helping these youngsters develop more positive racial attitudes and self-images. This is true because children can accurately percieve the teacher's attitudes, and because teachers are "significant others" for all children. In our society we acquire identity from other human beings who are "significant" to us and incorporate it within ourselves. We validate our identity through the evaluations of those who are influential in our lives. A study by David and Long indicates that the assessment a child makes of himself is related to the assessment "significant people" make of him. The study showed that a pupil's self-appraisal is significantly related to his perceptions of his teacher's feelings.[20]

Social studies teachers must also develop *higher expectations* for black and poor youngsters. Research indicates that teachers typically expect little from the urban poor child. Teacher expectations function as a self-fulfilling prophecy. The seminal research by Rosenthal and Jacobson illuminates the cogent impact that teacher expectations have on pupil achievement. These researchers selected a random sample of elementary school children and told their teachers that these pupils were potential "spurters." At the end of the year when they were tested, they evidenced unusually high intellectual gains. Write the authors, "The results indicated strongly that children from whom teachers expected greater intellectual gains showed such gains."[21]

A "New Negro" is in the making, one who is trying to reject his old identity, shaped to a large extent by white society, and to create a new one. This "New Negro" is wearing African tikis, sandals, and costumes. He is screaming for "Black Power" and fighting to gain control of his schools, communities, and his destiny.[22] Social studies teachers must promote this identity quest by encouraging black pupils to inquire into the extent to which racism has permeated our written history and our society, to become familiar with the contributions that black people have made to American life, and by developing more positive attitudes and higher expectations for black youth. Making the social studies curriculum more relevant for the black pupil is imperative if we are to help mitigate the mounting racial crisis in our cities and help the black child gain a more positive "self."

NOTES

1. George Fitzhugh, "Negro Slavery," in *American Issues: The Social Record*, Merle Curti, Willard Thorp, and Carlos Baker, eds., New York: Lippincott, 1960, p. 522.
2. Jefferson Davis, *The Rise and Fall of the Confederate Government*, New York: Crowell-Collier & Macmillan, 1961, p. 329.
3. See Vincent R. Rogers, "Using Source Materials with Children," *Social Education*, **24** 1960, 307–309.
4. Frederick Douglass, "The Plight of the Slaves," in *The Negro in American Life: Selected Readings*, Richard C. Wade, ed., New York: Houghton Mifflin, 1965, p. 27.
5. An excerpt from a fifth grade American history textbook.
6. James A. Banks, *March Toward Freedom: A History of Black Americans*, Belmont, Calif.: Fearon Publishers, 1970.

7. John Hope Franklin, *From Slavery to Freedom: A History of Negro Americans*, New York: Alfred A. Knopf, 1967, pp. 178–179.
8. From "Phillis Wheatley's Poem on Her Own Slavery," *Eyewitness: The Negro in American History*. William L. Katz, ed., New York: Pitman, 1967, p. 39.
9. James A. Banks and Ermon O. Hogan, "Inquiry: A History Teaching Tool," *Illinois Schools Journal*, **48** 3 (Fall 1968), 176–180.
10. David C. Epperson, "Making Social Critics of Disadvantaged Children," *The Social Studies*, **35** (1966), 52.
11. Kenneth B. Clark, *Dark Ghetto*, New York: Harper & Row, 1965, pp. 63–67.
12. James Baldwin, "A Talk to Teachers," *Saturday Review* (Dec. 21, 1963), pp. 42–43.
13. Epperson, "Social Critics," p. 51.
14. James A. Banks, *Teaching the Black Experience: Methods and Materials*, Belmont, Calif.: Fearon Publishers, 1970.
15. Russell L. Adams, *Great Negroes Past and Present*, Chicago: Afro-Am Publishing Company, 1964.
16. These pictures were taken from the set *Negroes in Our History*, Afro-Am Portfolio Numbers One and Two, Afro-Am Publishing Company, Inc., 765 Oakwood Blvd., Chicago, Illinois 60653. Each set contains 24 laminated portraits drawn by Eugene Winslow.
17. Larry Cuban, "Black History, Negro History, and White Folk," *Saturday Review* (Sept. 21, 1968), p. 65.
18. David Gottlieb, "Teaching and Students: The Views of Negro and White Teachers," *Sociology of Education*, **27** (1964), 245–253.
19. Howard S. Becker, "Career Patterns of Public School Teachers," *Journal of Sociology*, **57** (1952), 470–477.
20. Helen H. Davidson and Gerhard Long, "Children's Perceptions of Teachers' Feeling Toward Them Related to Self-Perception, School Achievement and Behavior," *Journal of Experimental Education*, **29** (1960), 107–118.
21. Robert Rosenthal and Lenore F. Jacobsen, "Teacher Expectations for the Disadvantaged," *Scientific American*, **218** (1968), 19–23.
22. James A. Banks, "A Profile of the Black American: Implications for Teaching," *College Composition and Communication* (December 1968) (in press).

A SPEAKER MODELS PROJECT TO ENHANCE PUPILS' SELF-ESTEEM

Donald Hugh Smith

A Negro child raised in an urban slum does not have nearly the same chance for the promise of America that other children, Negro or white, have who are born into more fortunate circumstances. The Negro slum child is both a product and a victim of a culture of poverty.

Inhabitants of America's slums are dreadfully poor. Most of them have little education and few skills that are marketable in an automated society which is rapidly phasing out jobs that call for simple manual skills. To be Negro and poor—and most Negroes are poor—is to have the added burden of being denied the opportunity to hold a decent job and to earn a decent living. Racist customs and gentlemen's agreements which deprive the Negro of job opportunities also enforce invisible housing codes which force the Negro to live within narrowly confined ghettos.

The child who grows up in the ghetto has his view of life filtered by rat infested tenements; by crime and vice, co-evil effects of deprivation; by fathers and older brothers who daily stand on street corners instead of having jobs to go to; and by the picture of himself that the ghetto reflects. The child who sees only poverty and squalor all about him, and who also sees that everyone around him is Negro begins to conclude that poverty and being Negro go hand in hand. Very early in life Negro children become aware that their race is different, and frequently they believe that being Negro is something to be ashamed of. The social-psychological research of Clark and Clark[1] was the pioneer study of racial identity in Negro children. The Clarks found that as early as three years of age Negro children have a negative awareness of race. When the Clarks offered young Negroes their choices of Negro or white dolls, the children invariably selected the white dolls, even in instances where the white dolls were dressed unattractively and the Negro dolls were beautifully adorned. The more recent research of Goodman,[2] of Morland,[3] of Stevenson and Stewart,[4] and of Trager and Yarrow[5] confirm the Clarks' findings of self-deprecation and self-rejection of Negro children.

Society communicates in many ways to the Negro child that he is allegedly inferior. A father who cannot get a job, racial epithets, brutality from police,

---

Donald Hugh Smith, "A Speaker Models Project to Enhance Pupils' Self-Esteem," *Journal of Negro Education* (Spring 1967), 177–180. Reprinted by permission of the author and the publisher.

and history books which omit the deeds of Negro Americans all help to inculcate and reinforce a self-image of worthlessness. An experience I had when I taught elementary school will help to amplify the point. I was a substitute teacher, fresh out of college, temporarily assigned to teach first grade in a disadvantaged area. Like all newly assigned teachers I decided to give my children a sociogram. Therefore I asked these Negro, Spanish, and white first-graders the following question: "Suppose I were to change your seat tomorrow. Write the names of the two students you would most like to sit next to." The results were illuminating. Without exception the Spanish children chose other Spanish children. White children were about even in their choices of the Spanish children and of other white children, but no Negroes. The Negro children most often chose Spanish children and occasionally white ones, but almost never themselves, and this in a class where Negroes were in the majority. Within this little first grade classroom I found a phenomenon which has been well documented in social science research on American life: not only are Negroes rejected by others but frequently they reject themselves and others like themselves. It is probably a normal reaction that in a social order which constantly tells a people they are inferior, those people seeing little evidence to the contrary will begin to believe in their own unworthiness, and they will develop hatred for themselves and other unfortunates like themselves. Convinced that their low station in life is just in the nature of things, their concept of self and their aspirations of progress will be accordingly low.

In June, 1961, I was informed by the principal of the disadvantaged high school where I taught that the following September I would be privileged to teach a freshman honors English class, all but one of whom were Negroes. The other child was a Japanese boy who had been riased by Negro foster parents. During the summer as I pondered what I would teach those freshmen I was aware that what I tried to communicate in the way of literature, grammar, and composition was only a part of the teaching job I had to do. Unless I could also convince those youngsters that they were important, worthy human beings and that life had more to offer them than it had offered their parents, they might never realize the potential their test scores indicated. The ghetto has a way of reaching out its tentacles and reclaiming those who try to escape. Many able youngsters who enter high school desperate to find a path to a better life soon become discouraged by a society that expects them to fail and by a school system that is insensitive to their needs. I have known many cases of bright students who should have gone to college, who should have been able to make a large contribution to society but who instead dropped out of school to haunt the streets and become part of the social dynamite to which Mr. Conant refers. What could I do to help my freshmen beat the incredible odds against escape? Perhaps the most important thing I could do would be first to give them hope that with diligent study and achievement in school they might have their chance and second, to give them the courage to set their aspirations high. Hope and aspiration are the springs to vault the ghetto wall. Michael Harrington has expressed this idea poignantly in his sensitive social document, *The Other America*. Harrington states passionately: "If a group has internal vitality, a will—if it has aspiration—it may live in dilapidated housing, it may eat an inadequate diet, and it may suffer poverty, but it is not impoverished."[6] And so it was my clear duty to help these children cling to whatever aspirations they had, while at the same time raising their sights to levels they never imagined possible. One of the measures I took is the title of this paper: a Speaker Models Project to Enhance Pupils' Self-Esteem.

Once a month, for an entire year, I brought to our class outstanding Negroes, most of whom were themselves former slum dwellers but who had managed to achieve outstandingly in spite of adversity. The purpose of the project was twofold: first, to bring live models of Negro achievement before the children. Success in the flesh is far more inspiring than an attempt by the teacher to communicate some abstract possibilities of the future. And second, to use the diverse careers these models represented as examples of professions that Negroes have been able to pursue.

The speakers who participated were either personal friends of mine or were recommended by friends. In selecting the speakers I tried to choose models who were credible. A Willie Mays would not do, for Willie Mays is superhuman and not even a white boy, except perhaps a healthy Mickey Mantle, could hope to be the Giants centerfielder. Included among the speakers were a teacher in the school who was also a civil rights activist, an engineer, an anthropologist, a journalist, an attorney, a poetess, the secretary of a U.S. Congressman, a doctoral divinity student, and a psychologist. Each speaker talked for about twenty minutes, giving biographical details and telling something about his work. Following this the pupils asked questions for about twenty minutes. There was never any lack of response on the part of the students. Sometimes their questions were so penetrating I was thankful that the guest, not I, had to answer.

Perhaps the high point of the program was the presentation of Pulitzer Prize winner Gwendolyn Brooks. In addition to relating events of her life Miss Brooks read some of her poetry, and the children were enthralled. During the course of the year the pupils were to do some writing of their own. Six had their essays published in the High School Essay Anthology and one young poet published in the High School Poetry Anthology.

These twenty-four children and I were together for a year, and it was my great pleasure to see them grow intellectually, and to perceive what I hope was a strengthening of their self-concepts. It would be both unscientific and unrealistic for me to contend that this project alone was responsible for any behavioral change among these students. I have no scientific data to support my assertion that among other influences the speaker models project helped to convince these youngsters that it is all right to be a Negro and to have lived in a slum, that in spite of their physical destitution America promised them prospects of a good life. I have only inference to support my conclusion that they began to think more of themselves because of the speaker models. I believe they also reasoned that if their teacher thought enough of them to have such a project, and if those important people thought enough of them to come at 8:00 A.M. then they must be pretty good little people. One indication of the program's value is that when, at the end of the year, I asked the students to write a course evaluation, not a single child failed to mention the program and most of them expressed praise.

I was unable to be with these children after the one year, but I have followed their progress. In a school whose dropout rate is greater than 50 per cent, twenty-one of the twenty-four are known to have graduated, though three completed their work at another high school. The whereabouts of three others who transferred are not known. The class produced two valedictorians, one who graduated a semester early. In a school where less than 25 per cent go on to college, fifteen of the twenty-one graduates are known to have entered college. One brilliant girl who scored at the 99th percentile on the freshman Differential Aptitude Test won a National Achievement Scholarship. She was accepted by Smith College, but lacked adequate financial support so she enrolled at Carleton College. An exceptional boy, who later transferred on scholarship to a private school, is now a scholarship student at Dartmouth and a member of the freshman football team. Other students are enrolled at Knox College, the University of Illinois, Southern Illinois University, Bethel College, and various junior colleges in the Chicago area.

I will not guarantee that anyone who attempts a program such as I have described will be successful. I cannot even be sure that I was successful with my own project. As in the case of the classic Hawthorne Effect we can never be sure whether the real influence is the elaborate projects we set up or is simply that the children are responding to the fact that someone thinks they are worth doing something special for. Perhaps it really doesn't make any difference. Sometimes faith in a fact can help to create the fact.

In spite of the personal joy I derived and in spite of the apparent good the project accomplished, as I reflect upon it I cannot help but think of its tragic aspect. For I submit that it is a deep national tragedy that any American children should be so badly scarred and humiliated by racial prejudice that part of their school curriculum must be devoted to the rehabilitation of crushed egos. If their fathers had iobs and received a decent wage and if unfair housing practices were abolished so that these children could live beyond the walls, in time the scars would heal. But without the chance to belong to a family that is self-sustaining, the children's wounds will grow deeper. As

Daniel Moynihan, former assistant to President Johnson, put it: "Employment ... is the primary source of individual or group identity. In America what you do is what you are: to do nothing is to be nothing; to do little is to be little. The questions are implacable and blunt, and ruthlessly public."[7] And I might add to Mr. Moynihan's statement they are also "ruthlessly private."

Until the practitioners of government and the titans of industry and the American people at large decide to remove the psychological and physical barriers that maim and distort the self-images of children, we who teach must be as concerned about their emotional development as their intellectual development; we must paste and patch and do whatever else we can to give these children the same chance for happiness that is promised to all Americans.

NOTES

1. Kenneth B. Clark and Mamie P. Clark, "Racial Identification and Preference in Negro children," in T. M. Newcomb and E. L. Hartley, eds., *Readings in Social Psychology*, New York: Holt, 1947, pp. 169–178.
2. Mary E. Goodman, *Race Awareness in Young Children*, Cambridge, Mass.: Addison-Wesley, 1952.
3. J. Kenneth Morland, "Racial Recognition by Nursery School Children in Lynchburg, Virginia," *Social Forces*, **38** (1958), 132–137.
4. H. W. Stevenson and E. C. Stewart, "A Developmental Study of Racial Awareness in Young Children," *Child Development*, **29** (1958), 399–409.
5. Helen G. Trager and Marian R. Yarrow, *They learn What They live*, New York: Harper and Row, 1952.
6. Michael Harrington, *The Other America*, New York: Macmillan, 1962, p. 10.
7. Daniel P. Moynihan, "Employment, Income, and the Ordeal of the Negro Family," *Daedalus*, **94** (1965), 746.

"NOT UNTEACHABLE—JUST UNTEACHED"

Lawana Trout

"Wop. Nigger. Cracker. Chink!" "Like man, I'm tellin' you, there ain't no land of the free and home of the brave, and we gotta move."

I was teaching a unit on prejudice and propaganda to disadvantaged high school juniors in the Institute for Advanced Study for Teachers of Disadvantaged Youth held at Princeton University. Since that first class, I have taught the unit in several cities to classes that were all Negro, all white, and Negro-white, and to multiracial classes that included Puerto Ricans, Mexicans, Indians, and others.

President Kennedy said, "Those who make peaceful revolution impossible will make violent revolution inevitable." I wanted to evoke a peaceful revolution in my classroom—a revolution in thinking, a revolution in feeling, and a revolution in teaching. I ignored IQ scores and observed student performance. I forgot reading grade levels and searched for selections that spoke to the students. I was unconcerned about haircuts and dress styles, but I did care about what students thought and how they felt. At times I became a student, and each student became a teacher. I lost books, but I did not lose students.

During our study, I stopped periodically to discuss how different kinds of material should be covered. Should it be taught to everyone? to some? to which ones? I asked the students, "What problems do you think we will have to overcome as this class studies race problems?" The first day one boy asked, "Hey, you gonna let us talk about *Whitey* the same as us?"

Students were encouraged to disagree with anyone's ideas, including the teacher's. The one rule was, "You may say anything you like, but you must listen to everything anyone else says."

This English unit reveals how a speaker or writer achieves his goals through careful manipulation of words. It shows students the relationship between words and emotions. I selected *prejudice, propaganda*, and *protest* because they are live topics for the students and they offered illustrations of the language situations I needed. The response of many students to the unit can be stated in the reaction of one: "I wasn't board a time." Some *were* bored, but the materials were more effective than most traditional ones.

We started by finding out how words are used to evoke feelings. Since the

Lawana Trout, "Not Unteachable—Just Unteached," *NEA Journal*, **56** (April 1967), 26–29. Reprinted by permission of the National Education Association and Lawana Trout.

students were familiar with advertising, I used ads to make them aware of the "feeling" of words, I asked them to choose from a collection of pictures (Hondas, cigarettes, cars, record albums) something that they would like to sell, and then to write several types of ads about it.

The ads they wrote were serious, satirical, and humorous—for radio, television, magazines, or newspapers. Students "sold" their products to the class through reading and role playing. They slanted one ad in several different ways to appeal to different groups—teen-agers, poor people, middle-aged women, young men.

The class compared different ways of expressing one idea—finest quality filet mignon: first class piece of dead cow. They played with personal slanting: "*I* daydream. *You* run away from the real world. *He* ought to see a head-shrinker."

After we had written slanted descriptions of people and places, one student commented, "You can *make* people and things be anything you want them to be with the words you use."

Since the material was sometimes inflammatory and since I was a stranger to the students, tension was present until the class accepted me and my materials. Humor was my most vital ally. For example, one day I showed a cover of a popular magazine which pictured a boy carrying a small table and chair during the riot in Watts. "You are working for a magazine and you use this picture. Write one caption that will slant it positively and one that will slant it negatively."

After the class had provided several positive captions like "Innocent victim rescues furniture," I asked for some negative ones.

Student: "Boy makes off with loot."
Teacher: "Make it more negative."
Student: (all Negro class) "*Negro* boy makes off with loot."
Teacher: "More negative." (Hoping to get a word like *hoodlum, thief*) "What is the worst thing you could call this boy?"
Student: (With a playful glint in her eye) "WHITE boy makes off with loot."
Teacher: "I'm glad to see we've lost our prejudices in here."

From advertising we moved to the study of propaganda, which is, as one girl pointed out, another kind of selling. She noted, "Advertisers sell products, and propagandists sell ideas." We examined local newspapers for propaganda, and formulated a list of propaganda techniques.

Students examined simple editorial cartoons. Each student explained his cartoon to the class and we listed observations about what makes a cartoon. The class decided that symbolism is often used and that whether or not captions and situations have meaning often depends on the reader's familiarity with past events. Some questions were: If you were going to show hate in a cartoon, what would you use? How would you show love, peace, anger or fear?

Our study of propaganda was not limited to newspapers; we looked at it in films like *The Twisted Cross*, which shows Hitler's rise to power, and in paintings like Picasso's "Guernica." The class was asked to give a one-word reaction to this painting. They listed *confusion*, *frustration*, *fear*, *struggle*. When one shy girl said, "Loneliness," the class roared with laughter. They stopped laughing when she argued, "These people are in trouble and afraid; fear makes people lonely."

We opened the study of prejudice with the book *Two Blocks Apart*, which reports the contrasting views of two New York boys from families of very different backgrounds—one, a poor Puerto Rican family; the other, a stable Irish Catholic family—on their neighborhoods, homes, schools, political views, and future plans. The book provoked many questions: Where do people get their views of others? Why do they accept them?

Students were asked to list various racial groups and to write, anonymously, positive and negative comments about each. We duplicated the combined comments and the class discussed the prejudice profile. One student observed, "People don't think about bein' prejudice. They just *be* it."

A boy reading *Black like Me* played the role of Griffin and talked to the class about his trials in trying to understand and cope with prejudice. Hemingway's short story, "Ten Indians," and "A Question of Blood" by Ernest Haycox showed the Indian as a victim of prejudice. Several students read and liked *Letters from Mississippi*, accounts written by white students who went to Mississippi for the Student Nonviolent Coordinating Committee.

In an attempt to understand intolerance, we examined words that are weapons of prejudice. I asked for names referring to groups of people. Students supplied: Krauts, Kikes, Gooks, Frogs, Spiks, Crackers, Wops, and others. After discussing their answers, I introduced Dick Gregory's autobiography, *nigger*. Since several copies had disappeared from the display table, I assumed that some were interested in his treatment of prejudice.

We listened to a record of Gregory's jokes about civil rights issues. I cut up his joke books, *What's Happening?* and *From the Back of the Bus*, and gave each student a joke to tell to the class. Then we talked about Gregory. Why did he entitle the book *nigger*? Who will buy this book? Why did he say, "Dear Momma . . . if ever you hear the word 'nigger' again, remember they are advertising my book"?

Students prepared roles from *nigger* and read them for the class. One part dealt with prejudice in the classroom, and I asked how a teacher shows prejudice.

One boy responded immediately: "I once had a teacher who was always screamin' and yellin' at us. 'You dirty little colored kids are ruining our schools,'" he mimicked.

Others joined in. Some defended teachers, but others countered with comments like, "Yeah, but some teachers don't have to say anything to show they don't like you. They just give you that certain look."

Later in the lesson, I role-played several types of teachers, and the class reacted. Armed with a strong stare and a belligerent voice, I threatened, "I know all about you. I've heard about how tough you are. I want you to understand I can be just as mean as you can."

"I hate you!" exploded one boy.

After seeing the film *A Raisin in the Sun*, students discussed how the lines reveal the self-image of the characters. How did this image affect the characters' actions? What are some Negro self-images today? What are some white ones? How do these self-images affect individuals' actions regarding civil rights? What problems do they create? What is your image of the Indians? Of other races? Where did you get that image? How does one remain true to his own race and at the same time learn to live with other races?

By reading "The Odyssey of a Wop," the class got the picture of an Italian boy who denied his people until he reached manhood. Books relating to the search for identity included *When Legends Die* (Indian), *A Walker in the City* (Jew), *Autobiography of Malcolm X*, and others.

An examination of protest climaxed the unit. I searched for techniques that would help the students release their feelings. After we had looked at books of paintings and discussed expression through color and form, I had the students express some of their feelings about the civil rights struggle through finger painting.

A girl scratched her nails down the page—fingers tense, face tight. "This is hate," she said.

"This is King and his sissies being smothered by black power," said a boy as he distorted the quiet routine he had traced.

With a soft rhythm, a girl's finger traced human outlines. The rhythm flared as dark patterns of terror cut over the bodies. She titled her picture "Birmingham Sunday."

When the students had finished painting, they wrote brief interpretations of what they had sought to express and put them on the paintings.

As we evaluated possible solutions to the civil rights problems, we investigated the basic principles of several groups—Ku Klux Klan, Black Muslims, believers in black power, the defenders of the nonviolence movement, and others.

They read the constitution of the Klan, and they examined copies of the Black Muslims' newspaper. They explored multiple definitions of black power, and they reacted to the newspaper put out by the National States' Rights Party, "Thunderbolt: The White Man's Viewpoint." They took notes as they listened to recorded speeches by Malcolm X, Martin Luther King, and others. From these notes, they refuted the main arguments. Students also conducted interviews, television shows, and trials. One day when I praised them for good work, a boy flicked a half grin at me with, "We ain't unteachable . . . just unteached!"

The study concluded with a debate that opened by having a representative from each group present his basic ideas. Students were allowed to join any group or to remain independent. The different factions had filled the room with propaganda, signs, slogans, pictures, and projects. As members of the class played Martin Luther King, Malcolm X, the Imperial Wizard of the Klan, Stokely Carmichael, and others, students exploded like fire-crackers all over the room.

"You mean to tell me you're gonna try to move the Negroes from the South to the North? They don't want us there, either."

"Man, Malcolm and his cats just yell and scream. We cool it." (A nonviolence speaker.)

We also read from *Our Faces, Our Words*; *The Negro Protest*; *To Kill a Mockingbird*; *Huckleberry Finn*; *Crisis in Black and White*; and other books. Students read "Jew-town" from *How the Other Half Lives*, by Jacob Riis, and the article, "A Spanish Harlem Fortress" (*New York Times Magazine*, January 19, 1964). They acted scenes from *In White America* and read several poems.

This unit allows every student to be an observer, a hero, a martyr, a crusader, an avenger. He is Jew *and* Gentile as the class reads Alfred Kazin's struggle to "be a Jew" and "become an American" in a *Walker in the City*. He is Indian *and* white as a student gives Tecumseh's speech against the white man's stealing Indian land. He is black *and* white as he discovers the meaning of Kenneth Clark's words:

> The great tragedy—but possibly the great salvation too—of the Negro and the white in America is that neither one can be free of the other. . . . Each one needs the other—the white to be free of his guilt, the Negro to be free of his fear. . . . The poetic irony of American race relations is that the rejected Negro must somehow also find the strength to free the privileged white.

In the classroom, students may bare their frustrations and fears, their loves and hates, their disillusionments in the past and their hopes for the future.

"Our English class was more instring then during the regeler time. I feel that if we had nonvolins we could all work together in one union."

"You're wasting your time. Whitey ain't chang and we are gonna get him."

"I don't think I'll ever be afraid of the word *nigger* again."

SOCIODRAMA AS A TEACHING TECHNIQUE

Grace Graham

Not long ago a young man whom we shall call John Jones, a West Coast college student, applied for a teaching position in a small Eastern city. After submitting his recommendations and exchanging several letters with the superintendent of schools, he was given a contract which he signed. John and Mary, his wife, bought a trailer in which they made a leisurely trip across the United States, arriving at their destination a week before the opening of school.

The next morning John visited Mr. Brown, the superintendent.

Mr. Brown was very upset when he saw John Jones. "You did not tell me you are a Negro," he said. "We have never had a Negro on our faculty and the community would not stand for it. I don't know what we can do about you. I'll call a meeting of the School Board to discuss the matter. But I can assure you, Mr. Jones, you will not be allowed to teach here."

John Jones went home to tell his wife the bad news and to discuss with her what they should do.

A story such as this is ideal for the implementation of sociodrama as a teaching method. After telling the story, the teacher would tell her class:

"Now we shall act out possible solutions that John and Mary might find to their problem. Tim, you play the role of John, and Jane, you play the role of Mary. Remember, you decide what you are going to do and also how you think the person whose part you are playing will *feel* and talk."

The teacher then chooses one or two other casts and sends the couples out of the classroom to discuss the problem briefly. While they are outside, the rest of the class quickly list various possible solutions, such as these:

1. Sue in court for a year's salary;
2. Plead with the Board for a chance, agreeing that John will leave after a trial period if he does not make good;
3. Appeal to the National Association for the Advancement of Colored People for help;
4. Get another job in the vicinity;
5. Settle for compensation for time and expenses of trip;
6. Get a job in a Negro school.

Grace Graham, "Sociodrama as a Teaching Technique," *The Social Studies*, **51**, 7 (December 1960), 257–259. Reprinted by permission of the author and *The Social Studies*.

The casts return and *extemporaneously* discuss the problem and decide what they will do. Often the couples hit upon the same or a combination of the same solutions that the class suggested, but sometimes they act out an entirely different ending. The feeling that each pair puts into the dramatization usually varies from belligerency to dejection on the part of one or the other of the characters.

Following the role-playing, the class analyzes the solutions and the feelings portrayed in terms of reasoning, psychological authenticity, and possible consequences of alternate courses.

This sociodrama is an example taken from a college course in Social Foundations of Teaching where problems of minority groups are studied. The setting is present-day America, but any problem situation involving human relationships—current or historical—can be studied through sociodrama.

Classes in social studies that have learned the issues in a labor-management controversy might use a situation involving a meeting of leaders from both groups. A class might enact a scene in which the local town council discusses a problem. The mock United Nations meetings attended by high school representatives in many states are actually large-scale sociodramas. Family living courses offer innumerable problems of parent-child, brother-sister, child-peer group relationships that are natural plots for sociodramas. In sociodramas such as these, the primary purpose might be to present opposing views rather than arriving at a solution to the problem.

While stories for role-playing may come from today's headlines, they may be as old as recorded history. For example, the dilemma of Hans Van Loon, a wealthy patroon in New York who must choose sides in the American Revolution, or of Tom Smithson, a Northern States-Righter at the time of the Civil War, might be emphasized through sociodrama. In historical settings, probably imaginary characters in hypothetical situations are better material for role-playing than well known personages because the choices actually made by the latter tend to restrict creativeness.

Perhaps you are thinking, what is the advantage of this method over the usual informal class discussion beyond the fact that it adds a little variety? The chief advantage is that frequently the players and perhaps the class, too, *identify* with the roles being portrayed. In studying current affairs, their social sensitivities are developed because they learn how it feels to be in someone else's shoes. Identification with the aspirations, disappointments, troubles, and fears of others is especially important today when so much of our society is living in tight little subcultures of suburbia.

Sociodrama may help also to make everyday people who lived long ago come alive, problems seem real, and social history become more significant. They may, furthermore, add another dimension to good teaching of history: the concept of social change. Although problems of human relationships are as old as man, the solutions chosen by persons long dead might have been different had they known what we know today. Consequently, pupils must orient their thinking to that of the period being studied. Part of the evaluation of the sociodrama would entail the historical accuracy of the data cited in support of a decision. At the same time, children would be reminded that in like manner, some of the choices we make today might be unwise from the vantage point of 2500 A.D.

HOW TO TEACH USING A SOCIODRAMA

Planning. Select a problem of human relationships that fits the maturity level of your pupils. If you are lucky you may find a short story that serves the purpose which you will read to the class. You may, however, write your own story or simply describe the characters and the situation in which they are involved to your class. In any event, the number of characters should be limited, how the story ends will not be suggested, and several different endings are possible.

Procedures. 1. Prepare the pupils to identify with the characters by explaining that you will choose some of them to act out the ending of the story you are about to tell or read.

2. Read or tell the story. This should not take more than fifteen or twenty minutes.

3. Choose the cast or casts. (At first, you may find it helpful to choose the actors before you tell the story.) Since you want your first sociodramas to be successful, you might choose boys and girls who would cooperate willingly and be able to talk readily. After you have used the technique a number of times, you should then choose pupils who would gain most from playing the role. For example, when you know a boy has no sympathy for unions, you would cast him in the role of a labor leader. The assumption is that he would learn something of labor's point of view from taking the role.

4. Send the actors out of the room for a three to five minutes' planning session.

5. Let the class suggest solutions. Some teachers may prefer to omit this step, but others find it useful in getting involvement from the whole class.

Perhaps with first attempts, you might prefer to spend the time in helping the class think through how they will evaluate the role-playing. At this time, you would also suggest that the class should be sympathetic with the performers and refrain from laughing.

6. Students act out the conclusion of the story. While the play is in progress, you should sit with the class and not interrupt the players unless they are

obviously changing the facts of the situation as described. You should, however, recognize when a decision is reached, end the scene, and thank the performers. Sometimes the pupils themselves do not seem to realize when this point is reached.

7. Evaluate in terms of (a) emotional reactions portrayed; (b) facts cited; and (c) consequences of various courses of action. Sometimes teachers assume that they can evaluate their pupils' emotional reactions, too, on the basis of how they play roles. Thus they confuse sociodrama as a teaching method with psychodrama, a projective technique used by psychiatrists and psychologists. Since analyses derived from projective techniques are sometimes questionable even when made by expert psychologists, teachers should beware of amateur diagnosis. After all, you asked the pupil to play a role. Let's assume that he is doing just that.

A Final Word. Plan carefully so that you will establish a clearcut problem situation that is interesting. Nevertheless, don't be discouraged if your first effort fails. Sociodrama will work on any age group from kindergarteners to adults, but older persons are more likely to laugh and be self-conscious and less likely to identify on first tries than younger children. After a little experience, the chief limitation of the technique is the lack of ingenuity of the teacher.

STUDY QUESTIONS

1. Joyce asks, "Should textbooks and tradebooks expose children to the injustices endured by American minorities? Should they tell the story of America 'like it is?'" How would you respond to these questions? Are there other, perhaps more significant issues that the author may have overlooked? If so, what might these be?
2. Joyce argues that traditionally, children's books have projected distorted images of American minority groups. What are the reasons for this? Do newer books differ significantly from the older ones? If so, in what ways?
3. Joyce asks, "Do educators have the right to expect that publishers should serve as agents of social change?" How would you respond? What are the obligations of publishers toward teachers and pupils? Of teachers and pupils toward publishers?
4. Banks describes how a teacher used the topic of slavery as a vehicle for helping his pupils develop inquiry and problem-solving skills. What specific skills were emphasized? If most of the pupils in this class were poor readers, what other types of media might have been used?

5. Numerous studies suggest that a close relationship exists between cognitive and affective elements of learning. In what ways does the Banks article lend credence to this belief? How might the lessons described in this article change the self-concepts of the pupils? for the better? for the worst?
6. Banks maintains that the study of history can help black children forge new identities. What does this mean for pre- and in-service training of teachers?
7. Did the results of Smith's sociogram surprise you? Under what circumstances might Smith have achieved different results? Would you expect that older children might respond differently than Smith's first graders? Why or why not?
8. On what basis did Smith believe that his Speaker Models Project was successful? What type of follow-up activities would reinforce the learnings acquired by Smith's students? Would Banks' strategies reinforce those of Smith?
9. Why did Smith attempt to select speakers who were credible? What are some of the pitfalls to be avoided in selecting speakers? Would it be desirable to invite speakers with widely varying backgrounds?
10. What were the major goals of Trout's unit on prejudice and propaganda? Do you regard these goals as defensible? Why or why not? What does the author submit as evidence that she accomplished her aims? What additional evidence might be useful for evaluative purposes?
11. What roles did Trout's pupils assume? Which roles would tend to be most disconcerting to students? Why? What type of teacher would be most likely to make Trout's unit a meaningful learning experience?
12. What are the various teaching strategies Trout used? Would there be any value in attempting to modify these strategies for use with upper elementary or junior high pupils? If so, how might this be done?
13. What does Graham regard as the primary advantages of sociodrama over more traditional methods of instruction? Is her rationale for using sociodrama consistent with some of the basic principles of learning?
14. Why do young children respond better to sociodrama than older children? What does this imply about the planning and organization of sociodramas? To what extent do Graham and Trout agree regarding the purpose of role-playing?
15. What are the roles of pupils and their teacher in evaluating a sociodrama? To what extent are they alike and different? Do you agree with the evaluative criteria recommended by Graham? If not, what additional criteria might be useful?

SUGGESTED READINGS

Arnold, Richard D., "Social Studies for the Culturally and Linguistically Different Learner," *Social Education*, **33** (January 1969), 73–76

Banks, James A., and William W. Joyce, *Social Studies for Culturally Different Children*, Reading, Mass.: Addison-Wesley, 1971

———, "Relevant Social Studies for Black Pupils," *Social Education*, **33** (January 1969), 66–69

Crowder, William, "Teaching About the American Indian," *Civic Leader*, **46** (April 22, 1968)

Crystal, Josie, "Role-Playing in a Troubled Class," *Elementary School Journal*, **69** (January 1969), 169–179

Gearing, Frederick O., "Why Indians?" *Social Education*, **32** (February 1968), 128–131

Gibboney, Richard A., "Socioeconomic Status and Achievement in Social Studies," *Elementary School Journal*, **59** (March 1959), 340–346

Johnson, David W., "Freedom School Effectiveness: Changes in Attitudes of Negro Children," *Journal of Applied Behavioral Science*, **2** (1966), 325–330

Joyce, Bruce R., "The Primary Grades: A Review of Textbook Materials," in C. Benjamin Cox and Byron G. Massialas, eds., *Social Studies in the United States: A Critical Appraisal*, New York: Harcourt, Brace & World, 1967, pp. 15–36

McLendon, Jonathon C., *et. al.*, *Targeted Communication (Interpretative) Study of Research and Development in Social Studies and the Disadvantaged: Phase One—Analysis and Implications*, Athens, Ga.: University of Georgia, 1970

Misiazek, Lorraine, "A Profile of The American Indian: Implications For Teaching," *College Composition and Communication*, **19** (December 1968), 297–299

New York Board of Education, "Teaching About the Puerto Rican," in *Teaching About Minorities in Classroom Situations*, Curriculum 1967–1968 Series, No. 23

Peter G. Kontos, "Revolution and Justice: Role-Playing in Social Studies," in Peter G. Kontos and James J. Murphy, eds., *Teaching Urban Youth*, New York: John Wiley & Sons, 1967, pp. 92–98

Skeel, Dorothy J., *The Challenge of Teaching Social Studies in the Elementary School*, Pacific Palisades, Calif.: Goodyear, 1970, pp. 93–107

Webster, Staten W., "Social Studies for Disadvantaged Students," in Staten W. Webster, ed., *The Disadvantaged Learner: Knowing, Understanding, Educating*, San Francisco: Chandler Publishing Company, 1966, pp. 586–594

PART THREE/ PROLOGUE TO CHANGE

The major thrust of this section is toward the future. Part One of this text dealt with problems and issues affecting the language development of culturally different children. Part Two described promising strategies for classroom instruction. Part Three serves a different function: it offers the reader an opportunity to take a long, careful look at the future implications of current and emerging trends in this field.

It is difficult—perhaps impossible—to predict with any certainty how the language arts will be taught five, ten, or fifteen years from now. But are there not emerging trends that enable us to make some well-reasoned conjectures? Are educators beginning to formulate sound, defensible approaches to dealing with the language problems of culturally different children? Do these answers provide us with empirically sound bases for planning for the future?

These questions governed the selection of readings for this section. Chapter 9 focuses on the triad of society, community, and school, with a view toward suggesting important philosophical considerations impinging on curricular reform. The readings examine these in terms of their relevance for pre-school as well as elementary instruction.

CHAPTER 9 EMERGING IMPERATIVES

Previous chapters dealt with a broad spectrum of problems and issues concerning the language development of culturally different children. Because the readings presented many different—often conflicting—perspectives regarding this topic, there is the danger that the fundamental issues may have become blurred. These issues need to be redefined, not only because they directly affect classroom practice, but also because they tend to have long-range implications for the future.

We are notoriously short-sighted in our diagnosis and treatment of language disabilities. In our fervent desire to meet current problems head-on, we may overlook other related problems that are only beginning to manifest themselves. For example, in our preoccupation with teaching the "standard language of society" to all children, we frantically cast about for techniques that will enable us to achieve this goal in the quickest, most efficient way. But in doing so we may be arbitrarily denying the integrity of the language patterns that our children bring with them to school. Can we defend the imposition of one unvarying, inflexible "standard English" on our children? Does it promote the upward mobility of disadvantaged sectors of our population? And, most important of all, what *is* "standard English?" If educators have still not reached consensus on its definition, can we expect them to do so five years from now? Ten years from now? At what point in a child's life should language instruction begin? Is kindergarten too late? Too early? Clearly, questions such as these should command our attention; they are germane to our present, pressing problems as well as those of the future.

The first reading, by Esther P. Edwards, raises many questions concerning the intellectual development of pre-school children, and proceeds to outline a series of proposals for the reader's consideration. In "Disadvantaged Student? Or Disadvantaged Teacher?" San-su C. Lin renders an incisive appraisal of short- and long-range problems confronting teachers and administrators. The chapter closes with an article by William W. Joyce which considers some of the broader issues raised in the preceding readings.

KINDERGARTEN IS TOO LATE

Esther P. Edwards

Education of the young child has come with a rush and a swirl out of the quiet backwater where it sat so long in its own reflection and has swept into the mainstream of American concern and controversy. At last we are hit hard with the fact that young children's experiences in their first years are of crucial creative importance for their total future lives. The heredity-environment dilemma having been laid to rest with the recognition that both are significant in continual interaction, we are ready to accept the thesis that intelligence is not fixed once and for all at birth but can be shaped by experience. We are just beginning to look seriously at the kinds of stimuli we provide for children. What should these be? When should they occur? How should they be presented? By whom? In what setting?

But what is the basis for this growing awareness that the early years are of incalculable significance? Any attempt to give a capsule explanation will be an oversimplification; yet the attempt must be made.

The word "cognition"—knowing—became respectable in American psychology in the Fifties. Piaget in Switzerland and Vygotsky in Russia had shown as long ago as the Twenties and Thirties that human intellectual functioning could not be sufficiently explained in any purely mechanical fashion. American psychology of the ruling behaviorist school came more reluctantly to recognize that thinking, learning, and behaving as we know them cannot be reduced wholly to a direct stimulus-response hookup.

What gives an intelligent adult the ability to focus his attention on *this* rather than on *that*? What allows him some degree of choice, of voluntary control? What gets him out from under the domination of his environment—not always, not entirely, but in part, and part of the time? Why can the

---

absorbed reader fail even to hear the clock tick in the corner, the rain on the roof, the hiss of the fire, yet leap to instant attention when his child cries out softly in its sleep? Why, and how, have we human beings attained waking consciousness, that demanding burden and endless delight? What gives us alone of all life on this planet symbolic language—created, shared, used to build and sustain our cloud-palace cultures that float from generation to generation on the mind of man?

D. O. Hebb of McGill University has shown that there is a relation between the level of complexity of a species, the slowness and difficulty of early learning in its members, and the ease and speed with which they can deal at maturity with complex ideas. Whatever an ant learns—if it learns anything at all, functioning as it does chiefly through instinct—may be learned in the first moments of its life, learned once and for all. Thereafter it functions well as an ant, but with no possibility of varying its set pattern. "Go to the ant, thou sluggard"—but not for help with calculus. A rat reared in darkness, Hebb tells us, is capable of a selective visual discrimination, definitely learned, after a total visual experience of less than fifteen minutes; within an hour or so it has learned to function as well as its peer reared normally. A rat is an ingenious and canny beast, but calculus is not its meat either.

The young human creature spends months and years completing the intellectual structures which at his birth are present only as possibilities. Slowly he develops, with little visible change from hour to hour or day to day. His early learning is more laborious than that of neurologically simpler creatures. It is not only that the baby's period of development is longer than the ant's or the rat's, but that the human child is involved in a more difficult task. So difficult, indeed, that his first learning is less efficient, less fluent than any other creature's. It has been said: "The longest journey in the world is the journey from the back of the head to the front of the head." The infant is building the pathways that will make this journey at first possible, then easy, then lightning swift and marvelously effective. What pathways these, through what trackless jungle? Connected and interconnected systems of neurons, branching and coiling back, going off in new directions and returning, making patterned avenues through the forest of nine billion nerve cells that lies between the incoming sensory areas of the brain and the outgoing motor centers. Without this development, conceptual thought is forever impossible.

So at maturity the intelligent adult, whose potential has thus been translated into reality, perceives with understanding, speaks and thinks symbolically, solves problems, categorizes, appreciates, and does all this with an instantaneous flash of insight that is alone of its kind in nature. He deals conceptually with the universe—a universe he first had to construct for himself. How does he do this? As each of us must, he has built it during his earliest years out of the myriad perceptual cues coming into the nervous system from "out there"—cues impinging continually on nerve endings, but meaningless until his system has built the structures that allow a reading of the signals and response to them.

This is what the infant in his cradle is doing. We adults, rushing about harassed and busy, look at the baby and think: "How restful—to be fed, kept warm and clean, to have nothing to do but play with a toe, eat, cry a little, sleep. . . ." But the infant lying there is building his universe, and building himself. He must do both of these things, do them *then*, do them *at once* (for one is the converse of the other), or never do them at all. Never to do them is never to develop, to be cut off, to be a thing and not a man.

How construct a universe? The new-born baby possesses a nervous system which already receives and responds reflexively to signals from the outer world—to light, sound, temperature, pressure, and other stimuli. But though he responds through reflex action, the baby does not yet understand the signals: he cannot *read* them. He must learn to interconnect sets of cues—to see what he hears, for instance, and to learn that a light and a sound may describe one and the same object. So he begins to define reality. He must develop ability to deal with more and more signals at once. In time, perceptual cues gain meaning: the baby has begun to know what they signify. Memory, judgment, intention all stem from this moment in his intellectual life. First he acts as a purely physical being and learns how to solve problems by means of bodily acts. Then he learns to represent physical action by mental symbol, and thought has begun.

His first symbols are images, pictures which allow him to hang on to fleeting reality ("I remember my mother's face though she is out of the room"). Then the child learns a word, and another, and another, and begins to put words together. At eight months, or a year, he has begun to grasp the shorthand which allows him to hold in his head the whole of reality and to manipulate it, to solve the problems it sets him, through mental operations. Until he is five or six or older, the chief intellectual task of his life will be the creation of a symbolic vocabulary, or several of them (words, numbers, images, musical notes), which become the medium of his life as a human being.

How vital this is to human development is implied by the linguist's suggestion that the supremely difficult feat of building language recognition and response which takes place during the first years of life can occur because there is a built-in neurological mechanism for language learning present in every normal human organism. But like the image on the sensitized negative, this potential will not appear as reality unless the proper circumstances develop it. Experience—the right experience—is essential.

Heredity and environment interact. Hereditary possibilities are shaped by the influences that only human culture can provide; they are potentialities that must be developed while the young neurological organism is still rapidly growing, malleable, open to stimulus. If the "critical periods in learning" hypothesis applies to human beings (as we know it does to other creatures—dogs, for instance—and as evidence increasingly indicates it does to us), then the right experience must come at the right time, or the potential must remain forever unrealized.

Benjamin Bloom of the University of Chicago implies this when he says that the early environment, during the first five to seven years of life, is the significant one for intellectual development. This is why we are finally realizing that the young child's experience is of indelible importance, not only for his emotional life, but also in the formation of that aspect of man which is perhaps most crucially his own—his sapience.

If all this can be accepted as in some degree reflecting truth, where are we? We are at a point where we can see why education for the young child can matter enormously. It matters not as much as the family. The family is basic. But the good family is good precisely because it provides so much of the young child's education. Still, other appropriate experiences can add to what even the best family can do.

For the child born into a family which cannot give him what he needs in emotional security or intellectual stimulus, such experiences may act as a lifeline to essential development. What early education is offered to what children becomes, therefore, of first importance. Perhaps the right choices here can make a difference comparable to the release of nuclear energy—a release of human potential energizing our whole society.

This sense that the choices matter tremendously is why the present debate as to what constitutes good education for young children is more a battle than a scholarly discussion: Montessori—or not; "Teach your child to read at two"—or don't; imaginative play as the focus of the preschool experience vs. structured cognitive stimulation. Every aspect of the preschool is up for reconsideration, defended with zeal, attacked with fury. Partisanship is prevalent, the grounds for decision-making uncertain.

Part of this malaise stems from the attempt of psychologist and teachers to create activities appropriate for the thousands of urban—and rural—slum children who have come into preschool classes through such programs as Head Start. Once these children would never have seen the inside of a nursery school classroom. Now they are here. Teachers are responsible for them. And teachers have found that their tried and true techniques don't work with these children. How do you make contact with a nonverbal, uncooperative, frightened, dirty, doleful, thumb-sucking four-year-old dragged to school by a slightly older sister who can't tell you anything about him except that his name is Buzzer?

So it is perfectly true that many Head Start programs are not making a significant difference in the intellectual capacities or the academic readiness of children thrust into them for a brief six to eight weeks the summer before they go to "real" school. Head Start has been oversold in an effort to enlist citizen support: "It will bring the slum child up to the level of his middle-class age mates in one quick and easy exposure." That was a line that salved the taxpayer's conscience with a minimum of damage to his bank account. But it was a lie. No one with the faintest understanding of the realities of mental, social, and emotional growth ever thought it could do any such thing. Head Start may be better than nothing (in some cases even this is questionable), but it is vastly less good—and *less* than is needed.

The solution, however, is not to damn previous educational goals and means across the board. New circumstances and children with new needs do not prove that the established ways of going at the education of young children are valueless—only that we now are dealing with a wider range of children and must supplement the older ways with different aims, content, and techniques. We need a more varied repertoire. We need to know when to do what, and why. That's all. But that's a tall order.

The situation, then, calls for a plea to the embattled camps in preschool education to beat a few swords into plowshares, to leave their respective strongholds, to stop maintaining that each holds all the truth, and to begin to share questions and insights. A vast amount of hostility can be dissipated if we can accept two basic truths:

1. There is no one method of teaching young children which is ideal for all of them. Like the rest of us, they differ in temperament, in background, in needs, in readiness for this or that experience. As children vary, so must educational approaches.

2. Human beings are totalities: they have bodies, and they have minds; they exist in social contexts within which they act and feel. Small children are people, and their life in school needs to be a whole life in which physical, emotional, intellectual, and social aspects of the self are all given adequate nourishment. It is wrong to leave out any major segment, though emphasis can and should vary with the particular set of circumstances.

Perhaps the first step is acceptance of the individual differences among children. Some of these are genetic in origin; others are caused by environmental accidents. Within groups of children from similar cultural and social strata are wide ranges in health, energy, temperament, aptitudes, and innate potential. Even among children in the same family this is so. Dozens of factors can affect the quality of early experience. One child's mother was sick when he was at a vulnerable stage; another child had an illness that required hospitalization; for a third, everything went along smoothly and success bred success. The gap between one socioeconomic group and another magnifies the differences. The early life histories of children living within a few blocks of each other in an American city may be as remote from one another as is the

Arabia Desert from Manhattan. How foolish then to think that any one approach can be the best, much less the only one for such diverse bits of mortality, so variously shaped by their three or four years of life.

Proponents of cognitive preschool experience have recently leveled severe criticism at the less-structured types of nursery school curricula. "Only play," they say, "only messing around with finger paints . . ." The Montessori schools point to their abundance of graded materials which can be used by the individual child to move step by step from growing mastery of sensory-motor skills to a knowledge of letters, of numbers, of ordering and labeling. The child's attention span increases. He learns to work independently, systematically, following a coherent pattern established by materials and setting. For children from the often chaotic homes of poverty this may mean a significant gain.

O. K. Moore, of the University of Pittsburgh, uses his "talking typewriter" (actually a total language environment, rather than a typewriter in an ordinary sense) as a tool whereby children as young as three years have learned to read and write in the natural way in which they learn to talk—inductively—with personal choice of activity and pace. Carl Bereiter and Siegfried Engelmann, formerly of the University of Illinois and now of the Ontario Institute for Studies in Education, have created what is perhaps at the moment the most controversial program in pre-school education. It has been called a "pressure-cooker approach." In this setting, under direct academic force-feeding, groups of four- and five-year-olds from lower-class families are taught verbal and number patterns:

> This is a ball.
> This is a piece of clay.
> Is this a ball?
> Yes, this is a ball./No, this is not a ball.
> This is a what? This is a ball. . . .

The aim of this exercise is to develop the ability not merely to label "ball" and "clay," but to know the use and significance of such essential carriers of meaning as the simple word "not." Verbal skills, numbers, and reading are taught. Drill is the medium. The adults unashamedly pressure children to learn. Hopefully their own desire to achieve competence will be fired by the sense that they are doing something tough and important, but praise, exhortation, and tangible rewards and punishment are freely used. The atmosphere is intense. These children have no time to lose. They must move into the world created by adult society. The whole thrust of the program is to make this possible for them.

These and other preschool programs focused on cognitive development add a dimension that was underplayed if not lacking in the older nursery schools, organized as these were around the child's social and emotional growth, his creative activity in the graphic arts and in music, and (with varying degrees of effectiveness) around introductory experiences in those areas recognized at a higher level as the basic disciplines (literature, mathematics, sciences, social sciences). Such a curriculum assumed that the young child entering preschool brought with him a fund of organized sensory and motor learnings. His language development was already well under way, chiefly through many months of interaction with an intelligent, loving, verbal, and attentive mother. Often what he needed most was to be a child among children in an environment which allowed him to explore and to play. He had already been molded and stimulated by the adult world, represented by his vitally concerned parents, and every day he went home to continue this part of his education.

But the Head Start children come from homes which have failed to nourish them in health, in emotional stability, in intellect. They need desperately to develop language, to learn to think. For these children such a program as Bereiter and Engelmann's can perhaps give the all-essential forward thrust without which nothing else can have meaning. They come to school late in the day to establish basic learnings. Their tendency is *not* to listen, *not* to focus. They know in their bones that no one is paying attention to them. They have to undo false beginnings. From a mile behind the starting line they have to start the race their more fortunate peers are already running. Under such circumstances, if pressured instruction will get them ready for school, blessings on it and let them have it.

But young children are being made ready for more than the first grade, and there is more to them than a brain, however vital that may be. William C. Rhodes of the National Institute of Mental Health writes in *Behavioral Science Frontiers in Education*:

> The imposition of culture upon the child, without relating the culture to his inner substance, is forcing a foreign body into his being . . . He will only mobilize defenses against the culture in an attempt to neutralize its harsh, abrasive denials of what he is.

This we must not make children do by being too demanding in our concern for cognitive growth. There are other values also of major importance.

Maya Pines, in her October 15, 1967, *New York Times Magazine* article "Slum Children Must Make Up for Lost Time," quotes disparagingly from the Head Start *Guide to a Daily Program*, which advocates that children:

> . . . learn to work and play independently, at ease about being away from home, and able to accept help and direction from adults . . . learn to live effectively with other children, and to value one's own rights and the rights of others . . . develop self-identity and a view of themselves as having competence and worth.

This is not mere cant. It is not necessarily accomplished, but these are worthy goals. Anyone who has worked with young children, whether they be culturally deprived or not, knows it to be the most sober of cold facts that such children do need to develop independence, social competence, and a sense of self. Until they do, their growth toward other sorts of learning is enfeebled. The child who lacks adequate ego development neither cares nor dares to learn.

Hopefully children can learn both to use their minds and to become more fully human. Social and intellectual growth are not mutually exclusive. The valid criticism of the Bereiter and Engelmann program is not made on the ground that it gives drill in cognitive patterns, but that it gives little else except such drill, in a setting where teacher imposes and child conforms. This is too narrow a segment of experience. It ignores vital components of the totality that is a child. What the end result for these children after some years will be, no one knows. But one must wonder whether so intense a focus on the growth of knowledge and the means of its verification will not diminish other aspects of personality.

Preschool educators criticize the Bereiter and Engelmann program because of its frank admission of dependence on rewards (cookies, praise) and its use of punishment (physical coercion, isolation in unpleasant surroundings). These are gross inducements toward learning. If they are used only to prime the pump, as is recommended, then one may consider them symptomatic not of the program so much as of the damage already done to the child by his stultifying early experience, a damage demanding heroic measures to overcome. But if they must remain in the teacher's repertoire, if they are not left behind in favor of satisfaction from the achievement itself, then they form an indictment of the meaningfulness of this approach to children. A learning that takes place only when the teacher doles out candy or brandishes a switch (hypothetical or not) is a learning without intrinsic satisfaction. Performance can be evoked temporarily through pressure, but will not last. This is one touchstone of valid education.

But why must we wait so long, and then resort to pressure? Already there are several experimental programs which are attempting significant intervention before the age of two in the lives of "high risk" children (the younger brothers and sisters of academically retarded children from deprived homes, or children from markedly nonverbal backgrounds). Appropriate education must be made available to every child as soon as he can benefit from it. We know that as early as eighteen months disadvantaged children start trailing their middle-class age mates in tests of general intelligence and language development. Already the subtle undermining brought about by inadequate experience has begun. It is simply not true that all lower-class children are lacking in potential compared with their middle-class peers. Some, no doubt, are. But for many, if not most, the deficit that so early becomes visible is more likely caused after conception by various environmental lacks (poor nutrition, the mother's ill health during the baby's intrauterine life, and inadequate sensory-motor stimulation after birth). Such lacks can be reversed, and they ought to be.

We are going to have to make educational stimulation available from babyhood on for the children whose families cannot provide it for them. Whether tutors should go into the homes, whether children should be brought into carefully planned, well staffed *educational* (as distinct from baby-sitting day-care) programs, we do not know. Experiments going on in several places in the country should help us decide. But however we do it, intervention by the age of eighteen months should be the rule for the children of deprived inner-city or poor rural families. As it is now, few children reach Head Start before the age of four. We are not making use of the golden period when we can most easily and effectively work with children without using pressure, without having to force on them a culture already so foreign that it cannot be learned unless, as William Rhodes says, we make the child "give up completely the content of the self." We are not coming to children when there is still time to help them build effective roadways through the neurological labyrinth, to help them create a universe rich, diverse, satisfying. We can, if we will. And we must.

We must build programs designed to amplify the child's world as the middle-class child's parents do, when he is still an infant in the crib. We must do this not to cut the lower-class child off from his home and his family, but to assist his overburdened mother, to help make the family milieu better for the child. We must create kinds of stimulation that become a constant part of his life, involving him daily in meaningful interactions, just as the child from a more fortunate home interacts with his mother every day for years, until the time that the thousands of exchanges, each modifying and adding to his understanding, give him mastery of thought and speech. We know that this is the most deeply meaningful education for the one-, two-, or three-year-old child. We must try to approach it for every child.

Such special interventions are not yet widely available. Large numbers of deprived children remain, in a sense, accident victims in need of first aid. Perhaps the Bereiter and Engelmann type of program is that first aid. Perhaps it is the best solution to an unfortunate situation. Perhaps it can build in children who have missed out on the normal growth toward competence some of the abilities they would have developed more gradually had their backgrounds been more intellectually stimulating. Perhaps it cannot. We do not know, but surely it is worth trying, with the sobering thought that force-feeding programs, though they rescue the starving, do not make up for deficits already incurred.

But because people who have been hurt need first aid is no reason to prescribe first aid as the all-important component of everyone's experience.

Because deprived children may benefit from intensive work in the cognitive areas where they lack development does not mean that a broader, more inclusive type of program which meets the equally real needs of the intellectually advanced child deserves ridicule. What we really want is to bring into our repertoire a much wider range of experience from which we may select intelligently those aspects which are most useful and appropriate for each group of children—indeed for each child.

Here we take issue with Miss Pines's description of the "established" nursery school, quoted from her *New York Times Magazine* article but similar in tone to what she writes in her new book, *Revolution in Learning: The Years from Birth to Six*. Miss Pines states:

> Middle-class nursery schools operate on the theory that they can directly influence only the child's emotional and social development—not his mental growth. They assume that if they build up a shy child's confidence, or redirect an angry one's aggression, the child's intellectual development will take care of itself, following a sort of built-in timetable. Therefore they concentrate on teaching children to "get along with others" and "adjust to the group."

Undoubtedly this neglect of the cognitive dimension is true of many preschools, but it is not true of the good ones, and certainly it is false to the philosophy behind early education. It overlooks a range of experience which is very present when young children are well taught by intelligent teachers who are themselves cultivated and concerned people. Children do not get over being shy; they do not learn to redirect their anger or interact with others in a vacuum. They are able to develop as people, in the social and emotional sense, most effectively when their minds are occupied with challenging ideas. "Why does the ice cube melt? What is *melting*? Why does the wind blow, and what is air, and what are the words that let me talk about it? How can I draw a picture of what I felt like when I was in the hospital? What is a dream? Why am I afraid? How many nickels do we need to buy fresh food for our guppies if a box of fish food costs a quarter? What makes my baby brother cry at night and wake me up? How can a rocket go around the world so fast? When is tomorrow? How far is far?" These, and the millions of other questions small children ask every day, are *intellectual* challenges. The preschool exists to help children formulate them, examine them, and, in some degree, answer them. It can only do this by giving children some of the multiplicity of interlocking experiences through which they can move slowly toward mature answers. As nursery-school children they will not arrive, but they make progress.

Because in the past the intellectual component of the preschool has been implicit rather than explicit, this does not mean that it has been lacking. It means that the skilled preschool teacher has done a good job only when she has turned every experience to the benefit of intellectual growth as much as to social or emotional growth. It has given her the task of picking up the children's leads and building her program about these, on the presumption that children are readiest to learn in areas where they already show interest.

Let us not be so foolish as to say that the established nursery school curriculum—if it is taught well—lacks intellectual content, or that it ignores children's growth toward cognitive ability, for it does not. It has been subtle in its approach to these. Perhaps it has been too subtle to allow the critics to recognize the presence of these strands of experience, but not too subtle for children to learn from them—provided the children were ready to do so.

But let us also admit that children who have lacked the requisite preparatory growth are *not* ready for such a program and need something else, something with a more explicit structure, something which is geared specifically to their level of attainment and their deficits. If these children are not always to be accident victims, they need educational intervention years sooner than we are giving it to most of them now. But in trying to do this, we must also bear in mind that to teach is not to bulldoze. Nonverbal, immature, dirty Buzzer is still a person, not a thing to be obtusely shoved into any mold we choose. This is why we need teachers to create programs that as yet do not exist, programs which can combine structured cognitive stimulation with full respect for the inalienable right of each human being to be himself.

Let us admit, also, that when we create these new approaches to cognitive growth, they may also be able to add something vital to the multiple stimuli offered by the middle-class nursery school. To object to an exclusive focus on structured intellectual learning for the middle-class child is not to say that he cannot gain from some of it. No one is talking in terms of taking the bloom off frail butterfly wings. Children who have learned how to learn are eager and resilient, and gobble up new information, skills, and insights in every conceivable way. If they are given some leeway to choose those aspects of a program on which they will spend most of their time, they can only benefit from encountering a wider range of possibilities. Teachers should know all the materials—the fullest spectrum of approaches—and should not be afraid to use them.

We are wasting time and energy, good humor and understanding, in opposing each other. No school of thought has all the light. There is no one ideal approach to learning for all young children. Instead, there are many possible variations of emphasis which can make the preschool experience maximally valuable for a wide range of children from differing family backgrounds, social strata, and levels of development. Let's stop this fruitless squabbling and instead fight ignorance (our own as well as that of others) and the limitations to children's potential growth, however these may occur. Let's be grateful for every addition to the armament of techniques and tools which we can use to help children. Let us try to find out how best to employ each approach: when, with whom, for what reasons, under what circumstances. And for heaven's sake, let's get going.

DISADVANTAGED STUDENT? OR DISADVANTAGED TEACHER?

San-su C. Lin

A disadvantaged student is one who is isolated from the mainstream of culture in a given society by the accident of birth or upbringing. A child who grows up in a family and a community which are economically deprived or socially stigmatized, or both, has a disadvantaged start in life. The school, which is supposed to bring him back to the mainstream of culture, has generally failed to achieve this goal because the teacher is not equipped to handle him and his problems.

What are the problems or what are the disadvantages of a school child from a disadvantaged background? First, he usually has a negative self-concept growing out of the neglect, indifference, or downright hostility which he experiences. Second, he and his teacher usually fail to understand each other, because each has a different set of values. Third, he usually has very limited experience with the use of language, particularly the kind of language he is expected to use in school.

Let us take the language problem first. The child who lives in an over-crowded home where everybody has to shout to be heard and where the child is always told to shut up, the child who is left alone all day because the mother has to work to make ends meet, the child who has nobody to care enough to talk to him or to listen to him—all these children have not had an opportunity to use language in a normal give-and-take pattern which is essential to their social adjustment and intellectual development, both highly important for success in the American society.

Another form of the language problem is the dialect problem. The disadvantaged child usually uses a local dialect which is considered unacceptable

San-su C. Lin, "Disadvantaged Student? Or Disadvantaged Teacher?" *English Journal*, **56** (May 1967), 56–61. Reprinted with the permission of the National Council of Teachers of English and San-su C. Lin.

by the teacher and the members of the prestigious group who use standard English. The disadvantaged child, therefore, has an additional task to cope with, the task of learning standard English in school, whereas the middle-class child has already learned it at home. He also has greater difficulty in learning to read, because, among other things, his reading materials are written in standard English.

The child who speaks a different language, such as the Indian child from the reservation or the Spanish-speaking child from Mexico or Puerto Rico, presents another kind of language problem, that of learning a language entirely different from his native tongue. This task of learning English, not an easy task in itself, is often complicated by the child's learning from another disadvantaged child of his age, the nonstandard dialect, which, instead of winning him the encouragement of the teacher, only brings him the teacher's disapproval and a subsequent sense of confusion and futility.

These problems, underdeveloped language skills in the use of one's first language, the use of a nonstandard dialect, and the problem of the non-English speaking child, are difficult problems; and they tend to become more difficult because they tend to become entangled with the value judgment of the teacher. When a teacher takes language retardation for mental retardation, or attributes the persistent habit of using a different language or a nonstandard dialect to an inferior intellect or to corrupted morals, both teacher and student are caught in a conflict of values which aggravates the child's sense of rejection and negative self-concept. Many teachers who know enough not to blame the child blame, instead, the child's home background. When a four-year-old comes to the Head-Start Program knowing only his first name, we can perhaps say that the neglect is in the home; but what about the seventh-grader or the tenth-grader who has failed to achieve after having been enrolled in school year after year and exposed to the instruction of teacher after teacher? How do we account for the accumulative deficiency or the declining I.Q. when the child has gone through the mill of formal education? If a child is shackled by his environment, isn't it the purpose of education to free him? If he is held back by circumstances over which he has no control, isn't it the responsibility of the teacher to give him a start, a sense of direction, and a sense of value in himself and in what he is doing? If we see a disadvantaged home behind a four-year-old who needs a head start, who is behind a disadvantaged student who remains disadvantaged in school? Isn't it the disadvantaged teacher who has contributed significantly to the disadvantage of the student?

A teacher is disadvantaged in the same way that a student is disadvantaged. First, if the disadvantaged child is one who has a negative self-concept, the disadvantaged teacher is one who has a negative concept of the child he is supposed to help. Second, like the disadvantaged child, a disadvantaged teacher has a value scale very much limited by his own cultural or class orientation. Third, the disadvantaged teacher lacks adequate background to help him understand the nature of language and the functions of literature and their unique place in the education of the disadvantaged child.

Let us take the language problem first. Some otherwise highly sophisticated teachers, for instance, believe that one cannot think efficiently or logically in a nonstandard dialect, not realizing that deficiency in a child's language training cannot be construed as a deficiency in the language itself. Certainly words like *and*, *but*, *or*, *if*, *then*, *because*, *unless*, *although*, and the like—words that denote comparison, contrast, choice between alternatives, cause and effect, tentativeness, conditioning, and other logical relationships—are present in a nonstandard dialect as well as in standard English. If a child has not learned to use these words, it is because he has not been taught to make use of all the facilities in his native dialect, which is very different from saying that his dialect has no facilities to express logical reasoning.

Some teachers consider the lack of inflection in nouns and verbs or the omission of the verb *to be* in a sentence like "he sick" or "he been away" in a nonstandard dialect as a manifestation of laziness or slovenliness which they associate with the poor or the lowly. Such teachers violate the basic linguistic principle that every language or dialect has its own system, and that one should never judge a language or dialect in terms of the system of another. They also fail to understand that a language or dialect is a social convention, the product of a particular interacting social group, not the product of an individual or his character traits. It is just as futile to generalize that a language or dialect reflects the virtue or vice of a certain race or class as it is to generalize that a certain virtue or vice is inherent in any ethnic or social group. In fact, contemporary literature, particularly the works of Mark Twain and William Faulkner, is full of examples to illustrate that magnanimity or depravity of the soul cannot be correlated with the standard or nonstandard dialect that the individual happens to speak.

Standard English, no doubt, is a great value in our society, and every child should be exposed to it as soon as possible and helped to master it sooner or later. Many teachers, unfortunately, do not fully understand how language learning can best be achieved. Many, evidently, believe that standard English can be mastered by workbook drills, or by goading and "correcting" the child, or by diagramming. Furthermore, while all English teachers know the value of standard English, it takes a teacher with psychological insight or some linguistic orientation to understand the value of a nonstandard dialect to the disadvantaged child, who sees it as an essential means to maintaining communication and rapport with his family and peers. To attack this dialect, whether directly or by implication, is to attack his loyalty to his group, his identity, his worth. The disadvantaged teacher, who fails to see the values of the disadvantaged child, tends to conclude that the child has no values to speak of, thus rejecting the child as he rejects the nonstandard dialect.

This tendency to repudiate anything different from one's own cherished values reflects an emphasis on strict conformity which is a narrowly conceived middle-class value. To enforce strict conformity, one is likely to lose sight of other values, to become inflexible, intolerant, self-righteous, and, when the standard becomes too rigid and unrealistic, superficial and pretentious.

In the English class, literature is an area of information to be dutifully covered, or a hunting ground for the figures of speech or other technical devices, or narrowly conceived moral lessons dressed up in flowery language. Traditional school grammar, with its imposing array of definitions and rules invested with an authority not to be questioned, plays its role in discouraging intellectual curiosity and critical judgment. The disadvantaged child, thrown into this class, a world irrelevant and alien to him, finds it as difficult to accept the values of this class and its teacher as it is to reject his own.

Are there other, more significant values in the American culture? Are there values which both teacher and student can cherish, regardless of class? Are there values that encompass all classes, all human beings—values that provide a meeting ground for teacher and student? These are questions which every teacher of the disadvantaged should ask himself. The teacher is most probably the first significant person the child encounters outside his disadvantaged home and his small community. The teacher, by profession, is the key person to lead the child into the larger society in which he expects to live if he is not to remain disadvantaged all his life. What is this larger society? What qualifications and training must one have before one can be accepted as a rightful member? These are questions to which teacher and student together must provide the answers.

Everybody knows that the American society is a democratic society, in which everybody is born equal, in which everybody is expected to think for himself and to make his own decisions, in which governmental policies and actions are mapped on the basis of consensus of the majority through a process of communication and persuasion. Further, the American society is a humanistic society, in which human freedom and human dignity are the highest values. Education in this country is education for democracy and humanism.

With this broad view of the larger society, the teacher who adheres to his middle-class values at the expense of democratic and humanistic values is as disadvantaged as the disadvantaged child who derives his values from his subcultural group. When a teacher says, "If a student doesn't speak good English, he doesn't know what is good for himself and you just have to force him," he is throwing the baby away with the bath, or rather throwing the baby away and keeping the bath, since the nonstandard dialect cannot be eliminated by resorting to dictatorship. Similarly, a teacher who stops the student every time he reverts to his dialect pattern is blocking the communication line and, in so doing, rendering a disservice to democracy as well as to the student, who must learn to communicate if he is to take his part in a democratic society.

How, then, can a language teacher help the student learn the democratic way? First, the teacher and the student can explore together how a language works to convey meaning, not only the lexical meaning one finds in the dictionary, but also the structural meaning which comes to light when words are arranged in certain grammatical relationships. For example, they can discuss the difference between saying, "The man hurt the dog," and "The dog hurt the man;" or between "The boy eats breakfast at seven," and "The boys eat breakfast at seven;" or between "The wind blew up the hill," and "The bomb blew up the hill." They can further examine how a language conveys attitudes and feelings as in "He is a Negro," versus "He is a nigger;" or "John is firm," versus "John is stubborn." They can study the stylistic difference in "He reads with adequate comprehension," and "He understands what he reads," and "He digs the jive." Or, they can discuss the social implications in "I saw those books before," and "I seen them book before."

Freedom means freedom of choice which presupposes a knowledge of a full range of alternatives, and English is a field rich in alternatives for us to explore. In the multi-dimensions of grammar, usage, semantics, and style, the place of standard English and a nonstandard dialect can be examined in an impersonal, detached manner. Once a student becomes aware of all the possibilities and their consequences, he should be permitted to make the decision which he and he alone can make for himself.

Second, the teacher can help the child experience the power of words. Language is the cornerstone of civilization; it is what distinguishes the human from the animal. To acquire the power of words is to become civilized, or humanized, and a lack of opportunity to develop this power early in life is what constitutes the greatest disadvantage of the disadvantaged child. To restore the child to the larger culture, he has to be helped to cultivate the power of language.

Power comes from knowledge and skills. A child should be given many opportunities to use the language he can use, while at the same time being exposed profusely to the language he should use. Rich language experience can thus include the use of both standard English and the child's dialect; one need not be rejected in favor of the other. Neither does the teacher need to be the only model of standard English; records and tapes can provide good models in many voices, styles, and regional variations. The purpose of such experiences is to help the child become involved in the actual process of communication, to help him develop language skills through assimilation and without self-consciousness, and to become proficient, adaptable, and confident in their use.

An older child whose mental abilities are developing and who understands the value of standard English can study its syntactical, morphological, and phonological patterns and the way words are invested with meanings. This study should begin with observation; the sharpening of sense perception, particularly auditory and visual perceptions in listening and reading; an awareness of similarities and differences leading eventually to an ability to make classifications and generalizations based on observed facts. As the child learns to observe, classify, and generalize, language patterns emerge, concepts take hold. This process of internalization will help clarify or redefine his image of the world and the image of the self. In addition to his intuitive insight, he is learning the steps of inductive reasoning, and, as he becomes more skillful in the manipulation of language symbols, he also becomes more skillful in the manipulation of concepts, relationships, alternatives, possibilities, and probabilities. The child who was the slave of circumstances is now his own master, because he is attaining at the same time the power of language and the power of thought.

The power of language to impart democratic and humanistic values can best be illustrated through the study of literature. Language not only helps us internalize the world, it also helps us externalize our feelings. The child who says "I hate my mother" not only releases his pent-up feelings; he hears what he is saying and immediately becomes his own judge. By putting his feelings into words, he externalizes them, and enables himself to see them more clearly, to judge them, and eventually to accept or repudiate them. Thus the impulsive outburst is really a little drama, in which the child is both actor and audience.

One of the purposes of literature is to deal with human emotions, which are dramatized and intensified for us by the creative writer. The writer subjects his characters to all sorts of stress and strain, exposes them to all types of situations to test their strengths and weaknesses and to examine their emotional reactions. In so doing, he illumines the hidden motives of human behavior and probes the depth of human nature for the reader.

The disadvantaged child, with his more than usual share of frustration, is helped through literature to release his emotional tension vicariously. This cathartic function of literature is beneficial to everyone. For the disadvantaged child, it is a powerful force of rehabilitation.

Literature, however, has yet another function, that of educating our feelings by helping us understand them. In imaginative literature, we see people not only through appearances and overt actions, but intimately, right into their hearts and into their minds. We see life stripped to the core and human nature revealed through carefully selected patterns of details. We watch the characters laugh, weep, suffer, doubt, hope, fear, and despair as they surmount or succumb to temptations and obstacles, and we recognize these same feelings in ourselves. We not only recognize but understand them, because they have been objectified for us in such a vivid way that we are willing to suspend disbelief even though we know these characters who present themselves for our scrutiny are but fictitious figures. The double nature of the characters is very important. They are real on the one hand but fictitious on the other, and this double exposure makes it possible for us to become personally involved and retain our critical judgment simultaneously. Does this character deserve this kind of suffering? In what way or to what extent is he responsible for the consequences? What are the alternatives open to him? What forces or motives influence his decisions? What are the values behind these decisions? Thus, in addition to educating our feelings, literature shapes our value judgments. Life is a series of choices. We are constantly presented with alternatives and forced to make choices. Freedom to make choices, however, is often denied a disadvantaged child in his actual experiences, and he needs vicarious experiences to help him see the possibilities and the consequences imaginatively and examine the validity of the values people hold on to. In the process he will achieve a measure of moral discrimination and an understanding of the value scale that prevails in the individual or the society.

When a disadvantaged child more and more deeply immerses himself in the world of literature, he comes out with deeper insight into human nature and human values, including his own. He is one of humanity. He is no longer isolated. He is no longer disadvantaged.

Disadvantaged student? Or disadvantaged teacher? If we are concerned about the disadvantaged child, we must not forget the disadvantaged teacher, who, like the disadvantaged child, is disadvantaged not because of a lack of ability but because of a lack of proper training. Finally, let us beware of the disadvantaged teacher, not the one who teaches in the next room, but the one that lurks in ourselves.

CHILDREN, TEACHERS, AND THE LANGUAGE ARTS: SOME UNANSWERED QUESTIONS

William W. Joyce

PROLOGUE

As he left his home on the first day of school, his thoughts were of the children he would be working with during the coming year. What would they be like? Would the challenges be any different from those he had faced before? True, earlier conversations with the principal had convinced him that many of his pupils did have learning problems, but still, these kids were fifth graders, and he had taught this grade before, so why worry? Perhaps the principal had exaggerated, as administrators often do when they want to impress a new teacher. Today he'd find out for himself.

Any lingering doubts he might have had became intensified as he neared his destination. By now the neat, trim homes with their manicured lawns that are so unmistakably suburbia abruptly gave way to a neighborhood of sleazy taverns, empty storefronts, decaying tenements, and junk yards piled high with rusted relics of abandoned cars. As he paused for a stop light the sights, the sounds, the smells of the neighborhood engulfed him. Surrounding him was the filth, the squalor, the poverty, the despair of the urban ghetto. The traffic light changed and he caught a fleeting glimpse of his destination: an aged elementary school, its massive, ugly hulk looming high above the forlorn neighborhood that surrounded it.

As he crossed the playground his misgivings began to evaporate. Boys busily engaged in a noisy game of football, girls playing hopscotch, others clustered in tight, little groups, regarding him shyly. "Why am I so jumpy?" he reasoned. After exchanging small talk with the principal and a few teachers, he entered the room and began reviewing his plans for the day's work. His thoughts returned to last week's orientation session for new teachers.

"Don't expect too much of these kids," the principal had cautioned him, "Most of them are in school only because the law requires them to be here. Their parents would rather have them stay at home, helping out. If they give

The author is particularly grateful to Dr. Ray G. Harper, Chairman, Department of Elementary Education, Northeastern Illinois State College, for his assistance in the preparation of this article, written especially for this volume.

you a rough time, belt them in the behind with your 'pursuader.' Believe me, that's the only language they understand."

His gaze shifted to a long, flat wooden object resting on top of his desk. This was the "pursuader" that the principal had given him. Was he expected to use it? Was discipline as much of a problem as the principal had indicated, or was this an initiation rite sprung on all teachers new to the school?

Within a few days most of his questions had been answered. Yes, these children were different from those he had taught before. He could barely understand them when they spoke—despite the fact that they seemed to communicate quite effectively among themselves. Their reading was but a step beyond the pre-primer level. They could barely decipher the words in science and social studies text that until recently had lain on the book shelf, presumably untouched by previous fifth grade classes. Their writing was barely legible, consisting of painfully immature scrawls and scratches.

The results of a group-administered test of mental ability seemed to confirm these impressions: I.Q. scores for twenty-five of his twenty-nine pupils were between 60 and 75, three scored between 75 and 85, and one reached 105. Shortly after he had received these results the teacher next door chided him, "On paper, most of the kids in this school are eligible for placement in E.M.H. (Educably Mentally Handicapped) classes, but you're stuck with them for the year."

His pupils' day-to-day behavior patterns were similarly disconcerting. Jake, Rosemary, and Richard could barely keep their eyes open. Clarence day-dreamed while Miles brooded in sullen silence. Richard paraded back and forth to the "baffroom." Ronald and Carlos, the most aggressive ones, seized upon the slightest provocation as an excuse to create a disturbance Darlene, Cynthia, and Larynette wriggled and giggled throughout the day, obviously savoring the admiring glances they elicited from the boys. Mary would be working quietly at her desk, and suddenly lapse into uncontrollable sobs. Henry and Jim quietly masturbated at their desks, heedless of the taunts of classmates.

Another persistent problem was the curriculum. By administrative decree, all pupils in the school system were expected to follow with unvarying regularity the same program of studies, with specific periods of instructional time allocated to each area of the school program. His instructional materials consisted of a set of textbooks for reading, language arts, arithmetic, social studies, and science, a collection of aged readers, and spelling workbooks. The school possessed some supplementary materials, but all records, films, and film strips had to be ordered three to four weeks ahead of time, with no guarantee that they would be available when needed. The school library was a dank, dimly-lit room tucked away in a distant corner of the basement. Although well-stocked with various trade books of uncertain vintage, it was open only by special request of the teachers, each being permitted to use these facilities one-half hour per week. There was no librarian, although the teacher was assured that "A lady from the central office stops by now and then." Who this lady was or what she did on her infrequent visits to the school remained a mystery to him, for he never saw her during the year.

Somehow the teacher stumbled through the year. Along the way he lost eight pupils—one became pregnant, two were committed to the state reformatory, and four moved away without leaving any forwarding addresses. Three pupils who had been suspended from another school in the district were transferred to his room ostensibly because "The change of scenery might do them some good." Each passing day brought more unexpected problems and frustrations. Increasingly, he felt his efforts thwarted by an unsympathetic administration, by pupils who seemed incapable of "academic" learning, and by his own feeling of inadequacy.

Throughout the year it became increasingly apparent to him that the major source of difficulty for his pupils was the language arts. The children hated their reading, spelling and language arts texts with equal passion. Grammar, penmanship, and word drills were sheer drudgery. Despite the seeming futility of teaching the conventional skills of communication, he knew that they had to be taught—somehow. But try as he might, his pupils were not showing any appreciable progress in these skills. For this teacher and his pupils the year was becoming a nightmare.

These naive, superficial reactions of a new teacher in a ghetto school are not unusual. Indeed, our colleagues who have taught under similar circumstances tell us that in varying degrees they typify many of their own initial impressions, gleaned from experiences that seemed intolerable at the time. Who is to blame? Were these children at fault, because of their inability to learn? Was the school at fault because of its inability to provide teachers with adequate leadership and resources for meeting the needs of its pupils? Was the teacher at fault because of his failure to understand his pupils—their problems, needs, and aspirations? Was the community at fault for allowing the school to dispense a third-rate education?

CHILDREN AND PROGRAMS

Today the situation is improving. In recent years educators, supported by grants from public and private sources have begun to formulate realistic, defensible strategies for meeting the educational needs of children who for various social, economic, and biological reasons are often termed "disadvantaged!" Increasingly, they are recognizing the fundamental, pervasive influence of the language development—not only as it impinges upon achievement in other school subjects, but also because of its relevance for all avenues of human endeavor. For the most part educators have channeled their efforts in three directions: toward studying the underlying causes of language deprivation, toward analyzing the locii of learning problems, and toward designing new instructional programs geared to the perceived needs of children. Because these efforts are in their initial, exploratory stages, far too many questions remain unanswered. Some of the more perplexing questions confronting language arts teachers are:

1. How successful have been our E.S.E.A. Title I language programs for disadvantaged children? By what standards have these programs been evaluated? What are the characteristics of successful programs?

2. Can children acquire the skills of communication in spite of their psychosocial problems? Does psycho- or sociotherapy need to precede instruction in listening, speaking, reading, and writing?

3. What areas of language development should receive maximum attention? To what extent should language programs focus on auditory discrimination of sounds in words and visual discrimination of letters?

4. If it is true that most retarded readers tend to be visual rather than auditory readers, what does this mean for the development of reading programs?

5. Is the perceptual development of retarded culturally different children in the early grades as impaired as many authorities would lead us to believe? If so, are there any specific corrective measures of demonstrated effectiveness?

6. What is the relation between a child's self-concept or self-image and his language development? At what stage in a child's education are these factors most closely related?

7. Should teachers gear language instruction to standard English models, to ethnic or racial dialects, or should they teach English as a second language? Are there any other alternatives? Under what circumstances would one of these approaches or a combination of them be most useful?

8. Can existing language programs be employed successfully with culturally different children? If not, can they be modified accordingly, or should separate, distinct programs be developed?

9. Is there a literature for culturally different children? How effective are fictional and factual stories, biography, fantasy? What criteria should be employed in selecting, using, and evaluating children's literature? To what extent does literature enhance the self-concept of children?

These are but a few of the many questions confronting teachers and administrators. That educators are striving to produce defensible, empirically-sound answers is evidenced by the abundance of articles, research reports, and textbooks published in recent years. But these efforts toward dealing with the language problems of culturally-different children may be too narrowly-conceived, too short-sighted. They have centered almost exclusively on pupils, their social environments, and on instructional programs—at the expense of neglecting a pivotal figure in the teaching-learning process, the classroom teacher.

VALUES AND EXPECTATIONS OF TEACHERS

To date there have been few authoritative articles and even fewer research reports dealing with the role of the teacher. Those that have appeared in the professional literature seem to have been an afterthought of scholars who for various reasons are suddenly moved to momentarily thrust the teacher into the limelight. But if we acceed to Wolfson's proposition that ". . . as a teacher interacts in the classroom she is communicating in both obvious and subtle ways the fabric of her personal values,"[1] it becomes axiomatic that her attitudes and predispositions toward pupils largely determine her ultimate effectiveness as a teacher of the language arts, or of any other school subject.

That a close relationship seems to exist between teacher attitudes and pupil achievement was dramatically illustrated by Rosenthal and Jacobson in their seminal report, *Pygmalion in the Classroom.*[2] These researchers began with the premise that the basic reason given for the poor academic performance of the disadvantaged child is merely that he is a member of a disadvantaged group. Yet their studies with low-income children in San Francisco revealed that there might be another reason: the child does poorly in school because that is what his teacher expects of him! That is, a child's academic deficiencies may be attributable not to his different ethnic, cultural and economic background, but to his teacher's response to that background; in this way a teacher's expectations for his pupils' academic achievement become a self-fulfilling prophecy.

Rosenthal and Jacobson found that teacher expectations have both positive and negative implications for achievement. If a teacher expects a child to be intelligent, he will actually demonstrate greater intellectual capacity. Similarly, when a teacher holds a low expectation for a child's intelligence, the child will show lower intellectual capacity. These researchers summarize their conclusions in these words:

> To summarize our speculations, we may say that by what she said, by how and when she said it, by her facial expressions, postures, and perhaps by her touch, the teacher may have communicated to the children of the experimental group that she expected improved intellectual performance. Such communications together with possible changes in teaching techniques may have helped the child learn by changing his self-concept, his expectations of his own behavior, and his motivation, as well as his cognitive style and skills.[3]

The results of these studies are by no means conclusive. But they do serve to illuminate a highly significant variable that previously had gone unnoticed: teacher expectations. Are there additional variables that are likely to influence a teacher's effectiveness in the classroom? Here too the evidence is at best spotty, but the literature does suggest several potentially fruitful avenues of inquiry:

1. To what extent are a teacher's cognitive competencies, character traits, and personality attributes a function of his societal position? To what extent do religious affiliations, community of origin, and other elements in a teacher's social class background affect his attitudes toward culturally different children?
2. To what extent are teacher attitudes influenced by what pupils and their parents *appear to be* and by what they *appear to do*? How does a teacher react to his pupil's language patterns, hygiene, physical appearance, and general deportment in the classroom? To what extent do these factors affect a teacher's expectation regarding the achievement of his pupils?
3. How do the levels of aspirations teachers set for their pupils compare with those pupils set for themselves? Do these vary in accordance with a child's socioeconomic background? Are they tied in with certain cultural constants? Do similarities and dissimilarities between these levels affect pupil achievement?
4. How does systematic training in counseling in classroom behavior enhance the language arts teacher's effectiveness? Do interaction analysis, micro-teaching, simulation, and other techniques enable teachers to develop new perceptions and expectations of themselves and more control over their classroom behaviors?
5. Does sensitivity to elements of social systems beyond the classroom enhance the language arts teacher's effectiveness? What type of experiences in the local community are most likely to promote realistic, humane relationships with parents and children outside of school? How can we insure that these experiences will encourage teachers to reexamine basic assumptions about culturally different children, and assess them through individual contacts?
6. Can personal attributes of successful language arts teachers be identified and quantified? Should behavior models based on these attributes serve as criteria for selection, recruitment, and training of teachers?

These questions barely scratch the surface, but they are offered in the hope of offering some beginning lines of inquiry to assist educators in coming to grips with the broad, fundamental issues impinging on their work with culturally different children. But many unforeseen problems lie on the horizon;

this is amply illustrated by Burton Clark:

> The large and continuing growth of Negro and other dark-skin minority populations in northern cities make teacher reaction a critical aspect of the education of minorities. The northern urban situation is one in which prejudice alone is not the major factor. It is a matter of the way in which the characteristics (other than skin color and race) of the minority child affect teachers and the operation of the schools. In an important sense, doing away with prejudice would not do away with the minority problem; for as long as a sizable share of the children from culturally deprived and lower-class backgrounds are dirty, violent, and unmotivated—or appear so in the eyes of their teachers—the teachers are likely to handle them differently, teach them less, and want to escape.[4]

POSTLOGUE

That blacks, Puerto Ricans, Mexican-Americans, Indians, and other minorities are now beginning to acquire equality of opportunity in business, education, and politics is largely a matter of record. Some observers regard these as highly significant advances, unprecedented in the history of our nation; others regard these as mere tokenism, as concessions offered in a pathetically transparent effort to compensate for the many centuries of injustices endured by minority groups. The nature of these gains and the rapidity with which they have occurred tends to obscure two inescapable facts: (1) equality of opportunity for all Americans, irrespective of race, creed, or national origin will not become a reality until educators make a concerted effort to work toward this end; and (2) more than any other social institution, the schools can become a dynamic, potent force for initiating social change.

Are schools at the local level shouldering this responsibility? Are teachers and administrators serving as agents of social change? Educators readily acknowledge the necessity of providing for the learning problems of culturally different children. They flock to conferences on educating the disadvantaged. They create new programs, design new teaching strategies, and undertake impressive research projects, all the while convincing themselves that they are in fact discharging their responsibilities toward their pupils. But this is not enough. Conferences, curricula, and research tend to be a needless expenditure of time, money, and effort if they fail to produce positive, enduring changes in the value systems of educators. Educators need to first look within themselves. They need to examine their own value systems by analyzing the source and status of their own beliefs and predispositions toward minority group children. Only then can they acquire the sense of commitment, of involvement that is so essential to their task.

NOTES

1. Bernice J. Wolfson, "Values and the Primary School Teacher," *Social Education*, **31** (January 1967), pp. 37–38, 47.
2. Robert Rosenthal and Lenore Jacobson, *Pygmalion in the Classroom*, New York: Holt, Rinehart & Winston, 1968.
3. *Ibid.*, p. 180.
4. Burton R. Clark, *Educating the Expert Society*, San Francisco: Chandler Publishing Co., 1962, p. 99.

STUDY QUESTIONS

1. What is the "critical period" in learning hypothesis? Does it support Edwards' argument for pre-school programs? Does it negate the author's position regarding variability among children? Are there any additional hypotheses that might be deduced from the author's analysis of differences between pupils?
2. How does Edwards' opinion of Head Start compare with the results of research studies? What does Edwards' suggest as alternative experiences for disadvantaged children? Does she have reservations about cognitively-focused programs? If so, what are they?
3. Why does Edwards believe that educational stimulation for children of deprived inner-city or poor rural families should occur by the age of 18 months? Does this proposal seem feasible? What agencies would be best equipped to provide such stimulation? If implemented on a broad scale, how would this proposal affect existing teacher training programs?
4. Lin maintains that "a teacher is disadvantaged in the same way that a student is disadvantaged." How does he defend this allegation? What are his criteria for assessing the competencies of teachers of the disadvantaged? Do you accept these criteria?
5. In Lin's opinion, what characteristics are most commonly found in disadvantaged students? How do these characteristics compare with those given by other authors in Chapters two, three, and four? Would you conclude that Lin would define disadvantaged in narrow or broad terms?
6. What does Lin regard as the major advantages of using literature with disadvantaged children? How does his position compare with positions expressed in Chapters seven and eight? Do the opinions expressed by these authors differ with regard to the nature and purpose of literature?
7. In what ways could a pupil's expectations for his teacher's behavior

become a self-fulfilling prophecy? Does Rosenthal and Jacobson's thesis have relevance for teacher-teacher, teacher-principal, or teacher-parent relationships?

8. Is Joyce's description of the perceptions of a ghetto-school teacher believable? Are the problems that he identifies as prevalent today as they were a decade ago? Have teachers encountered other problems in the intervening years?
9. What is your appraisal of the "unanswered questions" raised by Joyce? What questions would you add or delete from his list? What questions are most germane to pre-service training in teacher education? To in-service training? Which of these questions can be stated in terms of researchable hypotheses?

SUGGESTED READINGS

Baldwin, James, "A Talk to Teachers," *Saturday Review* (Dec. 21, 1963), 42–44, 60

Davidson, Helen H., and Gerhard Lang, "Children's Perceptions of Their Teachers' Feelings Toward Them Related to Self-Perception, School Achievement, and Behavior," *Journal of Experimental Education*, **29** (1960), 107–118

Dumont, Robert V., Jr., "Cherokee Children and the Teacher," *Social Education*, **33** (January 1969), 70–72

Goldberg, Miriam L., "Adapting Teacher Style to Pupil Differences: Teachers for Disadvantaged Children," *Merrill-Palmer Quarterly*, **10** (April 1964), 161–168

Greene, Maxine, "The Teacher and the Negro Child: Invisibility in the School," *Educational Forum*, **29** (March 1965), 275–280

Hamilton, Charles V., "Race and Education: A Search for Legitimacy," *Harvard Educational Review*, **38** (Fall 1968), 669–684

Melbo, Irving R., and David W. Martin, "Building Morale in Teachers of the Deprived," *The Educationally Retarded and Disadvantaged*, Sixty-Sixth Yearbook of the National Society for the Study of Education, Part I, Chicago: University of Chicago Press, 1967, pp. 328–349

Ornstein, Allan C., "In Defense of Slum-School Teachers," *Teachers College Record* (May 1968), 759–766

Riessman, Frank, "The Overlooked Positives of Disadvantaged Groups," *Journal of Negro Education* (Summer 1964), 225–231

Rosenthal, Robert, and Lenore Jacobson, *Pygmalion in the Classroom*, New York: Holt, Rinehart & Winston, 1968

Schueler, Herbert, "The Teacher of the Disadvantaged," *Journal of Teacher Education*, **16** (June 1965), 174–180

Smith, B. Othaniel, Saul B. Cohen, and Arthur Pearl, *Teachers for the Real World*, Washington, D.C.: American Association of Colleges for Teacher Education, 1969.

TEACHING THE LANGUAGE ARTS TO CULTURALLY DIFFERENT CHILDREN

Edited by

WILLIAM W. JOYCE
Michigan State University

JAMES A. BANKS
University of Washington, Seattle

ADDISON-WESLEY PUBLISHING COMPANY
Reading, Massachusetts · Menlo Park, California
London · Amsterdam · Don Mills, Ontario · Sydney

This book is in the
ADDISON-WESLEY SERIES IN EDUCATION

 Printed in the United States of America. Published simultaneously in Canada. Library of Congress Catalog Card No. 78-136123

ISBN 0-201-03403-4
BCDEFGHIJK-CO-7987654